# Socialism and Religion

There is much talk of the 'return of religion' these days. This is frequently conceptualised in terms of 'post-secularism', a perceived move away from what Richard Rorty has described as (and as a resolute secularist defended) 'the compromise that the Enlightenment reached with the religious', namely that religion be confined to the private sphere and that public discourse be grounded on the basis of a common rationality shorn of the metaphysical and ethical particularities of religious doctrine.

Thinkers as varied as Jürgen Habermas and Charles Taylor have argued that a necessary defence of the achievements of secular modernity needs to be combined with a recognition of the fundamental value of religious traditions, and of their legitimate place in public life. The global resurgence of a new religious politics – graphically symbolised by 9/11 – has added a new urgency to this project; how is religion to be integrated, and if necessary contested, in such a time? As this study shows, the desire to integrate religion into a 'progressive' politics, or even to make it the very basis of such a politics, is not new; Geoghegan argues that ideas and practices generated in these earlier moments have an inherent interest, and even a degree of relevancy to contemporary concerns about the nature and scope of religion.

Providing a comprehensive analysis of the Common Wealth movement, this work seeks to bring together for the first time the religious and political commitments of four of the leading thinkers in the movement, bringing to light the significance of the relationships between them.

**Vincent Geoghegan** is Professor of Political Theory at Queen's University Belfast.

# Routledge Studies in Social and Political Thought

1. **Hayek and After**
   Hayekian Liberalism as a Research Programme
   *Jeremy Shearmur*

2. **Conflicts in Social Science**
   *Edited by Anton van Harskamp*

3. **Political Thought of André Gorz**
   *Adrian Little*

4. **Corruption, Capitalism and Democracy**
   *John Girling*

5. **Freedom and Culture in Western Society**
   *Hans Blokland*

6. **Freedom in Economics**
   New Perspectives in Normative Analysis
   *Edited by Jean-François Laslier, Marc Fleurbaey, Nicolas Gravel and Alain Trannoy*

7. **Against Politics**
   On Government, Anarchy and Order
   *Anthony de Jasay*

8. **Max Weber and Michel Foucault**
   Parallel Life Works
   *Arpad Szakolczai*

9. **The Political Economy of Civil Society and Human Rights**
   *G.B. Madison*

10. **On Durkheim's *Elementary Forms of Religious Life***
    *Edited by W.S.F. Pickering, W. Watts Miller and N.J. Allen*

11. **Classical Individualism**
    The Supreme Importance of Each Human Being
    *Tibor R. Machan*

12. **The Age of Reasons**
    Quixotism, Sentimentalism and Political Economy in Eighteenth-Century Britain
    *Wendy Motooka*

13. **Individualism in Modern Thought**
    From Adam Smith to Hayek
    *Lorenzo Infantino*

14. **Property and Power in Social Theory**
    A Study in Intellectual Rivalry
    *Dick Pels*

15. **Wittgenstein and the Idea of a Critical Social Theory**
    A Critique of Giddens, Habermas and Bhaskar
    *Nigel Pleasants*

16. **Marxism and Human Nature**
    *Sean Sayers*

17. **Goffman and Social Organization**
    Studies in a Sociological Legacy
    *Edited by Greg Smith*

18. **Situating Hayek**
    Phenomenology and the Neo-liberal Project
    *Mark J. Smith*

19. **The Reading of Theoretical Texts**
    *Peter Ekegren*

20. **The Nature of Capital**
    Marx after Foucault
    *Richard Marsden*

21. **The Age of Chance**
    Gambling in Western Culture
    *Gerda Reith*

22. **Reflexive Historical Sociology**
    *Arpad Szakolczai*

23. **Durkheim and Representations**
Edited by W.S.F. Pickering

24. **The Social and Political Thought of Noam Chomsky**
Alison Edgley

25. **Hayek's Liberalism and Its Origins**
His Idea of Spontaneous Order and the Scottish Enlightenment
Christina Petsoulas

26. **Metaphor and the Dynamics of Knowledge**
Sabine Maasen and Peter Weingart

27. **Living with Markets**
Jeremy Shearmur

28. **Durkheim's Suicide**
A Century of Research and Debate
Edited by W.S.F. Pickering and Geoffrey Walford

29. **Post-Marxism**
An Intellectual History
Stuart Sim

30. **The Intellectual as Stranger**
Studies in Spokespersonship
Dick Pels

31. **Hermeneutic Dialogue and Social Science**
A Critique of Gadamer and Habermas
Austin Harrington

32. **Methodological Individualism**
Background, History and Meaning
Lars Udehn

33. **John Stuart Mill and Freedom of Expression**
The Genesis of a Theory
K.C. O'Rourke

34. **The Politics of Atrocity and Reconciliation**
From Terror to Trauma
Michael Humphrey

35. **Marx and Wittgenstein**
Knowledge, Morality, Politics
Edited by Gavin Kitching and Nigel Pleasants

36. **The Genesis of Modernity**
Arpad Szakolczai

37. **Ignorance and Liberty**
Lorenzo Infantino

38. **Deleuze, Marx and Politics**
Nicholas Thoburn

39. **The Structure of Social Theory**
Anthony King

40. **Adorno, Habermas and the Search for a Rational Society**
Deborah Cook

41. **Tocqueville's Moral and Political Thought**
New Liberalism
M.R.R. Ossewaarde

42. **Adam Smith's Political Philosophy**
The Invisible Hand and Spontaneous Order
Craig Smith

43. **Social and Political Ideas of Mahatma Gandhi**
Bidyut Chakrabarty

44. **Counter-Enlightenments**
From the Eighteenth Century to the Present
Graeme Garrard

45. **The Social and Political Thought of George Orwell**
A Reassessment
Stephen Ingle

46. **Habermas**
Rescuing the Public Sphere
Pauline Johnson

47. **The Politics and Philosophy of Michael Oakeshott**
Stuart Isaacs

48. **Pareto and Political Theory**
Joseph Femia

49. **German Political Philosophy**
The Metaphysics of Law
Chris Thornhill

50. **The Sociology of Elites**
Michael Hartmann

51. **Deconstructing Habermas**
Lasse Thomassen

52. **Young Citizens and New Media**
Learning for Democratic Participation
Edited by Peter Dahlgren

53. **Gambling, Freedom and Democracy**
Peter J. Adams

54. **The Quest for Jewish Assimilation in Modern Social Science**
Amos Morris-Reich

55. **Frankfurt School Perspectives on Globalization, Democracy, and the Law**
*William E. Scheuerman*

56. **Hegemony**
Studies in Consensus and Coercion
*Edited by Richard Howson and Kylie Smith*

57. **Governmentality, Biopower, and Everyday Life**
*Majia Holmer Nadesan*

58. **Sustainability and Security within Liberal Societies**
Learning to Live with the Future
*Edited by Stephen Gough and Andrew Stables*

59. **The Mythological State and its Empire**
*David Grant*

60. **Globalizing Dissent**
Essays on Arundhati Roy
*Edited by Ranjan Ghosh and Antonia Navarro-Tejero*

61. **The Political Philosophy of Michel Foucault**
*Mark G.E. Kelly*

62. **Democratic Legitimacy**
*Fabienne Peter*

63. **Edward Said and the Literary, Social, and Political World**
*Edited by Ranjan Ghosh*

64. **Perspectives on Gramsci**
Politics, Culture and Social Theory
*Edited by Joseph Francese*

65. **Enlightenment Political Thought and Non-Western Societies**
Sultans and Savages
*Frederick G. Whelan*

66. **Liberalism, Neoliberalism, Social Democracy**
Thin Communitarian Perspectives on Political Philosophy and Education
*Mark Olssen*

67. **Oppositional Discourses and Democracies**
*Edited by Michael Huspek*

68. **The Contemporary Goffman**
*Edited by Michael Hviid Jacobsen*

69. **Hemingway on Politics and Rebellion**
*Edited by Lauretta Conklin Frederking*

70. **Social Theory in Contemporary Asia**
*Ann Brooks*

71. **Governmentality**
Current Issues and Future Challenges
*Edited by Ulrich Bröckling, Susanne Krasmann and Thomas Lemke*

72. **Gender, Emotions and Labour Markets – Asian and Western Perspectives**
*Ann Brooks and Theresa Devasahayam*

73. **Socialism and Religion – Roads to Common Wealth**
*Vincent Geoghegan*

# Socialism and Religion
Roads to Common Wealth

Vincent Geoghegan

LONDON AND NEW YORK

First published 2011
by Routledge
2 Park Square, Milton Park, Abingdon, Oxon, OX14 4RN

Simultaneously published in the USA and Canada
by Routledge
711 Third Avenue, New York, NY 10017

*Routledge is an imprint of the Taylor & Francis Group, an informa business*

First issued in paperback 2013

© 2011 Vincent Geoghegan

The right of Vincent Geoghegan to be identified as the author of this work has been asserted by him in accordance with the Copyright, Designs and Patent Act 1988.

All rights reserved. No part of this book may be reprinted or reproduced or utilised in any form or by any electronic, mechanical, or other means, now known or hereafter invented, including photocopying and recording, or in any information storage or retrieval system, without permission in writing from the publishers.

*Trademark notice*: Product or corporate names may be trademarks or registered trademarks, and are used only for identification and explanation without intent to infringe.

*British Library Cataloguing in Publication Data*
A catalogue record for this book is available from the British Library

*Library of Congress Cataloging in Publication Data*
Geoghegan, Vincent
  Socialism and religion : roads to common wealth / Vincent Geoghegan.
    p. cm. – (Routledge studies in social and political thought)
  Includes bibliographical references and index.
  1. Socialism. 2. Christian socialism. 3. Christianity and politics. 4. Religion and sociology. 5. Macmurray, John, 1891–1976–Political and social views. 6. Ingram, Kenneth, 1882–1965–Political and social views. 7. Stapledon, Olaf, 1886–1950–Political and social views. 8. Acland, Richard, Sir, 1906–1990–Political and social views. I. Title.
  HX73.G46 2011
  261.8'5 – dc22
                            2010049346

ISBN: 978-0-415-66828-6 (hbk)
ISBN: 978-0-415-83022-5 (pbk)
ISBN: 978-0-203-81478-9 (ebk)

Typeset in Times New Roman
by Taylor & Francis Books

For David Gregory Burgess

# Contents

| | | |
|---|---|---|
| | *Acknowledgements* | x |
| | Introduction | 1 |
| 1 | John Macmurray: Christ and Marx | 15 |
| 2 | Kenneth Ingram: The Christian and the sexual – homosexuality, bisexuality, pederasty | 53 |
| 3 | Olaf Stapledon: Religious but not Christian | 85 |
| 4 | Sir Richard Acland: The conversion of a Liberal MP | 109 |
| 5 | The moment of Common Wealth | 142 |
| | Conclusion | 183 |
| | *Notes* | 195 |
| | *Bibliography* | 224 |
| | *Index* | 234 |

# Acknowledgements

I would like to thank the British Academy for awarding me a Small Research Grant which enabled me to visit various archives around the UK. The staff at these archives were all unfailingly helpful in providing me with access to their relevant holdings; my thanks therefore go to the following collections: Exeter University (the Acland Papers), Sussex University (the Common Wealth Papers), Edinburgh University (the Macmurray Papers), Liverpool University (the Stapledon Papers) and the Liddell Hart Centre for Military Archives, King's College London (the Wintringham Papers); also to Lambeth Palace Library for sending me a copy of the Temple/Ingram correspondence. Queen's University Belfast kindly allowed me a sabbatical leave in late 2008 to carry out most of the above visits; and I have been actively assisted in my research by the last three heads of the School of Politics, International Studies and Philosophy at Queen's, whom I also value as friends, namely Shane O'Neill, Rick Wilford and Richard English. In the years in which this book has slowly trickled out I have benefited from the comments of a number of individuals who have either read parts of earlier drafts, or have commented on presentations at conferences and seminars: Ruth Levitas, Tom Moylan, Susan McManus, Laurence Davis, David Boucher, Larry Wilde, Lyman Tower Sargent, Michael Freeden, David Leopold, Michael Bacon, Patrick Parrinder and the five anonymous referees provided by Routledge. Thanks also to Macmurray's biographer Jack Costello for kindly sending me a copy of the list of contents of the John Macmurray Collection, Regis College, University of Toronto. Among my colleagues at Queen's I would like to thank the following: the members of the Political Theory cluster, Keith Breen, Cillian McBride, John Barry (and Shane and Susan); also Debbie Lisle and my old friend Graham Walker; two of my former PhD students, Joly Agar and Philip O'Sullivan, have continued to have conversations with me on the nature of modern secularism. At a more personal level the book is dedicated to my partner of two decades, David Gregory Burgess, who remains the centre of my life.

An earlier version of parts of Chapter 3 was published as 'Olaf Stapledon: Utopia and Worship', *Utopian Studies*, 16:3, 2005, 347–63, and I would like to thank the editor of the journal, Dr. Nicole Pohl, for permission to use this material.

# Introduction

Common Wealth was a left-wing political movement which emerged in Britain in the Second World War, and became for a period a real presence on the political landscape. This book is not an institutional study of this movement. It is only in the final chapter that there is an extensive discussion of Common Wealth, and this is done with a very specific focus on the religious controversies that animated the leadership of the movement. This is not an arbitrary or tendentious point of concentration for the debate about the fundamental values of Common Wealth was central to its political project of transforming Britain. The earlier chapters are concerned with the emerging ideas of four individuals: the philosopher Professor John Macmurray (1891–1976), the novelist and writer Kenneth Ingram (1882–1965), the science fiction writer and philosopher Olaf Stapledon (1886–1950) and the Liberal MP and baronet Sir Richard Acland (1906–90). Again, the focus is on the religious thinking of these individuals, for the religious was, or was to become, central to their modes of thought. The link between the political movement and these four men is that all were to become prominent members of Common Wealth, with Richard Acland as the effective founder of the movement. The final chapter therefore traces the complex interactions between the four men in Common Wealth as they took up varying positions in the battles over religion. The aim is both to show the intrinsic theoretical interest of many of the ideas discussed and to illuminate a fascinating period in the intellectual and political history of Britain.

Let us begin by saying a few initial words about Common Wealth, for the name probably suggests relatively little to present-day readers. Formed in 1942 out of two earlier movements, Forward March and The 1941 Committee, it had at its peak somewhere between ten thousand and fifteen thousand members, and over three hundred branches around the country. While its policy was broadly socialist, it attracted support from a wide spectrum of political opinion, and from people who had previously little or no interest in political matters. To further its political cause and to ensure that the coalition government had to face the tribunal of a public vote it broke the wartime electoral truce and either fought by-elections in conservative seats with its own candidates or, where this was not possible, supported acceptable anti-conservative candidates. In the process it chalked up some considerable achievements, regularly achieving significant swings in its favour, despite the fact that two potentially significant sources of support were, until 1945, disenfranchised (21- to 25-year-olds, since the 1939 Electoral Register was still in place, and the armed forces). There were also three outright victories by its own candidates, principally Chelmsford in April 1945 which converted the 1935 Conservative majority of 16,624 into one of 6,431 for Common Wealth, a swing of over 28 per cent. Apart from this, Common Wealth also published and distributed large quantities of propaganda, organised talks and lectures the length and breadth of Britain, and sought to use its small parliamentary group to get an alternative voice heard in the Commons. One little illustration of its visibility is that when troops held a mock election in Cairo towards the end of the war Common Wealth came second, securing 55 votes to Labour's 119, with the Liberals third (38 votes) and the Tories taking the wooden spoon with a mere 17 votes;[1] it is also an indication of its energy in that Common Wealth had been actively responding to, and further building up, support in the services. The political programme of Common Wealth was centred on two themes – Common Ownership and Vital Democracy – which boiled down to social ownership of all the main sectors of the economy, fundamental constitutional reform, and the extension of democratic participation to both the economic and the social level. In the process it provided a focus and a space for the aspirations of a range of different constituencies who saw the movement as a vehicle for moving beyond the barren politics, social inadequacies and international madness of the 1930s towards something better. Largely the creation of the maverick Liberal MP Sir Richard Acland, Common Wealth held a particular attraction for those like Acland himself who wanted to restore a moral basis to politics. Often, again as in Acland's own case, this was linked to a belief that the religious needed to be at the centre of such an enterprise. This concern with religion was also to be a source of considerable strife in the organisation, not simply between differing conceptions of the religious, but also between the latter and those, such as Marxists, who were not happy with what they considered religiosity and moralism.

In what follows there will be an examination of three individuals that eventually joined Acland's movement – Macmurray, Ingram and Stapledon – and a study of Acland's own development. Concentrating on central themes in their work which help illuminate their conceptions of the religious, the goal is both to get a sense of what sort of *mentalité* each brought to Common Wealth, and how these fed into the subsequent battles over religion in the movement, but also to show that each has striking things to say about the relationship between the religious and the social and political. There is much talk of the 'religious turn (or return)' these days. This is frequently conceptualised in terms of 'post-secularism', a perceived move away from what Richard Rorty has described as (and as a resolute secularist defended) 'the compromise that the Enlightenment reached with the religious',[2] namely that religion be confined to the private sphere and that public discourse be grounded on the basis of a common rationality shorn of the metaphysical and ethical particularities of religious doctrine. Thinkers as varied as Jürgen Habermas and Charles Taylor have argued that a necessary defence of the achievements of secular modernity needs to be combined with a recognition of the fundamental value of religious traditions, and of their legitimate place in public life.[3] The global resurgence of a new religious politics – graphically symbolised by 9/11 – has added a new urgency to this project; how is religion to be integrated, and if necessary contested, in such a time? As this study should hopefully show, the desire to integrate religion into a 'progressive' politics, or even to make it the very basis of such a politics, is not new. In this respect it is a piece of historical reconstruction. But – a claim the reader will have to test – there is also a supposition in the book that the ideas and practices generated by these individuals have an inherent interest, and even a degree of relevancy to contemporary concerns about the nature and scope of religion.

There were linkages between the four men before they all became members of Common Wealth. Macmurray and Stapledon knew of, and referred to, each other's work in the 1930s, Ingram became importantly influenced by Macmurray and joined forces with him in the Christian Left, while Acland was a student of Macmurray, a friend and political ally of Ingram, and got to know Stapledon in the very early days of Forward March. Although all were concerned with the validation of the religious, their religious trajectories were distinct. As a youth Macmurray fervently embraced the Scottish evangelical Presbyterianism of his family, while Ingram was an active and vocal Anglo-Catholic – both were later to adhere to a form of immanentist materialist Christianity. Acland abandoned his boyhood Christian beliefs as a teenager, and it was only many years later, in 1940, that he became a passionate Anglican. Stapledon fairly early on decided that he was no longer a Christian, and maintained this stance until his death; instead, he espoused what he sometimes referred to as a 'pious agnosticism' centred on a philosophically unknowable 'spirit'. These very different religious understandings and beliefs were to determine the patterns of conflict between them over religion, most notably in the skirmishes and battles in Common Wealth concerning religion; they also drew fire from yet other positions in the organisation, as from the Marxists and theologically conservative Christians.

The first three chapters are primarily concerned with the theoretical contributions of, respectively, Macmurray, Ingram and Stapledon. Acland's interest is somewhat different. He had a very sharp political brain, a radical intuition and the capacity to articulate, and dramatise, powerful ideas; to a number of his critical colleagues in Common Wealth, however, he thought and wrote quickly, too quickly – as Tom Wintringham (of whom much more later) put it in a letter to Ingram, Acland 'can write a book in the time I need for an article'[4] – and he undoubtedly was not theoretically dextrous, knew it, and it pained him; from his perspective there was the pique of a practical politician at what could seem the self-indulgent theoretical fastidiousness of intellectuals when by-elections had to be won, and effective propaganda produced. His skilful establishment of Common Wealth is dealt with in Chapter 5, and the other three are reintroduced into the picture as they become associated with his project, and as they participate in the struggles over the foundational values of the movement. The big geopolitical events of the time variously recur in, and to an extent frame, the separate chapters: Fascism's rise, the Spanish Civil War, Soviet Communism, the drift to war, war itself, its immediate aftermath and the emergence of the Cold War. By the late 1940s one has reached the end of what one might term the 'long inter-war years' and the terminal boundary of the study is reached. Olaf Stapledon's death from a heart attack in 1950 is the boundary stone.

The first chapter's subject, John Macmurray, was an academic philosopher who, after a couple of early appointments, was based in turn at Balliol College, Oxford, University College, London, and the University of Edinburgh. He could also be called a public intellectual, particularly in the 1930s and the subsequent war years, notably through the broadcasts he gave on the BBC and the publications that flowed from them. Thus when a book came out in 1944 entitled *Ten Modern Prophets* Macmurray was deemed to be one of them (as was Olaf Stapledon).[5] Also included was someone who had died over sixty years earlier – and therefore hardly modern – namely Karl Marx, included, as the introduction put it, 'because of his great influence on our times'.[6] And it is Macmurray's engagement with this figure which is the focus of the first chapter. He was initially drawn to Marx's work in the early 1930s as he attempted to get to grips with the nature of Soviet Communism. But what he found in Marx, particularly in the early works, a number which had just been published for the first time, was a powerful theoretical resource for progressing his own project, the development of a refurbished Christianity, shorn of idealism and politically relevant. This involved a radical re-reading of the figure of Jesus, stressing his rootedness in the integrated culture of the Jews and his role in the universalising of the living elements of this culture in the form of Christianity. This intermingling of Jesus and Marx animates his most important work of the 1930s, *The Clue To History* (1938), with a dazzling, if at times perverse, account of the process of European development. Central to this is an understanding of the religious dimension in phenomena often deemed non- or anti-religious, as in, for example, science and socialism, and of the integral role these dimensions must play if an adequate religion is to emerge. Religion is here understood not as one separate mode of human activity among many – for this indicates a still fragmented society and culture – but as the informing essence of an eventual Kingdom of Heaven on earth, for 'if a society … has a religion it is not religious. If it is religious it cannot have a religion.'[7]

Macmurray was to become a major influence on the subject of the second chapter, Kenneth Ingram, novelist and writer, a man we know relatively little about, despite his having written over seventy books and being an active member of numerous political organisations. The chapter traces the development of his ideas through a focus on one particular aspect of his work, his reflections on sexuality, not his work on sexuality in general but on his analysis of 'deviant' sexuality – what he referred to as 'abnormal' but not 'unnatural' sexuality – homosexuality, bisexuality and, way out of most people's comfort zone, pederasty or boy love. This focus is justified partly on biographical grounds: Ingram was a homosexual, in days of illegality and moral censure, and one senses the burning centrality of the issue to him in his writings. As one reviewer noted: 'it is on the subject of homosexuality that the author becomes most expansive.'[8] For a variety of reasons he does at various stages critique the name, the concept and the practice of homosexuality but, as he sees it, in the service of a more adequate conception of that which is of value in the homosexual, and against the inadequate, as for example in an overly sexualised notion. His sexual orientation would also appear to be pederastic, evidenced by both the distinctly homoerotic portrayal of young males in his fictional works and his willingness to validate this orientation in his theoretical work. Pederasty was to him a spiritual phenomenon, and not a sexual activity, which he rejected as immorality and vice. This was to cause him theoretical and moral headaches when in his later work he came to the conclusion that sexual activity outside of marriage could be justifiable. Finally, bisexuality featured in his work as an ideal or aspiration that he believed was *the* appropriate mode of human sexuality. The other reason for the focus on these forms of sexuality is that, as both Macmurray and Ingram recognised, sexuality was an issue that went right to the heart of how Christianity saw itself, and that its sexual exclusions spoke of deficiencies in its conception, and evaluation, of the personal and the interpersonal. That today the issue of homosexuality is threatening to tear Ingram's Anglican Church apart is perhaps some evidence of how deep the issue of sexual behaviour goes in the issue of what constitutes an authentic Christianity. Ingram's pursuit of these issues was to result in a call to him to withdraw his final comprehensive statement on sexuality, *Sex Morality Tomorrow* (1940), from William Temple, the Archbishop of Canterbury, an attempt by the Bishop of London to have the book repressed, and an approach to the police by some members of the Church of England to have him prosecuted. In terms of Ingram's political and ideological development the chapter shows how he moved from an early neo-Medievalist feudal socialism with a very ugly and explicit anti-Semitic dimension, to a socialism that bears, under the influence of Macmurray, a marked Marxist inflection.

With Olaf Stapledon, in the third chapter, we ascend to the cosmic. He came to public attention in the 1930s with a series of science fiction novels, notably *Last and First Men* and *Star Maker*, the latter having as their subject matter conjectural histories of the universe in which beings and planets and galaxies flourish and die and where the ultimate terminus is utter extinction, the death of the universe itself, and with it all memory of the billions of years of sentient life and the teeming expanses of space. At first sight this doesn't seem promising territory for a positive conception of religion, but Stapledon was adamant that an authentic religion was both possible and very necessary.

This was not to be Christianity. Although sympathetic to some elements of Christianity he viewed it as hopelessly enmeshed in doctrines that he believed could not be validated philosophically because they asserted things far beyond the capacity of the human mind to know. This was the rigorous philosophical dimension in Stapledon's work, honed in his PhD in philosophy, and in his extra-mural classes in the subject in his days as an adult education lecturer, and that made his imaginative works very much ideas-based. His religion had two principal components. One was the normative principle of 'personality in community' which was the focus of his political and social radicalism, itself self-consciously socialist with a critical sympathy for Marxism. In this respect he shared with Macmurray and Ingram the notion that the seemingly irreligious could be profoundly religious. This is designated as the 'utopian' pole of his thinking, not in the pejorative sense of the impossible, but in the sense of an informing vision of a better society. His second religious conviction was a deeply personal sense of an awesome spirit in reality, one unconcerned with humanity and its purposes, and one that humanity could and should embrace, even though it was the effective author of the destruction of their highest hopes and ideals. Unknowable, it was the object of an 'agnostic piety' which Stapledon denoted as 'worship'. His problem, as he acknowledged throughout his life, was that there was a considerable tension between these two religious convictions, for how was one to worship something that was constantly undermining the search for personality in community, and would ultimately visit an obliterating nothingness on aeons of striving? We can see the tension in his notes for a lecture in 1934: 'Conflict between Love and Worship/love demands fruition for the beloved/worship qualifies this demand/and accepts tragedy gladly/ ... Admit a logical conflict/between striving and worship/ between "Love thy neighbour" and "Thy will be done".'[9] And it was a tension still unresolved at the time of his death.

Chapter 4 seeks to chronicle the political and religious development of Richard Acland, a man who, though sadly lacking a biography, left no fewer than three drafts of autobiography in his papers.[10] The product of generations of Liberal politicians, Acland was elected Liberal member for North Devon at the 1935 General Election, aged 25. His views became increasingly socialist over the next five years. In the Commons and in his first publications he attacked the social conservatism and the foreign policy of appeasement of the National Government, and aligned himself with those seeking to create a Popular Front of those opposed to that administration. Still an atheist, he began to stress the moral dimensions of his politics, and religious language began to enter his vocabulary. It was only in 1940 after reading John Hadham's *Good God*, and an ensuing mystical experience, that he regained a Christian faith, initially attracted to, though significantly misinterpreting, Kenneth Ingram's views. Quite quickly, though, he developed a belief in a personal God, and this was to be the basis of his religious stance in Common Wealth. The publication of *Unser Kampf* (Our Struggle) in early 1940 was a huge popular success (rapidly selling over 150,000 copies) which triggered the

Introduction 7

beginnings of the popular movement that was to lead via Forward March to the establishment of Common Wealth.

This sets the scene for the final chapter, which charts the development of Common Wealth, and shows the roles Macmurray, Ingram and Stapledon played in the new organisation; Macmurray entering via the 1941 Committee, J.B. Priestley's group of notables, and Ingram and Stapledon via Forward March. Their roles were significantly different. Macmurray, according to Angus Calder, whose unpublished 1968 PhD thesis on Common Wealth is still far and away the most detailed and thorough account of the organisation,[11] acted as an *éminence grise*, his views consulted on foundational matters such as the movement's constitution and, as we shall see, on its philosophical basis; he sat on an Appeals Committee but was not an active day-to-day member of Common Wealth. Ingram, however, was very much a hands-on member. For the effective life of the movement he was a very senior member, sitting on the ruling Executive Committee, and was spokesman on foreign affairs. He was also a member of Acland's 'ideational team' (as was Macmurray) which was meant to formulate policy. Stapledon was primarily a regional member of Common Wealth based in the North West of England. Although involved in the talks in London that brought about the merger between Forward March and the 1941 Committee, his main political activity was on the Wirral and Merseyside where he was an active branch member and officer. From here he wrote his contributions to Common Wealth publications and canvassed in elections, and this was where he travelled round contributing talks and lectures on policy matters at public and branch meetings. Finally, the role of all four men in the multi-faceted religious controversies in Common Wealth is charted, bringing in important new characters who played key roles in the debates, especially, from the Marxist wing, Tom Wintringham (veteran of the Spanish Civil War, former member of the Communist Party and leading figure in the establishment of the Home Guard) and his wife Kitty (née Bowler), a formidable figure in her own right, and two figures relatively close to Acland on religious matters, the Rev. John Parkes (who under the *nom de plume* John Hadham was the actual author of *Good God*) and Tom Sargant. Acland came under attack from theologically conservative clergy for his early associations with Ingram and Macmurray, and from Olaf Stapledon for what he took to be Acland's hegemonic claims for Christianity. Above all, coming to a head in November 1943 was a clash for the soul of the organisation that pitted the Wintringhams and their Marxist distaste for Christianity and the vocabulary of the moral against what they saw as the conservative troika of Acland, Parkes and Sargant. Both sides sought to win over Macmurray and Ingram, for to Acland they were fellow Christians, and to the Marxists they were sympathetic to the claims of historical materialism. Macmurray decisively sided with the Wintringhams; Ingram, whose whole attempt to theorise homosexuality had centred on its *moral* status, though supportive of a number of the Wintringhams' ideas, assisted Acland in his attempt to validate the moral appeal of Common Wealth. No one was able to engineer an outright victory, and time was anyway running out for Common Wealth. The decision of the Labour Party to pull out of the government coalition and field candidates in the post-war General Election sounded the death knell of Acland's movement; slaughter at the polls followed.

In the conclusion, after briefly sketching the lives of Macmurray, Ingram, Stapledon and Acland after 1945, an attempt is made – again briefly – to relate our subjects and their movement to some contemporary thinking on the emergence, and significance, of modern secularism. The ideas of the four men discussed in the previous chapters represent an historically earlier round of thinking about what is distinctive about secularism, and what stresses and strains have been generated in its emergence. In this sense Macmurray's *The Clue to History* is not doing dissimilar work to Charles Taylor's *A Secular Age*. Furthermore, like the contemporary theorists referred to in the conclusion, these earlier writers were not simply commentators but partisan writers who wished to defend the precious gains of modernity, correct perceived weaknesses, and rejuvenate, particularly through a reworking of religious resources. The recent theorising also allows us to get a fuller picture of why Macmurray and the other three felt that a reconsideration of the relationship between the religious and the secular was so necessary. Thus, although historical figures, they have a very modern resonance.

The particular conjuncture in which Macmurray, Ingram, Stapledon and Acland operated was framed by the two world wars. Macmurray, Ingram and Stapledon were all at the heart of the fighting in France during the First World War, the former two as combatants in the infantry, Stapledon as a member of the Friends' Ambulance Service. The horrors they experienced, and their growing perception of the whole disastrous context and direction of the war in varying degrees, distanced them from previously held assumptions and beliefs, and forced them to ponder alternative conceptions. There was a stark contrast between the relative realism and camaraderie of the front line (with a degree of respect for even 'enemy' troops) and the illusions and animosities of the civilian world left behind. In Macmurray's case his experience of the jingoism of institutional Christianity during the war precipitated his redefinition of himself as a Christian outside the Churches;[12] Ingram was to talk of his experience of 'war hysteria', and 'the welter of hates and enthusiasms' that poisoned public opinion and led to a vindictive and self-defeating foreign policy towards Germany;[13] Stapledon, appalled by the bellicosity of relatives on one of his spells of leave, wrote that it was up to those who had experienced the reality of the war to counterbalance the fantasies of those who had not: 'The only hope is that the people who have been *in* the furnace may not be so mad and venomous and blind as the people who sit around the furnace and talk politics.'[14] Acland was only a schoolboy when the war started,[15] but the war was to cast a long, long shadow on his politics, particularly in the 1930s when a re-run looked increasingly a possibility. The current generation, he argued, had a duty to those who had perished in the war to prevent a further war setting their ultimate sacrifice at nought. He was very conscious of being a part of that young generation who had found themselves heirs to the insecure peace of the interwar years.

They all arrive at various points and in various ways at some form of socialism, but, as we shall see, each one's ideological development is markedly different, as are their understandings of the nature of socialism. What distinguishes them from most of the socialists of the period – again noting variations between them – is the desire to subsume socialism into a broader foundational concept of the religious – socialism as an integral part of an essentially religious project. We see them engaging with, and contesting, a range of leftist currents, all the time looking for some form of vehicle that could make a practical political difference, a need that Common Wealth at the time met. Although attracted to socialism as a very young man it was really in the 1930s that Macmurray, greatly influenced by his encounter with the work of the early Marx, became a serious exponent of socialist theory and practice.[16] Convinced as he was of the underlying Christian impulse behind the Bolshevik Revolution, he found the Communist repudiation of religion erroneous and pernicious and viewed the Communist Party of Great Britain as a snare for the unwary. From 1935 to 1941 he sought to build up the 'Christian Left', a small offshoot of an offshoot of the Student Christian Movement, to offer true political leadership in Britain[17] (and Kenneth Ingram was to become actively involved). Ingram in the 1920s developed an Anglo-Catholic feudal socialism which he was eventually to abandon and, under the significant influence of Macmurray, move much closer to a Marxist conception of history. He was not, however, a mere populariser of Macmurray's work. His life-long reflections on the *moral* status of homosexuality made him more sympathetic to the use of moral argumentation than was Macmurray, who was not at ease with talk of 'oughts'. Politically he was prepared to work with the Communists, but found their minds to be closed and their attitudes intolerant, confessing in 1941 that 'I have secretly prayed that I should never again be associated with a campaign which enlisted communist support.'[18] He himself was a member of the Labour Party in the 1920s and 30s, though we also know that like a number of leftists (such as C.E.M. Joad and John Strachey) he was attracted by Oswald Mosley's 'New Party' before it became Fascist – though whether like them he was an actual party member is unknown.[19] Stapledon on the other hand throughout the 1920s and 30s remained outside of all the political parties, describing himself in 1939 as 'one who has never been able to identify himself with any party'.[20] He had been a socialist since at least the age of 24, recognising himself in H.G. Wells's *New Worlds for Old*,[21] and he told a 1930s audience in a talk entitled 'Why I am a Socialist' that although the term 'socialist' could be misleading he was happy to adopt the title for it seemed to him to be a shibboleth for progressive views; it was 'the great *touchstone* today ... if you accept essential Socialism ... you are politically useful ... if not, not'.[22] But the way he chose to engage in political activity was through a host of campaigning organisations agitating primarily on the causes of international peace and co-operation; these included the 'No More War' movement, the

'League of Nations Union', the 'International Peace Campaign' and the 'Federal Union';[23] he tirelessly spoke at their meetings or on their behalf to whatever groups would listen to him. Acland's reading of Keynes in 1936 started his road to socialism, though his liberal roots were still apparent, and it took him some time before he was comfortable with describing himself as a socialist. He was also anomalously the Liberal MP for North Devon (elected in 1935), and did not formally leave the Liberal Party until a couple of months after the foundation of Common Wealth in September 1942; 'London Liberal headquarters,' he was later to write, with some understatement, 'was naturally concerned at having one of the few Liberal seats represented by a Socialist.'[24] Although stimulated by a book his socialism, unlike the other three, owed relatively little to the literature of socialist theory; he recalled that he was totally ignorant of this literature before reading Keynes,[25] and even afterwards seems to have done little to familiarise himself; it was only under the pressure from his Marxist colleagues in Common Wealth in 1943 that he made some effort to read Marx (and Macmurray). He saw himself as a practical man who thought issues through as they emerged in everyday experience. Thus his admiration for John Macmurray as a thinker was not untinged with an element of scorn for the philosopher's perceived unworldliness.

The central religious concern linking all four men could be called a recognition that religion is too important to be left to the religious. One aspect of this was a shared conviction that contemporary organised religion had lost touch with what should have been its animating spirit. All, in differing ways, found current Christianity deficient in this respect. In Stapledon's case this was a belief that the religious core of Christianity, which it shared with other faiths, had been smothered by empty speculative doctrine; for Macmurray and Ingram the Christian materialism of Jesus had been turned by institutional Christianity into a conservative transcendentalism; even for Acland, who was burning with enthusiasm for his rediscovered faith, and relished his new communion within the Anglican Church, the contemporary Church had failed in the social duties entailed in faith by declining to bring its morality to bear on the disabling inequalities of a capitalist society. In these responses Stapledon saw himself as a person outside the current patterns of faith, while Macmurray deemed himself to be a Christian outside the Churches; Ingram and Acland, committed to their shared Church, sought to generate internal renewal, as in their participation at the 1941 Malvern Conference called by Archbishop Temple to equip the Church for the coming post-war world. All four believed that 'religions' contained resources for the renewal of the religious. Thus even Stapledon acknowledges that the ancient spiritual vocabulary of Christianity has both a poetic potency and referential precision lacking in the concepts and vocabulary of secular rationalism, and he embraces words such as 'worship' and 'spirit'; he sees no reason, furthermore, why existing faith communities should have a monopoly of, let alone a veto on, the religious heritage of all. Macmurray and Ingram attempt a form of critical hermeneutic on biblical texts seeking to uncover intentions marginalised or suppressed by subsequent hegemonic readings which can then both enrich and correct the very necessary and historically progressive methods and categories of modern thought. Finally, Acland wants the Bible to be read not just as a repository of timeless spiritual truth but as an authoritative source of a morality that is mocked in merely private projects of individual salvation.

Underpinning these responses, though again in varying degrees, is an expanded conception of the religious. It is most marked in the cases of Stapledon, Macmurray and Ingram, but, partly in response to criticisms of his 'orthodoxy' within Common Wealth religious debates, it can also be seen in Acland. Stapledon is keen to detach the religious from 'faiths', which to him undermine their religious dimensions with specious metaphysical invention. As he put in some lecture notes:

> religion is one and perennial/religions are many, fleeting, and all false ... 'The religions' (Christian, Buddhist etc) are in part local and temporary expressions of true religion/ (and in part sheer opium of the people, dope)/ every religion contains a pinch of true religion/sometimes a lot of it/but always with adulteration.[26]

Religion is about openness to the universe and all its possibilities and limitations not sets of prescribed ontological 'beliefs' – it is therefore concerned with 'a feeling that something is sacred/not a God, but a way of life/a feeling that we are instruments/on which divine music must be played'.[27] He also uses the term 'religious' to characterise a political openness and energy in the service of genuine community. Macmurray and Ingram, although they privilege Christianity, have a very capacious conception of the meaning of authentic Christianity. Macmurray's historical narrative is full of the Christian manifesting itself in forms that appeared to the institutionalised Christianity of the time as deeply unchristian or even anti-Christian, as in the religious roots of the Enlightenment, and the Enlightenment roots of the contemporary religious. For Ingram a particular concern was to bring affections and practices historically condemned by Churches – notably homosexuality – within the moral parameters of Christianity by excavating from the depths of biblical Christianity morality's foundation stone of love. In the case of Acland creedal adherence and theological rectitude is no guarantee that one is doing God's will, nor atheism and hostility to religion a sign that one is necessarily not; of Tom Wintringham, his relentless opponent in the religious debates but a man whose idealism and hard work he greatly admired, he was to write: 'although we differed about morality he really does qualify for "They who do the work of God shall be called the children of God".'[28]

The tumultuous international context of the 1930s gave edge and immediacy to these concerns. Soviet Communism and German Fascism seemed in a variety of ways to put the deficiencies of the Western democracies into high relief. In the case of Fascism both Stapledon and Ingram drew attention to the way that this ideological movement was able to draw upon and channel the energy and enthusiasm of their populations. Although deeply hostile, as they all were, to the expansion of German National Socialism, and conscious of the role of manipulation and terror, Stapledon was convinced that it was not simply a matter of lies and brute force, and that Fascism in a perverted manner offered a vehicle for aspirations that the existing social structure failed to nurture. These yearnings were for Stapledon at root religious, for

> the peoples of Italy and Germany, in their despair and bewilderment, obscurely but rightly felt a need for some kind of real values, something more compelling than the goal of economic prosperity ... The Fascist and the Nazi faiths offered him in a crude and barbarous form the very thing that he craved.[29]

In contrast the forces of socialism were simply not open to these dimensions and were politically surpassed. Ingram, also, points to the capacity of Fascism to mobilise a religious desire without a home – Fascism is triumphant 'not because the masses are cowed or apathetic' but rather because they 'are filled with religious fervour', 'there is new hope, a new purpose in their lives'.[30] In this respect, therefore, Fascism both exposed a fatal blindness to the potency of religion in hyper-rationalist leftism and pointed to the dangers within capitalist economies of reducing everything to the private and the utilitarian. There are similarities here with the type of analysis the utopian Marxist Ernst Bloch was developing at this time in his attempt to understand events in Germany; the Nazis had moved into the territory abandoned by the Left; 'vulgar Marxism had forgotten the inheritance of the German Peasant Wars' and 'the Nazis streamed into the vacated, originally Münzerian regions';[31] in Acland's words, 'Nazism exploited the opportunities which Socialism neglected.'[32]

But Fascism was clearly an international threat and nowhere was this more dramatically instantiated than in the great passion play of the 1930s left – the Spanish Civil War. From the opposition benches in the Commons Acland harried the government over what he considered its mendacious, naïve and self-interested policy on Spain. Between November 1936 and July 1938 he spoke in the chamber on Spain on twenty-nine separate occasions, all premised on the belief that Britain and France were cowering behind the doctrine of non-intervention while Italy and Germany actively assisted General Franco's rebellion against the elected Republican government; he also tried to perform a difficult political balancing act as regards Soviet policy on Spain, stressing both the commitment of the USSR to the Republican government *and*, compared with Fascist intervention, its relatively limited actual intervention. In April 1937 Macmurray and Ingram were part of a group of Christians invited by the Spanish government to Spain to investigate claims by the Francoists that the Republicans were systematically trying to eradicate religion. The emotional heart of the joint report subsequently published is the delegation's experience of the Basque country. While there they witnessed at first hand the second aerial bombing of the little town of Durango by Franco and his allies (hundreds had perished in the first attack, among them 'twelve nuns and two priests, one of whom had been killed while saying Mass'[33]), a prelude to the bombing by the German Condor Legion of Guernica shortly afterwards. Members of the group were able to broadcast a refutation of the nationalist claim that 'the Reds had blown up churches in Durango and killed the nuns'.[34] The nationalists are portrayed as the enemies of real religion, the republican closure of churches and attacks on clergy are construed as a response to the reactionary *political* stance of the religious and not an attack on religion as such; indeed, the Basques are portrayed as embodying all the virtues of a truly religious society: 'All of us who were in this part of Spain agreed that we had never been in a country anywhere in Europe in which religion was more real and more alive as a social force.'[35] The political mood is upbeat, Franco has missed his opportunity and is facing defeat despite his Fascist backers; likewise in the Commons at more or less the same time Acland saw the resistance of the Spanish as the first serious check the Fascists had experienced in the 1930s, no thanks to the craven behaviour of the British and French:

> Until recently the Fascist powers went calmly on their way, and they succeeded unless we, the non-Fascist powers ... were prepared to do something which might, in certain circumstances precipitate a conflict; and as we always failed to do anything of that kind, the Fascists up to quite recently, seemed to be having it all their own way. Now they have met the Spanish People's Army, and the position to-day is much more serious.[36]

Up in Merseyside Stapledon threw himself into supporting the republican government, lending his pen and his voice to the cause, and, along with his wife, Agnes, helping to arrange the evacuation of Basque children following the German bombing raids.[37] The fading of optimism and the acceleration towards global war is tracked through Acland's eyes in Chapter 4. In the narrowing and darkening space that remained, Acland's desperate search for some process or vehicle that could provide political hope was to culminate in the emergence of Common Wealth.

In the case of Soviet Communism the response could broadly be characterised as critical support. This was partly a willingness, often deeply credulous, to see the new socialist experiment in the USSR in the best possible light, and also a belief that in the absence of any moral backbone in the leading Western democracies the Soviet Union alone seemed willing to stand up to Fascism – most notably in the Spanish Civil War. There was also a perception that anti-Sovietism was an important weapon in the ideological armoury of anti-socialist forces in Britain. Internal repression was noted and deplored but was softened by notions of Russia's historical 'backwardness' and international hostility. These considerations were of sufficient strength to survive the Nazi–Soviet pact and the USSR's invasion of Poland, when a whole host of mitigating circumstances were identified (though Acland did, with some equivocation, condemn the invasion of Finland).[38] Expanded notions of the religious provided a theoretical space for this stance. Writing in the Second World War when, following the Nazi invasion of the USSR, philo-Sovietism was at its height, Macmurray opined that since 'the leadership of progress is in Russian hands ... the religious issue in Russia is the decisive question, not only for the Christian Church, but for world-civilization'.[39] He viewed the militant atheism of the USSR as, in effect, Communism's belief, though not expressed in these terms, 'that Christianity is the enemy of every effort to establish the Kingdom of Heaven on earth'.[40] But this assumption, true as regards institutional Christianity, is itself the expression of an authentic Christian impulse towards both science, itself so necessary to overcome the underdeveloped conditions of Russia, and community. Macmurray's assertion of this point clearly impressed Stapledon, though he replaced 'Christian' with 'religious': 'the Russian revolution ... though consciously anti-religious ... was unconsciously a religious movement, as has been pointed out by John Macmurray'.[41] Macmurray himself argued that progressive Christianity had the task of making the Soviets conscious of the deep Christian roots of their great experiment; the corollary of uncovering the dark atheism lurking in the Christianity of the West.

Common Wealth thus provided a space that proved hugely attractive to a host of different voices, an organisation that actively encouraged an aspirational politics, and was sufficiently capacious and open to allow a huge diversity of opinion; Irene Wagner, who was to become librarian of the Labour Party, expressed the exciting sense of possibilities that Common Wealth offered: ' So like many other socialists we were attracted to the Commonwealth [sic] Party ... here we could hear and say, and do, what the Labour Party was officially not allowed to be concerned with.'[42] The titles of Acland's books in this period convey something of the sense of anticipation, hope and a forward-looking optimism that could be found at all levels of the movement – *Unser Kampf* (Our Struggle), *The Forward March*, *What It Will Be Like* and *How It Can be Done*. His own moral and ultimately religious grounding of politics made the space of Common Wealth alluring to the religious/political projects of Macmurray, Ingram and Stapledon, yet its modern, socialistic outlook could make it an acceptable home for refugees from the Communist Party such as Tom Wintringham. Common Wealth brought together people with some pretty big dreams. The contrast is clearly great between these personal, sexual, global, even cosmic, aspirations, and the relatively modest reality and achievements of a small political organisation. And yet it is a tribute to Acland's creation that there was no sense of incongruity, or of bathos. Common Wealth took ideas very seriously, for it had itself grown out of analysis and debate, vision and values. In its short life, in a time of mortal peril, it did what it could to effect political and social change while never losing a desire for the sublime.

# 1 John Macmurray
## Christ and Marx

In 1994 Tony Blair, the newly elected leader of the Labour Party, publicly identified himself with the Scottish philosopher John Macmurray: 'if you really want to understand what I'm all about,' he had said, 'you have to take a look at a guy called John Macmurray. It's all there.'[1] Since then much ingenuity has been deployed trying to identify the nature of this 'it',[2] for Blair has never been particularly precise on the matter.[3] His highly visible endorsement has been distinctly double-edged – on the one hand he significantly helped to rescue Macmurray's name from the obscurity that had descended upon him even before his death in 1976, but on the other hand the philosopher was to an extent wrenched out of context, his name linked to an issue of which he knew nothing, New Labour. The impression created was that Macmurray was some kind of pious social democrat, when the reality was so different. Since Blair's intervention there has been a growing literature seeking to redress this imbalance, attempting to place Macmurray's work in the turbulent intellectual and political conditions of his time. This chapter endeavours to do this through a consideration of his interwar exploration of the relationship between Christianity and the work of Karl Marx, where, a lifetime away from Blair, in a world context of Soviet Communism and international Fascism, Macmurray attempted his ambitious synthesis of radical socialism and highly heterodox religion.

### 'Here I Stand'

Some time around 1934 John Macmurray (born 16 February 1891),[4] Grote Professor of the Philosophy of Mind and Logic at London University, decided to commit to paper his deepest convictions.[5] It is a token of the seriousness of the resulting document – especially from one raised in a staunchly protestant household in Scotland – that it begins with the words of defiance traditionally attributed to Martin Luther at the Diet of Worms: 'Here I Stand'. The typescript, which Macmurray never published, can be found in the Macmurray Papers at the University of Edinburgh, where he was to become Professor of Moral Philosophy in 1944. It is a little spiritual autobiography dealing with the erosion of the faith of his childhood and youth, and its replacement by a new Christian certainty:

> I STAND as a Christian, outside every Church. I stand outside the Churches because I am a Christian. If I am to explain the position I take up as an individual, or as a citizen, in philosophy, or politics, in any department of human life, theoretical or practical, it is this I have to explain. Everything else follows from it. It is, to me, the fixed centre of an experience in flux. Of this I am certain. I am sure of other things, only to the point where I can see their necessary relation to this.[6]

He looks back to his days as an undergraduate at Glasgow University (1909–13) and to the evangelical Protestantism he then vigorously espoused:

> That faith today is in rags and tatters. I should rather go naked than be seen in it. Even though I find a good deal of its language still useful, the meaning behind the words has been transubstantiated. In its traditional meaning, it has become frankly incredible.[7]

This is attributed not to a gradual and largely unconscious process of loss but to 'a conscious and continuous re-examination of its substance, in the light of history and science and philosophy, as well as of concrete personal experience'.[8] He indicates the current direction of his thinking in enigmatic, even paradoxical, language: 'The experience that has led me to this declaration, that I am a Christian, is the same kind of experience that has led a considerable number of my own generation to declare themselves atheists.'[9]

That this intense credo was written at this time is indicative of Macmurray's sense that his thought was going through a significant shift, and is a testimony to the impact that a couple of years' intensive study of the young Marx had had on his ideas. As he suggests in 'Here I Stand', his thinking had been evolving since his undergraduate days, in his time studying philosophy at Balliol College, Oxford, and as a university teacher at Manchester and Witwatersrand, before his return to a fellowship at Balliol (1923–8). Significant among his 'concrete personal experience' had been his active service in the First World War where he was wounded (indeed permanently scarred), and his company wiped out, at the battle of Arras (he was subsequently awarded the Military Cross for his actions in the battle). There was also his painful experience of the hostile reception he received when, on sick-leave after the battle of the Somme, he preached a sermon on international reconciliation in a London church, an event which determined him to renounce membership of any institutional Church.[10] Thus, as we shall see in more detail later, a good deal of his thought in the 1930s had roots that predated his encounter with Marx, but his deep engagement with that thinker's work was an undoubted watershed. Reminiscing in the 1960s Macmurray pinpointed his decision to begin an in-depth reading of Marx's early work to a conference held in

October 1932 which brought together a number of leading religious and lay thinkers to ponder the question of the rejuvenation of Christianity in the modern world. In Macmurray's account the conference concluded

> that before we could discover what Christianity is we should have to study seriously two other questions. The first of these was the nature of modern Communism, the other was the problem of sex. We then decided that we would tackle Communism first ... It was this conference which led me to undertake a thorough study of the early writings of Karl Marx, with an eye to discovering, in particular, the historical relation between Marxism and the Christian tradition.[11]

The fact that the conference decided to discuss *Communism*, and not Marx specifically, is indicative of the impact of broader social and political factors on public perceptions at the time. Soviet Communism, for better or for worse, was increasingly on the public agenda. Macmurray's study of Marx was initiated, and was to be coloured, by the beginnings of the geo-political tensions between Communism, Fascism and the Western democracies that was to dominate the decade and precipitate a world war.

## Macmurray and the early Marx

What is especially noteworthy about Macmurray's study of the early Marx in the 1930s is that he had access to texts only recently published for the very first time, particularly the groundbreaking *Economic and Philosophical Manuscripts of 1844*, with its classic discussion of alienation, which had appeared in the German original in 1932 (in a collection entitled *Der Historische Materialismus: Die Frühschriften*). Given that the first freely available English translation of the text did not appear until 1956 Macmurray had access to material virtually unknown to the English-speaking world.[12] Encouraged by his new friend the Hungarian thinker Karl Polanyi, Macmurray's reading bore fruit in a remarkable essay (published in 1935) entitled 'The Early Development of Marx's Thought' which must constitute one of the earliest discussions of the *Manuscripts* in the English language.[13] It also included a very insightful reading of another early text of Marx, *On the Jewish Question*, where Marx presents a bravado analysis of the dualism inherent in liberal democracy. These texts laid bare the link between Marx's analysis of religion and his critique of capitalism, and provided a context for understanding the ambiguities of the compressed critique of religion in the *Contribution to the Critique of Hegel's Philosophy of Law. Introduction*.

Marx's early work was decisively shaped by his encounter with Feuerbach's critique of religion.[14] The structure and methodology of Feuerbach's *The Essence of Christianity* positively invites contrasting readings. It is divided into two parts, in which the first part deals with 'the true or anthropological essence of religion', while the second seeks to reveal 'the false or theological essence of religion'. In a later preface, Feuerbach expresses this distinction as a contrast between the 'human' and the 'unhuman' aspects of religion.[15] Put baldly, Feuerbach's overarching argument is that humans use religion to think and speak about themselves. Building on the atheist axiom that the transcendental realm is an illusion, he argues that religious language must be a form of human language, and must therefore be a form of conversation humanity holds with itself. In this sense 'God' can never be higher than the underlying humanity.[16] However, the differing strands in *The Essence of Christianity* emerge in Feuerbach's attempt to analyse in depth the nature of the religious conversation. On the one hand religion involves an expression of the most sublime perceptions and hopes of humanity, but on the other it articulates self-loss and spiritual impoverishment.

Between early 1843 and mid-1844 we find Marx at his most Feuerbachian; it is also in this period that he produced his most detailed critique of religion. Never again was he to devote this degree of energy to the topic, for in these months he came to believe that he had definitively sorted out the question of religion. In the course of his deployment and development of Feuerbach's critique of religion, Marx began to fashion some of his most important concepts, and these, as a consequence, were grounded in the overcoming of religion. Marx's whole emerging project therefore rested on his stance towards religion.

The concept of ideology was to emerge out of his analysis of religious consciousness. He runs with Feuerbach's notion that religion reverses real relationships, arguing that 'man makes religion, religion does not make man' and that therefore religion inverts the world; religion is 'an inverted world-consciousness'.[17] This image of inversion became central to Marx's fledgling concept of ideology. Likewise Feuerbach's notion of self-loss in religion is fundamental in the genesis of Marx's concept of alienation. The ideological inversion of relationships in religious consciousness is the first form of alienation Marx considers. In a direct echo of Feuerbach, he argues that 'the more man puts into God, the less he retains in himself'.[18] All his subsequent expansion of the concept of alienation comes in the wake of the initial discussion of religious alienation, and he acknowledges that it was the examination of this form of alienation which was achieved first: 'The immediate *task of philosophy* ... once the *holy form* of self-estrangement has been unmasked, is to unmask self-estrangement in its *unholy forms.*'[19] Feuerbach's characterisation of the egoistic individualism of Christian religiosity also informs Marx's first major attempt, in *On the Jewish Question*, to develop a theory of the state. Marx argues that, historically, the secular project of liberal democracy has resulted only in emancipation from state religion, not religion as such. In the USA, which he considered the most developed form, to date, of liberal democracy, religion positively flourishes. Paradoxically it is not the religious state which represents the triumph of Christianity, but the modern secular state. This is because the division between civil society and the state in liberal democracy is an expression of the egoistic individualism dominant in civil society, and this egoistic individualism is at the heart of modern Christianity.

Liberal democracy is thus profoundly Christian. For Marx the fact that in liberal democracy individuals acknowledge themselves via the intermediary of the state means not that they are merely doing something *analogous* to religious behaviour, but that this activity is itself religious.[20] Put another way, religion represents how far *political* emancipation falls below *human* emancipation.

When Macmurray began his intensive study of Marx the best known and most easily available text by the young Marx on religion was his *Contribution to the Critique of Hegel's Philosophy of Law. Introduction* (late 1843, early 1844). The actual remarks on religion only occupy a brief few sections at the very beginning of the work, but found here is Marx's most quoted statement on religion – that 'It is the *opium* of the people'. In fact this statement is embedded in a discussion in which *both* aspects of the Feuerbachian analysis of religion are present – the negative and the positive. Thus religious distress is deemed to be 'the *expression* of real distress and also the *protest* against real distress'; it is 'the sigh of the oppressed creature', 'the heart of a heartless world' and 'the spirit of spiritless conditions'. But then comes the killer: 'It is the *opium* of the people', and despite ingenious attempts to put a positive gloss on the narcotic metaphor, the negative connotation is surely deliberate. All the surrounding passages are resolutely negative: 'the struggle against religion is ... indirectly a fight against *the world* of which religion is the spiritual *aroma*', or 'the criticism of religion disillusions man to make him think and act and shape his reality like a man who ... has come to reason'.[21] And yet it was possible to assemble out of these early works elements towards a much more positive appreciation of religion, and one, furthermore, that could also use Marx's critique of dualism to distinguish an authentic from an inauthentic religion. As Macmurray threw himself into a detailed reading of the early Marx, this possibility became clear to him.

At the same time as Macmurray was engaged in his close reading of Marx, Isaiah Berlin was working on his biography of Marx, *Karl Marx: His Life and Environment*, which was to see the light of day in 1939 – but what contrasting readings of the early Marx they provide. Berlin claimed that he had read everything Marx had written – in the multi-volumed collection of Marx's original-language texts (the so-called MEGA edition)[22] – but it is clear that he was either unfamiliar with the *Economic and Philosophical Manuscripts*, which is not mentioned, or failed to see the significance of the text, a fact attested to by the complete absence of any discussion of the concept of alienation. His account of Marx's views on religion lacks nuance in its characterisation of Marx as simply hostile to religion, which is explained in terms of a psychological reaction to his father's opportunistic conversion from Judaism to Lutheranism, and the influence of Feuerbach's materialist critique of idealism.[23] Berlin has no understanding of the complexities of Feuerbach's project (describing the thinker as one of the 'mediocrities' in the history of thought whose 'contribution to philosophy is jejune and uninspired'[24]) and no sense of the linkage between religion and alienation; hence his total lack of appreciation of *On the Jewish Question*, where he merely notes Marx's rejection of Bauer's liberal solution to the Jewish question, before making the astonishing judgement that 'it is an essay of little value'.[25] In introductory notes to later editions of his book in the 1960s and 70s, Berlin acknowledged the lacuna on alienation, and also admitted that he was 'perhaps too deeply influenced' by two sources.[26] The first of these was what he termed the 'classical interpretations' of Marx produced by Engels, Plekhanov and Mehring. This, however, deepens the mystery of his treatment of the early Marx, in that Engels always retained great respect for Feuerbach, and in *Ludwig Feuerbach and the End of Classical German Philosophy*, a work which he described as the payment of 'an undischarged debt of honour' to the older man, he included 'a full acknowledgement of the influence which Feuerbach, more than any other post-Hegelian philosopher, had upon us during our period of storm and stress';[27] this influence is, moreover, closely detailed in Mehring's *Karl Marx: The Story of His Life* (1918), along with copious material on the religious struggle of the left-Hegelians, and a lengthy appreciation of the virtues and importance of *On the Jewish Question*.[28] With Plekhanov, the founder of Russian Marxism, the case for influence seems stronger, in that although he spends time in *Fundamental Problems of Marxism* rebutting those who wish to denigrate Feuerbach's theoretical achievements and reject his lasting influence on Marx, he, like Berlin, is primarily concerned with Feuerbach's theorising of materialism.[29] The second source of undue influence highlighted by the later Berlin is E.H. Carr's 1934 book on Marx, which rejoiced in the engagingly tendentious title of *Karl Marx: A Study in Fanaticism*. What immediately strikes one when reading this book is the perfunctory and disparaging treatment of Feuerbach, who while acknowledged as a teacher of Marx is nevertheless characterised as merely a muddled-headed materialist whom Marx rapidly out grew; given, as with Berlin, that the focus is on Feuerbach's materialism, it is interesting to note that in Carr's bibliography 'the standard work on Marxist philosophy' is deemed to be Plekhanov's *Fundamental Problems of Marxism*.[30] This perhaps casts a new light on Michael Ignatieff's claim about Berlin that 'having fluent Russian gave him a route to Marx barred to most other scholars, with the exception of E.H. Carr'[31] – such facility possibly misled them both! In the 1978 preface to the final edition of *Karl Marx: His Life and Environment*, Berlin called Carr's book 'admirable';[32] his view in the 1930s, expressed in a private letter, was less charitable: although acknowledging Carr's attempt to try to answer questions 'about M[arx]'s ideological evolution', and admitting that Carr was one of his sources, he nonetheless called the author 'frivolous' and 'patronising', 'always superficial, intolerably jocose, & usually wrong'.[33] Carr, in a memoir of 1980, expressed his own negative feelings about his early book: 'I knew nothing about what was really important in Marx ... It was a foolish enterprise, and produced a foolish book.'[34] The only real sign of Berlin's reappraisal of the young Marx in subsequent editions of *Karl Marx: His Life and Environment*, given that the author concluded that it was best to leave the book as a product of the time, is a softening of the patronising language used to characterise Feuerbach. All of this puts into relief Macmurray's achievement in recognising that the Feuerbachian critique of religion had a mighty and persistent effect on Marx, decisively shaping the latter's conception of alienation – a concept invisible to both Berlin and Carr.

Even after Macmurray had gone into print with his reading of the early Marx, some critics found the presentation of Marx so much at variance with conventional understandings of this thinker that they accused Macmurray of failing to grasp the nature of Marx's project. Thus Elizabeth Lam in a long critical essay, 'Does Macmurray Understand Marx?' (1940), while noting the importance for Macmurray of the texts collected in *Der Historische Materialismus: Die Frühschriften*, remarks vaguely that 'certain aspects of Marx's thought hitherto unknown come to light in this recently published volume', without outlining the nature of these 'aspects', before effectively downgrading these writings by asserting that 'it is necessary to take into consideration [Marx's] other writings of the same period which give us a more adequate clue to his total intellectual development'.[35] Showing no sign of understanding the true importance of the new collection (there is, for example, no mention of alienation, or the debt to Feuerbach), a collection which she only seems to know in French translation, Lam accuses Macmurray of fundamentally misunderstanding Marx, contrasting 'Macmurray's view of Marx and the real Marx'[36] – the latter confection, in its silence on the complexities of the trajectory of the early Marx, being not markedly different from the portrayal to be found in Berlin and Carr.

## Before Marx

Macmurray's intellectual development in the years before the 1930s was such as to generate significant potential bridgeheads to the work of Marx.[37] Like Marx he was clearly shaped by idealist thought, broke with it, but continued to be marked by that legacy. British idealism was the dominant philosophical force in Macmurray's student days prior to the First World War; as Bevir and O'Brien note, 'Balliol, together with the Scottish universities, was a birthplace and stronghold of British idealism.'[38] Although a 'realist' reaction set in after the war,[39] and Macmurray was happy to use this term to describe himself, he threw himself into a close study of the German idealists in the 1920s, and the influence can be seen in his political theorising just prior to his serious study of Marx. In 'The Conception of Society' (1930–1) he defended what he termed an 'adjectival' conception of society, where society is viewed as an aspect of human personality, involving 'the mutuality of human life',[40] namely the sharing of experience with others. This was to be an enduring element in Macmurray's philosophy and is deeply rooted in idealist conceptions of the constitution of the social, conceptions which had energised the young Marx's critique of abstract individualism.

Like Marx, Macmurray had consciously broken with idealism, and the term itself became a signifier in his work for the debilitating illusions to be found in the political, philosophical and religious life of modernity. In 'The

Conception of Society', the 'adjectival' conception of society is contrasted with the 'substantival' conception which defines society in terms of group life, and effectively idealises the group – most recently in terms of the nation state – but at the expense of the actual needs of real individuals:

> It seeks to justify the obligations of the individual to society through a conception of society as an ideal entity, while the individual who is saddled with these obligations remains an actual individual. In Rousseau's phrase, it takes 'men as they are and States as they ought to be'. As a consequence it is continually involved in fruitless efforts to equate the society as an ideal entity with the society as an actual entity.[41]

Likewise, Marx in *On the Jewish Question* had analysed the dualism at the heart of liberal democracy between the formal equality and community of the state, expressed as citizenship, and the substantive inequality and atomism of life in civil society. For both Macmurray and Marx a repressive top-down ideal had usurped the place of authentic bottom-up activity.

In the *German Ideology* Marx had characterised this misperception of reality as seeing the world through a *camera obscura*; perceiving the world upside down was the very essence of ideology. Macmurray also became increasingly concerned with the nature of unreality, and began to move towards another position which was to facilitate his appropriation of Marx – the unity of theory and practice. In the late 1920s Macmurray was gradually unifying the disparate elements in earlier theories of the individual – mind and body, reason and emotion, individual and social – in a resolutely anti-dualist frame of mind. His early thoughts on theory and practice revolved around the scientific methodology of verification through practice: 'things are only discovered to be unreal *in use*. The only test of unreality is a practical test. This is the secret of science.'[42] His first extensive development of these ideas is to be found in *Interpreting the Universe* (1933) where the living wholeness of 'immediate experience', taking the form of practical activity, is contrasted with the abstraction from such action to be found in 'reflection'; immediate experience is therefore 'our consciousness in living rather than our consciousness of living',[43] and therefore 'thought divorced from life is inherently unreal and untrustworthy'.[44] Shortly he was to call the unity of theory and practice 'the first fundamental principle of Marxian philosophy ... Everything else in communist thought dwindles into insignificance beside it.'[45]

## The dialogue with Marx

Once Macmurray began to immerse himself in the writings of the early Marx he was clearly excited by the fact that Marx's radical social theory emerged out of his analysis of religion, and he alighted on a phrase from the *Contribution to the Critique of Hegel's Philosophy of Law. Introduction*: 'the criticism of religion is the beginning of all criticism'.[46] He also recognised the centrality of

Feuerbach's radical analysis of Christianity in Marx's development from left-Hegelian to Communist materialist. This perception of the religious roots of the Marxian project suggested to Macmurray a criterion for judging that enterprise, for if the analysis of religion was flawed, was not the ensuing social theory? 'Marx ... would have agreed, I feel certain, that the correctness of his final position stands or falls by the correctness of his interpretation of religion'.[47] And it was indeed to be over the interpretation of religion that Macmurray signalled his fundamental disagreement with Marx.

Given Macmurray's prior appreciation of the phenomenon of idealism in political life, it is not surprising that he found particularly illuminating a passage in *On the Jewish Question* where Marx is attempting to describe the dual life individuals experience in a capitalist liberal democracy, and where he deploys a religious imagery: 'When the political state has achieved its true completion, man leads a double life, a heavenly one and an earthly one, not only in thought and consciousness but in reality, in life.'[48] Macmurray appreciates that Marx isn't merely deploying a metaphor here, but is rather describing a real social process in which the projection of human needs on to the state is a continuation of religious projection, and that these religious processes in liberal democracy had to be unmasked and socially overcome. However, for Macmurray, Marx's general irreligion was itself part of a greater religious moment, with the move to Communism an aspect not of the death but of the apotheosis of religion:

> When ... the ideal development is complete, and seeks its realisation in actuality, the pressure in human life to the realisation of religion necessarily takes the form of an attack upon religion. It is impossible at once to maintain the separation of the two worlds, and to unify them. To realise the Kingdom of Heaven on earth necessarily involves the disappearance of the idea of Heaven as another world in which the wrongs of this world are righted.[49]

Idealistic, institutionalised religion dies, but not authentic religion itself.

Macmurray alights on those elements in the early Marx which validate not merely religion but, more specifically, Christianity. He is taken by Marx's parallel endorsement of the historical achievements of Christianity and democracy, with Christianity's deification of the human in the figure of Jesus, and democracy's recognition of the social potential and needs of humanity; and he quotes Marx in the *Critique of Hegel's 'Philosophy of Right'* – 'Christianity is the religion *par excellence*, the essence of religion, deified man as a particular religion. Similarly democracy is the essence of all constitutions of the state, socialised man as a particular constitution of the state'.[50] He places Marx and Feuerbach in a tradition commencing with Hegel, in which Christianity is viewed as the cutting edge of humanity, reminding his readers that 'Hegel considered that his philosophy expressed abstractly the essence of Christian theology'.[51]

Macmurray's project here has some points of similarity with the German maverick Marxist philosopher Ernst Bloch, who in the 1930s was working on his own positive evaluation of religion, which was to form a fundamental dimension of his post-World War II classic *The Principle of Hope*. There is the recognition in Bloch of the achievement of Feuerbach who is 'a turning point in the philosophy of religion; from him onwards the final history of Christianity begins'; but this is not a simple act of destruction, for Feuerbach was acutely sensitive to the inheritance contained in religious traditions: 'he did not want to be merely a gravedigger of traditional religion ... on the contrary, he was fascinated by the problem of the religious heritage'.[52] Furthermore, his anthropological analysis of religious consciousness was of unique importance, and represented a culmination of a radical humanist element in religious thinking:

> No one has made a more concerted effort than he did to turn the flow of human ideals away from the Beyond and back to man whom these ideals reflect. One can even say, with some exaggeration, that no one, so far as *method* was concerned, was as indebted as he to the radically human line in Christianity.[53]

Bloch also places Feuerbach in terms of the latter's position on the Hegel/Marx axis; at one point, and in a notable phrase, he says that 'Feuerbach lies ... on that German salvation-line which leads from Hegel to Marx' (in distinction to the German 'disaster-line' taking in Schopenhauer, Nietzsche and, ultimately, Fascism),[54] and he quotes the young Hegel's remark that 'it has remained primarily the task of our day to vindicate, at least in theory, as the property of man, the treasures which have been squandered on heaven'.[55] A concern with the religious heritage of humanity is of fundamental importance in Bloch's own approach. He posits a 'utopian surplus'[56] among the ideological material of religion, the gold-bearing seam containing the potentialities and possibilities of the 'not-yet' world to come, a world which, in Marxist mode, he designates as Communism, but which differs from, and far exceeds in conception, Marx's own fragmentary notions. Bloch sees the turning point for religion as the moment when the elements invested in the external divinity are repatriated to their true home. This is not construed as reductionism, but rather as enrichment. Atheism is deemed to be the triumph of religion: 'the religious kingdom-intention as such *involves atheism, at last properly understood atheism*';[57] or as he put it in one of his typically paradoxical aphorisms: 'Only an atheist can be a good Christian; only a Christian can be a good atheist.'[58] In this sense, religion or, more specifically, 'meta-religion' remains: 'not simply no religion but ... the inheriting of it, meta-religious knowledge-conscience of the final Where To, What For problem: *ens perfectissimum*.'[59] Of course, there are major differences between Bloch and Macmurray, especially the former's explicit atheism and total commitment to Marxism, but the points of similarity are striking and represent parallel attempts to use the thought of Marx and German idealism to craft a socialism grounded in the rich resources of religion.

But Bloch is a utopian; he places utopianism at the very heart of his thought. What is Macmurray's stance on the utopian? The answer is that methodologically he is fiercely anti-utopian, and the term 'utopian' is consistently used in a pejorative manner. His philosophical assumptions made him particularly sensitive to the dangers of certain forms of imaginative 'oughts' which seemed to him to be the very definition of utopia. Specifically, his conception of the primacy of 'action', conceived of as the unity of thought and practice, disposed him to reject any attempt to validate thought as an autonomous and authoritative realm, a source of free-floating conceptions of the good life which could judge reality, and to which the world was somehow meant to conform. This wariness extended to a general suspicion of talk of 'ideals', which inhibited the open experimentalism that characterised the best practice of Christianity and Communism by trying to establish in advance that which could only emerge in the process of action. In his 'Here I Stand' document he denied that his statement about being a Christian outside Churches was 'in the ordinary sense of the term, a confession of faith' because he was 'concerned with facts, not with theories, not with ideals or aspirations, but with the making of history'.[60] This approach, he maintained, was that adopted by Jesus. In an unpublished manuscript which sought to explore the points of commonality between authentic Marxism and Christianity he argues that Jesus:

> pointedly abstains from laying down general principles of conduct as maxims to be followed ... There is nothing in the teaching of Jesus remotely resembling a philosophical system or a moral code ... He does not think of life as the realisation of an ideal ... Thus his statements about action are never definitions of an end to be realised, but either of the spirit which should animate action or of the means of achieving anything worth while.[61]

Likewise,

> the Communist spirit condemns ideals. It is not merely that Communism has no ideal and is not guided by ideals, it is that ideals are condemned as such ... Communist doctrine is therefore not a theory of ideal society, but a programme of social action.[62]

However, as the history of Marxism shows, the lack of a normatively informed conception of a future society is not sustainable at either the methodological or the existential level, and is invariably smuggled back in some form or other.[63] So it is with Macmurray. His critique of utopianism is really a critique of *abstract* utopianism, in the manner of Marx's critique of the utopian socialists. Thus in *The Philosophy of Communism* (1933) he echoes Marx's characterisation of the 'utopian socialists' in the *Communist Manifesto* as individuals who thought their own universal, undetermined insights could be the basis for a new creation:

> I am assuming that society is plastic in my hands, as if I were God making the world afresh ... Idealism in this form rests upon the delusion that in thought I can lift myself out of the stream of history and think in a way that has no relation to my way of life. It is to think that whenever I please I can come down from the clouds and push the world-process in the direction I should like it to go.[64]

What he doesn't rule out – for this would surely rule out politics itself – is an historically grounded future orientation which in *The Clue to History* (1938) he conceptualises in terms of a distinction between an 'ideal' and an 'intention', where intention is the conscious, purposeful dimension in human action, and 'ideal' a self-regarding abstraction from action.[65] In Macmurray's elaboration of the concept of intention a *future orientation* is clearly present, but this must take the form of action which is both thought and practice; goals, ends and purposes are all entailed but they have to be embodied in practice, and be generated, regenerated and validated on the basis of that practice: 'An intention is something that I am, *in fact*, trying to realize in action, not the conception of something that I might, or ought to, realize.'[66] This is not an issue of the scope or ambition of these purposes and intentions, as in many anti-utopian critiques, for Macmurray's intention, which he considers to be in historical continuity with the intentional activity of Jesus Christ, is no less than the establishment of the Kingdom of Heaven on earth. From this perspective Macmurray is not rejecting a future orientation, but merely seeking to establish the legitimate basis for its establishment.

Macmurray's conception of intentional activity forced him to consider that perennial issue of a goal-orientated politics, the relationship between ultimate and intermediate goals. He accepts that large important goals are likely to take quite some time to achieve, and will need to be approached via shorter-term objectives. He further maintains that the achievement of these more immediate goals will 'normally' involve 'the limitation of attention', a concentration on the immediate tasks, in which we 'forget, for the time being, the full intention to which it refers, and of which it forms part'.[67] Given that it is likely that the movement towards change will be made up of a variety of agencies each concentrating on its own specific intermediary goals, 'it is quite possible' that this 'may lead them to fail to recognize the underlying harmony of their separate efforts'[68] – a statement born of the tumultuous leftist politics of the period. Whether or not the insertion of the word 'normally' into his reflections on limiting attention was meant to exempt himself from this amnesia, it is the case that ultimate and intermediate goals co-exist in his work, with the former informing the latter.

At the existential level Macmurray was as much a dreamer as any other social thinker, or for that matter any other human being. The concept of the

Kingdom of Heaven provided a space in which his own deep longings and aspirations could inhabit. Because he rejected dualistic Christian notions of supernaturalism and 'otherworldliness', his focus was necessarily on the potentialities of this world, with the virtues of the authentic Christian tradition conceived as constitutive elements of the good society, one which, given the malformations of capitalism, lay in the future. The Kingdom of Heaven was deemed to articulate the deepest possibilities of humanity, which were to be concretised by purposeful activity. Herein lay Jesus' significance – his articulation of this properly religious conception of the Kingdom:

> We find in Jesus the paradigm of this coming to maturity of the religious consciousness in man … It meant straight away that he recognized his mission as the establishment of the Kingdom of God among men, the creation of the Kingdom of Heaven on earth.[69]

Furthermore, the great good society to come seemed to be borne along, and no longer blindly, by structural tendencies in modern society. Thus he was prepared to commit himself to stating the social form of the new reality:

> Communism is, therefore, the necessary basis of real freedom. Marx was perfectly right in describing the new form of society as a human society. For it is the only possible form of social relationship in which human development ceases to be merely an organic process and becomes an activity of rational beings.[70]

The two kingdoms, the realm of freedom and the Kingdom of Heaven, are not synonyms for Macmurray, the latter is a much fuller and richer concept, but Communism will be an integral aspect of its reality.

It is at this point that we reach the core of Macmurray's own utopian longings. From the late 1920s onwards Macmurray had been working with a triadic conception of modes of understanding of being. In the modern world, at the time of the scientific revolutions of the sixteenth and seventeenth century, reality had been conceived in 'mechanical' terms as discrete substances that could be understood through physics. The inadequacies of this model led to the development in the nineteenth century of an 'organic' conception of the world as a living organism, obeying a dialectical logic, initially knowable through biology but in time through the reformed conceptions of other disciplines. This conception now was itself inadequate to understand all the complexities of reality. Specifically it could not grasp the highest form of relations between people, which needed a new form of understanding, one he termed the 'personal'. These three modes of understanding thus refer to three forms of being, or more exactly relationships within being, for there are indeed mechanical and organic relationships as well as personal ones. But although all three are constitutive of reality there is a clear rank ordering in Macmurray's mind with personal relations entailing the true flowering of the world. He used various words to signify these relationships but most frequently he settled on the term 'friendship'. Friendship was the canvas on which he painted *his* vision of the good life, at once affirmative and critical; in these moments his style became almost lyrical:

> Friendship ... is the essence of morality ... Ultimately our own reality consists precisely in our ability to know people as they really are and to love them for what they really are. Everything that prevents that – fear or pride or the passion for wealth or power or position in men, the subordination of human beings to organizations and institutions, an unjust distribution of wealth or opportunity in the community – everything that opposes or denies the inherent right of a human individual to be himself and to realize and love the reality of other human beings, is the enemy of morality. To be oneself freely and spontaneously, to realize oneself – that *is* to be a good man or woman.[71]

This is the utopian heart of Macmurray's project.

His attempt to ground this great normative beacon created problems in his dealings with the Marxist tradition. Nothing could be allowed that threatened to particularise or historicise friendship; it was deemed to be essentially the same in any historical or geographical context: 'Friendship ... is just friendship in England or in equatorial Africa, in the twentieth century AD or in the twentieth century BC.'[72] To reinforce this point he brings to bear a word full of religious resonance – friendship is 'eternal',[73] not in the sense of everlasting but rather as immutable. But mutability is inscribed into the very substance of historical materialism; that friendship, a fundamentally *social* relationship, could somehow lie outside the process of historical change would have struck Marx as deeply unsound. From Macmurray's perspective the failure to appreciate that friendship was 'superorganic'[74] indicated an unacceptable application of an organic model to an arena in which it had no real purchase. This charge he levelled against Communist dialectical materialism; his attitude towards Marx was more complicated.

The Communists were quite right, he argued, in attributing a dialectical logic to succeeding modes of production in history; their mistake was not to realise that Communism created the basis for a society where non-dialectical 'personal' relations would flourish. Because Communists assume that mutual co-operation is the highest form of human relationship they are trapped in an organic approach to such relationships, and believe, therefore, that a Communist mode of production is necessary *and sufficient*, whereas for Macmurray it is merely necessary. In the case of Marx he cannot quite make up his mind whether he too is tainted with organicism. The element of dubiety comes from an insightful reading of Marx's stance on dialectics. He rightly realises that for Marx dialectics in history is an indication of primitiveness, not sophistication – modes of production proceed dialectically because history lacks a controlling subject, hence conflict and revolution. Macmurray interprets Marx's remark that the period before Communism is mere prehistory and that only in Communism will history actually *begin* to mean that Marx had an inkling of Macmurray's own position, that 'a truly human society would follow a process of development which could not be interpreted dialectically'.[75] This does seem a plausible reading of Marx, but Macmurray was not sure.

The designation of friendship as 'eternal' was neither metaphor nor rhetoric but expressed Macmurray's belief that friendship was a profoundly religious experience. The Communist desire to abolish religion was thus indicative of deep confusion as to the nature of reality. Communism, following Marx, was aware of the idealist dimensions of religion; its mistake was to assume that all religion was idealist, and that a post-capitalist religion was a contradiction in terms. The Communist rejection of religion in Communist society speaks of an impoverished conception of humanity where mere social reform is sufficient for the good life. It also ignores the Feuerbachian insight, embedded in the early Marx, that humanity's deepest hopes and fears have always taken a religious form. Why, Macmurray asks, should this cease with the passing of capitalism? The idea that humanity can get by without recourse to religion is utopian in the sense of foolish idealism; the hopes and fears surrounding love and death are not going to disappear simply because of a new mode of organising society, and neither therefore will religion:

> Religion has always been specially bound up with the fear of death in particular, and it seems to me that only a mad idealist could suggest that the socialisation of the means of production will make an end of that fear and of the ramifications of its effects.[76]

More positively, a non-idealist, non-dualist religion would be a vehicle for the full flourishing of personality in a Communist society. This, however, as Macmurray recognises, would be a step too far for Marx, for whom 'the total rejection of religion as such, is an essential condition of the acceptance of Communism'.[77]

And yet Macmurray cannot resist baptising the Communists despite their heartfelt espousal of atheism. Compared with dualistic, idealistic Christians whose actions reveal that they don't have a real belief in God, the Communists, with their confidence in a beneficent power in history, and a willingness to sacrifice their own lives for the benefit of suffering humanity, show by their practice a genuine faith in the Godliness of reality; a faith, moreover, rightly disgusted by the pious religiosity of orthodox Christianity: 'nothing is left for him but a total repudiation of religion. Only by a profession of atheism can he maintain his own faith.'[78] This is not intended by Macmurray to suggest that the Communists are now the true way forward, for their atheism is indicative of an inadequate grasp of reality, but rather that Christianity must regain its belief in God, and begin the job of creating the Kingdom of Heaven on earth.

## Jesus

Macmurray's understanding that the thought of Hegel and Feuerbach, and ultimately Marx, was shaped by its engagement with Christianity provided further evidence for his long-standing conviction that the life and teachings of Jesus represented the world historical discovery of the riddle of human salvation. Criticisms from orthodox Christians that he was pandering to the Marxists by attempting to *manufacture* a Communist Jesus, or from Communists that he was engaged in tendentious historical regression would, he believed, miss this central point. He insisted that his attraction to the work of Marx and the modern Communist movement was ultimately the product of his finding in Marxism echoes of material first encountered in the Gospels. In *Creative Society* (1935) and *The Clue to History* (1938) the figure of Jesus moves centre-stage in the development of Macmurray's radical vision, and in his attempt to show the ways in which Marxism needed to be supplemented and critiqued.

Macmurray's anxiety that, in his characterisation of Christ, he might be thought too accommodating to Communism perhaps reflects an awareness that he had gone out of his way to show Jesus' affinity to significant elements in Communist praxis, to the extent of tracing out key historical materialist themes in the biblical narratives; a project clearly driven by the political need to engage positively with British and international Communism. Thus he describes as 'structural ideas in the religion of Jesus': 'the unity of theory and practice, the dialectical nature of social development, the importance of class conflict, and the fundamental part played by economics in the social process'.[79] In a reading of the parable of the prodigal son which shows the influence of Marx's analysis of alienation in the *Economic and Philosophical Manuscripts*, Macmurray argues that Jesus was highlighting the dialectical process whereby humanity becomes estranged from itself, and can only regain unity by going through a process of complete loss. Thus the prodigal son is lured by wealth and luxury away from the community of his father, and it is only when he ultimately succumbs to total poverty that he realises what he has lost, and returns to his home:

> The long process of impoverishment and slavery was required to overcome his self-alienation from his own community and to reveal to him the fact that he was starving in the midst of plenty, and that he had only to return to his father's house to have enough and to spare.[80]

This, Macmurray insists, is not a mere secular analogy of a religious phenomenon, for his Jesus is acutely aware of the economic roots of spiritual malaise, and the Kingdom of Heaven brings with it an entirely legitimate material prosperity, where 'the meek shall inherit the earth'. Jesus was thus engaged in a process which embodied the unity of theory and practice. Convinced of the unreliability of the rich, he chose 'from amongst the common people a band of disciples' and thereby created 'the nucleus of a party', and with this 'proceeded to extend the circle of his adherents through missionary propaganda'.[81] Finally, abandoned by the people when he refused to be a national Messiah, he gained 'full insight into the dialectical process through which the Kingdom of Heaven must be established' – his own death would be the basis of ultimate triumph, and to effect this 'he decided to challenge the ruling classes in a final dramatic fashion.'[82] The conceptual and linguistic resonances of this material could not have been lost on anyone at the time.

Macmurray grounds Jesus' achievements in his Jewishness, and Jewishness itself is inserted into a dialectical triad of Jewish, Greek and Roman that provides a historico-philosophical framework for his analysis of the development of Western society. In the years before his engagement with Marxism, Macmurray had sought to craft a philosophical history of the contributions of religion, art and science to the creation of the modern world. These attempts took different forms but all showed his idealist heritage in their attempt to invest triads of historical individuals or cultures with world-historic philosophical significance. By 1930, in a pamphlet introducing a series of radio broadcasts he was due to present on the BBC, he was able to provide a sketch of the terrain that he was to explore throughout the rest of the decade:

> Three old civilizations have been mixed together to form the culture of which we are the heirs – the Hebrew, the Greek and the Roman, a religious, an artistic and an organizing, administrative or scientific civilization. These three streams of experience have never really fused. Indeed the main problem of European civilization hitherto has arisen from the strain that their antagonisms have set up, and from the effort, never successful, to unite them in a single culture.[83]

By the time he came to write *The Clue to History*, which finally emerged in 1938, the effects of the dialogue with Marxism are apparent in his analysis of the three civilisations, seldom in terms of explicit reference to Marx, but significantly informing much of the controlling argument.

Macmurray's construct of the biblical Hebrews was to bear a good deal of weight in his speculations of the 1930s. Drawing on decades of intensive reading of the Old and New Testaments, Macmurray produced a personal *mythus* in which ancient Judaism served as both historical master key and fount of normativity – part Golden Age, part historical *geist*, part ultimate *telos*. As the decade developed and Fascism's threat to the values espoused by Macmurray became more and more evident, he viewed the centrality of virulent anti-Semitism within German National Socialism as further confirmation that a global struggle between the forces of light and darkness was approaching a climax. Hitler, he argued, instinctively recognised that Judaism constituted a root and branch rejection of his barbaric will to power. But Macmurray's enthusiasm for ancient Hebrew society was grounded in a clearly Christian perspective, for it was Macmurray's conviction that Christianity was the efflorescence of Judaism. The 'rejection' of Jesus by established Judaism was, for Macmurray, the point at which the spirit of Jewish culture began its tortuous historical ascent towards universality.

## History

In Macmurray's speculative history, ancient Hebrew society retained its religious form while all other societies abandoned theirs. A religious civilisation is one in which there are no autonomous spheres – as is, for example, art, science, morality, law *and* religion. Rather, religion is the synthesis of all these practices – it is not merely one other distinct practice. All societies apart from the Hebrews have religions, but only Hebrew society is genuinely religious, because it does not have a religion: 'if a society ... has a religion it is not religious. If it is religious it cannot have a religion.'[84] This is another way of stating that ancient Hebrew society is radically anti-dualist in its make-up – there are no dualisms between the religious and the secular, the spiritual and the material, reflection and action, the ideal and the actual, this world and the next. Time and again Macmurray reiterates the claim that the biblical Hebrews had no conception of an afterlife, that their religious project was entirely concerned with this life. Their God was a fellow worker in the real world, not a distant aristocratic deity in some transcendental realm. The Old Testament narrative is construed as a struggle of the Jewish people against tendencies towards dualism in their society, as in their resistance to the kingship of Saul, the prophetic struggle against attempts to develop a priestly ruling class, and the Jubilee redistribution as a means to undermine class polarisation in the economy. In Macmurray's treatment Jesus is deemed to have understood that this was his inheritance from the Jewish people, and that his task was to renew this essential dimension. Hence Macmurray reads Matthew 22:35–40, where Jesus intimately links love of God with love of neighbour, as both cultural heritage and radical imperative:

> Master, which *is* the greatest commandment in the law? Jesus said unto him, Thou shalt love thy God with all thy heart, and with all thy soul, and with all thy mind. This is the first and great commandment. And the second *is* like unto it, Thou shalt love thy neighbour as thyself. On these two commandments hang all the law and the prophets.

The political demand Macmurray extracts from this is that society must be 'equalitarian and democratic', conceived in his personalist sense as 'the inner democracy and equality of friendship'.[85]

In an implicit critique of Communist class reductionism, Macmurray situates this call for a new religious civilisation in a strongly voluntarist conception of agency. Dualism in thought is not ultimately caused by class dualism in society; rather, it is the 'social acceptance' of class division that is the real cause. If this were not the case then people would be simply prisoners of their social position. The rejection of class division is thus the beginning of the royal road to the abolition of all forms of dualism; it is therefore possible 'to recover the religious form of consciousness even in a dualist social order, by rejecting the social dualism and working for its abolition'.[86] What is not clear here is whether or not the criticism is addressed simply to Bolshevik theory or is meant to also encompass Marx's conceptions.

Immediately striking in the presentation of the historical vicissitudes of the Jewish spirit in *The Clue to History* is the markedly dialectical cast of the analysis – a dialectic owing much to Macmurray's recent immersion in the work of Marx, but also to the idealist dialectics of Marx's youth – and his own. An epic drama of the emergence of modernity out of the ancient and Medieval worlds is presented via the concepts and language of negation and contradiction, at times, it has to be said, verging on a schematic scholasticism, with the messy historical particularity marshalled into neat formations where negations are negated, contradictions sublated, and 'necessary' dynamics unfold. From the definite article in the book's title onward there is also a degree of assumed historical omniscience in the authorial tone – an assurance that palpably shades, on occasions, into the dogmatic, as spectacularly partial political judgements are presented as self-evident truth.

The rewarding core of this analysis is a nicely nuanced exploration of the double-edged nature of modern secular society that anticipates current 'post-secular' concerns. Deeply critical of the modern dualistic understanding of the relationship between the religious and the secular, he attempts to uncover the historical projects that brought this distinction into being, and those that promise its ultimate transcendence. In a manner akin to Feuerbach and the early Marx he seeks to reveal the social roots of contemporary conceptions of the religious and its boundaries, as well as the internal resistances to undistorted comprehension of the limitations of these conceptions. The aim, as with Feuerbach and Marx, is not to apportion blame or praise to historical actors, but to bring out the controlling social logics underpinning the actions and self-understandings of these groups and individuals.

At first glance it might seem that Macmurray is not looking forward to the overcoming of the distinction between the religious and the secular but to the total annihilating victory of just one of the elements – the religious. It is certainly the case that he does conceive of the society of the future as a thoroughly religious one, in the sense that ancient Jewish society was inherently religious. First, however, as his characterisation of the biblical Hebrews indicates, his conception of the religious is a capacious one: in ancient times it was the point prior to the breakdown of integrated society, and the emergence of religion as a distinctive set of beliefs and practices apart from other aspects of life. In this sense a future 'religious' society is a form of the return of the integrated society. Furthermore, this new society isn't simply a 'return', where history is a circular process of the re-establishment of the Golden Age. The intervening history between the two moments of ancient and future religion is not a dead time, nor a desert to be endured, but rather provides the social, economic and cultural basis for a religious society of immensely greater complexity and sophistication than its ancient Jewish forbear – including all the valuable dimensions of the 'secular' aspects of preceding times. A parallel conception, but a very far from exact one, can be found in late nineteenth-century Marxist theories which, building on the anthropological speculations of Engels in *The Origin of the Family, Private Property and the State* (itself indebted to the anthropological work of Lewis Morgan), conceived of future Communist society as the return, at a higher level, of the supposed primitive communism of prehistoric times.

It is not too fanciful to argue that Macmurray attempts to overcome the rigidities of hyper-secular discourse in the very way he argues and writes. The philosopher Charles Taylor has acknowledged that in the past he kept his deeply held Roman Catholic convictions out of his philosophical writings because he believed that such material was out of place in the process of secular philosophical conversation.[87] This convention is part of the legacy of what Richard Rorty has described, and defended, as the liberal deal between the Enlightenment and religion, since religion threatens to contaminate the inclusive conversations of a liberal society. 'The main reason religion needs to be privatised is that ... it is a conversation-stopper.'[88] To provide what he considers an analogous example, he cites the hypothetical case of a person in a gathering of professionals who suddenly says: 'Reading pornography is about the only pleasure I get out of life these days'; 'the ensuing silence,' Rorty comments 'masks the group's inclination to say, "So what? We weren't discussing your private life; we were discussing public policy. Don't bother us with matters that are not our concern."'[89] Macmurray, however, cheerfully mixes religious and secular modes of argument, and traditions of thought and presentation, with, for example, a biblical text sitting cheek by jowl with a complex philosophical argument drawn from Hegel and Marx, or moral exhortation, reminiscent of the pulpit, embedded in a passage of technical social analysis. Given what we know of Macmurray's life, notably the fervent evangelical Protestantism of his youth, one could view his texts, psycho-analytically, as transcripts of unresolved tensions, in which atavistic currents break through the surface of secular reason. But this interpretation would do Macmurray a disservice. Rather, one senses a conscious intention to address perennial issues in a new way, which draws upon the historical achievements of both the secular and the religious, and breaks up existing academic and literary divisions of labour. And it was the case that this sense that Macmurray was subverting existing paradigms contributed to his growing influence throughout the 1930s.

*The Clue to History* uses biblical texts as sources of metaphor, as means of bringing out levels of meaning and significance that mere historical analysis cannot convey, and as a form of linkage to the remarkable religious society that produced them. Insofar as there is an overarching text in *The Clue to History* it is, or to be exact, they are two interrelated passages: Matthew 13:33, 'The kingdom of heaven is like unto leaven, which a woman took, and hid in three measures of meal, till the whole was leavened', and 1 Corinthians 5:6, 'Know ye not that a little leaven leaveneth the whole lump?' Macmurray deploys the imagery of the leaven and the lump as a dynamic metaphor for the immanent transformation of society occurring through ancient and modern history. Furthermore, the fact that this is a parable of Jesus invests it with the authority of a truly paradigmatic religious life. This, in turn, enables Macmurray to ground his analysis of the development of the modern world in a deep ontology of the divine – in God itself.

Quite what Macmurray means by God is not easy to determine.[90] The analysis deals less with 'is' (which, frankly, is largely left to inference) than with 'isn't'. His desire to distance himself from conventional 'dualist' conceptions of God results in a good deal of negative definition, stating what God is not: not a potentate, not outside of history, not the gatekeeper for a blissful or agonising afterlife, not a deity who can be cajoled into granting special favours – not, in short, a wholly transcendent God. What remains, turning to the positive (and which, to repeat, seems rather unspecified), would appear to have roots in European idealist philosophy (Hegel and Spinoza come to mind); God would be the ground and the process of reality itself, where, to use Kenneth Ingram's gloss, the whole is more than the sum of its parts, and therefore transcendence is within immanence:[91] an unfolding of potentiality in which humanity is an integral component. Macmurray makes this point in his 1936 critique of Karl Barth's emphasis on the transcendence of God: 'The emphasis on the transcendence of God is itself a denial of the transcendence of God. For the transcendence of God *is* his immanence; and his immanence is his transcendence. God in action is the history of the world.'[92] God-talk, though it has its uses, can lead one's search for God in an unfruitful direction, for the divine is to be known in the profane:

> the truly religious man will talk little about God – he will leave that to the speculative philosopher and theologian – and much about the empirical life of personal relationships. He will realize what Blake meant when he wrote: 'God only exists and is in existing beings or men.'[93]

Anything more than this, or, in Macmurray's sense, less than this, as in an external God, would be to succumb to an erroneous and enervating dualism.

Three levels can be identified in the historical narrative of *The Clue to History*. There is a meta-narrative outlining the basic plot of European history. According to this story, Christianity, as the inheritor of the communal egalitarianism of the Jews, has historically been the leaven in the lump of society, the cutting edge of progress, be it in religious or secular form, propelling Europe through ever more advanced social forms towards the true community of the future:

> Christianity remains itself, as the intention to realize the universal community which is the reality of human life. That intention, which comes

from the Hebrew culture, is embedded like leaven in the races of Europe, and works as a ferment in them.[94]

The second level is an account of the structural dynamics of European history that draws heavily on Hegelian and, crucially, Marxist understandings. The analysis isolates structural constants in the rise and fall of social formations, notably the way the intentions of dominant groups become self-frustrating, thereby weakening the society, which allows social forces from below, the natural home of the essential egalitarianism of Christianity, to bring about a more advanced social form, which, in turn, goes through the same pattern of ascent, decline and supersession. For Macmurray, Christianity provides a degree of vision to rising social forces which are largely motivated by less-exalted aims, and thereby the destructive and frequently blind energies unleashed in dialectical conflicts issue forth in progress:

> It is, in fact, Christianity which saves the substance of societies which destroy themselves by dualism, and carries it over into the society which follows it in a higher form. The history of Europe is a continuity of progress and not a mere succession of unrelated societies precisely because the Christian intention of creating a universal community of equality and freedom is embodied in its substance.[95]

The final level, and in many ways the most interesting and distinctive, is Macmurray's exposition of the specific dynamics of each period, the particular concatenation of ideas, movements and structures, be it the Christianisation of the Roman Empire, the emergence of dual authority, spiritual and political, in the Middle Ages, or the rise of individualist capitalism and the world-historical conflict between Soviet Communism and Fascism.

In effect, Macmurray perceives a golden thread of authentic Christianity running through the fabric of European history. The interpretive task he sets himself is to track the often elusive trajectory of this intention, its presence in forms not merely not religious, but deemed anti-religious, and its frequent absence in the formally religious. The problem for anyone attempting to reconstruct this historical process is that the three levels of analysis developed by Macmurray are not actually fully integrated into a comprehensive, coherent and consistent approach. What one actually gets is a sequential juxtaposition of the levels where, for example, a passage dealing with the internal dynamics of an historical society is succeeded by one offering elements of a general structural explanation, with glimpses of the meta-narrative interspersed throughout. The result is that there are significant explanatory lacunae and troubling inconsistencies. The best one can do, therefore, is to follow Macmurray's own idiosyncratic focus.

For Macmurray Christianity's first major step towards universality was its move beyond Palestine into the broader Roman Empire. This, however, also occasioned a double fall from grace. First, Christianity eventually became the official religion of the Empire and thereby began an uneasy relationship of dual power with the state. With this fateful arrangement 'it ceased to be possible to identify Christianity with the Church'.[96] Second, at the level of theory, Christianity became corrupted by Greek Stoic conceptions in which a fundamentally contemplative orientation generated enervating hierarchical dualisms centred on the notion of a divine soul imprisoned in a fallen body, where the spiritual and the ideal were privileged over the practical and the material. Thus at the very beginnings of European Christian history Macmurray wishes to distance authentic Christianity from its dominant institutional and doctrinal forms. Thus the foundation is laid for his later historical contention that authentic Christian confrontation increasingly took the form of a secular critique of social and political institutions – 'why we habitually associate the forces in European history which aim at equality and freedom with secular and political action, and yet can find that they have their origin in the teaching of Jesus and nowhere else.'[97]

Rome is succeeded by the 'higher' social formation of Medieval Christendom, though Macmurray is very vague as to precisely how this came about. Given his claim that ruling classes ultimately frustrate their own intentions and thereby allow progressive egalitarian (i.e. authentically Christian) currents from below to prevail, one must presume that he believes something like this happened with the Roman Empire. This must be the meaning of his bald statement that 'The Roman will to power destroyed itself. The meek inherited the earth',[98] though who the 'meek' were, or how precisely they inherited the earth, is not explained. The Medieval world is deemed to be a higher social formation than Imperial Rome because of the element of conscious Christian universality at work in its midst, whereas Roman universality had arisen out of 'blood and soil' and 'organic impulse'.[99] But Macmurray's intention was not to praise the Medieval order but to bury it, for within that world ripened forces that would usher in the modern world. The Church, the spiritual power, is the dominant force in the Medieval world, but the inner dynamics of this institution leads to self-frustration and the eventual triumph of the temporal power of the secular state. Part of the ground is prepared by the Church's need to maintain and promote spiritual authority, which leads it down the path of temporal authority as it seeks to discipline, and bring order to, European society. This threatens the division of labour which maintains the dual leadership of Christendom. Within the Church, moreover, and specifically within the monastic system, Macmurray argues, what in effect is a new reality principle is developing, one which taps into the creative forces of authentic Christianity. The underlying desire here – to credit Christianity with the creation of the modern world – involves Macmurray in making some very large claims for Medieval monasticism. Thus while the claim that the Reformation sprang from the monk Martin Luther, if simplistic, is nonetheless relatively plausible, this cannot be said of the accompanying assertion that the Renaissance owes its origin to another Medieval 'monk' – Francis of Assisi! Ingeniously he also argues that the roots of modern individualism are to be found in monasticism, in that spiritual discipline involved a suppression of the self and that this led to a concentration on that self, thereby preparing the way for a positive approach to the self: 'the effort to suppress the self will disappear and the demand for self-fulfilment and self-satisfaction will take its place'.[100] The monasteries, in this reading, were not simply powerhouses of creativity, they also embodied powerful elements of economic egalitarianism, which linked them to the aspirations of subordinate classes in the temporal world, links facilitated by the social services of education and healing provided by the monasteries. Thus dangerous energies were building up whose focus of discontent was the Church itself. This fact was not lost on the temporal powers,who took the opportunity to channel this energy in the direction of temporal superiority, with purely national churches firmly under the control of nation-states; thus 'the building up of this secular ideal, and the impulse to break with the Church, is the work of the Church itself'.[101]

Macmurray's arguments about the positive (and religious) aspects of secularism anticipate the recent work of the Roman Catholic philosopher Charles Taylor, whom we have encountered earlier. Taylor is in no doubt that the secular project was both necessary and desirable. In 'Modes of Secularism' he speaks of the 'inescapability of secularism',[102] and in 'A Catholic Modernity?' argues that not only has this phenomenon brought the benefits of political accountability (via a liberal 'rights' programme), but that the break with 'Christendom' which this involved actually developed elements of Christianity which were blocked by the old order; in short that 'this process ... made possible what we now recognize as a great advance in the practical penetration of the gospel in human life'.[103] This has not, however, come about without a cost, namely the marginalisation of the religious and spiritual, prompting the question: 'Do we really have to pay this price – a kind of spiritual lobotomy – to enjoy modern freedom?'[104] The negative answer he provides to this question moves him into the ambit of postsecularism, and into the territory explored by Macmurray over half a century earlier.

In Macmurray's account of the development of the modern world the stress is on the religious core of progressive secular thought and practice, and therefore, necessarily, the secular dimensions of the religious. Secularism is not, therefore, some kind of unconscious tool of a religious project but is itself part of the substance of a fully human and consequently religious society. To conventional (i.e. dualist) religious consciousness secularism will appear as a deadly foe; and this is not an illusion, for it does aim at the destruction of that debased form of Christianity:

> the secular movement which is the bearer of the Christian intention tends towards the destruction of organized religion. The Christianity which comes to consciousness in the modern world is not recognized as Christian, and tends more and more to be considered anti-Christian and anti-religious.[105]

The analysis of the destructive dynamics of modern society would seem to owe much to Marx, and focuses on the self-frustration of the individualist pursuit of freedom. Macmurray's more distinctive contribution lies in his characterisation of the various counter-currents (both theoretical and practical) which he believes will bring about the new social order. Conscious of the historical antagonism between religion and science, he provocatively describes science as the theoretical cutting edge of the religious impulse. This is deemed to flow from the experimental character of modern science which overcomes the theory/practice distinction: 'it is action based on theory and determining theory ... it has overcome dualism: it is therefore the expression of the full achievement of the Christian intention.'[106] The Enlightenment scientific virtues of predictability, control, universality, co-operation and progress are extolled as expressing Christianity's finest theoretical manifestation to date. But in modern dualist society science is in reality still trapped in a debilitating realm of pure knowledge, whose power is exploited by interests inimical to human flourishing; as in (an example much on Macmurray's mind at this period in the 1930s) the destructive project of the burgeoning armaments industry.

Turning to the realm of 'practice', Macmurray's desire to establish the theoretical primacy of Jesus, and possibly an element of authorial hubris, results in a degree of faint praise for Marx, who is merely credited for his explication of the ideological processes of modern society: 'Our interest,' Macmurray confides, 'lies in seeing how the process achieves its opposite, and destroys the system which it sets up, from the point of view of the law of self-frustration which Jesus discovered',[107] which is to do a disservice to the influence of Marx on the subsequent analysis. Again, the main interest here, and Macmurray's achievement, is in re-baptising the seemingly Godless and uncovering the human in the divine. His *leitmotif* of the link between the authentic Christian impulse and the 'common people' is now deployed in his account of the emergence of socialism. Against its conscious intentions the employing class effectively collectivises the working class through industrial organisation, and begins the process of consciousness-raising through elementary education, and political organisation through its democratic institutions. Still itself in the grip of dualist thinking, the working class develops successively more advanced, but still inadequate, forms of socio-economic, political and cultural forms, from trades unionism through the establishment of workers' parties and the development of socialist programmes. With no doubt the experience of the collapse of Ramsay Macdonald's Labour government and the formation of the National Government in 1931 very much in mind, Macmurray argues that the working class is now on the threshold of uniting theory and practice and a move towards a collective society:

> One further step in the development will compel theory and practice into unity, and it can do it most simply by revealing the contradiction between the theory and practice of a socialist government which makes the attempt to introduce socialism without unifying the political and economic functions of social life. If they make an attempt they must inevitably produce an economic crisis. If they still persist in their idealism they must

combine with the representatives of the ruling classes to achieve a purely political unification of parties at the expense of the workers.[108]

In response to these developments the employing class is forced to organise amongst itself to try to resist working class progress thereby undermining the whole individualist project of this class. Thus the two great classes of modern society are swept along by an inner logic which propels them into two very different ideological directions: 'The working-class movement tends towards communism in practice but rejects the intention of it; while the employing class tends equally in the direction of fascism against its intention.'[109]

## Communism

As we have already seen, Macmurray's study of Marx in the 1930s had been part of a response to the phenomenon of world Communism, which meant inevitably that he was also drawn to the task of analysing the nature of the Soviet Union. If the Gospel metaphor of the leaven and the lump seemed apposite for his exploration of European history in general, in his account of the progressive movement in modern Europe, and specifically in his reflections on the USSR, he utilised Matthew's metaphor of the good fruit: 21:43, 'The Kingdom of God shall be taken from you and given to a nation bringing forth the fruits thereof', and 7:16, 'Ye shall know them by their fruits.' The first passage suggested that the original vessel for human salvation (Christianity) could lose this capacity, and that the mission might pass to a more worthy vehicle (Communism), while the second stressed the importance of actual results as opposed to intentions and theories (Communist practice as opposed to Christian rhetoric). In his writings of the 1930s Macmurray wants both to distinguish the Soviet Union from the full Communism of the future *and* defend the Soviet experience from a range of attacks, especially those from a religious perspective. In pursuit of the first objective he deploys the internal Marxist argument that the dictatorship of the proletariat (which he equates with the Soviet stage) is a transitional stage which uses the state to create the conditions for the withering away of the state in a truly classless society. However, using Rousseau's image of people being forced to be free, he creates distance between himself and the Soviet experiment by articulating the negative consequences of employing the repressive instrument of a state. This analysis is itself embedded in a recognition that the USSR emerged out of largely feudal, not capitalist, conditions which bequeathed the new society a special inheritance, some of it positive ('the communal traditions of pre-capitalist society'[110]), some negative (it has to make 'a heroic effort to provide the conditions' necessary for further development[111]). Soviet Russia is therefore deemed to confound many of the perspectives of orthodox Communist opinion in being both greater than those expectations, given its status as a truly new and complex reality, and lesser, in that it cannot function as a universal model for developments elsewhere. The USSR is not therefore the end of history but the introduction of a very important new element into the historical pattern, one which has a crucial role in future developments worldwide.

Macmurray was also prepared publicly to defend the Soviet Union. In March 1934 he joined a certain Professor Wood in addressing the Council Members of the Industrial Christian Fellowship, the Bishop of Malmesbury in the chair. Wood's speech was strongly anti-Marxist and highly critical of the USSR, and rested on a rather conventional Christianity. Macmurray's stated method was not to contrast the realities, as he saw them, of the Soviet Union with the theoretical values and aspirations of Christianity, but to contrast the USSR with the actual social system of a supposedly Christian Britain. Thus he is quite prepared to condemn the revolutionary violence of the Bolsheviks – 'the atrocities and barbarities that were involved in the revolutionary activity itself, and still are. They cannot be condoned, they cannot be justified, they are definitely unchristian'[112] – but insists that this has to be set against the Black and Tan campaign in Ireland, British repression in India, and the slaughter of the First World War. When, however, he turns from contextualising bad practice to illustrating good, a different voice emerges, one bursting with utopian energy. For it is the case that one can utopianise an existing society. Thomas More's island of Utopia, although imaginary, was a geographical not an historical construct – it lay elsewhere, not somewhere in the future. Think too of the British radicals' response to the French Revolution. Such a society *need not* be perfect, merely a considerable improvement on existing arrangements – not the best but the better. Many studies have shown how the Soviet Union in the 1920s and 30s attracted people who really did want to believe that something significantly better was occurring in that society, and who convinced themselves, or were convinced by others, that this was really happening.[113] In Macmurray's case, with his dislike of abstract utopianism and concern with the practical and the actual, one senses a strong impulse to believe in the Soviet transformation. There is naivety here and credulity, but not duplicity. He presents the 'evidence' as steely fact, but the excitement is there. Read, for example, the last sentences of his address:

> There is already in the world, covering one-sixth of the globe, a great people building a system of human society, which is far nearer, in many respects, to the Christian ideal of what society ought to be than anything the world has yet seen. We have already dropped to second place in the order of civilized life.[114]

Likewise his claim that 'the fundamental principle of social organization on which the reorganization of Russia has been carried through ... is expressed in a simple principle – the Bolsheviks express it themselves – there shall be no exploitation of one man by another',[115] or his panegyric to the Russian leadership:

> the rulers of Russia themselves live at a standard of life, which is probably no higher than that of a working man in this country, and ... they work

overtime day in and day out for years. For what reason? What is their motive? Their motive is simply the motive of service, of building a society in the world that they believe to be just.[116]

Jews are emancipated, women liberated, racialism punished, individualism cherished, criminals reformed, full employment reigns, and, for good measure, 'there is probably no country in the world where children are treated with such care'[117] (the latter from the one source he mentions – the Rev. Sherwood Eddy's *Russia Today: What Can We Learn From It?*). This is real enthusiasm.

To the question of why this is happening in Russia, and not in the industrialised West as Marx envisaged, *The Clue to History* provides an answer. Unfortunately it is not a particularly good answer. Or, perhaps with a little more charity, the answer could be described as ingenious. Its interest lies in Macmurray's attempt to slot all forms of progressive modernity, including the Russian Revolution, into a great religious drama. The key historical fact as regards Russia was the split between the Eastern and Western Churches in the Middle Ages, which Macmurray views as a division between a contemplative and mystical Greek consciousness in the East, and an intellectual Roman consciousness in the West. In Russia, where Orthodox Christianity became the state religion, the essentially contemplative nature of the faith inhibited any effective opposition from below to the political and religious elites, and prevented any serious conflict between the temporal and spiritual powers. This, for reasons far from clear in the text, meant that the self-frustration of the ruling classes took far longer than in the West, but when it did happen it brought down both the political and the religious establishments simultaneously and allowed a new world view of freedom and equality to come to the fore:

> the process by which the will to superiority in the governing classes destroys itself is not ... avoided. It works only more slowly and more surely; and it had the result that in Russia, when at last she was forced into action by the impact of the Western world, it destroyed both the ecclesiastical and political ruling classes at one blow, and discovered a will to equality and freedom in the suppressed classes all the more effective and creative for the form and length of its suppression.[118]

The precise meaning of 'more slowly and more surely' and 'all the more effective and creative for the form and length of its suppression' remains unclear. Elsewhere in the text a little more flesh is placed on this skeletal explanation. A quasi-hydraulic model of mass psychology is deployed. In Russia, we are told, a 'reservoir of emotional energy for the accomplishment of the revolution was built up'.[119] This needed the assistance of Western intellect in the form of Marxism to add method to drive: 'It was the penetration of the Marxist theory by the emotional driving force of the Russian people that alone could produce that unity of theory and practice in action which was involved in the practical realization of a socialist society.'[120] Here again there are major explanatory lacunae, notably any more specific designation of the nature of this 'emotional energy'. Certainly the impression is given that there is something elemental, something not quite civilised about this energy, and that this coming together of Western intellect and Eastern emotion was not without problems: 'Marxist theory was a fairly recent introduction into Russia, and the fusion ... was very imperfect at the time of the revolution and remains still very incomplete.'[121] Macmurray, unsurprisingly, wants to highlight the deleterious effects of the negative approach of the Soviet regime to religion (though it is not clear what the relative contributions of Marxist theory and Russian emotional energy are to this approach) for the true unity of intellect and emotion, theory and practice, is only possible in religion. His conclusions on Soviet development are ambiguous. There is a path to virtue: 'so long as the intention of achieving communism remains it must necessarily produce a process of development which will negate the unconscious dualism and bring the continuity of Christianity into consciousness';[122] however, the 'danger point' is that this communist intention becomes idealised and formulaic, the ideology of a new ruling elite with 'a new form of the will to power'.[123]

## Fascism

In his 1930s writings on Fascism Macmurray's frame of reference in the early years of the decade is the statist Fascism of Italy, but as the years pass the anti-Semitic Nazism of Germany begins to occupy centre-stage. This change of focus leads to new perspectives on the nature of Fascism, and the role of this ideological movement in the struggle for authentic Christianity.

In the early 1930s Fascism is presented as exemplifying and further developing the deficiencies of the Soviet system – particularly the emphasis on state power and economic efficiency. This explanation is couched in the language of dialectics: Fascism 'derives its meaning as well as its existence from the limitations inherent in the thesis which it negates'.[124] The Soviet dictatorship, transitional in Communist theory, is made permanent in Fascist ideology, and one of its principal uses in Fascist hands is to stabilise the crisis-ridden economy – the basis of its support among the working class. This latter point flows from Macmurray's further claim that 'it is not for fraudulent purposes that fascism considers itself to be a socialist movement'.[125] But it is an impoverished conception of reality with a debased economistic approach to human development – something it has taken from the vulgar materialism of Soviet theory with its insistence 'that economics was the determining factor in human life and that politics was merely an expression of the economic organization'.[126] Fascism thus involves the evaporation of politics from society – 'politics is swallowed up in economics ... Fascism is not a new form of politics. It is the negation of politics';[127] this, for Macmurray, is what the Fascist doctrine of the corporate state is really about. Fascism is thus the living proof that the Soviet Union in its current form does not represent the end of history. The existence of Fascism betokens a new dialectical moment in human history, and indicates those features of contemporary Soviet practice that need to be overcome if genuine Communism is to emerge: 'The true communist revolution remains, therefore, to be achieved at a higher level, and therefore through the negation of that limitation in current communist action which becomes explicit in fascism.'[128]

In the years immediately following the National Socialist accession to power in Germany the focus of Macmurray's analysis of Fascism alters. The extreme nationalism, virulent anti-Semitism and the cult of leadership centred on Hitler impelled Macmurray to anatomise the psychology of Nazism. The position of the USSR in the analysis also changes. The earlier claim that Fascism was the expression of the deficiencies of the Soviet Union gives way to the proposition that Fascism is a fearful response to the potentialities of the Russian Revolution. Fear indeed becomes a growing motif in these texts as the international situation worsens and world war becomes a real possibility.

In *Creative Society* (1935) the impact of Macmurray's recent intensive study of Marx's early texts, particularly his analysis of the inadequacies of liberal democratic citizenship, is evident (if unacknowledged). The success of the Soviet Union, Macmurray argues, dramatically exposes the gap between the formal equality of liberal democracy and the substantive inequality of liberal capitalism. Since real community does not exist, which is another way of saying that real religion does not exist, a 'pseudo-religion'[129] of aggressive patriotism is pumped out to bolster the illusory community of citizenship. The socio-economic context is deemed to be the growth of mass unemployment – most notably in Germany – which erodes the image of a liberal community and favourably highlights the real community-building process in the USSR. The power of the state is used to both inculcate this nationalist propaganda and physically repress any centres of dissent. Thus Nazism

> seeks to unify the German nation in terms of sentiment by the creation of a myth of nationality disseminated by propaganda designed to create a purely psychological and ideal sense of community; and on the other hand by suppressing the expression of all internal discord and unifying the nation on the military plan with defence through power as the organizing principle.[130]

Thus the attempt of the USSR to transcend the traditional national community has had the effect of exacerbating national sentiments elsewhere. This undermines any possible united pan-capitalist front against the Soviet Union, and fuels, instead, attempts by states to create international alliances with the USSR to strengthen their own nationalist designs:

> In these national tensions Russia becomes not the common enemy but the potential and increasingly important ally of one side or the other. This process has already brought Russia into the League of Nations and into qualified alliance with France, and it tends to range Great Britain also, though less easily, on the same side.[131]

The reference to the League of Nations is part of the dimension of hope in the work. He reiterates his call for the creation of real community – that is, real religion – which in the darkening international climate requires international co-operation. He is also certain that Russia is the key to any successful outcome:

> we must conclude that the practical issue of the contemporary situation depends upon the religious task of overcoming fear by strengthening the positive impulse towards the creation of community. It is in the field of the co-operation between nations and between the citizens of different nations that the main issue lies. Above all, it would seem to lie in the establishment of relations of co-operation between Russia and the rest of the world.[132]

In *The Clue to History* (1938) the psychological dynamics of Fascism are analysed in terms of the intellectual West/emotional East distinction previously discussed in relation to Russia. The psychological assumptions underpinning Macmurray's account would seem to have Freudian roots. Macmurray posits that emotion becomes suppressed in the intellectual and scientific West, but continues to play an important role, though negatively and unconsciously, by attempting to negate the intellect. Given that in the post-Enlightenment world the ideals of the intellect are freedom, equality and progress, then 'the impulses of the suppressed emotional consciousness will be anti-libertarian, anti-equalitarian and anti-progressive; in a word the unconscious, in which the motives to action are buried, will be blindly reactionary'.[133] However, in conditions of social and economic collapse, as was the case in post-First World War Germany, these unconscious impulses are liberated and use the technical and organisational achievements of the intellect to destroy the political and ethical norms and institutions of the modern Enlightenment world. This, he argues, is 'the spiritual character of fascism'.[134] The result is an anti-democratic and nationalist 'collective individualism' in which the individual and state are bogusly integrated into a mystical unity where the state becomes the true individual – a process facilitated by the leadership of an actual individual, hence the cult of Hitler and Mussolini. And since, for Macmurray, egoistic individualism is always self-defeating, then the desire of the Nazi German state for its supposed rights and freedoms will generate permanent international friction, and ultimate defeat:

> The nation which will have nothing to do with internationalism makes all political problems international. Fascism is the supreme example of the truth of the insight of Jesus. In Italy and Germany, if we have eyes at all, we can hardly fail to see the experimental verification of the law that he that saveth his life shall lose it.[135]

Macmurray makes interesting and telling points about the inherent problems of Fascist ideology and practice. The focus on the supreme leader in Fascism imposes an imperative on a Hitler or a Mussolini to provide ever more symbolic triumphs to sustain the illusory sense of unity, with the ever-attendant danger that perceived failure on the part of the leader could lead to radical disillusionment.[136] He thus effectively evokes the driven nature of Fascist policy, the endless drive for new successes. He also notes the tension between the anti-rationality of Fascist ideology and the need of all advanced societies for rational thought, technique and organisation, speculating that the former might undermine the latter with, again, potentially damaging effects.[137]

But in his discussion of anti-Semitism serious problems emerge, problems arising from the central assumptions of his philosophy of history and philosophical history. Primarily there is his refurbished Christian providentialism, of 'thy will be done', decked out in neat dialectical clothes. This leads to an almost Panglossian optimism that sees the saving hand of God in even the most negative of phenomena, and that saps sound political analysis and significantly takes the terror away from the truly terrible. Thus, since history is moving towards the unity of emotion and intellect, harbingered by the developments in Russia, it is incumbent on Fascism to play its part in the unfolding of the process. He proposes that Fascism is 'a kind of psycho-analytic process in society'[138] in which the release of unconscious material, the emotional heart of Fascist barbarism and unreason, begins to give individuals and society itself insights into the true nature of reality, though internal resistances to this process are still strong. Fascist anti-Semitism is thus, paradoxically, potentially part of the path to self-awareness, in that it registers the centrality of Jewish consciousness for an understanding of history and society. Hitler is therefore in this reading a 'genius' in that he understands that Judaism is a dagger at the heart of modern society, and therefore the central force to be opposed:

> Hitler's declaration that the Jewish consciousness is poison to the Aryan races is the deepest insight that the Western world has yet achieved into its own nature; and his capacity to realize this is the proof of his genius as well as the secret of his power and of the curious fascination which his personality exerts ... The only difference between us is that his will and mine respond to the truth in different ways. The thought of the triumph of the Jewish consciousness fills me with joyous exhilaration, while it casts Hitler into the depths of despair.[139]

Granted that the language here is ironic, meant to bait the Nazis with the, to them, unwelcome hidden consequences of their own ideology, but the underlying substance of the claim is in earnest, and was repeated by Macmurray elsewhere.[140]

At this point in the argument another central assumption of Macmurray makes its presence known in a distinctly perverse manner. Recall that although Macmurray talks about the Jewish spirit working its way through European history, he in fact means Christianity. The Jews, he claims, in their rejection of Jesus chose racial exclusion over universal community. This made them an anti-national force, since race is defined not territorially, a counter to modern nationalism, but in a negative exclusive manner. This is a springboard for the suggestion that Nazi Germany has taken its racism from the Jews, and that this is feeding the objective destruction of nationality by Germany, as in its activities in Austria, Czechoslovakia and Spain (presumably in the latter case, which is not a self-evident example, Macmurray is thinking of the Nazi role in the destruction of the legitimate Republican government of Spain as an attack on the principle of national sovereignty):

> The German consciousness is becoming Jewish in form and ... is destroying the European conception of nationality as the basis of political unity, and supplanting it by a *racial* basis. And the racial conception of society is essentially Jewish and non-Aryan ... The situation with which Europe is faced is this. At its very centre its most highly organised nation has suddenly turned on the Jews and said 'You are not the chosen race. *We* are the chosen race' ... It has substituted itself for the Jews, and in consequence has annexed the essential form of Jewish consciousness.[141]

An (unacknowledged) argument straight out of Marx's *On the Jewish Question* is used to bolster this line of argument. Just as Marx had belaboured Bruno Bauer for suggesting that liberal democracies could emancipate the Jews, resting as it did on the assumption that mere political emancipation was the equivalent of human emancipation, so Macmurray argues that the experience of Fascism shows that Jews cannot be emancipated in a liberal-capitalist national state. Again, Russia is said to show the way forward. In his critique of the citizenship option for the Jews, the wording, with the benefit of hindsight, is to say the least unfortunate:

> Individualistic societies can appear to solve the Jewish problem by the grant of equal citizenship ... But this is not a real solution. As soon as one of these societies is driven into fascism by its own development ... the Jewish problem is rediscovered. The Jews cannot be part of a real national unity. They may be German citizens but they cannot be Germans. The only real community in which the Jewish problem could be solved would be the community of humanity in which race was no longer a principle of unity. The disappearance of the problem in Russia rests ... on the acceptance of the intention by Communism to create such a universal community.[142]

Thus the terminus of the analysis is that racism has its basis in Judaism, and that the persecution of the Jews can be construed as part of a painful but necessary process of self-awareness and self-frustration in the West – the cunning of history indeed! Thus, *sub specie aeternitas*, the will of God is done.

*The Clue to History* does not descend from this analysis of general tendencies to suggesting in any detail what is likely to happen, or should happen in the near future. There is some suggestion that the matter will need to be resolved by international action: not on the basis of international agreement, for as Macmurray notes himself, Germany and Italy had destroyed the League of Nations by withdrawing from it in 1937. Rather, international *pressure* from the Western powers, and, above all from the Soviet Union, needed to be brought to bear on the Fascist powers. Thus Germany 'must' (in the dialectical sense of that word) 'unify the other nations against herself, and produce a situation in which Russia can intervene and determine the issue'.[143] He is silent on whether this means war, though on the closing page he talks of Europe blindly falling into 'self-destruction',[144] but immediately qualifies it by saying that it will not be civilisation that will be destroyed 'but only the modern form of Western society and its dualistic consciousness',[145] so his thoughts on this matter remain opaque.

## War and beyond

Once war arrived, Macmurray interpreted it as a working through of the contradictions of the interwar years. The old world was being destroyed, and the glimmer of new possibilities could be glimpsed among the terrible wreckage:

> What we are actually doing in this war, as the submarine slips out to sea and the bombers take the air, is to destroy the material fabric of our old European life ... As the ships are sunk, the factories and machinery broken, the churches and homes of the people pulverised or burned, there perishes with them more and more of the spiritual order which built them and expressed itself in them ... [T]he reconstruction has to be creation of a new civilisation.[146]

The hostilities were an aspect of a global revolution in which a positive outcome crucially relied upon the triumph of authentic Christianity. At the domestic level the interventionist wartime state was viewed as an acceleration of a longer-term trend in which liberal 'negative government' was transforming into socialist 'positive government'.[147] Macmurray's anxiety – one that was to be a significant *leitmotif* in his subsequent writings – was that mere political and economic reorganisation without prior 'personal' (that is, religious) transformation would run the risk of the cultural life of individuals being subordinated to the very different purposes of the state, an institution which in the past had been disciplined by a dispersed economic power. Indeed, experience elsewhere demonstrated the melancholy fact that 'the transition from negative government had resulted invariably in the loss of democracy and the substitution of some form of totalitarian or fascist government'.[148] This fear, when addressed at the international level, invested Macmurray's wartime reflections on the Soviet Union with a good deal of ambiguity. Even during the Nazi–Soviet Pact and the Soviet invasion of Finland, Macmurray claimed that he remained convinced that the USSR would necessarily eventually join a victorious fight against Nazi Germany.[149] Once the Soviet Union had entered the war on the side of the allies, Macmurray, building on some of his pre-war enthusiasms for the USSR, publicly reflected the fairly widespread British warmth towards the new ally. But, in line with his reflections on the potential dangers of the positive state, he felt obliged to also point to the inability of the Soviet people actually to use their democratic constitution and institutions to exercise genuine popular control of a party-dominated state. In *Challenges to the Churches* he explicitly links the British and Soviet contexts:

> If we bring the economic field within the control of political authority we lose our traditional instrument for keeping the government in its place ... This is the problem which Soviet Russia has so far failed to solve. That country is, we must not forget, the antithesis of the Fascist State. It is the product of a popular revolution and represents a definite advance in the democratic direction. But it has not discovered how the people are to control a government which controls the economic organisation and therefore the means of life, the wealth of the nation.[150]

The fulcrum of the solution to this conundrum is to be provided by religion, or more exactly by Christianity.

As should be clear by now, Macmurray, beneath remarks about the universality of Christianity, is actually calling for the hegemony of Christianity. There is nothing ecumenical in this conception. In *Conditions of Freedom* (1950) he claims that there are only three religions in competition for the universal allegiance of humanity, Buddhism, Islam and Christianity, but that the first two are ultimately vitiated by the dominance within them of what he terms the 'negative motive': Buddhism because of its desire for withdrawal from the world, and Islam because of its inherent 'aggression and compulsion'. Only Christianity is 'positively motivated' in that 'it seeks a universal fellowship realized in the actual conditions of human life, a brotherhood of mankind, a kingdom of heaven *on earth*'.[151] Hence his remark in *Through Chaos to Community?* (1944) that 'historians of the future may reckon the missionary movement of the nineteenth century one of the critical turning points of world development'.[152] In the same text he scanned the world, locating those areas where Christianity was the traditional religion – the Americas, Western Europe, the Soviet Union (given his argument about its Orthodox roots) and 'the white populations of their dominions, colonies and outposts' – and turning molehills into mountains elsewhere on the globe: China (on the grounds that its 'great leader ... is a Christian' who 'has commended Christianity to his people' and the fact of the 'conspicuous and impressive' virtue of Chinese converts), Japan (because with the likely collapse of emperor worship following military defeat 'it is certain that the Christian co-operative movement associated with the work of Kagawa will play an important part in the renewal of that great people'), and India (where once national freedom has effaced the link between colonialism and Christianity, India's 'Christian communities will play a notable part in the social transformation that will follow').[153] He answers his own slightly odd objection – that why then is Christianity such a spent force in the West – with 'perhaps that is because we have taken from [Christianity] all that we can take until it has brought the rest of the world up to our level of civilisation'! Macmurray's biographer, John E. Costello, in a discussion of a 1928 document where similar views are ventilated, is undoubtedly right that Macmurray had a capacious and unorthodox definition of Christianity,[154] but the privileging of Christianity, if mitigated, is not removed.

As Macmurray's references to the larger world suggest, he had become aware that the post-war world would be precisely that – a world. He registers what he sees as the passing of the old order of European hegemony, in his eyes the classic cradle of civilisation which, leaving aside his speculations on biblical Israel, had been the focus of his analysis and hopes. There is an elegiac feel to his reflections on this transformation: 'the history of Western Europe has *been* the history of the world ... Almost suddenly this has ceased to be true ... Our civilisation *has* come to an end.'[155] The USA, which had been virtually invisible in his earlier writings, is now deemed to be one pole of a new bipolar world, the other being the USSR. While Macmurray's writings in the 1930s had perceived a grand dialectical movement in the processes of European politics, in the post-war period he paints a picture of a global impasse, of an unstable tension between the two super-power blocs, where a third world war is a real possibility. International politics was about the politics of accommodation, namely to 'enable East and West to live together without excessive friction'.[156] This, then, was the terrain in which post-war reconstruction was to take place, and when he applied his mind to the specifics of this project his fears about mere organisational and political restructuring were once again to the fore. He argued that it was the West that was exacerbating world tensions by attempting to achieve the admirable and necessary goal of world unity by intergovernmental agreement and constitutional and institutional ingenuity. Just as he had argued that existing national states tend towards the curtailment of individual liberty, so he now maintained that some form of top-down global political institution would be, in effect, a form of tyranny: 'If we could set up now a world authority with power to enforce its decisions it would of necessity be a world dictatorship. Freedom and democracy are not to be created by organisation.'[157] For genuinely stable, effective and free institutions to emerge, a bottom-up process of cultural renewal, dialogue and agreement was necessary:

> A democratic solution can only be found at the *lowest* level – through the gradual formation of a common tradition and a common way of life throughout the world. We have started this process of overcoming the limitations of our own tradition where the task is simplest, by seeking agreement with Eastern Christendom.[158]

As ever, his mind was drawn to the fundamental religious dimension of this process.

## Distancing Marx?

After the 1940s, references to Marx in Macmurray's writings are few and far between, and when developed at all are largely critical. His main theoretical preoccupation in the 1950s was to articulate in a philosophically rigorous and comprehensive manner the underlying themes of his thought, which he presented, initially, in the Gifford Lectures at Glasgow University in 1953 and 1954, and subsequently in two monographs *The Self as Agent* (1957) and *Persons in Relation* (1961). The underlying thesis, which he expresses in its 'simplest' form as 'All meaningful knowledge is for the sake of action, and all meaningful action for the sake of friendship',[159] arches back to ideas developed before his encounter with Marx, and is Macmurray's attempt to demonstrate his own distinctive contribution to modern philosophy. He bows his head only to philosophical giants – above all Kant. The old strictures on the dangers of dialectical organicism are rehearsed at the expense of Communism and Marx, and the doctrines of the dictatorship of the proletariat and the withering away of the state are implicitly condemned as embodying the worst errors of Hobbes and Rousseau. Interestingly, he happily uses Marx's term for an authentic community – 'a truly human society'; his critical point is that what

> is both illusory and fantastic is the attempt to achieve it on the Hobbesian principle of the State as absolute power, in the hope that the State will then vanish away and leave the completely organic society of Rousseau's romantic phantasy.[160]

But *the* bone of contention for Macmurray, in these post-war thoughts, is Marx's ultimately negative appraisal of religion. In *Persons in Relation* Macmurray is acerbic in tone, focusing entirely on the negative dimension implied in the 'opium of the people' phrase, which he reduces to the bald claim that 'religion is a device ... for taking men's minds off their present miseries by the promise of a better life in a better world', a claim Macmurray calls 'almost grotesquely unscientific and *a priori*'[161] and which he subjects to a moment of speculative psychoanalysis: 'such a theory of religion surely betrays its origin in a subjective and emotional reaction, probably dating from early years. Such atheism, indeed, strongly suggests the projection of a childish phantasy upon the universe.'[162] Even here, however, he concedes that Marx's critique has some purchase on some forms of religious institutions and practice, but that this should have been the basis for a call for the reform and not the destruction of religion. The shift in tone towards Marx can, perhaps, be related to Macmurray's theme of the danger posed to the personal by the organisational and political, signalled by his recourse to the word 'totalitarian' in his texts. In 1950 he was arguing that the USSR sought 'freedom through justice alone' and that this was to be facilitated by the subordination of 'the freedom of fellowship to the patterns and the exigencies of economic co-operation', and he related this to a Marxist conception of base and superstructure, where a cultural superstructure is supported (or rather subordinated) to an economic base, thereby, in effect, robbing the cultural of its free autonomy, adding significantly of Soviet Marxism, 'It is this that is symbolised in its antagonism to religion.'[163] Underpinning this is the ultimately ahistorical concept of personal friendship discussed earlier. The personal, for Macmurray, although existing in history, somehow transcends history; it is grounded in a human essence which is fundamentally unchanging. As he put it in a wartime essay: 'The forms of life change and pass, but the substance remains the same. The forms vary from country to country ... but the substance is the same everywhere.'[164] And it is the religious sphere that somehow perennially validates and protects this essential and unchanging essence. Religion is therefore not like a snakeskin that can be cast off at the appropriate level of development, and thus Marx's vision of a world without religion is entirely unacceptable. And yet, at the age of 74, looking back over his life, Macmurray candidly acknowledged the significant effect that his study of Marx's work in the 1930s had had on him: 'I ... found that I learned a great deal about Christianity by this study, and especially by coming to understand the reasons behind Marx's rejection of religion.'[165] This, as we saw earlier, was facilitated by pre-existing themes in Macmurray's work which lent themselves to a dialogue with Marx; however, one should not underestimate the influence of Marx on Macmurray's subsequent development, most notably in the texts of the 1930s discussed in this chapter, but also throughout all his subsequent work, above all in his critique of economic, political and religious dualism, his understanding of the dynamics of modern history, and the vision of the Kingdom of Heaven *on earth*.

# 2 Kenneth Ingram
## The Christian and the sexual – homosexuality, bisexuality, pederasty

The conference on the nature of Christianity attended by John Macmurray in 1932 had decided that an adequate answer to the question 'What is Christianity?' depended on prior work on two issues – Communism and sexuality. Many years before this event Kenneth Ingram had been devoting a good deal of thought to the latter topic. As a homosexual in a time when all homosexual acts between males were illegal, and as a member of an Anglican Church that morally condemned such activity, he had unsurprisingly pondered on the nature, and moral status, of sexuality.[1] The result was a body of work over twenty years that provides, for this era, a very rare theoretical reflection by a male homosexual on what he was and what, at the erotic and emotional levels, he could or could not do. His sexuality deeply marked his exploration of the relationship between the religious and the secular and coloured his sense of what the good life should be, a fact to some extent obscured by the silences, dissimulations and evasions that understandably attended 'deviant' sexuality in twentieth-century Britain. As with his other fundamental concerns, he was driven to reflect in print on the nature of sexuality, notably in three specific texts – *An Outline of Sexual Morality* (1922), *The Modern Attitude to the Sex Problem* (1930) and *Sex-Morality Tomorrow* (1940) – and to join with others to promote a better understanding of the subject, as in his membership of the British Society for the Study of Sex Psychology. This might at first sight seem a somewhat particular concern, but in its examination of the relationship between the reality of one mode of a 'deviant' sexuality and the morality of Christianity it asked hard questions of that morality which have a more general resonance; indeed, Ingram's Anglican Church is today in danger of being irreparably split by the differing moral assumptions determining the categorisation of homosexuality. As Macmurray's conference would appear to have recognised, the Church's attitude to sexuality illuminated crucial aspects of its central beliefs. For Ingram this was to be a journey in which his views underwent considerable changes, and one on which he was ultimately to fall foul of his own Church.

These perspectives were of course an aspect of his broader theoretical and political projects. There was always to be a central religious core to these concerns. In the 1920s this took the form of an advocacy and defence of

Anglo-Catholicism. Alongside his one book on sexuality, *An Outline of Sexual Morality*, he produced in this decade over twenty other volumes with titles such as *The Anglo-Catholic Case* (1923), *The Pilgrimage of Mass* (1924), *A Portrait of Six Christian Heroes* (1926) and *The Sunday Mass and the Industrial Problem* (1929). With the 1930s, which began with *The Modern Attitude to the Sex Problem*, one sees the publication of a string of books which register the powerful effect of John Macmurray's work on his thought. The titles of some of these reveal this influence: *The Coming Civilization. Will it be Capitalist? Will it be Materialist?* (1935), *Christianity – Right or Left? Which Way will Religion Move in the World Crisis?* (1937), *The Christian Challenge to Christians* (1938) and *Towards Christianity: The Religious Progress of the World* (1939). By the end of the decade Ingram and Macmurray were very much linked together in the minds of both friends and foes as leading thinkers of the Christian Left.[2] This focus persisted into the war years. Thus, while there was *Sex-Morality Tomorrow* and a booklet, *Christianity and Sexual Morality – A Modernist View* (1944), there was also much reflection on the moral and social changes that the coming peace required, as in *Religion and the New Society* (1944) and the quaintly titled *Guide to the New Age: A Political Guide for a Young Soldier and his Girl* (1945).

This is not to suggest that there was a Chinese wall between his sexual works and his other productions. As we shall see, reflections on sexual matters are to be found in his other theoretical books, and there is sexual material – at times homoerotic – to be found in his works of fiction. It would also be wrong to deduce that this material represents a minor or peripheral element in his thinking – a mere curiosity, no more. On the contrary, it is clear that a concern with the moral status of sexual behaviour was a passionate and central impulse in his life. What is true is that the prevailing moral climate – particularly with regard to homosexuality – meant that any degree of sexual radicalism had to be advanced with a great deal of circumspection. This meant that Ingram was to enter Common Wealth under conditions different to those pertaining to Macmurray, Stapledon and Acland. The latter three brought their full range of fundamental concerns and interests openly into the movement – Ingram did not.

Without doubt Ingram is the least known of the four subjects of this study.[3] Unlike the other three figures Ingram does not have an entry in the *Oxford Dictionary of National Biography*. Biographical information is scanty: a few references here and there, the odd autobiographical statement in his own writings, sundry correspondence, and documentation connected with his political activity. He was born on 7 June 1882;[4] after schooling at Charterhouse, and with a period of war service in France during the First World War, he pursued a number of careers: reading for the bar, but never practising, employment in the Ministry of Labour, and director of a small publishing house. His desultory employment record is indicative of the fact that his real passions lay elsewhere. He was an inveterate joiner of campaigning organisations, devoting considerable time and energy to promoting their objectives. In his youth this was for the cause of Anglo-Catholicism – and he was to become editor of the Anglo-Catholic journal *Green Quarterly*[5] – but with his radicalisation in the 1930s he threw himself into bodies associated with the Christian Left, in time becoming an activist with Common Wealth during the Second World War, and a leading member of the National Peace Council in the post-war years. Alongside these activities, and frequently in the service of them, he was an extraordinarily prolific writer, author, according to the British Library's (incomplete) listings, of sixty-nine books, encompassing devotional literature, ecclesiastical polemic, political analysis, texts on sexuality, biography as well as a sizeable number of works of fiction, including detective novels and public school stories.

An important further thing to be known about Ingram is that his homosexuality appears to have been 'pederastic' in orientation, and we can find a palpable line of defence, indeed of affirmation, for this orientation in his work. 'Pederastic' is the word Ingram himself uses and it was a term that would have been understandable to his various audiences, though he did not publicly use the word to describe himself, for he was always to put authorial distance between himself and the orientations and activities he was discussing – always 'they', never 'I'. The word meant 'boy-lover', from the Greek *pais paidos*, 'boy', and *erastēs*, 'lover'. For Ingram this was essentially a spiritual phenomenon, not what he termed 'a physical vice'. This was consonant with both his Christian understanding of the proper boundaries of sexual behaviour, and the tradition of Victorian and Edwardian boy love of which he was a continuation, which in its poetry and tracts stressed the lofty and moral nature of this attachment. It was only in the later 1930s in the wake of his major rethink about the basis of morality, which opened up the possibility of sexual relations outside marriage, that he had to think through the implications of this in the case of inter-generational and youth-to-youth relations. What follows is an account of the development of Ingram's ideas on sexuality, and their position in the broader constellation of his thought, beginning with his early immersion in the world of Anglo-Catholicism.

## Anglo-Catholicism

'Beware of the Anglo-Catholics,' advises a character in *Brideshead Revisited*, 'they're all sodomites with unpleasant accents.'[6] Waspish and inaccurate as this statement was (even given its referent of Oxford University in the 1920s), it does convey an element of public perception of the movement, and registers the undoubted truth that quite a number of homosexuals were attracted to Anglo-Catholicism. Leaving to one side, for a moment, the issue of sodomy, there is no doubt as to Ingram's energetic participation in the Anglo-Catholic movement in the first three decades of the twentieth century: 'I was,' he later recalled, 'caught up in its interests and very largely absorbed in its concerns.'[7] In heavily didactic novels such as *The Faded Vision* (1915) and *The Changing Order* (1925) he had irrefutable Anglo-Catholic priests vanquish scoffers and religious opponents, and win over initially sceptical laymen to 'correct' doctrine and practices. The themes are the stock-in-trade of Anglo-Catholic thought: Protestant England's fall from Catholicism; Rome's unacceptable papal authoritarianism; the Catholic revival within Anglicanism; the integrity of Church of England ordination; the centrality of the sacraments; the necessity for ceremonial and appropriate liturgy and ritual; the virtues of monasticism, and so on and so forth.[8]

As other works reveal, however, these quotidian tropes of Anglo-Catholic discourse are embedded in an historical meta-narrative of Hellenism, deeply rooted in the homosexual milieu of nineteenth- and early twentieth-century Britain. Hellenism in its homoerotic form has its roots in the work of Walter Pater and John Addington Symonds, who, as Linda Dowling has persuasively argued, transformed the notion of martial citizenship at the heart of civic republicanism, by presenting it as rooted in the male erotic bonding of the ancient Greek armies. This eroticism was deemed to be a fundamentally spiritual phenomenon, informing the glories of Greek civilisation and providing a model for the regeneration of Victorian Britain.[9] In Ingram's hands the 'Greek' becomes one of the two predominant types of human nature in history. Among all the supposed fine attributes of this type – an affinity to the divine, love of beauty in all its manifestations, multi-faceted self-development – Ingram inserts knowing references to ancient lovers: Achilles and Patroclus, Diocles and Philolau and the Sacred Band of Thebes; and to the Battle of Chaeronea (a recurring image in homoerotic Hellenism), where the warrior lovers of Thebes were massacred by the forces of Philip of Macedon. It is indeed possible that Ingram was a member of the secret 'Order of Chaeronea' formed by George Ives to promote same-sex relationships; he certainly knew Ives, as both were founder members of the British Society for the Study of Sex Psychology (BSSSP), a body with a significant homosexual presence.[10] Indeed, Timothy d'Arch Smith has called the Order of Chaeronea 'an inner order' of the BSSSP, and contends that Ives, with his mania for secrecy, spiked the one and only issue of *The Quorum* (1920), a magazine of 'friendship' (a contemporary code word, among those in the know, for homosexuality) to which Ingram (along with other Chaeronea and BSSSP members) had contributed.[11] Certainly Ingram's characterisation of his Greek heroes (in his theoretical work *England at the Flood-Tide* (1924)) echoed the covert and exclusive ethos of Ives' order; these ancients were, Ingram asserted, 'an esoteric aristocracy, an inner circle of those who loved and had been initiated ... a masonry of comradeship which cannot be entered by the merely curious or the vulgar'.[12] In short, 'the key to the secret of the Greek spirit was the cult of comradeship'.[13]

The theoretical resources on 'homosexuality' available to Ingram at the time would have been predominantly British and German. In *An Outline of Sexual Morality* (1922), his first book, in which he has an extensive discussion of the issue, he refers to Havelock Ellis's *Studies in the Psychology of Sex: Sexual Inversion*, and Edward Carpenter's *The Intermediate Sex*. He has one reference to a German text by Magnus Hirschfeld – the then colossus of German sexual theory – but it is quite possible that he had simply lifted this from Carpenter's own citation of Hirschfeld in *The Intermediate Sex*; and the fact that he garbled some of the German title suggests that he was not especially comfortable with that language. Carpenter, on the other hand, was very much at ease in German, and his works were thickly larded with the findings of German-language theory – Ulrichs, Krafft-Ebing, Weininger, and the specialist articles contained in Hirschfeld's journal on scientific research into homosexuality, the *Jahrbuch für sexuelle Zwischenstufen* (Yearbook for Sexual Intermediates). Carpenter himself owed much to Hirschfeld's work, particularly the notion of homosexuality as a third sex, and Ingram, as we shall see, to an extent identified with this position.[14] Within German theory there were important divisions. Hirschfeld's medicalisation of homosexuality, stressing the inherent biological nature of the disposition, was vehemently opposed by a variety of writers associated with a group called the Gemeinschaft der Eigenen, the Community of Self-Owners (named after the individualist Anarchist Max Stirner's work *Der Einzige und sein Eigentum* [English title *The Ego and His Own*]) and its magazine *Der Eigene* (1899 to 1931). They upheld male/male love as a positive cultural trend, in need of no extenuating defence, and viewed Hirschfeld's stance as inherently apologetic.[15] Furthermore, *Der Eigene* was strongly pederastic.

To the extent that Victorian Hellenism was partially occasioned by a perceived crisis of religious belief, it could offer two contrasting responses – the supplementary, where the values and civilisation of ancient Hellas could help bolster-up or thicken Anglican Christianity, or the substitutory, a new post-Christian culture. Ingram, however, took a different tack, one that might be termed 'essentialist' in that he claimed that the fundamental essence of Christianity was Greek, and that the modern task was to cleanse the faith of those non-Greek impurities with which it had been adulterated. Here, however, a dark element enters the analysis, for the corruptions of Christianity are ultimately grounded in the second predominant type of human nature – the 'Jewish'. By Ingram's day the device of contrasting the Hellenic and the Jewish had a long pedigree, including, notably, Matthew Arnold's distinction between Hebraism and Hellenism in *Culture and Anarchy* (1869). In Arnold's usage both of these two poles have validity for human development, with Hellenism contributing 'spontaneity of consciousness' and Hebraism 'strictness of conscience'. The aim was to have both elements in equilibrium.[16]

Ingram's conception is a very different beast. Although he at one point refers to the Jews as 'this wonderful people'[17] his characterisation is in the main highly negative: they are obsessed with law, reliant on force, racially exclusive; the historical record, he claims, shows that 'the Jew had no eye for beauty'[18] and 'knew no mercy where the discipline of life was broken';[19] even his references to the endurance and tenacity of the Jews are rendered negative: 'persecutions and all the vicissitudes of life have failed to crush him out of existence. The persecutors have died forgotten, but the Jew lives on, outcaste and stranger, morose, jealous, and unyielding.'[20] A stark, conflictual binary is therefore established where Christianity's emergence from Judaism is portrayed as a form of spiritual emancipation, for 'though Christianity was born, physically, as it were, of Jewish parentage, its spiritual family is inextricably that of the Greek type'.[21] Although not an explicitly racial theory, Ingram's distinctions have a degree of family resemblance with certain debased forms of German Hellenism, whose ultimate malign fruit was the Aryan Christ/ Jewish Paul dualism to be found in some strands of National Socialism.[22] Ingram was, of course, far from alone in espousing what we really do have to call anti-Semitism – it could be found on all points of the ideological spectrum in Britain, was evident in Anglican discourse, and was clearly present in a man much admired by Ingram – the socialist and homosexual Hellenist, Edward Carpenter.[23]

With the assertion that Medieval Catholicism, at its best, embodies the Greek spirit – exemplified in the interpenetration of the religious and the secular, and the corporate, collective quality of social life – Ingram is able to make a bridge to matters English. The Reformation is deemed to have ushered in a Protestant individualism, and to have enabled the triumph within the national Church of a Puritanism which partook of the Jewish spirit in its repressive, philistinism – the 'Jew-Puritan'[24] as Ingram terms it. With the historic defeat of an attenuated Catholicism in the collapse of Jacobitism and the exit of the non-Jurors from the Church, Anglicanism was in no position to withstand the withering effects of scientific materialism in the nineteenth century, and the period of major religious decline set in, with the modern Catholic revival the only ray of light in the darkness.

At one point, Ingram says of the nature of community in Greek life that 'literally it is a brotherhood'.[25] The gendering present here isn't merely a reflection of linguistic usages of the time. All of Ingram's novels, even after his Marxist radicalisation, reveal a fundamental homosocial imagination; his focus is primarily on the relationships between men. Women are present but they are peripheral, or foils, caricatures, plot devices – props in the central male drama. In the theoretical reflections of his Anglo-Catholic period he registers the economic, social and political strides made by women since the nineteenth century, and considers himself a friend of the call for women's emancipation, but his conception of what this emancipation should entail is, to put it no stronger, idiosyncratic. Thus while espousing a critique of the Victorian family, with its debilitating effects on women, one of his main concerns is that domesticity undermines male bonding, keeping men too frequently in the home, in the company of their wives, away from spaces of potential male community. Consequently he is hostile to any efforts to integrate the sexes more fully, preferring instead parallel development, where women as much as possible inhabit their own space – an arrangement he considers admirably Greek in its embodiment of both independence and equality (by contrast the degradation of women is linked to 'the Eastern and Semitic'[26]). He even manages to construe the Medieval Catholic cult of the Virgin Mary as the creative and Hellenic source of the chivalrous attitude towards women. All of this rests on certain conventional assumptions about 'natural' gendered differences and dispositions.

This view of gender relations is readily apparent in his attempt to sketch a utopia in *England at the Flood-Tide*. Given what we have already learned about Ingram's general political and social assumptions in this period, it should not perhaps come as a surprise that he calls his utopian creation 'an aristocratic, neo-feudalistic, guild-union Utopia'.[27] In fact the device is more akin to a social and constitutional plan than it is to the more familiar fictional narrative utopia. It combines strong aristocratic features – dukes running guilds, and a Platonic-like Privy Council – with some democratic features, such as an indirect electoral system, and a continuing role for representative institutions. In terms of gender, women stand, and indirectly vote, for membership of a lower House of Women, while female aristocrats are appointed to the higher House of Ladies – both houses being concerned with 'Bills ... which concern women directly or indirectly'.[28] Likewise, in pursuit of creating as much distinct male and female space as possible he rules out in his proposed society co-education in all schools after kindergarten.

Ingram's earliest detailed consideration of sexuality and sexual behaviour, *An Outline of Sexual Morality* (1922), is very firmly in his Anglo-Catholic period. Its form and content reveal the constraints on writing about sexuality at this time. The title of the book itself grounds the enquiry into sexuality (especially 'deviant' sexuality) in the serious and respectable pursuit of the substance of private and public morality; there is an introduction by a doctor to give an additional medical imprimatur to the enterprise; and Ingram himself, though partisan, makes no personal identification with any of the forms of sexuality discussed (scrupulously using the third person plural) and carefully allows the voice of orthodox disapproval to be heard in a variety of contexts.

In the case of homosexuality, the medicalisation of the phenomenon, illustrated in the introduction to the text, had become increasingly important in public discourse since the end of the nineteenth century, and had infused the term 'homosexuality' with associations with which Ingram is ill at ease. He clearly does not like the term, but cannot contribute to a public debate on the issue without using the word. He thus tries to infuse it with alternative associations, and also explores other terminologies. The chapter dealing with the issue is called 'The Homosexual Temperament', the final word to an extent attempting to deflect the perceived harsh resonances of the second word, and thereby suggesting something cerebral or emotional, rather than sensual, something furthermore that indicated a perfectly natural variation.

The first part of the chapter is a call for understanding, tolerance and decriminalisation of this temperament against harsh and hegemonic legal, social, scientific and religious discourses. This plea rests initially on the assertion that while homosexuality is 'abnormal' it is not 'unnatural' and therefore there cannot be a legal or a moral case per se against a natural disposition. He bolsters this up with an argument that brings us back again to Victorian

Hellenism. To the early advocates of homoerotic Hellenism, notably Pater and the early Symonds, same-sex love was a spiritual, not a physical, phenomenon. Physical sexuality was deemed to be a lower, inadequate form of an *eros* whose finest form was a meeting of minds and hearts. This is the conception favoured by Ingram: 'Homosexuality,' he asserts, 'is a romantic cult rather than a physical vice.'[29] Within Victorian Hellenism, however, a belief in the validity of the physical aspects of homosexuality had emerged, and this conception, through the spectacular events of the Oscar Wilde trials, became the predominant one in the public mind, thereby dictating the terrain on which Ingram had to struggle. He tries, therefore, to differentiate spiritual 'higher' homosexuality by deploying a term used by, among others, Edward Carpenter – 'homogenic love'.

His defence of the homogenic also allows him to stay within the moral bounds of his Anglo-Catholic faith, which he summarises in the injunction 'that there can be no religious countenance for any physical sex-act outside the sacrament of matrimony'.[30] More positively he builds upon the notion of spiritual love to argue that the homogenic represents something deeply Catholic: 'Pure love, especially so intense a love as the homogenic attachment, is not profane but divine.'[31] Such sentiments would not have been out of place in some Anglo-Catholic circles, this being the small element of truth in Waugh's *Brideshead* gibe. As David Hilliard has argued in his study of Anglo-Catholicism and homosexuality: 'For many homosexual men in the late nineteenth and early twentieth centuries, Anglo-Catholicism provided a set of institutions and religious practices through which they could express their sense of difference in an oblique and symbolical way.'[32]

An important element in much Victorian homoerotic Hellenism was a validation of *paiderastia*, interpreted as the non-sexual (i.e. non-genital sexual) love of a man for a boy. Indeed, from the end of the 1880s there was a veritable efflorescence of poetry and prose, photography and painting, celebrating the beauty of boys.[33] Certainly the only occasions in Ingram's novels where there is a degree of erotic imagination is in the portrayal of boy characters; these are sometimes portrayed as adolescent, while at other times the age cannot be determined from the context. His earliest publications, dating from before the First World War (and written under the name of Archibald K. Ingram), focus on the theme of boyhood, with his thoughts on the 'sympathetic discipline'[34] of boys in *Boys: What They Are and How to Manage Them* (1911) (with a 'Preface' by fellow Old Carthusian and Scouter, Baden Powell – whose own sexuality has come under scrutiny of late)[35] and two public school novels, *The Greater Triumph: A Story of Osborne and Dartmouth* (1911) and *Basil Verely: A Study of Charterhouse Life* (1912) which centre on the close friendships of schoolboys.[36] In *An Outline of Sexual Morality* there is an unambiguous defence of what he terms 'child-love',[37] though, again, he insists that this must not involve any form of physical sexual activity beyond an embrace: 'The embrace of children must be natural but not too ardent. In fact the lover must diffuse his love and romp with children as a class rather than allow himself to appear emotional over one individual',[38] which sounds like experience. His conclusion is frank: 'The cult of child-love is in fact one of the purest and noblest of sex-expressions. But it is a difficult path, and he who treads it must beware of many pitfalls';[39] which sounds like advice.

One can only speculate on possible literary or theoretical influences on Ingram's pederastic reflections. It probably makes more sense to talk about a milieu of which he was a part. He moved in circles in which what was termed 'boy-love' was validated. One of his fellow contributors to *The Quorum* was the Anglican clergyman the Rev. E.E. Bradford (1860–1944) who in his poetry openly celebrated his love for boys he had met; the titles of these collections leave little doubt as to their theme – *Passing the Love of Women*, *The Romance of Youth* and *Boyhood*.[40] There was the exotic Montague Summers (1880–1948) who claimed, almost certainly fraudulently, to be a Roman Catholic priest (though he had been a deacon in the Church of England) and was an expert on, and possibly a sometime practitioner of, Black Magic. Summers was the secretary of a study group within the BSSSP devoted to the subject of homosexuality, and was the author of florid verse on, among other kindred subjects, a dead altar boy.[41] Or there was George Ives – the lynchpin of the Order of Chaeronea and the BSSSP; Ingram would very probably have heard his lecture on 'The Graeco-Roman View of Youth' at the BSSSP in 1920, which drew on a large range of ancient and modern encomiums to pederasty.[42] Timothy d'Arch Smith tentatively suggests a possible influence on Ingram from the shadowy writer William Paine, whose *Shop Slavery and Emancipation* (1912, with an introduction by H.G. Wells) and *A New Aristocracy of Comradeship* (1920) combined anarcho-syndicalism, a refurbished discourse of the aristocratic, and a vindication of love 'between two young men of equal age' and between 'a man and a youth'.[43] Among possible German influences there was a strong pederastic emphasis in *Der Eigene*. Under the pen-name 'Sagitta' the Scottish-German writer John Henry Mackay (1864–1933) contributed poetry to the journal and wrote novels about relationships between adult males and teenage boys; indeed, one of his objections to Hirschfeld was that he was attempting to gain sympathy for the repeal of the anti-homosexual laws by introducing a male age of consent at 16.[44] A range of other contributors supplied articles extolling the 'pedagogic eros' (*Pädagogischer Eros*, a term coined by Gustav Wyneken (1875–1964)) – the teaching role an older man could have on the youth in whom he was in love ('Only a good paederast can be a complete pedagogue', as one put it[45]). And it is quite possible that Ingram could have come into contact either directly or indirectly with the ideas of *Der Eigene* through the international linkages of the BSSSP (George Ives, for example, was in correspondence with Adolf Brand, the editor of *Der Eigene*; and the journal's main theoretical target, Hirschfeld, was himself an important founding member of the BSSSP).[46] Or Ingram might have come across some of their ideas via Edward Carpenter, also a member of the BSSSP. Carpenter's *Ioläus*, an anthology of world literature on homosexuality, including many extracts from ancient pederastic poetry and prose, would appear to have been inspired by an earlier work, *Lieblingminne und Freundes liebe in der Weltliteratur* (Love of Comrades and Friends in World Literature) by Elisar von Kupffer (1872–1942), a major theoretical influence on *Der Eigene* circles.[47] Carpenter includes an extract from von Kupffer's book dealing with love between boys, and again cites von Kupffer's work in *The Intermediate Sex* (a work with which we know Ingram was familiar).[48] More indirectly, *The Intermediate Sex* deals with the theme of the pedagogic eros in its chapter on 'Affection in Education'.[49] What would have made some of this German material unacceptable to Ingram at this period is that sexual activity is explicitly not ruled out (so long as it is infused with 'spiritual' purposes) by many of these writers (the English literature is much more coy on this issue), and he would have found the fierce anti-Christian cast of much of the material distasteful.

Note that in *An Outline of Sexual Morality* Ingram defends 'child-love'; he does not speak here of 'boy-love'; indeed, he asserts that 'a symptom of this temperament is that romantic attachments are formed towards either sex, because before puberty, the child is bisexual or sexless'.[50] This can be seen as part of a gradual distancing of himself not merely from the definitions of homosexuality of his day, but from the notion of a self-sufficient homosexual identity. This further emerges in his other speculations on the validity of bisexuality – a theme that was to be developed in his later work. His assumption is that most people have aspects of the opposite gender in them, and, explicitly building upon the work of Edward Carpenter, he conjectures that 'the homosexual is apparently a prototype, a preliminary attempt of nature to combine both sex-natures in one individual'.[51]

Ingram's 1924 novel *The Symbolic Island* incorporates many of the features previously discussed. The plot is thin: a group of people are stranded on an island off the coast of Britain by a poisonous cloud emanating from a massive explosion on an adjacent isle. The explosion is linked to the one Jewish character, and chief villain, in the text, Lord Steinher, who is very unsympathetically drawn as a grasping, selfish and devious plutocrat (complete with bulbous nose and 'slightly foreign'[52] accent), whose experiments in producing a super-weapon have occasioned the disaster. A whole constellation of negative features are thus given a Jewish signifier. The central drama is between that mainstay of Ingram's novels, the man in search of truth (a Mr Akley, stuck in a dull marriage), and the real heroes of the piece, an Anglo-Catholic priest (Father Everill) and his companion, a boy of about 16. The latter, Gerald, gets the full weight of Ingram's erotic characterisation – blond-haired, slim, graceful, boyish – the works! Akley is portrayed as being strangely drawn to the boy, which leads him into conversations with the priest, where further Ingramian themes are ventilated. Thus Everill describes the boy as 'Hellenic', a type, the priest continues, who 'have a much keener sense of comradeship' with 'a much more romantic and sacred element in friendship than I imagine we English have possessed for a long time'.[53] Such types are also 'bisexual' in the way Ingram had indicated in *An Outline of Sexual Morality*, not being 'wholly masculine in temperament' and combining 'some of the affectional sympathy of women',[54] though Everill hastens to add that they are not thereby 'effeminate'. Likewise Akley is used to describe the close bond between boy and priest:

> The figures of the man and boy, as they leaned over the fire, were cut clean against the sky-line ... They were natural and hospitable and free with him. But he was not one of them ... There was quite enough comradeship between them to make his presence utterly unessential ... There were curious little asides, random allusions to this religion of theirs, a language which they talked but which evaded him.[55]

The climax of the novel comes when the poisonous cloud is destroyed as the priest and boy celebrate Mass in the old ruined chapel, a ceremony unleashing a distinctly homoerotic epiphany in the attendant Akley, and centred on the golden boy Gerald:

> He was faintly and curiously sure of a great multitude of others, like Gerald, joining hands with hands, on and on into infinity. ... [A] sense of boundless youth – youth fair-haired, white-robed, full of laughter and happiness, linked in a chain of unconcerned comradeship ... He wanted to stretch out his hands towards them, yet he could not stir.[56]

Although it is a mundane deluge of rain which disperses the threat, the religious ceremony is clearly a fundamental aspect of the deliverance; these events also symbolise the triumph of the Anglo-Catholic Hellenism of Gerald over the evil designs of the Jewish Steinher.

Again, as in the Hellenised Christianity, in the very different conditions of Germany, this type of homoerotic and pederastic discourse could, and, in some cases did, feed into National Socialism.[57] A number of the contributors to *Der Eigene*, which was politically diverse, were sympathetic to National Socialism, and some were even Nazi Party members. Notions of male bonding, as in the comradeship of the trenches and the post-war *Freikorps*, and in the *Wandervogel* (the German Youth Movement), masculinity and the conception of distinct roles for women could easily find the patriarchal nationalism of Nazism attractive, and the dimension of homosocial/homoerotic Hellenism in its aesthetic compelling. Add to this an undoubted element of anti-Semitism and it is not surprising that when Hitler came to settle *political* scores with the leader of the SA, Ernst Röhm, on the Night of the Long Knives, he could use the existence of a homosexual circle centred on Röhm, long tolerated, to justify his murderous campaign, thereby giving the green light to the homicidal homophobia of important sections of the party (notably Himmler), leading ultimately to the death in the camps of between 5,000 and 15,000 male homosexuals. Not that Ingram could be called a proto-Fascist – though it is true to say that, like a number of leftists, he did display some sympathy for Oswald Moseley's New Party before it became Fascist[58] – merely that his thought in this period contained elements that in very different cultural, social and political circumstances could have been directed into a trajectory markedly differing from the one he was actually to take in the 1930s. An important element in the reformulation of his ideas was to be his encounter with the ideas and the person of John Macmurray.

## A period of transition

In the late 1920s and early 1930s Ingram's views underwent a process of significant reorientation. An increasing commitment to socialism made him aware of a growing gap between his religious and socio-political beliefs, a situation he was only to resolve with the help of John Macmurray's ideas in the early 1930s.[59] Ingram had been aware of, and not unsympathetic to, aspects of socialism, and in his 'utopia' of 1924 he used the device of guild property to enshrine serious limitations to the rights of private property. Inevitably, given the neo-feudalist cast of his alternative, Marx and Engels' category of 'feudal socialism' comes to mind. There is certainly a resonance in Ingram's 'aristocratic' disdain for the perceived divisive and class-ridden nature of bourgeois society, with a backward glance to the supposed community spirit of the Catholic Middle Ages. But, as ever, his critique is also fed by his concern with the quality of personal relations between (primarily) men. Thus one of his two contributions to the mayfly existence of the homosexual magazine *The Quorum* (1920) was entitled 'Class Hatred' and dwelt on the way men from different classes found it so difficult to understand one another owing to their carapaces of class prejudice. Interestingly, given Marx and Engels' attribution of feudal socialist perspectives to the 'Young England' movement, Ingram uses Disraeli's famous 'two nations' concept to characterise contemporary social relationships in Britain. His solution, in guarded and coded terms, implicitly echoes Edward Carpenter's perennial call for a loving comradeship between men, which will somehow undermine the disabling prejudices of class: 'The only bridge,' Ingram asserts, 'which will reach over the gulf is that of friendship, real affectionate, unaffected, and uncondescending friendship.'[60] The reference to condescension illuminates the class configuration of Carpenter's homoerotic transcendence of class – in his case the desire of a middle-class man to embrace and groom men and boys of the working class. This was a widespread syndrome among middle-class male homosexuals of Carpenter's time – the fantasy drawing on the economic reality of the class basis of available sexuality. In Ingram's case the class trajectory of his project is brought out in his analogy of a colonial official among 'natives' and his illustration of a caring officer and his men during the First World War.

Ingram's second specific book on sexuality, *The Modern Attitude to the Sex Problem*, appeared in 1930, and is thus firmly in this period of transition – before his detailed acquaintance with John Macmurray. The reference to modernity in the title is indicative of new currents of thought in Ingram's perspective. A critique of Victorian sexual mores is grounded in an awareness that broad economic changes are undermining the social structures that have underpinned that code; there is an emphatic assertion that the position of women has so strengthened (described as 'the most interesting and significant development of modern times'[61]) that many of the older gender assumptions are no longer tenable; and there is a recognition that new theoretical approaches, especially in psychology, are revealing new levels of complexity in the human psyche. But modernity is also threatening, in that it has generated a reaction to the old sexual orthodoxy; and with its emphasis on freedom and pleasure, Ingram considers it socially and morally corrosive. However, given his growing distance from the doctrinal certainties of his Anglo-Catholic youth, he is conscious of the need to create a new moral framework that can provide the necessary orientation among the dangers and the possibilities of the new sexual environment.

There is a development of three themes previously discussed in *An Outline of Sexual Morality*: there is a further distancing from the concept and the practice of homosexuality; a much more detailed and committed discussion of bisexuality; and elaboration on the theme of youthful sexuality, both inter- and intra-generational. In the case of the first of these, homosexuality, Ingram devotes a specific chapter, entitling it, using the language of contemporary psychology, 'The Invert'. He deploys the concept of the higher, spiritual 'homogenic' love to argue that while healthy adolescents go through a homogenic phase, homosexuals are somehow repressed at this stage and remain, as a consequence, immature and undeveloped: 'the invert is almost always someone whose development was delayed during the homogenic period. Something in that age caused a repression and blocked the way for further growth.'[62] This enables him simultaneously to pathologise homosexuality and validate adolescent same (though non-genital) sex. In the latter case he also uses the opportunity to critique those who argued that co-educational schooling was the solution to 'unnatural practices' – the opposite is the case, for 'the occasional passionate attachments, the hero-worship of masters and older-boys',[63] given their necessity for healthy development, are more readily facilitated in single-sex educational establishments.

These assumptions allow him, as in *An Outline of Sexual Morality*, to champion the claims of paiderastia. Non-sexual love of youth is deemed to be the proper concern of the homogenic: 'Love of youth, of boyhood and adolescence, is the legitimate and natural objective for which this temperament is designed.'[64] Indeed, he pens an encomium to the great service pederasts have rendered to the youth of Britain: 'many an invert ... has been able as schoolmaster, scoutmaster, or in some other capacity, to gain the sympathy of, and to wield an intensely valuable influence over those to whom he is attracted.'[65] Even in the case of more overtly sexual behaviour, Ingram is prepared to argue that, in psychological terms at least, 'paiderastia is less harmful than contemporary homosexual habits'[66] on the grounds that since – apparently! – habits acquired later in life are more likely to become permanent than those encountered earlier on, a homosexual seduction of a young man is likely to turn the victim into an invert, while a pederastic seduction will only have a temporary effect. Consequently the penal policy of 'adopting rigorous repression ... so far as the very young are concerned, but to be more tolerant where the vice is of a rather more contemporary character',[67] insofar as the aim is to reduce the spread of inversion, is misplaced. He is at pains to make the point that there 'are obviously the strongest of reasons for protecting children from sexual victimization',[68] but the degree to which he is prepared to minimise the effects of this kind of sexual behaviour is striking.

With the assertion that 'paiderastia is generally a bisexual symptom',[69] Ingram is able to anchor this disposition in his concept of bisexuality, a concept which has undergone further refinement since its initial outing in *An Outline of Sexual Morality*. What is interesting in his discussion of the inadequacies of exclusive homosexuality and heterosexuality is that his bisexual synthesis is actually asymmetrical. Thus, at one point, he says that 'the attractiveness of the modern girl is that she looks so much more like a boy, and is no longer athletically incompetent',[70] whereas the male 'has something of the female charm, and his mind possesses female qualities',[71] a combination which evokes a beauty ideal of an androgynous youth – an inference reinforced by his slighting references to 'severely masculine'[72] lesbians and 'abnormally effeminate'[73] homosexuals. Perhaps also of relevance here is that in his discussion of 'the Greeks', deemed by him to be bisexual (a highly gendered assertion), he asserts that 'if there is any such thing as objective value in physical beauty, the Greek youth was the most beautiful physical creation the world has yet seen'.[74]

The context for the proliferation of bisexual relations is, paradoxically, a radical downgrading of sexuality. Ingram repeatedly makes disparaging references to the animal and sensuous dimensions of sexuality, and contrasts it unfavourably with the human qualities of reason and sociability. Indeed, the thing that united his critique of the Victorian code of morality and the 'free love' code was that both overemphasised the importance of sexuality, the former by an obsessive concern with its dangers, the latter by an ardent pursuit of its supposed virtues. Likewise, an important aspect of his characterisation of the new emancipated woman was that she primarily wanted an intelligent companionship in marriage, with sex as a subordinate incidental dimension. The decreasing importance of sex is therefore a barometer of human development, for 'if the intelligence of the human race is to progress, man must become less sexual in his inclinations than he is at present'.[75] But clearly an important aspect of this case for relative desexualisation was that it facilitated the reclassification, and the legitimation, of a whole range of affective same-sex relationships:

> The modern will marry – marriage perhaps may be slightly less frequent – but the homogenic element of intellectual affinity, and not merely sexual dissimilarity, will be the tie which binds the partners. With this modern type marriage itself, indeed, will be of a homogenic as well as of a sexual nature. Moreover, both husband and wife will preserve homogenic ties within their own sex.[76]

Echoes of some of the themes in *The Modern Attitude to the Sex Problem* are discernible in Ingram's 1933 novel *Midsummer Sanity*, a curious genre-mixing work – part social satire, part tale of the supernatural. The central character, the recently retired Mr Lambourne, is in search of a new life in the country, giving Ingram the opportunity to populate the village Lambourne encounters with a suitably diverse cast of attitudes and opinions. Thus the local vicar, the unsubtly named Mr Bland, is used to illustrate the Church of England's loss of touch with modern conditions – his delight in the minutiae of High Church liturgical reform an implicit reproach to Ingram's own recent past. Fiercely antagonistic to the vicar is the militantly secular and materialist doctor – scourge of all things religious. This context of a weakened institutional Christianity and a facile secularism frames Mr Lambourne's personal encounter with the forces of the mysterious – an encounter, moreover, pervasive with sexual undercurrents. He thus meets Edith, who has two main functions in the book: to dramatise the possibility of otherworldly dimensions in the apparently mundane, and to embody a number of the characteristics of Ingram's youth-loving bisexual. Hints of both these features are conveyed in Lambourne's first meeting with her:

> She was dressed loosely in white. It was the white purity of her appearance which most impressed him, for her hair and her complexion were fair, and there was a unity, almost an ethereal unity, in her presence. It was not her physical beauty. She was slight, he thought, and very young. He was conscious rather of a grace, a charm in her movement and in her poise, an indefinable, unfamiliar charm.[77]

It transpires that Edith lives in a place where different planes of existence intersect, and that the denizens of one such plane, whom Enid calls 'the Little People',[78] have given her a 'Gift'[79] which is annually renewed at Midsummer. The Gift is the ability to enter 'the Kingdom'[80] – the Kingdom of childhood; Edith is able to develop a deep level of empathy with children that adults as a whole have lost, and children respond to her as if she is one of them. Ingram's delineation of the 'Kingdom' is clearly another stab at portraying *his* conception of legitimate inter-generational love relationships between adults and children. There is an articulation by Edith of the principle of generalised love – evoked in the non-specific 'romping' of *An Outline of Sexual Morality* – 'you mustn't centre your love on any one. It must be the Kingdom only that you serve.'[81] But this is deemed to be a difficult principle, for Edith admits that 'you forget, I forget that. You can't help love',[82] and acknowledges that she may have loved an Eton schoolboy, Roy, too much. There is also a theme that Timothy d'Arch Smith has identified as a perennial presence in the 'Uranian' poetry of the late nineteenth and early twentieth century, which he terms 'the fleeting days of boyhood'[83] – the awareness of the transitory nature of the beloved's attractions; in Edith's words: 'The children pass out of the Kingdom. They are always passing out. You have learnt to love them, perhaps some one of them. And then suddenly you find he has gone.'[84] In her case this is centred on the awareness that Roy is 'very near the edge. He doesn't know. But I shall lose him soon.'[85] The theme of love overcoming class, present in *The Quorum* article, is also here, for Lambourne notes how Enid manages to bring together both her Eton boy and the lower-class village children: 'she had been the centre, as it were, of a community of youth, a masonry which had naturally formed around her'.[86] Perhaps, not surprisingly, Ingram has Lambourne enthusing that it is 'a beautiful Gift',[87] and contrasting his own complete inability to be liked by children.

Lambourne's attempt to understand all of this is used by Ingram to ventilate his thoughts on the nature of the religious. He thus has his character argue with the reductive materialist doctor over the status of religion. Lambourne accepts 'that religion is often in the hands of the wrong people and used for wrong purposes'[88] but defends the claim of religion to have a more sophisticated and nuanced conception of reality, comparing the simplistic materialist case to a worm believing that there was nothing beyond the life of the soil. In an attempt to bring some 'evidence' for this assertion he tells the doctor of Enid's experience, only to be told in turn that *this* was an example of true delusion. A conversation with the vicar proves no more fruitful. Lambourne tries to explain his notion that religious truth emerges from the progressive development and modification of tradition, but finds the vicar lost in his own world of the formal ceremonies of the Church, literally uncomprehending Lambourne's discourse. Ingram's social radicalism is apparent in the repulsive Mrs Granby, the lady of the manor, whose late husband was a war profiteer and who lectures all and sundry on the rights of private property and the threats from socialism and Bolshevism. She is also thoroughly Victorian in her moral code, and seeks, with the support of the vicar, to close down the local pub and employ people to sniff out immorality in the village and its environs. Possibly Ingram was influenced here by a shift in policy of the Public Morality Council, an evangelical body which traditionally had concentrated on rooting out heterosexual 'immorality' in the capital, but which, in the first few years of the 1930s, began to focus on homosexual activity and had quite a number of commercial homosexual venues closed down.[89] Ingram ultimately links together all three characters – the vicar, the doctor and Mrs Granby – as rigid and intolerant, with secularism and Puritanism as merely two sides of the same coin, all enemies of the 'Kingdom'.

The denouement, given what one knows about Ingram, is somewhat predictable. Edith, evicted from her home by the grasping and censorious Mrs Granby, returns in Midsummer to have her 'Gift' renewed. Lambourne barges into the middle of the ceremony and finds himself invested with access to the Kingdom. The very next morning the grocer's boy comes to his door and tells him that he has the afternoon off:

> Mr Lambourne hesitated a moment. 'You wouldn't care to come up here this afternoon, I suppose?' he said ... 'You might bring a few friends. We could have some games.' 'Love to,' said the boy. 'What time?'[90]

Within minutes he bumps into Roy, the Eton schoolboy – same result:

> 'I wonder if you would care to come up and have tea? I'm asking two or three of the village boys in. There may be a girl or two as well. I don't know. Would you care to come?' 'Thanks awfully,' said Roy. 'I should love to. What time?'[91]

The cross-class masonry of the Kingdom thus begins to be reassembled.

From the perspective of today, what is striking about the subject matter of Ingram's work on sexuality is that whereas it has become considerably easier to talk about homosexuality the opposite applies in the case of pederasty. Let us return, for example, to the previously mentioned Rev. E.E. Bradford – Ingram's fellow contributor to *The Quorum* – and his poems to youths and boys. When a collection of his poems, *To Boys Unknown*, was published by the Gay Men's Press in 1988, Paul Webb in his introductory remarks assumed as a given that something needed to be explained here, namely how between 1908 and 1930 Bradford could publish eleven anthologies of such material and receive respectful reviews from mainstream journals and newspapers. The question gets its energy from contemporary notions of sexual taboo, above all the discourse of paedophilia. Webb's attempt to answer his own question casts light on Ingram's position. From the perspective of reviewer response, Webb posits a willingness at the time to view Bradford's celebration of inter-generational relationships as selfless, educationally enriching initiatives by older males towards younger:

> If people took his poetry to represent a platonic love between man and boy, of a temporary and helpful nature – such as a scoutmaster might enjoy with his charges – then the poems must have appeared delightfully straightforward or, as the *Times* put it, 'cheery and wholesome'.[92]

In the case of Ingram, given his sincere and explicit commitment to a Christian-infused and thoroughly chaste notion of a pedagogical eros, it would not be unreasonable to assume that the bulk of his readership construed his words in this way.

Second, Webb adduces class-grounded cultural assumptions – the centrality to the educated classes of classical culture with its unconcealable sexual practices and mores, and the degree of licence accorded to elite cultural forms (in this case poetry) – as to why Bradford would not be perceived as transgressive or threatening. Ingram also, was encased in the partial security of elite cultural production, and carefully strove not to prompt doubts as to his respectability. His erudite treatises with their nod to science, classical allusions, and patent religiosity rendered pederasty reassuringly remote from the world.

But this is not the full picture. Ingram clearly felt that his views, though radical, could find a positive response among the opinions of the day, or could at the very least be publicly articulated. If one looks at the three anonymous reviews of his main books on sex published in the *Times Literary*

*Supplement* between 1920 and 1940 one gets no sense of shock, or any sense that the books are taboo-breakers. They all think that he will antagonise some readers, but no more than this. The review of *An Outline of Sexual Morality* talks of 'some fresh and acute thought' in the book while acknowledging that 'on some matters the writer may startle those who hold conventional views on the problem of sex'; it concludes with the observation that Ingram has 'some rather original and suggestive views on the various sex abnormalities'.[93] In the case of *The Modern Attitude to the Sex Problem*, the reviewer suggests that Ingram's views on sexuality were likely to alienate the religious tradition with which he had long been publicly associated, noting and welcoming the fact that the 'author, a well-known writer from the Anglo-Catholic standpoint, should have the breadth and courage to put his ideas, which are decidedly not those of his co-religionists, into print'. It notes that he 'devotes considerable space to his ideas on the intermediate sex' but doesn't find much new in Ingram's discussion, no real advance on the work of Havelock Ellis and Edward Carpenter. Specific criticisms are focussed on his downgrading of sexuality ('Mr Ingram sees it as a frivolous pastime') and a belief that 'his ideas about women are curiously tainted by prejudices'.[94] Finally, the review of his 1940 text *Sex-Morality Tomorrow* again makes the point that while some audiences won't like it the work is hardly revolutionary; Ingram's analyses and solutions 'though heterodox to some extent, are by no means cataclysmic'; the book's achievements are therefore modest: 'although Mr Ingram has not, perhaps, anything startlingly novel to contribute to the problem, and not all his solutions are equally acceptable, his book should have a clarifying effect on his readers.'[95]

To be surprised that these reviews do no more, and don't specifically speak of the positive remarks on pederasty, is to be anachronistic. Matt Houlbrook has argued that one sees the beginnings in the interwar years of what was to become a hegemonic discourse after the Second World War: the notion of the paedophile violation of childhood innocence. This begins to displace the view that in inter-generational sexual relationships *both* adult and juvenile could share a degree of guilt. The dominant 'paedophile narrative', to use Houlbrook's term, makes it difficult for a modern audience accurately to comprehend Ingram and his particular trajectory, or even to feel comfortable talking about his views. The historical reality for Houlbrook is that 'while many people disapproved of relationships between men and boys ... those encounters possessed meanings that are very different from those today'.[96] Ingram was still in a space where alternative meanings held sway, as were many of his readers and reviewers. The rise of this new narrative meant that the post-war drive for homosexual law reform had to exclude anything that even remotely could be linked to paedophilia – the speakable had become the unspeakable. In this sense a reason why it is easier today to talk about homosexuality than pederasty is because the condemnation of pederasty was integral to the emergence of the post law-reform homosexual. The introduction of a male homosexual age of consent, where none had existed before, created a powerfully symbolic moral and legal frontier, grounded in age, demarcating the acceptable from the depraved – penalties, for example, were *increased* for a male over 21 having sexual relations with a young man aged between 16 and 21. And in the silences that were attendant on the noise of the paedophile narrative, the quotidian sexual abuse of children by parents, teachers and clergy found the stiflingly quiet environment it craved. For Ingram the shift in paradigms meant that his varying attempts to integrate the homosexual and the pederastic would be increasingly out of kilter with the homosexual reform movement.

## Marxism and John Macmurray

The choice of the word 'Kingdom' in *Midsummer Sanity* is surely not without broader significance. As the 1930s progress Ingram's work becomes more focussed on differentiating the radical social resonances of the Christian trope of the Kingdom of Heaven, from conservative, quietistic interpretations. Increasingly Marxist in his social analyses, Ingram conceptualises the looming menace of Fascism as the last line of defence of a crumbling capitalism whose crisis can only actually be resolved by a classless society. The superiority of socialist goals is indicative of divine intentions in history, intentions which include the establishment of the Kingdom of Heaven in this world. This means that Christians have a duty to ally with, and assist, those forces creating such a society, even if those forces are openly atheist and antagonistic to Christianity, for 'God may use the very forces which deny Him to vindicate His purpose';[97] furthermore, God's use of socialism might be part of a dialectical move on his part to overcome the idealist, supernaturalist emphasis of existing Christianity by introducing a materialist moment:

> It may well be that the materialist reaction is the medium which God is using to redress the balance, to remind us that the supernatural and natural are an indivisible unity, and that the spiritual is unattainable, except through action in the world in which we live.[98]

This emphasis on the issue of atheism and materialism in socialism reflects Ingram's growing (though still critical) admiration for the Soviet Union in the 1930s, and the attendant need to justify support on Christian grounds. He became increasingly visible in leftist Christian circles, forming part of a religious delegation (which also included John Macmurray and the Dean of Canterbury, Hewlett Johnson) which gave the religious policy of the Spanish Republican government a clean bill of health, and playing a leading and a vocal role (also with Macmurray) in the Christian Left, a loose ginger group of left-wing Christians.[99]

In autobiographical fragments Ingram registers the crucial importance of John Macmurray in reorientating his views:

> It was in the early thirties that I began to read and meet John Macmurray, to whom I owe more than to any other of my friends. My contact with

him and with the small group which had grown up around him, brought me to a further stage on my journey.[100]

His closeness to Macmurray has misled commentators into disparaging descriptions of Ingram as a mere 'popularizer'[101] of Macmurray's work, thereby both obliterating the distinctive trajectory of Ingram's work before he ever encountered Macmurray (especially around the theme of homosexuality), and effacing Ingram's distinctive reading of Macmurray, itself grounded in the earlier struggle to develop a Christian understanding of homosexuality.

But there is a problem in determining the nature of Ingram's reading of Macmurray – the virtual absence of any explicit references to Macmurray's writings in Ingram's books of the 1930s. Like Macmurray himself, Ingram did not tend to highlight sources of importance (Marx and the Bible being notable exceptions). In the case of homosexuality this reticence is compounded by his own distanced approach – homosexuality is about others, not oneself, a social issue, not an area into which one explicitly brought sources of personal inspiration; this in turn helps to explain why Ingram could be seen as a mere unproblematic populariser of Macmurray's work. One therefore has to infer why Ingram would have found Macmurray of value in thinking through his analysis of homosexuality.

Trying to reconstruct a homosexual hermeneutics of Macmurray in the 1930s and 40s enables one to see this writer in a different light. Macmurray's critique of the biological organicist paradigm which he maintained had dominated thought and behaviour from the nineteenth century onwards must have seemed a promising starting point for such a reading. From the organic perspective gender differences were of paramount importance, as were the appropriate sexual relationships between genders. Macmurray proposed a new paradigm grounded in the personal where gender differentiation was a subordinate property; primary relationships were between persons, not genders; this stance, moreover, had impeccable scriptural authority, for 'in Christ Jesus there is neither male nor female'.[102] One surmises that Macmurray's deployment of the term 'friendship' to denote authentic relationships between persons must have had interesting resonances for Ingram. 'Friendship' both de-gendered relationships *and* invoked a traditionally homosocial space – indeed, one of Macmurray's concerns was to suggest that men and woman for the first time could become friends. The essence of friendship is selfless love which can occur between men and women, women and women, and men and men. In one text Macmurray illustrates this point with two male characters, David and Jonathan, whose biblical provenance must have been intended by Macmurray, and who had an iconic status in the canonic homosexual history of the time. Macmurray is talking about 'a friendship, for example, between two men or two women' and continues:

> Two people are friends because they love one another ... To ask David what he expects to get out of his friendship with Jonathan is to insult him

by suggesting that he only associates with his friend from self-interest. No doubt he might answer that he gets everything that makes life worth living; but of course what he means is that he gets friendship out of it, which is exactly what he puts into it. This is the characteristic of personal relationships ... Their value lies entirely in themselves and for the same reason transcends all other values.[103]

What must also have appealed to Ingram was that this analysis of the personal was grounded in a Christian critique of Christianity. Macmurray contrasted the judgemental and rationalistic ethos of Roman stoicism, which he argued captured Christianity, from the non-judgemental, loving ethos of Jesus to show that modern Christian sex morality is wrong-headed and destructive. The concept of 'chastity', reduced in the modern Christian conception to a fearful obsession with sex, is traced back to the emotional honesty of Jesus ('Blessed are the pure in heart for they shall see God')[104] and fashioned into moral injunctions whose import could not have been lost on Ingram:

It is, then, a failure in chastity to express a feeling to someone that you do not feel; to express love for a person, for instance, when you do not feel it. It is equally unchaste to conceal your feelings from someone to whom it makes a real difference.[105]

Chastity in this sense, Macmurray concludes, is 'the true basis for *any* intimate personal relationship and applies universally between persons, whether they are of the same or of different sexes'.[106]

A final point to consider here is Macmurray's approach to Judaism. We have already discussed Ingram's anti-Semitic deployment of a Greek/Jewish dualism. Macmurray, in contrast, was, as we have seen, an enthusiast for what he took to be the distinctive qualities of ancient Israel. He uses a tripartite classification of the Jewish, Greek and Roman, and of the three considers ancient Hebrew civilisation to embody the only true *religious* culture. He is also at pains to stress the Jewish nature of Jesus: 'it is essential to insist again that Christianity is Jewish and that Jesus was a Jew.'[107] The evidence is clear that Ingram did adopt this new perspective; thus, in the same year as Macmurray published his remark about Jesus' Judaism, Ingram would also assert that 'the teaching of Christ ... is essentially empirical and Jewish'[108] and it does not seem unreasonable to assume here the effect of Macmurray's good offices. It is also the case that there is a growing awareness in Ingram's writings of the nature of the persecution of the Jews in Germany, and he develops an analysis of the pernicious role of racism in Nazi ideology.[109] Nonetheless, even in the 1930s, Ingram was not averse to dramatising the significant *discontinuity* between Jesus and Jewish society. Thus in his 1935 novel *'It is Expedient ... '* he retells the Gospel narrative in a modern setting with a fictional Asian country as ancient Palestine, the British as the Romans, and so on and so forth. There is a good deal of progressive anti-colonialism in his depiction of the imperial British, but what is striking is his portrayal of the relationship between the modern Jesus figure, Avalla, and the indigenous society (standing in for the ancient Hebrews). Avalla is thus presented as repudiating the superstition, partiality and false religiosity of Jewish society and articulating a new universal ethic of love. As in biblical accounts, Ingram has local elites, fearful of his radical message, engineering Avalla's death through the instruments of a native Judas and a feckless British administration. The one relatively homoerotic moment in the novel occurs in a section where Ingram unfavourably contrasts the sexual mores of the local society with the new ethos of Avalla. It begins with a description of a boy (age undisclosed) that is suffused with Uranian Hellenism:

> A native boy sat on the river bank, playing a reed pipe. His feet dangled in the water. His skin was bronze, his body lithe and delicately formed. Against the background of the rushes which leaned forward when the faint breath of air spurred them, he had become a nymph of the stream. His lips were curved in a faint smile. He was naked but for the cloth about his loins.[110]

Into this scene comes a visiting Englishman (Gibburn) and an old man dragging an unwilling girl. The visitor asks the boy to act as an interpreter, and it transpires that the old man wishes to get Avalla to bless his intention to send his daughter to her death in the desert because she has taken a lover despite being a temple virgin – a clear breach of ecclesiastical law. When Avalla arrives he turns on the father for his lack of love towards his daughter, and advises the girl to go and live with her lover. The old man turns on Avalla, asserting orthodoxy and promising vengeance: '"You have dishonoured the law of the Temple ... You will answer for this."'[111] Ingram hasn't finished with the boy yet, for in a coda to the episode there are a number of enigmatic interchanges which surely hint of the 'Kingdom' love evoked in *Midsummer Sanity*:

> The boy came forward. Instantly, Gibburn noticed, Avalla's face was lit with a smile. 'Master,' said the boy, 'will you come to my house again? My brothers and sisters ask for you.' 'Yes, I will come,' Avalla answered ... He laid his hands on the boy's head. The procession moved on down the road ... Presently Gibburn and the boy were alone ... 'You seem happy,' said Gibburn. 'Is it Avalla who has made you so happy?' The boy nodded his head. 'But he has not given you money?' 'He has better to give than money,' the boy answered. 'Oh you've discovered that, have you?' Gibburn remarked. 'You are wise, in spite of your youth.'[112]

If this interpretation is correct then one might speculate about a residual element in Ingram of the opposition between a religious *eros* of Greece and a moralistic legalism of Judaism. Again, if true, this suggests that the dynamic of his relationship with Macmurray is much more complicated than the notion of 'populariser' suggests. This remnant cannot simply be explained in terms of a vestigial anti-Semitism (if indeed this was the case). Of course, Macmurray was aware that Jesus was at odds with elements of his society, but in the case of Ingram, given the specifics of his erotic makeup, one senses that *his* Jesus *had to be* significantly more at variance with his society, and that Athens rather than Jerusalem was still providing the measure of this difference.

## *Sex-Morality Tomorrow*

In 1940 Ingram published his last large-scale analysis of sexuality. It was completed in the early days of the Second World War, a war which he saw as the outcome of the contradictions of an imperialist capitalism. He was convinced that the conflagration signalled the death of the old civilisation, and therefore he sought to explore the form sexual morality might (or even would) take if a better and more enlightened society emerged with the peace – hence the book's title: *Sex-Morality Tomorrow*. This future orientation also created a bit of space between the author and some of the radical material he was discussing. His thoughts on morality in this text reflect the growing unorthodoxy in his religious views throughout the 1930s, views importantly influenced by the work of John Macmurray. Specifically he rejects notions of a moralising personal God, whose authoritarian code of morality was enshrined in an infallible Bible. Instead there is an immanentist theology of the divine working through the human, but this immanence is simultaneously transcendence, because the whole process is more than its parts. From this perspective Jesus is to be read because what he said is true, not the fact that he said it – the authority lies in the message, not the source.[113] It also means that sacred texts, religious doctrines and institutional forms were fallible human creations, but that sparks of the divine could be glimpsed by the careful observer.

In terms of sexual morality Ingram now recognised that his old Anglo-Catholic insistence that Christian doctrine made sex outside marriage impermissible was now unsustainable. This was now denounced as 'legalism', in that a legal form (whether it be secular or canon law) determines what is moral and generates an absurd moral ranking in which a loveless marriage is deemed infinitely superior to a loving relationship outside marriage.[114] These two examples indicate the direction Ingram was travelling, in that the real differentiation between the cases was that love was evident in one case but not in the other, and this indeed is the basis of Ingram's alternative moral principle: 'the determining factor of sex-morality is not the vow and the legal solemnization of marriage but the presence or absence of the love-motive.'[115] This principle had been bubbling about in his thinking from the early 1930s, but from the very start there was an awareness of the problem of defining love. He was attracted by the idea of attaching the notion of 'permanence' to the definition, to distinguish love from temporary and less substantial motivations; thus, writing in 1933 he argued 'that love, ideally, is permanent because it is something more than infatuation'.[116] That little word 'ideally' says it all, for he recognised that permanence was far too stringent a condition, admitting in the 1940 text that 'from the moral standpoint there is no justification for asserting that only that type of love which is likely to be permanent may be sexually consummated'.[117] But this merely confirmed the difficulties inherent in defining the moral principle of love, and by the end of the book there is an admission of inadequate work:

> We have to disentangle, much more effectively than we have as yet succeeded in doing, pure love from the impulses for selfish satisfaction and domination which are the main motives underlying so many human relationships which masquerade under the banner of love.[118]

This shift of moral ground is itself linked to a changing appreciation of the nature of sexuality. In his earlier book, *The Modern Attitude to the Sex Problem*, Ingram had sought to reduce the importance of sexuality, stressing rational relationships, companionship, the life of the mind, and so forth. By 1940 there is evidence of a change of direction in this area. Although the language of a middle ground between overestimating and underestimating sex is still present, the middle has shifted towards a more positive stance towards sexual behaviour. There is also an awareness that in reality sexuality *is* important in people's lives, and will continue to be so. This added urgency to the search for a moral principle governing sexual behaviour, for a widespread desexualisation was evidently no longer on the cards. Citing the findings of 'scientific' psychology, Ingram argues that sexual abstinence has real dangers, that 'for the majority of human beings celibacy is undesirable and not beneficial: it is not a natural state, it ought not therefore to be enjoined',[119] and that a healthy sexual life, governed by the moral principle of love, is an important feature of a well-ordered society.

Needless to say, all of this had far-reaching consequences for his analysis of homosexuality. In the two earlier texts on sexuality the public policy voice of the author, when discussing homosexuality, had spoken the language of tolerance. In his role as a concerned and fair-minded commentator on the homosexual 'other' his line had been that although much of the public found homosexuality disagreeable they should on both moral and pragmatic grounds tolerate these types. In *Sex-Morality Tomorrow*, however, although the language of toleration is still spoken, there is also the presence of a much more pluralistic approach, a welcoming of sexual diversity, which in the earlier books had only been fleetingly glimpsed in the speculative thoughts on bisexuality:

> Human nature, including the sexual nature of man, is not uniform: it is infinitely varied. And if this conclusion is accepted, it follows that society is better served by the free contribution of these varied temperaments than by any attempt to dragoon man into one type. The architecture of human society, in fact, requires the existence of differing types.[120]

In the case of homosexuality the search for a pathology of the phenomenon is itself now deemed problematic. He discusses various theories as to the 'cause' of homosexuality, including the 'arrested development' theory he espoused in *The Modern Attitude to the Sex Problem*, but concludes that he is sceptical of 'any theory which professes to find a sole cause for homosexuality ... I doubt if there is any single cause which constitutes its origin. It arises, like most varieties, from a number of causes.'[121] It is this notion of homosexuality as one legitimate 'variety' among many that takes centre-stage in this text: 'homosexuality ... is a natural variety of human nature and ... the homosexual in any intelligent form of society has a useful contribution to make to society.'[122]

New thinking is also apparent in the way homosexuality is defined. The tradition that Ingram grew up in understood sexual desire in terms of gender, by looking for a gender source of desire. To people like Edward Carpenter male homosexual desire indicated that there must be a female source for such desire within that male and, likewise, that lesbian desire had its roots in a corresponding masculine dimension. Gendering is also apparent in the hostility aimed at homosexuals in this era, where their behaviour was frequently characterised in terms of deviant sexual identity rather than of distinctive sexual activity. Thus 'Sam', a contributor to Porter and Weeks's collection of homosexual reminiscences, recalled: 'They might call you queer, but probably only because of the way you talked, but they wouldn't think anything about sexually. They'd call you queer because they thought you was a bit girlish. But not because of the sexual act.'[123] A gendered approach is highly visible in both *An Outline of Sexual Morality* and *The Modern Attitude to the Sex Problem*. Elements of this sort of language can be found in *Sex-Morality Tomorrow*, where Ingram does refer to 'masculine and feminine qualities'.[124] However, at the theoretical level there are signs of the emergence of an approach which defines homosexuality not in terms of a supposed gender source, but in terms of the *object* of desire. Ingram posits a degree of sexual energy in subjects which can potentially attract itself to any object; homosexuality is merely the direction of desire to members of the same sex. This means that 'a homosexual' is simply a description of someone who predominantly or mainly engages in homosexual behaviour – it is a generalisation from behaviour, and not some sort of essential identity:

> The sex-force is of the same essence in every individual, the affectional quality is of the same nature. They vary in intensity and in the direction to which they happen to be turned, but in substance they are similar in every case. When we refer to different types of sexual temperament we mean, therefore, simply that these forces are being expressed in different ways. The sexual temperament in this sense is secondary rather than primary. It is a mode of expression, not an ultimate quality. Hence we frequently find that persons who up till a comparatively late age have exhibited marked homosexual tendencies suddenly revert to normal, marry and have children.[125]

Matt Houlbrook in *Queer London* argues that this shift away from gendered desire to objects of desire became widespread in the homosexual community from the 1950s. He refers to the changing experience of a waiter and merchant seaman, John Alcock: 'In the 1940s he conceptualized his desires within the gendered opposition between man and quean. In the 1950s, by contrast, Alcock began to talk of himself as "homosexual", articulating a subjectivity defined by his partner's biological sex.'[126] Houlbrook sees this as a reflection of a new binary opposition between 'homosexual' and 'heterosexual', in which 'rather than a womanlike character, the "homosexual's" difference was located in his choice of a male sexual partner'.[127] Ingram's distinction, however, was not intended to generate such a dualistic conception of sexuality, but to create a new theoretical framework for his perennial search for the grail of bisexuality.

The new moral principle of love completely opens up the issue of homosexual practices. In his earlier texts, first Christian doctrine and then desexualisation had made legitimate homosexual sex a non-issue in the face of a chaste high-mindedness. In *Sex-Morality Tomorrow*, although reticent as ever about talking about homosexual sexual practices, Ingram allows the logic of the new morality to suggest to the attentive reader its own conclusions on this matter. Having established in Chapter 3 the principle: 'wherever there is love, wherever the desire for sexual expression arises as a natural result of love, wherever that desire is genuinely mutual, there can be no immorality in sex'[128] he then proceeds to assert in Chapter 5 that 'love, and usually love of the most complete kind, is the substance of the vast majority of homosexual relationships, and where the love is sincerely mutual it is immoral to devalue it',[129] effectively handing over a recipe for moral homosexual sex to its constituency – mutual love, mutual desire for sex.

In the case of youth sex his new moral principle was a potential minefield. Again it is necessary to distinguish between intra- and inter-generational sex. There is only one discussion of specifically homosexual sex between schoolboys in the text. Ingram uses an anecdote about 'sex-irregularities' in a public school to highlight the difference between contemporary moral orthodoxy and the morality of a future society. A boy was expelled for his involvement 'in two or three sex-affairs with other boys' where he was 'the prime instigator'.[130] Ingram castigates the headmaster for his moralistic overreaction: 'not the boy but the headmaster should have been branded as the criminal. The morality of the future … would place the boy's conduct, at worst, on the same level as failure to control his temper',[131] though loss of temper could itself, in certain circumstances, justify exclusion. The 'at worst' is significant, for when Ingram comes to talk about an imaginary example of youth sex in the future the tone is even more liberal. In this scenario a headmaster is interviewing 'a boy who practises promiscuous intercourse'. The fact that the gender of his partners is not revealed is possibly an attempt to avoid using an explicit, and potentially more controversial, homosexual example, thereby allowing him to deploy more radical ideas (though as his later correspondence with the Archbishop of Canterbury about his book reveals, he did have a single-sex school in mind). The headmaster says that he does not believe that the boy is in love with any of his sexual contacts, though he accepts that the acts were consensual. His advice to desist is both conditional (till love is present) and libertarian in its (guarded) acceptance of future experimentation:

> My advice to you ... is that you should control yourself until you have learnt to fall in love ... It will be no use coming to me and telling me that you've found someone who is willing to share sexual experience with you, until I can see that this is a genuine case of love. The proof of this will soon be tested. If it isn't a genuine case, you won't want to share your school life together; you won't be happy together. You may not discover such a lover until after you have left school.[132]

The nature of informed consent, both intellectual and emotional, not really addressed in this example is even more important when the issue is intergenerational sex. Again the material is short on detail. He repeats his previous claim that 'paiderastic homosexuals' make good teachers, indeed it is strengthened to the claim that 'the most successful schoolmaster is one who possesses to some degree the homosexual temperament',[133] on the grounds that such men can appeal to 'interests and affections' while non-homosexuals 'must rely mainly upon the disciplinary approach'.[134] But he repeats his earlier warning that such affection should be generalised rather than particularised, though while rejecting 'homosexual attachments' between teachers and pupils he adds, 'when this occurs the results, save in the most exceptional circumstances, are unfortunate',[135] leaving us in the dark as to the nature of these 'attachments' and what the 'exceptional circumstances' might be. He is also in favour of a homosexual age of consent prohibiting sexual relations between an older man and a boy beneath this age, though he does not actually say what this age should be.[136]

As ever, bisexuality is proclaimed as the ultimate goal. The discussion of this in *Sex-Morality Tomorrow* echoes many of the themes previously examined in earlier works. One can detect, though, an attempt to provide a more systematic socio-economic analysis of the matter than in the earlier works, a reflection, it would seem, of Ingram's immersion in leftist circles and literature. The trend towards bisexuality is grounded in the changing division of labour between the sexes, as more women leave exclusive domesticity and become part of the work-force. This mixing of the sexes breaks down some of the old gender differences, and there is a convergence as both women and men are changed. Ingram begins his chapter on bisexuality by referring back to his 1930 text *The Modern Attitude to the Sex Problem*, and refers to 'some misunderstandings regarding it which I am anxious to remove.'[137] Although he does not spell out what these 'misunderstandings' might be, he does use the opportunity to backtrack to some extent on the desexualisation thesis in that book. Thus while maintaining that men and women can increasingly relate to one another in asexual ways, he is at pains to state that 'I am not suggesting that this development will ultimately destroy the sexual impulse ... Men and women are just as sexual as they ever were.'[138] His new emphasis on objects of desire rather than gendered sources of desire also allows him to re-ground his theory of bisexuality on a much more fluid play of forces. From a rather clunky ontology of gendered presences he is able to envisage, instead, a dynamics of shifting desire: 'men and women are naturally bisexual ... their sexual-affectional faculty can be turned towards the opposite sex or inwards towards their own sex';[139] this also opens up the possibility of differing sexual practices with differing groups – genital sexuality with one sex, for example, romantic relations with another: 'I find among many young people of both sexes ... a conscious recognition ... that many of their affectional experiences have been homosexual, even though ... their actual intercourse has been wholly heterosexual.'[140] Ingram has travelled quite some distance from Carpenter's 'intermediate sex' paradigm.

## Silence

Ingram was to live another twenty-five years but, apart from a short pamphlet of 1944 – *Christianity and Sexual Morality – A Modernist View*[141] (which did not go beyond the views of the 1940 book) – he did not produce another dedicated and detailed work on sexuality, though he continued to publish books on other subjects. One possible reason for this silence may have been a fierce response *Sex-Morality Tomorrow* provoked in the Church of England – a response which brought Ingram into direct conflict with the Archbishop of Canterbury, William Temple. One can piece the altercation together from the Temple correspondence in Lambeth Palace Library. On 3 July 1942 a certain Miss Lettice A. MacMunn wrote to the Archbishop asking him to do something about Ingram's book, since 'there has never been a time more unpropitious for such pernicious stuff to be set before our young people'.[142] She informed Temple that the Bishop of London had tried to get the book suppressed, and that she and others had sought, without success, to get the Public Prosecutor to take criminal action. The specific reason she said she was approaching Temple was that he had invited Ingram to speak at the Malvern Conference, and therefore might 'be able to influence him to withdraw' his book. In Chapter 4 a great deal more will be said about the Malvern Conference, which was held in January 1941. Suffice it to say here that it was sponsored by Temple (then Archbishop of York) who wanted to put post-war social change very much on the church agenda. Ingram and Richard Acland (the subject of Chapter 4) were the two key radical speakers at the conference. The reform-minded findings of the conference were not to the taste of large sections of the clergy and laity. In this context the past association between Ingram and Temple now put pressure on both men not to let the furore over the book harm the cause of reform.

Temple wrote to Ingram the very next day. The tone towards the book is not all critical – 'there is a good deal in it and in its attitude with which I am sympathetic and from which I think some good may result.'[143] His theological stance was, however, fundamentally different from the radical immanentist perspective of Ingram and Macmurray; thus, he found in Ingram's book 'a great deal that seems to me entirely pernicious in effect though I know not in intention and due to an intellectualist handling of the matter which involves ignoring some of the deepest factors'. He is also at pains to impress on Ingram the threat posed to the Malvern Reform initiative if he is forced to dissociate himself publicly from Ingram, thereby advertising 'a breach in the ranks of those eager for social progress on Christian lines'. He therefore asks Ingram to withdraw *Sex-Morality Tomorrow*. However, his hopes were not high that Ingram would do this; he responded to Lettice MacMunn that he didn't expect his letter 'to produce any effect'.[144] He also revealed that he had been aware of Ingram's 'extremely unsound and dangerous views' on sexuality for at least a couple of months prior to receiving her complaint – an indication, perhaps, of the broader campaign against Ingram to which she had referred in her letter. But in matters of sexual behaviour Temple is no Puritan, as he makes clear to Miss MacMunn: Ingram represents 'an extreme swing of the pendulum', but 'some swing was inevitable and in my judgment desirable'; furthermore, although theologically unacceptable, and in that sense 'worse in itself', Ingram's position is 'probably less dangerous in its effect than the Puritan extreme from which it is a reaction'.

The reply he got from Ingram on 7 July was ambiguous. On the one hand Ingram was concerned to protect his integrity – 'I should not want to do anything which would imply that I had not the courage of my convictions'[145] – but on the other he was very mindful of Temple's fears about undermining the forces of reform – 'But I am certainly very anxious not to persist in any line which will embarrass my friends, and I fully appreciate what you say in that connexion.' One should also note that this was a letter from the spiritual leader of the Anglican community, a community of which Ingram was a sincere member; Macmurray had turned his back on institutional Christianity, Ingram had not: 'I have every desire,' he was to write in 1943, 'to remain in communion with the Church into which I was born.'[146] He thus asked Temple for time to consider his response. While waiting for this Temple discussed the case with Hugh Cecil, Lord Quickswood (1869–1956), the Provost of Eton and a leading Anglican lay person, sending him a copy of Ingram's letter. The opening lines of Quickswood's response could not have been very heartening for the Archbishop:

> I could not of course express any opinion as to what is, or is not, wise from the point of view of those supporting the Malvern movement (as one may call it) for on the whole I do not sympathise with that movement.[147]

Temple therefore subsequently avoided using this consideration in their subsequent correspondence; instead, developing a fear Quickswood himself raised, he counselled the need to minimise publicity over the affair in terms of depriving Ingram of a notoriety that would increase the sales of the book.[148] The correspondence with Quickswood, as is the case with Miss MacMunn, is not enlightening as to which specific parts of Ingram's book are causing offence. There is, for example, no mention of homosexuality; indeed, there is a decorous absence of any sexual detail. Temple and Quickswood agree, at a high level of abstraction, that the book enshrines a rejection of the Christian doctrine of chastity – namely that any sexual relations outside marriage are sinful.

Three weeks after Temple's initial letter Ingram sent his considered reply. He was not prepared to withdraw the book. The integrity argument was repeated, supplemented with a wish not to let down correspondents who had found his book helpful, and the stated suspicion that critics would not be satisfied with a mere withdrawal of the book. Instead, Ingram proposed that he insert in the remaining copies a statement, the draft of which he enclosed, and, as a further concession, that he could 'also probably agree to issue no further edition'.[149] Temple's heart must have sunk when he read the draft insertion. Apart from a slight caveat on 'trial marriages' the document reaffirmed some of Ingram's most controversial propositions in his book. He notes that most of the criticism has been directed at his chapter on sex in schools. Plunging straight into the fire, so to speak, he takes the opportunity to counter a 'misunderstanding' contained in a review in *The Shield* that he approved of 'sexual intercourse between schoolboy and girl lovers';[150] the misunderstanding was that 'actually I had in mind the one-sex school, where, I should contend, homosexual practices are comparatively prevalent'. And, lest a broader point be missed, he added: 'It was in that context that I admitted that I found no evidence to show that such practices during school-life lead to subsequent injury of a physical or psychological nature.' As for heterosexual 'affairs': 'I am not in a position to judge ... ' He reiterated his rejection of 'any policy which assumes that sexual practices at school are abnormal, or which attempts to suppress them by discipline', asserts his moral criterion of love, and insists on what must follow from this approach: 'those who are prepared to take their stand on this principle must, however, be prepared to face its implications. There are cases where, even at an early age, mature love is an integral element in the situation.'

However, Ingram ends the covering letter to Temple with some significant lines indicating his understanding of their shared fear that his book could be used as a stick to beat the reform movement: 'I am anxious to save you and any other of our friends any possible embarrassment, and I would gladly do anything to help in this way, short of any course which would involve me in insincerity.'[151] He notes that the book was written at the end of 1939 when Malvern was not on the horizon; if it had been, 'I might have hesitated to publish a book of so controversial a character concerning an issue which had no direct relevance to the much more important issues of religious-social reconstruction.' His closing sentence is even more significant: 'that consideration would probably lead me to decide not to write any further book on this subject'.[152]

In this period Ingram was very active in the leadership of first Forward March, the movement brought into being by Sir Richard Acland, and then Common Wealth (see Chapters 4 and 5). In a letter of August 1942 from the Reverend George Jager to Acland, Jager, a member of Common Wealth, warned Acland that his connection with Ingram was not helpful in the eyes of sections of the clergy; this had a lot to do with Ingram's heterodox theology, but, Jager added, 'it is his books on sex which really damn him in their eyes'.[153] There is thus the possibility that the Temple episode was reinforced by the pressures of making Common Wealth popular and successful.

However, Temple died in 1944, to be replaced as Archbishop of Canterbury by a more conservative figure, Geoffrey Fisher, and Common Wealth itself was all but wiped out in 1945, yet Ingram did not return in any significant way to the fray on sexual reform. The post-war climate on homosexuality may have played a part here. After the relative freedom gay men had enjoyed in the vicissitudes of wartime Britain, the period from the late 1940s to the early 1960s witnessed a police and media offensive against homosexuality, but also, and partly in response to this attack, a growing sympathy in sections of elite opinion for law reform. This context structured the way gay men sought to respond at the political level. In *Sex-Morality Tomorrow* it is possible to see a harmony of two themes which, even in 1940, was becoming less and less possible. On the one hand there was a defence of homosexuality, which stressed the decency and relative normalcy of most homosexuals. This type of approach was to characterise the various subsequent campaigns for homosexual law reform culminating in the Sexual Offences Act of 1967. As Matt Houlbrook has argued, the central image of this movement was the respectable and private homosexual.[154] And it is the case that in his very last book, *Is Christianity Credible?* (1963), Ingram indicates his support for legal reform, referring to 'the injustice and moral absurdity of the existing law'.[155] Intergenerational and youthful homosexuality was quite another thing. Even by the 1940s the figure of that outcast of outcasts – the paedophile – was beginning to emerge, and to be associated with homosexuality, a situation perceived as highly damaging to the cause of homosexual law reform.[156] The tone can be gauged in Peter Wildeblood's 1955 book *Against the Law*; imprisoned in the wake of a famous homosexual 'scandal', Wildeblood, although obligingly self-lacerating about the 'abnormality' of the homosexual life, nonetheless seeks to contrast more favourably 'moral' homosexuality with more deviant practices: 'It seems to me very important to discriminate between the pederast or lover of boys, and the homosexual, or lover of men' (stressing the dimension of physical 'seduction' in the former), and within homosexuality to further discriminate between 'the pathetically flamboyant pansy with the flapping wrists' and the sober and conventional homosexual; it is the latter group for whom Wildeblood speaks: 'When I ask for tolerance, it is for men like these.'[157] Sex between 'consenting *adults*' (over 21) was the extent of the demand. It must surely have been the case that the last thing the reformers wanted was a homosexual defence of pederasty! Ingram's talk of schoolboys and teachers would have been anathema to this conception and strategy,[158] as would the restrained but defiant dignity of his approach to homosexuality. In this respect his sexual utopianism – the sex-morality of tomorrow – was well out of kilter with the times.

# 3 Olaf Stapledon
## Religious but not Christian

Born 10 May 1886, Olaf Stapledon[1] was best known in his day as the author of a number of remarkable novels which we call science fiction, but which he for much of his life called 'fantastic fiction' or 'scientific romances'.[2] In a series of books in the 1930s beginning with *Last and First Men* (1930) and including *Last Men in London* (1932) and *Star Maker* (1937), which many consider his masterpiece, he sketched speculative histories of the universe in which he articulated many of his key philosophical themes. 'Novel' is probably the wrong term for these works, given the relative paucity of characterisation, plot or dialogue; there is poetry – Stapledon published a number of verses over the years – the poetry of the temporal and spatial immensities of the cosmos; and above all there are ideas. Although he studied history at Balliol College Oxford (1905–9) he was drawn to philosophy, and was to complete a doctorate in this subject at Liverpool University in 1924, and publish books and articles in this field. The Liverpool connection was grounded in his family's roots, and the nearby Wirral peninsula was to become his adult home, and the very centre of his life; in this respect, although possessed of a national reputation, indeed an international one, he was more of a regionally based figure (the term 'provincial', sometimes applied to Stapledon, carries harsh misleading resonances) than the more metropolitan Macmurray, Ingram and Acland. In the First World War, like Macmurray and Ingram, he saw combat, but in his case it was indeed 'seeing' – though still hazardous (he was to be awarded the Croix de Guerre for heroism)[3] – for he registered as a conscientious objector and became a driver in France with the Friends' Ambulance Unit from 1915 to 1919. After the war, following a number of jobs, he became an adult education lecturer in philosophy and psychology, history and English literature, giving this up when his writing made it financially possible. The large number of novels, philosophical works, social and political commentaries, essays scholarly and polemical, that he produced are all vehicles for a number of key themes that he relentlessly articulated and re-articulated, themes he considered to be essentially 'religious'.

### Christianity

Of the four individuals considered in this book, Stapledon was the only one who not only refused to call his religious beliefs Christian but positively rejected this designation. Macmurray and Ingram, as we have seen, although highly unorthodox in their Christianity, proudly declared their adherence to this tradition and asserted its religious pre-eminence, while Acland, as we shall see, after moving from unbelief to belief became a passionate advocate of the Christian faith. Not so Stapledon, who had fundamental philosophical and political objections to characterising himself as a Christian. We might look, by way of illustration, at an exchange of correspondence in the first half of the 1940s between Stapledon and the radical Christian writer Ernest W. Martin (1912–2005). Martin was putting together an edited volume provisionally entitled *In Search of Christianity* and wanted Stapledon to contribute a chapter. In a letter of response Stapledon declined the invitation, citing the title of the book as one obstacle to his participation:

> As I am not a Christian myself I do not think it would be right for me to join in the enterprise ... It would put me, I feel, into a false position if I were to write under such a title as you have chosen for your volume.[4]

He also makes a more specific objection. While assuring Martin that 'I respect and in many ways sympathize with Christians' he nevertheless asserts that the existing world faiths are all too narrow individually to provide an adequate resource for modern spiritual development: 'I definitely feel that the approach to the spiritual problem of our time has to be made from a broader basis than that of any one of the great historical religions.'[5] In fact Stapledon did, in the end, contribute a chapter, 'The Great Certainty', but, perhaps significantly, the book's title was now *In Search of Faith*. Furthermore, Stapledon did not feel comfortable with some of the other contributions to the volume, as he candidly told Martin in later correspondence: '*In Search of Faith* had some interesting things in it, but a lot of rubbish too';[6] the fact that he added that the book 'badly needed a contribution by someone of the Haldane type to redress the balance'[7] indicates his estimation of the philosophical centre of gravity of the work.

This renewed exchange with Martin was occasioned by the latter seeking to commission a further chapter from Stapledon for a new collection. It is difficult not to believe that the asperity of tone palpable in Stapledon's responses is related to a degree of resentment towards his participation in the first book. Stapledon's initial reply is polite, but firm. He *might* contribute something if he finds something interesting to say *and* 'provided that the volume has not a definite Christian bias'.[8] He expands on his earlier rejection of Martin's vision of Christianity as *the* leading spiritual force, and, in effect, against the position of Macmurray, Ingram and Acland. Christianity as a bundle of doctrines cannot harmonise with the differing doctrines of other religions, 'unless, of course, by Christianity you mean that which is common to all those attitudes, in which case one might as well call it by any other name'[9] – Martin's assumption has therefore the potential to exacerbate religious conflict for it rests upon a Christian appropriation of what is common property. In his reply to this, Martin, rather unwisely, revealed the proposed title of the new venture – 'The Need of Christendom'![10] Stapledon's gloves now came off and he penned a letter he himself was to describe as 'perhaps rather crotchety'.[11] The word 'Christendom' he calls a 'disaster', indicative of a dangerous sectarianism that 'harks back to the Crusades, and suggests that what you want is not to find a new and purged expression of the eternal truth, but just to defeat the pagans'.[12] He then begins a demolition job on Martin's own essay in *In Search of Faith*, 'Faith and Reason': Christianity, far from being a universal, is actually a transitory and immature expression of only a section of humanity, and is riddled with bad philosophy and beliefs which fail to speak to the real needs of the moment. Christianity

> is vital only to a minority of human beings, a minority that has not been able to outgrow an emotional attitude which the circumstances of the modern world are steadily forcing all human beings to outgrow. You are failing to distinguish between what is important in religion and what is temporary, local, adolescent, and unnecessary. And because of this confusion you are forced to produce intellectual arguments which have a low degree of cogency to defend metaphysical beliefs which may or may not be true but are anyhow of no serious importance to the pure religious consciousness.[13]

Furthermore, in an argument that takes him closer to Macmurray and Ingram, while acknowledging that some believers are doing good progressive work, he asserts that 'most of the people who are doing such work are *not* believers' and the evidence he produces for this claim is the example of the Soviet Union: 'the greatest expression of the spirit in our time has been the Russian Revolution, with all its faults.'[14] Indeed, his final point against Martin's venture is that it is fundamentally hostile to Marx and Marxism. This he pursues in his next letter, one gentler in tone – a possibly slightly shame-faced response to what he acknowledges to be a 'friendly' reply by Martin to his own angry missive. He says that he is prepared to 'shrug my shoulders' over Martin's theism 'for the sake of all that we have in common', but the animus towards Marx is misdirected at a figure of profound religious significance, and the founder of a movement that is properly religious – though Stapledon does not see himself as a Marxist:

> your hostility to Marxism, and the obvious anti-Marxist temper of the whole symposium really makes it very unsuitable for me to cooperate. I am not a Marxist, but I have learnt much from Marxists, and I am not anti-Marxist. If I had to choose (which heaven forefend) between Marxism and Christian orthodoxy I think I should have to plump for Marxism, in spite of the fact that Christianity has the core of truth which Marxism lacks. Marxism and Christianity spring from the same emotional experience, but each in its way misinterprets, falsifies. Marxism by

simply denying its validity, Christianity by smothering it under doctrines. I should choose Marxism because I believe that it is pointing the way beyond *itself* to a deeper, more purged sort of spirituality than Christian orthodoxy can ever arouse in our day ... Roughly I may put it that Marx, with all his extravagance, made a positive contribution which we must not ignore. A contribution to a revival of the spiritual attitude, I mean. Frankly, I suspect that there was more of the true spirit in Lenin (or even Haldane) than in most bishops and certainly far more in some quite humble and in many ways objectionable Communists.[15]

And on this basis Stapledon definitively bows out of the project.

## Faith and religion

One wonders what went through Ernest Martin's mind when he first read the opening lines of Stapledon's contribution to *In Search of Faith*: 'Faith? In the strict sense of the word I have no faith, and need none'; not exactly a promising start.[16] Whether or not one accepts it as a 'strict' definition, Stapledon's use of the word 'faith' is certainly very specific: it is

a conviction which reaches beyond the range of ordinary experience, yet which rests not on intellectual proof but on a mysterious, far-reaching and more or less explicit intuition. So far does faith claim to reach, that it makes definite assertions about the universe as a whole and about its fundamental nature, of which ordinary experience knows nothing.[17]

This is the 'faith' Stapledon rejects, on the basis of personal experience and philosophical analysis. Intuition, he says, has never revealed to him important truths about the universe or connected him to a deeper level of reality underpinning the quotidian. He accepts that this conviction cannot amount to certainty, and acknowledges that others do have 'faith' in this sense, but, lacking any firmer foundation, he has to go along with the way he sees the matter, which includes the judgement that those others are mistaken. Furthermore, although resting on intuition, faith is actually expressed in distinct propositions, and Stapledon, on the basis of an assessment of human capabilities, rejects the possibility that the human intellect to date is able to perceive, grasp and adequately express the metaphysical principles governing the universe: 'for to suppose that any profound factor in the hidden nature of existence can be caught upon the crooked pin of human conceptual thought is to exalt man fantastically'.[18] Finally, as propositions, these products of faith must face the tribunal of rational scrutiny, and in their literal form they do not seem plausible to 'the temper of our time', while as metaphor 'they evaporate in a mist of subtleties'.[19]

Faith is one thing, religion is quite another. There is a terminological difficulty in examining Stapledon's conception of the religious in that he uses the word to refer sometimes to just one of his two fundamental beliefs, and sometimes to both. In his contribution to *In Search of Faith* he designates one of these beliefs as a 'certainty', namely 'the intrinsic virtue of ... personality-in-community'; the other, which is neither faith nor a certainty but a deep personal experience, he terms a 'sense of "at-oneness" with something beyond me'.[20] When he uses the term 'religious' solely to refer to this latter experience it is usually because he wishes to bring out the one authentic commonality shared by himself and the people of faith, an intense feeling of rapport or connection with some awesome external other. When he includes 'personality-in-community' within the religious it is to stress the paramount importance of genuine community for human flourishing. Construed in either its single or joint meaning, religion was tenaciously defended by Stapledon against attempts by certain sceptics and materialists to characterise all forms of the religious as bogus and pernicious. Indeed, Stapledon himself was of the opinion that his reflections on the religious, defined broadly, constituted his most original contribution as a thinker.[21]

Stapledon's position that humans are unable adequately to comprehend the nature of reality entailed a large degree of modesty in the authentically religious. Macmurray's missionary zeal to universalise Christianity (however unorthodox) would have struck Stapledon as perverse. He accepted that many people developed 'genuine' religion in specific doctrinal forms, but these forms were contingent, and carried the danger of seducing adherents into barren and dogmatic belief systems. If anything, he believed that 'the Eastern religions' with their lack of the infantile wish fulfilment he detected in Christianity were, in this sense, 'more adult than the Western', but, adding with characteristic scrupulousness, 'not in others'.[22] Indeed, in his 1940s writings Stapledon began to use, out of Chinese traditions, the concept of 'Tao', which he understood as 'the Way' to designate his own conception of authentic spirituality.[23] Taoism's non-theistic awareness of the limitations of the human mind chimed well with Stapledon's own dispositions. In contrast, Martin's desire to delineate and promote the essential beliefs of Christianity struck Stapledon as pure hubris, and deeply delusional: 'unlike you I see that the truly spiritual attitude involves a very thorough intellectual agnosticism'.[24] In 'The Great Transformation' he refers to the need for 'agnostic piety',[25] a concept meant to convey both the negative dimension of the inadequacy of human understanding *and* the positive aspect of standing before something truly and vastly incomprehensible, and of immense worth:

> In that experience of at-oneness I feel that to make any demands whatever on the universe is impious. It is what it is, and I am a minute factor in it. And even if in its ultimate nature it is such as to blast all my longings and ideals, and the most developed and refined hopes of the human species, yet I cannot but accept it with joy, though dreadful joy ... I accept it unconditionally, with dread of what it is and what it may be in its hidden

regions be, but also with joy ... In this mood my emotional attitude ... is best expressed by the words 'Thy will be done'.[26]

And here is the rub. The problem for Stapledon – perhaps his supreme theoretical and existential problem, for it was one that he was acutely aware of throughout his life – was that his two fundamental beliefs were significantly in tension with one another. His belief in personality-in-community can, perhaps, be loosely described as the 'utopian' element in his thinking. It is utopian, not in the sense of the pursuit of an impossible dream, but as a theoretical and imaginative exploration of what constitutes the good community. The experience of 'at-oneness' can be designated as 'worship' because this was (among others) a term Stapledon used when discussing the phenomenon. The issue is clear. How can one joyfully contemplate the utter destruction of one's most precious dreams? The relationship between these two elements in his work now needs to be considered.

## Utopia and worship

Time is a great brooding theme in Stapledon's work – not the benign time of Enlightenment optimism, but a feral time rather, harsh and uncompromising. Time passing is the central structuring device of his novels, be it biographical time or cosmic time. But there is also a craving to find the eternal in this relentless change – the 'now', the fulfilled moment – not as a substitute for utopian yearning, but as a primary form of personal orientation in the midst of endlessly deferred hope. In his fictional cosmic narratives, notably *Last and First Men* (1930) and *Star Maker* (1937), Stapledon depicts the slaughter-bench of history, with painfully acquired achievements swept away time after time, and in his frequent speculations about future history he contemplates the death of the universe itself and the real possibility of a consequent total and irretrievable loss of all memory – absolutely *nothing* remaining of the aeons of time. This contemplation evokes two responses from Stapledon. There is a resolutely utopian approach – albeit he usually uses other terms to designate this orientation. His literary works are full of depictions of better worlds, and his theoretical and political works are suffused with a whole range of plans for improving society. But there is a second response, 'worship' – a form of delighted contemplation of the universe in all its aspects, good and bad. This is the universe as numinous and awesome, with processes, and possibly purposes, far beyond the theoretical and moral understanding of mere humanity. In articulating this vision, as astral poet, and philosopher of the immensities of time and space, he produces his most effective artistic effects. But it is also the element which gives him the most headaches to justify, for he sees a tension between this amoral contemplation and his utopianism. This juxtaposition is at the heart of his artistic and theoretical concerns, and the strains and stresses of attempting to effect a reconciliation between the two elements are evident in virtually everything he ever wrote.

We can see the presence of the utopian and worship in Stapledon's very first published book, a collection of poems entitled *Latter-Day Psalms* (1914). As the title suggests, the language is religious. A sense of the transient nature of the universe is manifest in the poem 'Time', with the poet reproaching God for creating a world he will ultimately destroy:

> Wherefore hast thou made the world that it shall die, and the heavens that they shall burn out like a flame? ... The sons of man have builded for themselves a house of beauty. It is continually embellished. The last of the generations shall dwell therein and die ... The home that seemed eternal is broken up and scattered ... I am heavy of heart because of fleeting time, and because all things come to nought.[27]

In 'Satan', however, Lucifer is praised as a Promethean deity who refuses to be broken by the imperious Jehovah:

> Thou who rebellest against the Almighty in all his dominion, scorning to be a slave even under him; Who puttest bitterness into the cup of his victory, and laughest in his face out of Hell; Who art for ever overpowered and never conquered ... It is thou that makest the uprooted tree to sprout, and the stag at bay to be terrible ... Thou art the god of heroes, and of those who battle against fate ... We hail thee, thou God in Man! We magnify thee against God in Heaven.[28]

Finally, in 'God' we get the attempt at a reconciliation which anticipates his later thoughts on this matter – that the transient is an integral part of the beauty of the whole, and plays a necessary part in the ultimate fulfilment of that whole:

> The voice of God spake out of his creation: I have made a law, that is my law of beauty. I have ordained my heavens that they shall blossom and wither away. The flower shall die, but the seed shall flourish. Like a flower, the world shall perish, but the spirit that is born therein shall live.[29]

The floral metaphor deployed here can be seen as Stapledon's attempt to provide a sustaining imagery for a position he himself found it difficult to justify with any degree of public plausibility, particularly in concert with his utopian aspirations. In a poem of 1923, 'God the Artist', he tries another metaphor, one that would be used a number of times in his later work – the universe as a great melody in which dissonance is an essential part of the composition:

> Bitter to us is God's song. He sings not for us. ... Yet we are heirs of God's own passion. Our will is that the Good be, that the song be sung.

> Therefore, though fate sound harshly to us, let us at least die glad to have been a syllable in so great a music.[30]

In wrestling with this tension, Stapledon felt a strong affinity with the philosopher Spinoza. Spinoza also conceived of the universe as substance in development – '*Natura naturans*', naturing Nature – the composition of which allowed one to talk of 'God or Nature'.[31] Spinoza also contrasted the divine or universal perspective '*sub specie aeternitas*' ('under the aspect of eternity') with the human perspective of '*sub specie durationi*' ('under the aspect of time') and posited the possibility of human access to the eternal.[32] He too believed that this cosmic drama properly stilled human judgement. Thus, writing to a correspondent in the midst of another round of European war, he asserted:

> I do not think it right to laugh at nature, and far less to grieve over it ... I realize that it is merely through ... lack of understanding that certain features of nature – which I thus perceive only partly and in a fragmentary way, and which are not in keeping with our philosophical attitude of mind – once seemed to me vain, disordered and absurd. But now I let everyone go his own way.[33]

Stapledon saw in Spinoza's work an anticipation of his own central dilemma, his inability to reconcile satisfactorily awe and struggle, and the apparent consequence of holding two utterly divergent positions:

> he [Spinoza] was pre-eminently conscious of two seemingly incompatible aspects of experience ... One is the intuitive and non-rational perception of the beauty or rightness of the experienced universe as a whole. The other is the intuitive and non-rational devotion toward the human enterprise within the universe. Intellectually he failed to reconcile these two experiences, but he lived in loyalty to both.[34]

One should note here, something to be returned to later, that Stapledon calls both of these two experiences 'religious', and in this vein he places Spinoza in the lineage of Buddha, Socrates, Jesus Christ and Mohammed.[35]

There is a deep anti-humanist element in Stapledon. He vehemently rejects all forms of ethical subjectivism, espousing a strongly objective theory of moral obligation ('consciousness ... awakens in the service of ends prior to it, and objective to it').[36] In his fiction, he is constantly undermining the category of the human. He destabilises the borders between the human and the non-human, as in his man/dog in *Sirius* (1944) or in the human mutations in *Odd John* (1935).[37] He cuts the human down to size when he explores the plethora of non-human sentient beings in his science fiction, with, for example, the conscious stars and nebulas in *Star Maker*, or the highly spiritual flame in *The Flames* (1947),[38] and almost takes delight in contemplating the end of humanity – the 'last man'. He does maintain that there is a deep unity between all sentient beings, and this belief is the ontological foundation of his objective ethics, but he refuses to reduce this belief to the merely human. In short, he finds something pervasively parochial in humanism: 'Pure humanism, or the acceptance of Man as the *final* object of admiration and loyalty, is after all in essence loyalty to our own nature, though perfected; and as such it is apt to seem prosaic and tiresome.'[39] And yet his political idealism is clearly marked by the traditions of liberal and social humanism. His political rhetoric speaks of the need to consolidate and accelerate the political and economic reforms of the past centuries, and to promote a rich and flourishing humanity – 'individuality-in-community'.[40] Again this bifurcation in his makeup – the centrality of humanity and its needs, and the relative insignificance of the human in the great scheme of things. He is simply unable to avail himself of the false comforts of a Hegelian reduction of cosmic history to human history.

His utopias are transitory. They are portrayed as good societies, immensely better than those of his own time, but they do not endure. They are not, however, early examples of what Tom Moylan has called 'critical utopias'.[41] Stapledon was not attempting to subvert the traditional idea of the good society by deliberately introducing dynamic imperfections. He had firm ideas about what was good and what not, and passionately wanted good societies to succeed. His point was an ontological one – good societies will for some reason or other always ultimately collapse. Thus, while he has examples of such societies disintegrating owing to internal imperfections, he also has examples of simple external bad luck being the cause – some natural disaster or other. The transitory utopia merely reflects a transitory universe. In *Last and First Men* there are at least two recognisably utopian societies. The first is that created by the 'fifth men' – a far-advanced form of humanity living millennia ahead in the future – which lasted for millions of years, and was destroyed by a move to Venus – necessitated by the coming destruction of the earth by the moon – where a combination of war and natural and technological disasters led to total degeneracy. In its wake, the 'sixth men' had to start the long process of social evolution all over again. At the very end of the human story, the society created by the 'eighteenth men', now on Neptune, embodies Stapledon's most exalted values and aspirations, but its population is annihilated by the Nova effect of a nearby star. And that was that! All that was left was Stapledon's ambiguous 'worshipful' voice:

> Great are the stars, and man is of no account to them. But man is a fair spirit, whom a star conceived and a star kills ... and for man the best is that the Whole should use him. But does it really use him? Is the beauty of the Whole really enhanced by our agony?[42]

In *Star Maker*, Stapledon self-consciously deploys the word 'utopian' as a category of transitoriness. In the explanatory notes he planned to be included with the work, but which remained unpublished, he has an entry on the 'utopian stage'. This is a state which struggling humanity hopes to achieve, but its creation elsewhere in the universe actually turns out to be a simple interval before struggles for an even higher stage – 'communal mentality'.[43] Stapledon uses the terms 'utopia' and 'utopian' in the actual text to talk of 'a Galactic Utopia',[44] and (in the wake of further cosmic disasters) of an even more advanced 'symbiotic society' of conscious stars and worlds which 'was in many ways utopian'.[45] The even higher goal of a 'cosmical community' is precariously gained only to encounter the eponymous Star Maker, who, it turns out, creates universes as an artist creates pictures, moving on from work to work. 'Our' universe is just one such attempt, and by no means the most advanced. On this note the universe fades away and dies with, as ever, the cosmic spirit 'compelling adoration'.[46]

The image of the Star Maker making various attempts in creation brings to mind Hume's *Dialogues Concerning Natural Religion*, a work with which Stapledon, with his undoubted admiration for the great Scottish philosopher, would surely have known. Indeed, there is a distinct parallel between the two texts. Hume's work ventilates a strong critique of the fashionable Deism of his time, with its central theme of God the divine architect, creator of a benign and rational universe. The anthropomorphism behind this conception is belaboured, and indeed mocked. If indeed a being is responsible for our universe, why must it be the divine watchmaker of Deism, why could it not be 'only the first rude essay of some infant deity, who afterwards abandoned it, ashamed of his lame performance'?[47] Hume throws in a couple of other alternatives: 'it is the work only of some dependent, inferior deity; and is the object of derision to his superiors: It is the production of old age and dotage in some superannuated deity; and ever since his death, has run on'.[48] Although proposed merely to dramatise the absurdities of the Deist conception of God, the pitiless cosmos evoked in them is pure Stapledon terrain, and the similarity between Hume's 'infant deity' and the ultimate plotline of *Star Maker* is striking. At the very least, *Star Maker* contains an echo of the philosophical moment when some species of theism ceased to be the default position of advanced thought, and the cold universe of Nietzsche and of Stapledon became a possibility.

## H.G. Wells

Given that Stapledon was writing what we would now call science fiction, the question inevitably arises of his relationship to that colossus of the genre, H.G. Wells. When Stapledon began publishing these works in the 1930s he was in his forties, while Wells was into his sixties with a large body of published work, including notable science fiction, to his credit. Historians of science fiction have differed in their estimations of the extent to which Wells might have influenced Stapledon *as a science fiction writer*, with some arguing for a considerable influence, others less so.[49] He undoubtedly admired Wells' skills as an author, ruefully acknowledging that Wells left him standing in this respect, noting in one review that 'Mr Wells can compress into a phrase what some of us would take pages to describe.'[50] But on the broader question of the influence of Wells' ideas on Stapledon the pioneering work of Robert Crossley, in his biography of Stapledon and in his publication of the correspondence of the two men, demonstrates that Stapledon's intellectual relationship with Wells was ambiguous and difficult to interpret, but that there were significant philosophical differences between the two which made their relationship an uneasy one, with Stapledon openly taking issue with a number of Wells' assumptions, and Wells responding with rebuttals and counter-attacks which, on occasion, crossed the line into the tetchy, if not downright angry.

That Stapledon had read a good deal of Wells there can be no doubt, though interestingly enough he claimed to Wells in 1931, in his first letter introducing himself as the author of the newly published *Last and First Men*, that he had only read two of Wells' 'scientific romances', *The War of the Worlds* and *The Star*.[51] Quite what Stapledon got in the way of ideas from Wells does not admit of an easy answer, for while he spoke fulsomely of Well's influence on him in letters to the older man he did not descend from vague, unhelpful metaphors – 'A man does not record his debt to the air he breathes in common with everyone else'[52] – to specifying the precise nature of Wells' influence. One should also note that Stapledon was attempting to establish good relations with Wells, and was clearly anxious that the latter might feel slighted by the lack of any reference to his work in the preface to *Last and First Men*. Crossley does speculate about possible Wellsian influence, but at the level of fundamental ideas these are at best tentative suggestions (Crossley speaks of the influence of 'Wells the utopian and the public educator'[53]) and refer to themes (socialism, internationalism and so forth) that, to use Freud's concept, are almost certainly 'overdetermined' in that they could come from a plurality of influences. Wells himself, as Crossley reports, bluntly told Stapledon that he could see nothing of himself in *Last and First Men*: 'It is all balls to suggest *First & Last Men* [sic] (which I found a very exciting book) owes anything to my writings. I wish it did.'[54] On the other hand Stapledon is clear and to the point when, in print or in letters to Wells, he spells out his profound disagreement with the Wellsian *mentalité* of the 1930s and 40s, and fundamental to this critique is his conception of the spiritual in human affairs.

From Stapledon's perspective, Wells exemplified the afterlife as it were of the intellectual agenda of an earlier moment of progressive thought where there was a perceived need for a humanism that stressed the biological nature of humanity against various strands of idealism; 'this purely biological view of man was a very wholesome reaction from the pre-scientific view'.[55] This involved, of necessity, a confrontation with religious theistic idealism, and Stapledon is with Wells in his struggle against clericalism – 'when clerics expound their faith, I fly to line up behind Mr Wells'.[56] But the virtues of this moment of thought had accompanying vices, notably a tendency towards a reductive and exclusive biologism which ignored and excised significant dimensions of human capacity and need, and left a profoundly impoverished conception of the human; as he wrote in *Waking World*: 'Mr Wells ... does not take the whole of man's nature into account ... I would suggest ... that the insufficiency of Mr Wells lies in the superficiality of his view of human nature and the consequent triviality of his particular kind of humanistic ideal.'[57]

Stapledon struggled to find metaphors to express his relationship to Wells. Thus immediately following his remark about lining up behind Wells, Stapledon describes himself as an 'an erring disciple',[58] and when writing directly to Wells about this issue his metaphorical language totally breaks down (though he was clearly not one to waste paper by starting again!):

> I have thankfully followed you a long way, but with occasional excursions, hither and thither beside the track which you have made and so many have since pursued. And by now I seem to be mostly on a more or less parallel way on the other side of the valley, so to speak. But the metaphor is getting in a muddle.[59]

Wells was well aware what all these tortuous constructions were about – religion. And he was quite right. Wells knew a good deal about religion. In the first couple of decades of the twentieth century he himself had attempted to articulate a religious perspective in works such as *First and Last Things* (1908) and *God the Invisible King* (1917). Although it was explicitly non-Christian in its orientation, Wells used the concepts and language of the Christian tradition to try to provide a degree of depth to his philosophical and political orientation. Thereafter he began significantly to retreat from this project, adopting a much more secular, positivist and 'scientific' approach, and displaying a distinct impatience with those who continued to place religion at the heart of their enterprises. It was at this stage in Wells' thought that Stapledon began his period of direct engagement with the older man. For Stapledon, Wells' hyper-secularism junked not merely objectionable religion, but wholly positive religious dimensions fundamental to the contemporary struggles of humanity. To Wells, Stapledon was still in the clutches of a superstitious metaphysics, and he was very abrasive when Stapledon's *Saints and Revolutionaries* appeared in a series entitled 'I Believe', with a preface by Ellis Roberts that deemed Stapledon to be one of the 'children of the spirit' as opposed to one of the 'servants of the machine' – Stapledon had allowed himself to play into the hands of the Christians, Wells thundered, and entered testicular mode once more: 'Why do you lend yourself even by implication to the marketing of such *balls*?'[60] And he attempted a bit of his own historical placing, positioning Stapledon in the place he had occupied in the first decades of the century, when he had had his own spiritual moment: 'your book ... reminds me (in spirit & phase) of me in my *God the Invisible King*. And I don't believe a word of it ... I've been through it all. I've been no worse than you. I am still quoted from the pulpits.'[61] Wells' remarks provided further confirmation for Stapledon, if any were needed, of the very delicate and, to many critics of religion, implausible balance he was struggling to maintain of a spiritualism that was not theistic. But in his reply to Wells, while noting the difficulties of this stance, he nonetheless reiterated it once more:

> I have in some ways been going badly astray, from your point of view. I have even at times been called a Christian, which is a bit disturbing, I confess. But at least I have come to realise that, silly as the Christians are, in their way, the pucker [sic] scientists are quite as silly in theirs ... However, it is easy to see that both lots are silly, and not so easy to escape being silly oneself, and very likely I've been it in appearing to side with the clerics. Certainly Ellis Roberts's blurb does jar.[62]

Whether the gap between the two men on this issue was as great as both, at times, suggested is probably doubtful. Wells was indignant that Stapledon didn't recognise that he (Wells) was a 'monist' who maintained that 'the opposition of "the material" and "the spiritual" is a fundamental mistake'.[63] And Stapledon was also to acknowledge that Wells did not reject religion in its totality, noting in a review of *You Can't Be Too Careful* that for Wells 'a stable community needs "religion"', by which he meant 'the binding system of ideas and practices which holds a community together'.[64] But a gap there still was, and their correspondence ended in 1942 with it still very much in place.

## Marx and Marxism (and Macmurray)

Stapledon was given to prefacing his remarks on Marx and Marxism with a deal of self-deprecation, insisting that he had come late in life to a study of the subject, had a relatively sketchy knowledge of the essentials, and was not sure he entirely understood the underlying theory.[65] Part of this would seem to be self-protective, given the heated discussion of Marxism generated in the 1930s and 40s, but it also possibly reveals a self-awareness that, indeed, his acquaintance with Marxist theory, especially the work of Marx himself, was neither extensive or deep. In booklists and guides to further reading he suggested that interested readers should look at the *Communist Manifesto* and *Capital*, but most of the suggestions were for secondary texts and anthologies of readings. Throughout, he was at pains to stress that Marx was an infinitely more flexible and original thinker than most of those who wrote in his name, but wasn't very specific in backing this claim up with detailed citation. There is nothing equivalent to Macmurray's deep immersion in Marx's work, especially the fundamental early works, of which Stapledon does not seem to be aware.

Passing references aside, his mode of analysis was to extract what he took to be core doctrines of Marxism, and then interrogate them as to their adequacy. That he was bothering to do this at all is indicative of his belief that Marxism was on to something valuable, noting in 1939 that 'Dialectical Materialism is in our day one of the main growing points of thought', and that its proponents 'will be content to know that their doctrine is an immensely fertile principle', but – and here is the rub – they should be content 'without insisting that it is gospel truth'.[66] His use of the term 'gospel' here isn't simply metaphorical, for he maintained that the scope and radicalness of Marxism's claims gave it a 'religious or quasi-religious aspect', which, in turn inspired 'religious veneration or religious hate', and therefore there was an imperative for serious seekers after the truth to avoid the uncritical stance of many Communists and the wilful blindness of their opponents. For Marxists, he argued, there was a particular theoretical problem in carrying out this injunction – a pragmatic tendency within the ideology linked knowledge to successful action, and thereby undermined a conception of objective truth, and encouraged 'the glorification of bias', which 'is bound to lead to an abandonment of intellectual honesty, and finally to the destruction of civilisation by barbarism'.[67] He did, however, take comfort from the fact that Marxism *was* committed to a notion of objective truth, and that this could act as a brake on the pragmatic turn.

While applauding the Marxist emphasis on the role of economic factors in history, he believes that Marxists have frequently distorted and simplified history in their attempt to create a comprehensive doctrine, under-estimating the role of mere chance, and underplaying the contribution of prominent individuals (like Lenin and Marx, for example). Economic determinism, he insists, surely works through 'the impact of the environment on human *motives* or needs'[68] and these motivations need not be economic, even if economic factors were involved in their genesis. Thus, he speculates that 'irrational herd mentality' may have had an economic utility in the past, but there must have been a pre-existing human or sub-human capacity for this mentality, which, as in wartime, can act as an independent variable, even at times undermining economic necessities – the 'environment has *evoked* it; not simply *created* it'.[69] The same can be said, he argues, of the sublime motivations to be found in the 'will for genuine community' and in some other religious aspirations. He accepts that economic factors are important for understanding religion, but, especially given the relatively underdeveloped nature of the study of human psychology, this need not be the full picture:

> It is at least possible that in the best kind of religious experience there is a core, probably impossible to describe accurately in any human language but none the less actual, which is not derived in this [economic] manner, but is a genuine apprehension at the upper limit of human capacity. It is possible that experience of this kind, in outstanding individuals, has played a not inconsiderable part in influencing the conduct of the masses at critical moments of history.[70]

This, he believes, is not a view incompatible with Marxism, since Marxism repudiates mechanical materialism and allows for the qualitatively new to appear in the course of history. Furthermore, as Macmurray recognised, so also does Stapledon believe that economic determinism is a feature of an undeveloped society, where nobody is fully in control of social affairs, and that its day will surely pass with the establishment of a properly human society:

> Economic Determinism, though perhaps the most useful principle for the interpretation of history during the past and the present, may cease to be the supremely significant principle in the not very remote future, when men (we hope) will have gained far greater facility and power of control over the economic environment.[71]

It is possible that Stapledon was influenced by Macmurray in his understanding of Marxism and Communism. He had read a number of Macmurray's works and recommended no fewer than four of these in his annotated reading list at the end of *Philosophy and Living* (1939), namely *Reason and Morals, Creative Society, The Structure of Religious Experience* and *The Clue to History*, but his was a critical respect, for he notes, 'I find his work sometimes ambiguous.'[72] Some sense of what he means by this can be gleaned from his 1939 review of *The Clue to History*. He applauded the broad intention of the historical narrative in the text, to show the creative resilience of the human spirit across history; of this, he says, 'the story is dramatic, tragic, yet full of hope. It contains, I believe, a truth of high importance', adding, 'as a historical study of mental integrity the book is magnificent, and exciting'.[73] He recognised Macmurray's religious heterodoxy, and took his part against Alexander Miller's Christian strictures in the latter's *The Christian Significance of Karl Marx*: 'Because he insists on Christian dogma, including the Trinity, the Virgin Birth, the remission of sins and individual immortality, he rejects Macmurray's identification of the classless society with the Kingdom of God.'[74] *But* Stapledon did not accept Macmurray's strong claim about the singularity of the Hebrews, and countered with the claims of humanity – 'the practical religious temper was surely not confined to the Jews. Even at the outset, the drama was being vaguely enacted in the mind of Everyman'[75] – nor was he happy with Macmurray's concept of God, which he found ill-defined, ambiguous and reeking of the metaphysical. However, he was clearly struck by Macmurray's contention that the genuine 'Christian' spirit, in the modern world was not to be found in the Churches but in science and in the Russian Revolution. We can infer this because this theme is subsequently much in evidence in his later work, and he does, on at least two occasions, link this insight with Macmurray – 'the Russian revolution ... though consciously anti-religious ... was unconsciously a religious movement, as has been pointed out by John Macmurray'.[76] As with Wells, we have to be aware of the potential overdetermined nature of influence but, at the very least, Macmurray's formulation evidently stayed in his mind.

## Ideology

Like his contemporaries Mannheim and Bloch, Stapledon also saw a close link between the visionary and the ideological. Like Bloch in particular, he was convinced that ideologies could never be simply lies, they had to tap into genuinely positive and visionary dimensions in the populace.[77] Throughout the economic and political crises of the 1930s and in the succeeding years of war, he deployed this insight in his characterisation of that darkest of ideologies – Fascism. He was always aware of the elements of deceit, manipulation and sheer tyranny in Fascist movements, but was convinced that they could not sustain themselves on these alone. Thus, writing in 1934, he could say, albeit with some equivocation, that Italian Fascism and German National Socialism, 'in so far as these depend on youth and seek to revitalize society with a new devotion and a new protest against the mechanic's mentality' were attempting to articulate elements of a 'new world'.[78] On the eve of war in 1939, he asked why Communism and Social Democracy had 'failed to capture the imagination of the peoples' while 'Fascism and Nazism [had] succeeded.' His answer was that:

> The peoples of Italy and Germany, in their despair and bewilderment, obscurely but rightly felt a need for some kind of real values, something more compelling than the goal of economic prosperity ... something which could restore man's conviction that his function on earth was more than personal pleasure ... The Fascist and the Nazi faiths offered him in a crude and barbarous form the very thing that he craved ... And this was the reason why the great organization of the Social Democrats and the devotion and resolution of the Communists were powerless against the new movement.[79]

Even after the war, although more convinced than ever of the barbarism of Fascism, he still maintained his pre-war analysis of the authentic utopian moment in the reactionary phenomenon of Fascism.[80]

His stance on the principal ideologies of the age reflects his distinctive ethical, epistemological and metaphysical assumptions. We have already referred to his belief in an 'objective' ethics. This belief necessarily entailed that people could be ethically mistaken. In the case of Stapledon, a hierarchical conception of truth was the particular result. Using a metaphor which he deployed on numerous occasions, he talked of 'awakened' individuals, who had escaped the somnabulance of their contemporaries; these more advanced people, in turn, were conceived in terms of a cosmos of potentially higher and higher forms of being. Thus, although Stapledon was a democrat, this was not out of a belief that every person's position *was* equally valid but because the majority *could* with the right measures become awakened, and an awakened democracy was necessary to resist tyranny. His conclusion was unambiguous: '*some* form of ultimate democratic sanction is now seen to be absolutely necessary ... But democracy cannot work successfully unless the great mass of the citizens are educated up to it.'[81] Indeed, he did not shy away from explicitly adopting and adapting the concept of aristocracy. The awakened aristocrats were legitimated by their high educative purpose:

> For my part, though I see little value in a social aristocracy, I am convinced that an intellectual, or rather cultural, aristocracy is necessary for the healthy life of a society; but its members must regard themselves as specialists in a particular form of social service, not as superior persons.[82]

Since, in Stapledon's view, no one ideological tradition has a monopoly on truth then it must be possible, he argues, to extract valuable material from across the ideological spectrum. In *New Hope for Britain* (1939), he looks at the four main British political parties with the eyes of a gold prospector, seeking to extract the precious metal from the dross. These elements are not the exclusive property of particular parties, for they may be found in a number of the traditions. From the Conservative Party he digs out a 'belief in the English spirit', which he defines as a 'spirit of mutual respect' between (in line with his own previously discussed aristocratic leanings) 'friendly organizers and those whom they organize ... between equals and between the humbler and the more responsible workers for the common weal'.[83] In the case of the Liberal Party, Stapledon applauds its historic 'fundamental value ... the intrinsic value of the individual human being',[84] conceived, at its best, as a defence of individual autonomy against both tyranny and conformism. The Labour Party has a grasp of the central importance of 'the social,' that 'the social environment moulds individual minds',[85] and that, as a consequence, the economic and the social need to be under the control of the people. Finally, in the case of the Communist Party, there is the strong commitment to revolution and to the creation of a new society based on 'comradeship'.[86] The conclusion Stapledon draws from this exploration is that the old party divisions will have to be abandoned, and an ecumenical unity created; a move, in other words, and to quote the title of his 1942 book, *Beyond the Isms*. This move, to return to our starting point in this discussion of Stapledon on ideology, will involve 'something even of Nazism'.[87]

We can thus say that, again like Bloch, Stapledon attempts to unlock the authentic utopian content within the ideological. He recognises that ideological traditions are shaped by dreams, which, in turn, are themselves shaped by those traditions. He understands the urgency and power of human hopes and aspirations, and their resilience in the face of social and economic disappointment. He recognises that progressive political forces which fail to speak to this dimension of human existence will be unable to make any effective breakthrough. They abandon society to reactionary political groupings that are skilful at manipulating and channelling human aspirations in disastrous directions. The theme of the dangers of ideology can also be found in his fictional work. In *Star Maker*, the first planet visited by the narrator – 'the Other Earth' – is made to mirror the intense ideological conflict characterising Europe in the 1930s. By making the denizens of this world focussed on the sense of taste, Stapledon seeks to satirise the arbitrary and irrational features of the ideological mindset. The dominant group valued saltiness, despite there being very few actual genuine salty types, and despised and persecuted a bitter-sweet tasting pariah group. In opposition 'was a movement among the intelligentsia for conditioning infants to tolerate every kind of human flavour'.[88] These oppositional elements further espouse the goals and values that we have seen in Stapledon's non-fictional reflections. Significantly, 'much of their doctrine was a re-statement of the teachings of religious seers of a time long past, but it had also been deeply influenced by contemporary science'.[89] This passing reference to a possible new relationship between the religious and the scientific reflects Stapledon's attempt to reconfigure the historic relationship between the religious and the secular.

## The religious and the secular

In *Waking World* (1934), Stapledon distinguishes between 'sham' and 'genuine' religion. Characterisations of 'sham' religion abound in both his fiction and non-fiction and centre on the philosophical nullity of most of the dogmas, the base psychological motivations underpinning conventional religiosity, and the pernicious economic, social and political consequences of such beliefs. In *Star Maker*, Stapledon allows the taste-orientated people of the 'Other Earth' to exemplify one such absurdity:

> there had seldom been any widespread agreement as to the taste of God. Religious wars had been waged to decide whether he was in the main sweet or salt, or whether his preponderant flavour was one of the many gustatory characters which my own race cannot conceive. Some teachers insisted that only the feet could taste him, others only the hands or the mouth.[90]

In quasi-Marxist fashion, Stapledon in *Waking World*[91] charts the emergence among the rise of the bourgeoisie of a scientific materialism; this emergence provides the intellectual weapons against religion, as commercial individualism undermines its traditional social base. Conventional religion survives but in a deeply weakened state. On the 'Other Earth' a similar process is at work: 'nearly all the churches were destroyed or turned into temporary factories or industrial museums. Atheism, lately persecuted, became fashionable. All the best minds turned agnostic.'[92] For Stapledon, this modern dialectical process has involved both gain and loss – modern science has indeed been of immense value, but it has rendered largely invisible the vital spiritual resources of the old religious world view. The people of the 'Other Earth' exemplify the necessary moment of synthesis of the dialectical triad: 'More recently ... apparently in horror at the effects of a materialistic culture ... the most industrialised people began to turn once more to religion. A spiritistic foundation was provided for natural science.'[93] This turning is the context for Stapledon's exploration of 'genuine' religion.

His critique of 'sham' religion does acknowledge the work of the great de-mystifiers of modern thought, Marx and Freud, and their insights into the economic and psychic dimensions in religious belief. Stapledon, however, always sought to utilise an anti-reductionist methodology, one which refused to allow knowledge of the genesis of phenomena to be definitive. Something is always more than its origin, its essence can never be reduced to its earliest form. Indeed, he reverses the flow of the argument – should not the earlier moment be seen as an inadequate form of the later adequate mode, rather than the 'true' exemplar of the type? Thus in a discussion of Freudian accounts of the ecstatic, he writes: 'Thus, supposing the Freudian "aetiology" to be in a sense true, we might yet interpret its account of the ecstatic experiences so as to dignify the "disreputable" rather than vilify the sublime.'[94] In this sense, he is closer to Bloch's notion that genesis occurs at the end and not at the beginning of processes. Marx and Freud, Stapledon believes, do not *capture* religion in their explanatory nets, and their followers have only done so in the negative hunting sense of confining, and possibly destroying, a living creature.

But, Stapledon asks, has the association of religion with a conservative theism so contaminated it as to render it unusable in a modern form? More specifically, can the traditional language and symbolism of religion be refashioned to express a new content? Stapledon feels the force of the objection that the old language is full of the most negative connotations. 'Worship', a word of immense usefulness from his perspective, has been debased in institutional Christianity:

> It was once a good word; but to-day it calls up for many of us images of hymn-books and collection plates, and the whole gloomy business of soul-saving. Yet if we could strip it of these associations, 'worship' would be the right word.[95]

Likewise 'spirit', which to many minds 'suggests self-deception, flight from reality, wishful thinking, hypocrisy, unctuousness, and so on'.[96] His decision is to keep on using these terms. One reason is that these terms are the most appropriate, and accurate, ways of expressing certain sublime truths. Underpinning this view is the assumption that religious language is a distinctive way of articulating certain matters – a way that cannot be achieved in other kinds of language. He thus sets his face against attempts to reduce religious language to more 'real' or 'basic' vocabularies, that 'God' is *simply* disguised talk about humanity, or 'soul' *merely* an imprecise formulation of the concept of personality. Religion has its own things to say, and needs to be heard. Thus, in the case of 'spirit' he says: 'But I cannot find any other word to express the thing that is recognised by all the religions at their best.'[97] He also recognises that to eschew religious language is, in effect, to allow the traditional abusers of religion, the religious, to have a veto on the use of this language. This recognition is dramatised in his novel *Sirius*, which charts the intellectual and spiritual struggles of an artificially created beast, part human, part dog, the eponymous 'Sirius'. Sirius wishes to explore the realm of religion, but is driven out and excluded from the services he attempts to attend. He finally, however, persuades a sympathetic clergyman to enable him not simply to witness the ceremonies but to sing his own passionate hymn:

> The strange music that Sirius put forth ... spoke of bodily delight and pain, and of the intercourse of spirits ... It spoke of love and death, of the hunger for the spirit, and of Sirius's own wolf-mood. It spoke of the East End and the West End, of the dockers' strike and the starry heaven ... All this it did for Sirius himself. To most of the congregation it was an inconsequent mixture of music and noise, and moreover a mixture of the recognizably, comfortably pious and the diabolical.[98]

The hegemony of the dominant discourse is thus challenged, the monopoly of the religious on religion broken.

The content of Sirius's religious composition, with its mixture of the social and the metaphysical, is indicative of Stapledon's conception of the substance of religion, which, in turn, brings us back to the starting point of our examination – the dimensions of the utopian and worship. These, it can now be seen, are the two principal modes of the genuinely religious life; they are 'the two fundamental religious experiences ... the moral protest, which seeks to alter the universe, and the ecstatic acceptance of the universe, with all its glory and its shame, its joy and its distress, its beauty and all its squalor'.[99] The two dimensions are united by selflessness. In sham religion, according to Stapledon, here in line with the Feuerbach/Marx critique of Christianity, selfish egotism prevails, the goal is to save one's own soul, to broker a private deal with the almighty, while genuine social activists seek the salvation of others and are prepared to sacrifice, if necessary, their lives for this goal. This acceptance of sacrifice is one of the reasons Stapledon had good things to say about the Communists, whose professed contempt for religion masked a deeply religious motivation: 'a movement which trumpeted its irreligion yet sprang from a singularly pure religious motive, namely disinterested loyalty to the principle of true community, and therefore, unwittingly, from loyalty to the spirit'.[100] Although critical of the scientistic form of their materialism, which blinded them to the genuine dimensions in religion,[101] he appreciated that their irreligion also sprang from a contempt for the hypocrisies of much organised religion, for in genuine worship there is no broker God. As with the activist, disinterestedness can come at a great price, for the supreme object of worship, the universe itself, is not accountable to humanity, and humans cannot feel cheated if their own destruction is entailed in universal processes. Stapledon pulls no punches in this prayer to the universe:

> Use me, break me; but let my breaking be part of your dread beauty. Use and break this human species, this human world. Destroy it with fire or frost, or through the consequence of its own folly and half-heartedness, like the countless other lovely, tortured worlds that you have so gloriously

conceived and coldly discarded. But let the breaking of this human instrument somehow contribute to your music.[102]

This too is a moral act, in line with Stapledon's rejection of subjective ethics. Just as the morality of political activity demands harsh things, so too does the objective morality of the cosmos:

> it is foolish and impious to demand that the universe shall be moral, or that the universal spirit shall be moral, or that 'God' shall be good. These ... do not exist for the sake of morality. On the contrary, morality exists for them.[103]

In like manner, it is important for Stapledon to try to argue that the experience of worship is no mere subjective impression but a revelation of an objective reality. His most serious attempt to make this case occurs in the speculative ontology he outlines at the end of *A Modern Theory of Ethics* (1929), the most technically accomplished of his philosophical reflections. He acknowledges that his argument owes a good deal to philosophical idealism. In effect, he tries to overcome the tension between the utopian and worship by designating temporality as only one attribute of an ultimate reality which is 'supratemporal': that is, timeless or eternal. The Spinozian distinction between the eternal and the temporal perspectives is clearly evident. In worship, we briefly and inadequately see the temporal aspects of reality from the perspective of eternity. 'Not-yet', with its teleological tension between the moment of striving and the moment of achievement, is, therefore, merely an aspect of the limited temporal dimension, for 'in the supratemporal view events of different date are equally actual'.[104] That Stapledon had deep worries as to the coherence and plausibility of this argument is attested to by his references to it as 'dubious' and 'frankly extravagant speculation'.[105] However, his willingness to float these arguments is a testimony to the depth of his commitment to both the utopian and worship. He found it virtually impossible intellectually to square this circle, but his deepest intuitions told him that the circle was indeed square.

## Final thoughts

Stapledon was working on a manuscript when he died in 1950. This was subsequently published as *The Opening of the Eyes* (1954) by his widow in its unfinished form (and therefore it needs to be treated with some caution). It is significant as an example of Stapledon's attempt to use religious language to express more than the conventionally religious. At first sight, it might appear to be a piece of traditional piety – with a perplexed and suffering sinner seeking to fathom the will of the almighty. This reading would not be entirely incorrect, for Stapledon does appear to be using this traditional form to ground his own anguished search for meaning. However, this dialogue is not with the God of the Christians, but is a debate with the cosmos personified – or something like this, for one of the themes of *The Opening of the Eyes* is his perennial pious agnostic belief that the ultimate, whatever that might be, cannot be adequately grasped or expressed by mere mortals. After Stapledon's death his old friend E.V. Rieu, in the introduction he wrote to *The Opening of the Eyes*, presents a questionable picture of Stapledon, on the one hand re-baptising the writer – 'he was a better Christian than he knew'[106] – and on the other, on the basis of a last conversation, suggesting some final moment of clarity and serenity which brought closure to the dilemmas of his life: 'he had reached the goal of his thinking: he had come to terms with reality; and comprehension had been added to acceptance'.[107] Rieu's remarks cast a long shadow. Sam Moskowitz in an essay of 1963, explicitly following Rieu's steer, and citing some highly ambiguous words in *The Opening of the Eyes*, opined that Stapledon 'had accepted God' and that he 'died with his lifelong mental anguish resolved'.[108] When Moskowitz began writing an authorised biography of Stapledon in the 1970s, Stapledon's widow, Agnes, took the opportunity to advise him that she was not happy with Rieu's attempt to suggest that Stapledon had undergone some form of theistic epiphany, and had regretted not having taken action at the time. She was also clearly not totally convinced that Stapledon was as serene as Rieu suggested, and posited a different explanation if it was indeed true:

> it is much too simple and too final ... I hope that Olaf was actually as serene in his thinking as Rieu believed him to be – but if he was serene I don't believe it was because 'comprehension had been added to acceptance'. I believe, rather, that he came to terms with reality by preparing himself to surrender the struggle to comprehend and agreeing to accept the reality unquestionably whatever it might turn out to be.[109]

She also implicitly took issue with another of Moskowitz's 1963 assertions which suggested a quasi-reborn Stapledon – 'that he had renounced communism and socialism'[110] – pointing out that

> he had never been a member of the Communist party, but he continued to admire some things about the Communist philosophy, just as he continued to detest some attitudes and actions of the party members. He never abandoned the socialist ideal in which he included all that was best in Communism.[111]

In a letter of 1981 to Ernest Martin (who forty years on from his exchanges with Stapledon was still concerned with the latter's beliefs), Agnes Stapledon returned to the theme of Rieu speaking of how the latter had 'come adrift – perhaps more in line with his own beliefs than with Olaf's' and countered with a picture of Stapledon's character and philosophical outlook based on a lifetime together:

Olaf was not at all the sort of person to have a sudden "conversion" into orthodoxy after having been an inquirer and an agnostic for the greater part of his life, and he was never worried about his agnosticism. He thought it was a perfectly satisfying and satisfactory doctrine.[112]

Serenity in fact is signally absent in *The Opening of the Eyes*. The tension between utopia and worship is, if anything, more visceral and troubling, with Stapledon wildly oscillating between the two poles, seeking a reconciliation. All his voices are here, but with a striking vividness and power. His longstanding social and political aspirations are affirmed, but there is a new savagery in his depiction of the forces of destruction and suffering, as in a terrifying theophany, reminiscent of Krishna's revelation of his universal form in the *Bhagavad Gita*.[113] Stapledon's biographer, Robert Crossley, documents how horrified Stapledon was when he saw film footage of the liberated death camps in Germany, and the dropping of the atomic bombs added yet further fuel to his outraged imagination. At a more personal level he witnessed the slow agonising death from degenerative arthritis of his friend the poet Lilian Bowes-Lyon.[114] Religious, cosmological and natural images of devastation and suffering jostle with the recent wartime experiences of genocide and nuclear weapons – delight and torture, indifference and lust meld together:

> If I am God at all I am also Satan ... Whatever is terrible and whatever loathsome, that is I ... I am the ice-cold heart of the cosmos. I make lovely things for the lust of wrecking them ... I crush robins and chaffinches on the road; and on battlefields I trample the wounded under the corrugated tread of tanks ... I enjoy the flavour of Buchenwald and of Hiroshima ... My delight is to compel a lover to watch the beloved become living carrion, or disintegrate into idiocy. And it is I, I, who torture the myriad worlds, and destroy worlds in their prime as a man may crush a fly. And in the end I shall destroy the stars as a housewife shovels living vermin into the fire.[115]

But with the further darkening of his picture of the universe occasioned by these recent encounters with the seeming pitilessness of existence, Stapledon struggles to believe that the animating spirit of the cosmos is an object of worship. If God and Satan contain one another then C.S. Lewis's charge against *Star Maker*, that it approached 'sheer devil-worship',[116] has real purchase, and Stapledon clearly felt the force of this type of objection. He savagely mocks the type of aesthetic metaphor he himself had deployed in the past:

> if your nails were being torn back, or the nerves of your teeth drilled for sheer malice; or if you were compelled to watch this happen to your dearest, would you then imagine that such devilry was all part of cosmical poetry?[117]

His dead friend Lilian Bowes-Lyon is (anonymously) introduced into the work, her pain and despair indicting Stapledon's 'God' who has nothing tangible to offer to her: 'Oh God, you are no God for me. You are for the strong and healthy and fortunate, not for the weak and defeated.'[118] But none of these are meant as knock-out blows, but are rather offered as illustrations of the difficulty (indeed, the increasing difficulty), not the impossibility, of being a utopian and a worshipper. The bleak facts of the universe hurled at this 'God' link Stapledon's posthumous work with his early cosmological speculations:

> And even if by some miracle mankind achieves a happier state, what then? Sooner or later, some unimportant astronomical event will casually destroy us. Or may you not at any moment project upon us out of your supramundane sphere some immaterial and inconceivable fiat to annihilate our universe?
>
> And no matter what catastrophe destroys us, it will be no accident but the intended climax of your music.
>
> And in all other worlds in all your galaxies, the upshot no doubt will be much the same. Sparks and hints of joy are everywhere turned to grief.[119]

# 4 Sir Richard Acland
## The conversion of a Liberal MP

**Prelude**

The year is 1944. A detective novel, *Night's Cloak*, by the writer E.R. Punshon. A wealthy, and repellent, industrialist, William Weston, has been found stabbed to death in his home. Inspector Bobby Owen and Sergeant Payne investigate. On a desk in the dead man's study they find a number of objects: the murder weapon (a Japanese sword), a large roll of banknotes, gold watch, gold cigar-case, keys, fountain pen and a few other bits and pieces – and one more thing:

> a small book, of a size to slip easily into a coat pocket. It was entitled 'What It will Be Like', and Bobby picked it up to glance at it. Payne said:
> 'Political, seemingly. By someone called Acland or something. Do you know who he is?'
> 'Member of Parliament, I think,' answered Bobby, who had heard vague talk about a political movement called 'Common Wealth' – one of many formed by those who search so eagerly for that new world ... Bobby knew nothing about it, whether it was 'right', 'left' or 'centre' ... Turning over the pages, Bobby found many such pencilled ejaculations as 'Rubbish'. 'Pestilent.' 'Rot.' 'Fiddlesticks.' 'Drivel.' Occasionally the comments were even fiercer. In one place language seemed to have failed the commentator, and was replaced by thick underlining and a row of notes of interjection. This was against a suggestion that workers in a factory should be allowed to choose their own foremen from among themselves. Bobby put the book down. 'Mr Weston wasn't much impressed, evidently,' he remarked.[1]

**Introduction**

The one name associated above all others with Common Wealth, that political organisation that brightly, if briefly, blazed in the Second World War, is Richard Acland. Although others had a role in its founding, and there were a number of other powerful personalities involved in the movement, Common Wealth can legitimately be called the creation of Sir Richard Acland, West

Country baronet and MP for North Devon. The political space was created for Common Wealth by the wartime coalition government and electoral truce which left many people feeling effectively disenfranchised, and willing to support a body that forced by-elections on an unwilling administration. Its origins as a personal project of Acland are to be found in a series of intellectual, moral and ultimately religious concerns that characterise his evolution in the 1930s and early 1940s from atheist Liberal to Christian Socialist.

Richard Thomas Dyke Acland belongs to a different generation to our three other subjects. Born on 26 November 1906, he was fifteen years younger than Macmurray, twenty years younger than Stapledon, and twenty-four years younger than Ingram. Thus, unlike the other three he had no direct experience of the fighting during the First World War. His father, Sir Francis Dyke Acland, fourteenth baronet (which title Acland was to inherit in 1939), was a Liberal politician (and landowner), one in a long family line, based in the West Country, which had previously provided eight members of parliament.[2] Both his grandfather and father had served in Liberal administrations, the former as Vice-President of the Council of Education (in effect Minister of Education) in Gladstone's final government, and the latter as Financial Secretary to the Treasury in 1915; unsurprisingly Acland was to recall: 'I always assumed, quite uncritically, that I should become a Liberal candidate.'[3] He was educated at Rugby and Balliol College, Oxford, where he was a student of Macmurray,[4] graduating in 1927 with a degree in Philosophy, Politics and Economics. After university he sought to enter parliament as a Liberal, targeting the family stronghold in the South West; after failing to win Torquay in 1929 and North Devon in 1931, he succeeded in the latter in 1935.[5]

## Member of parliament

Over the next five years his free market liberalism gave way to socialism. In an interview with Alexander Calder in the 1960s Acland said that his move towards socialism occurred quite soon after his election to parliament, and was occasioned by reading Keynes's *General Theory of Wealth, Unemployment and Money* (on the suggestion of the Labour MP Ellen Wilkinson) in which he found the analysis compelling, but the solutions proposed unconvincing. In his memoirs he called this acquaintance with Keynes 'one of the decisive events of my life':[6]

> I had previously been brought up on the automatic, self-working, laissez-faire Liberalism, and this [i.e. Keynes's book] was demonstrating that the thing just *did not* work out as the theorists said it would ... [A]t the end the conclusions were to reduce the rate of interest and engage in public works. And I simply said ... 'This remedy is nothing like in scale to the disease which you have diagnosed, and nothing short of putting the resources into the ownership of the community as a whole will overcome the ills.'[7]

Elsewhere he recalled that he had been 'powerfully drawn' to Communism in the wake of his encounter with Keynes, but had been 'pulled back from the communist magnet' by an aunt, in the winter of 1936/1937, who used the argument of the then fashionable, but now largely forgotten, Gerald Heard that adaptable organisms will always have the advantage over the super-efficient – in this instance, 'the case-hardened ... communists'.[8] In his parliamentary speeches at this time there is a strong sense of outrage at the plight of the poor in contemporary Britain, and of the preponderance of the interests of capital. In November 1936 he castigated the imposition of Means Testing at the household level in the assessment of unemployment benefit, arguing that 'unemployment is a national calamity and ought not to be shouldered on to the backs of sons who happen to have unemployed fathers living with them' and spoke of how 'the derelict areas are to suffer in the interests of the manufacturers of booming areas'.[9] The Labour Party is attacked for its 'academic discussions' on nationalisation, part of a dogmatic utopianism, but is invited to 'co-operate with us upon a much harder task – not the task of bringing in the Millennium' but of 'finding out what are the practical steps ... for the improvement of the condition of our people'.[10]

This desire to co-operate critically with Labour has to be seen in the context of politics domestic and international at the time. From being the governing party in 1916 the Liberals had undergone two decades of political civil war producing, in effect, two Liberal parties, one of which, the Liberal Nationals, were part of the Conservative-dominated National Government coalition.[11] The 1935 election, which had brought Acland into parliament, was for his party (the Liberal Party outside the coalition) a major disaster, losing about a third of its seats including the seat of its party leader, Herbert Samuel, leaving a parliamentary party of just twenty-one, the overwhelming majority of which had slender majorities, and the party as a whole despondent about its future. As one historian of the Liberal Party has put it: 'the aftermath of the 1935 Election was arguably the lowest point for the Liberals in the Twentieth Century.'[12] The new party leader, Sir Archibald Sinclair, deeply hostile to the National Government's failure to oppose robustly the international menace of Fascism, shifted the party's policy away from disarmament to re-armament, and he displayed, along with a number of other prominent Liberals, real sympathy for the idea of a Popular Front.[13] In his interview with Calder, Acland spoke of his anomalous position as a Liberal MP who had been converted to socialism, but added, 'strangely enough, almost at once, this didn't matter. Because from at least 1936 the one and only issue, really, was collective security.' In Acland's recollection the attraction of a Popular Front strategy lay to him in its potential to bring to bear on the National Government pressure from an incredibly wide political spectrum stretching from dissident Tories to the Communist Party of Great Britain:

> The internal battle was to see whether it was possible to arrange some sort of line-up, from Churchill and even Eden on one side right across to

Harry Pollitt on the other, of all the people who at that time believed in standing up to the dictators and aggressors wherever they might be aggressing.[14]

Acland threw himself into various campaigns and initiatives to establish a Popular Front, even threatening in 1938 to leave the Liberal Party if the party conference voted against this measure.[15] In this frame of mind he became associated with another Popular Front partisan, the former Liberal publisher, Victor Gollancz, and his Left Book Club, becoming a member of its selection committee,[16] and publishing, in 1937, his first book, *Only One Battle*, in the LBC series.

Compared with Macmurray, Ingram and Stapledon, Acland is not a theorist. He is every inch the politician, preferring in his published works to engage in what he saw as plain speaking in which theoretical distinctions were to be made understandable to as many as possible, and where solid imagery and rousing slogans were to help hammer home his central political objectives. He recognised the need for conceptual rigour and sought to achieve it, but it was not his forte, and his at times testy relations with more sophisticated theorists testified to some self-awareness of his limitations in these matters. *Only One Battle* is framed by the dark international situation of the late 1930s. The 'National' Government, whose name, for Acland, is merely an ideological concealment of its Conservative essence, is indicted for its failure to seriously oppose the Japanese incursion in Manchuria, Mussolini's invasion of Abyssinia, and Italian and German support for Franco in Spain, thereby setting at naught the sacrifices of the First World War and making the possibility of a second such war more and more of a possibility; they have thus 'betrayed the dead, and ... are leading the living to destruction'.[17] Acland's later recollection that there was only 'one issue' at this time would be seriously misleading if it is taken to imply that domestic issues ceased to play a vitally important part in his thinking, for in *Only One Battle* the Conservatives are as roundly condemned for their domestic as for their foreign policy. What Acland does do, however, is to try to integrate the domestic and international contexts into an overarching critique of the contemporary world, linking, for example, tariffs policy to both economic stagnation and the rise of Fascist international aggression, and into two central objectives: 'to preserve peace, and to develop the resources of the world for the benefit of the whole community'.[18]

Again, his later assertion that being a socialist and a Liberal MP in a sense quickly ceased being a difficulty is not substantiated in *Only One Battle*, where he clearly feels it necessary to argue that there is nothing problematic about a Liberal MP advocating socially progressive policies, and to assert that the Liberal Party can play a pivotal role in a radical politics. One way he attempts to buttress these claims is by invoking the radical past of the Liberal Party, as in its jettisoning of dogmatic *laissez faire* policies after 1870, culminating in the great reform measures of 1906–13, which involved 'wholly State intervention'.[19] To the same end he deploys the distinction between 'Socialist' and 'Radical', defining the former as the call for total and immediate nationalisation, while the latter, the stance of progressive liberals like himself, is defined as a more pragmatic approach to change, where nationalisation may or may not be appropriate. At the very least there does seem to be some sense of discrepancy between his party location and his social and political aspirations.

This is not to say that his radicalism doesn't draw deeply on liberal traditions of thought. There is a strong strain of idealism in his thinking. This comes out in his characterisation of, and opposition to, Marxism. Leaving aside the question of the accuracy of his understanding of Marxism, his exposition lacks consistency. Initially he asserts that 'Marxian theory takes account only of the selfishness of man',[20] but after quoting John Strachey, he concedes that, for Marxists, 'Ideals exist and men act from disinterested motives', but, re-establishing his critique, adds that in Marxian theory: 'ideals and disinterested motives are never the prime movers',[21] thus necessitating a Marxist claim that the selfishness may exist at a 'sub-conscious' level in the individual. Acland wishes, against this doctrine, to validate the existence of an *independent* and historically significant capacity for disinterested ideals in individuals: 'I ... insist that in the end idealism will be found to be an independent prime moving force in history, and that history cannot be understood when its existence as such is denied.' He illustrates this claim through an examination of the struggles for parliamentary reform, and the abolition of slavery, where he denies that the reformers were 'unconscious' agents of economic interests, but were rather individuals driven by moral concerns. Thus in the case of the parliamentary struggle:

> What is wrong with my suggestion that, somewhere around 1735–40, somebody said to himself, 'It is morally wrong that votes in the House of Commons should be influenced by the promises of social or financial advancement'? ... Why should not someone have said around 1780, 'It is morally wrong that seats in the House of Commons be open for sale and purchase through the hands of the owners of the rotten boroughs' ... I claim that someone *did* say [these things], and I claim that the whole drive for parliamentary reform came from these moral causes, and not from any economic cause whatever.[22]

Note here that there is no attempt to give a religious basis to this theory of moral causes. He notes that the campaign to abolish slavery was initiated by American and British Quakers, but this is purely an historical and sociological observation. The approach is, as yet, secular humanist in cast.

The book registers an evolution in his thinking on bringing the opposition together to fight the Conservatives. He mentions his previous membership of the Popular Front Propaganda Committee, which, although credited with doing 'much useful work', is critiqued for merely concentrating on persuading the higher echelons of the political parties to co-operate, when the real need was to bring to bear on the parties the pressure of an insistent public opinion demanding that they co-operate.²³ He proposes the establishment of a 'Co-operation Committee' to start the ball rolling, an institution which must not become a new political party in its own right, since it would then tend to seek political hegemony rather than inter-party co-operation. In terms of electoral politics the goal would be to get the co-operating parties to agree to back a common candidate in a constituency, who would also get the public blessing and the support of the Co-operation Committee. Underpinning this strategy is a belief in the fluidity of the electorate: that people will work and vote for a candidate they would normally have nothing to do with, if that candidate has a sufficiently noble objective (the defeat of the existing Conservative administration), and that people who normally don't vote can be persuaded to turn out in such a context.

Acland's conception of 'Radicalism' allowed him to argue that there could be a degree of ideological agreement between socialism and radicalism, though the ideological differences between the Communist, Labour and Liberal parties meant that there could not be agreement on 'the ultimate shape of society'. His conception of this possible commonality had undoubted social bite: 'We can co-operate in an effort forthwith to abolish or control (by national ownership in suitable cases) the gross and outstanding evils and abuses which have grown up under the present form of private enterprise.'²⁴ In more concrete terms he outlined four 'promises' which he hoped would evolve out of socialist/ radical co-operation: (1) the nationalisation of the coal industry and the Bank of England; (2) the abolition of the Household Means Test; (3) the prevention of landowners exploiting 'site values' for their own gain; (4) the provision of cheap supplies of milk.²⁵ These broadly egalitarian measures, once in place, would then provide the new context for further change in the future.

In November 1938 Acland was able to test some of his electoral notions in practice – and with spectacular results. He had established that there were thirty-five constituencies in Britain where the combined Liberal and Labour vote was greater than that achieved by the winning Tory candidate.²⁶ Bridgwater, a constituency next to Acland's own seat in North Devon, was one such place, and in 1938 a by-election was called.²⁷ In line with a practice he was to follow throughout the following years – that of seeking out local advice and allies – he linked up with the chair of the Minehead Left Book Club, who, sign of the times, was the Vicar of Oare, the Reverend Cresswell Webb.²⁸ With Webb's assistance he was able to persuade the Liberal journalist Vernon Bartlett²⁹ to stand as an Independent Progressive. Having obtained local Liberal support for Bartlett, Acland demonstrated his swashbuckling attitude to electoral pieties by using local Left Book Clubs to establish new *Labour Party* branches ('a singular role for a Liberal MP', as Martin Pugh has put it!),³⁰ thereby helping to gain Bartlett local Labour endorsement. In the resulting two-party contest the sitting Conservative Party lost its previous majority of 10,500 and the seat, Bartlett obtaining a majority of 2,332 with 53.2 per cent of the vote. Acland's belief in untapped sections of the electorate would appear to have been borne out by the rise in turnout from 72.7 per cent to 82.3 per cent, and since the Tory vote fell by only 700 votes, the combined Liberal and Labour vote, on the basis of the 1935 election, was insufficient to deliver the victory.

Throughout 1938 Acland's anger and frustration at the government's response to the tide of Fascist aggression is palpable. In April 1938 he published a pamphlet, containing an extract from *Only One Battle* castigating Conservative foreign policy, updating on the recent German annexation of Austria and, on a brighter note, the dissent in the Tory Party exemplified by the resignation of the foreign secretary, Anthony Eden, and the robust 'realism' of Churchill's attack on government appeasement; but it is the dark tone that pervades its blunt title – *This Way to Death*.[31] In parliament in October, following the Munich Agreement, Acland continued his castigation of the international policy of the National Government. At Munich the prime minister, Neville Chamberlain, in concert with the French, had purchased the promise of peace by, in effect, agreeing to Germany's incorporation of the 'German' Sudetenland from Czechoslovakia – an agreement, it should be remembered, that was widely welcomed at the time in Britain. Within days of the agreement Acland travelled to Czechoslovakia, including the Sudetenland, and, as he reported to the Commons, he found 'the people ... less dispirited ... by the loss of their territory than by the desertion of their friends';[32] and, with an eye to the future he relayed a conversation he had had with a Czech army officer: '"What have you gained from all this?" he said. I said "An arbitration treaty with Germany." "God help you," he replied "because that is what we had."'[33] Many years later in an unpublished memoir Acland related the trenchant, earthy remark that a Czech waiter made to him on this visit, one that he did not share with the Commons in 1938: 'Zee Vrench have focked us and zey vill be focked zemselves.'[34] In his speech, and very conscious of the anti-Semitic dimensions of German National Socialism (and its broader appeal), he envisaged a flight of Jewish professionals from the Sudetenland to Prague, and a resulting rise in anti-Semitism in that city, and called on the government to face down the protectionism of the British medical profession, and allow 500 Jewish doctors a year to come to Britain from Czechoslovakia.[35] Acland was to recall those October days on 15 March 1939 when, on the day Hitler began his invasion of the rest of Czechoslovakia, he rose in the Commons to commend the former foreign secretary, Anthony Eden, for his acknowledgement of the bankruptcy of appeasement. Acland clearly saw this as the vindication of his own stance throughout the 1930s:

> Last October some hon. Members quite sincerely thought that appeasement might succeed and others that it might fail. Today it seemed to me the right hon. Gentleman [Anthony Eden] said, without one word of dissent in the House, that there was only one opinion, namely that appeasement had failed.[36]

Britain's declaration of war in September 1939 further energised the already highly energetic Acland. One feels the sense of urgency in his public pronouncements and his desire to be as forthright and as candid as possible in the presentation of his radical programme for winning the war and establishing a more just social order. Two notable examples are his pamphlet, *What Now? Memorandum on the World Situation September 1939 by Sir Richard Acland, MP* (The *Sir* Richard was a result of the death of his father in June 1939, whom he succeeded as the fifteenth baronet) and a speech he made in the House of Commons in December 1939. *What Now?* like all his wartime publications has the air of someone thinking on their feet – and thinking fast: 'it was written, printed and published in 27 days'.[37] In the thirty pages of the text principles are stated, but details as to practical implementation are almost entirely absent. The opening line sets the tone of social radicalism heard throughout: 'With the declaration of war I believe we heard, whether we understood it at the time or not, the death knell of private capitalism.'[38] Free-market capitalism has given way to monopoly capitalism, which in wartime poses a serious threat, but also provides opportunities for change; the war cannot be won under the existing economic system, but the need for common sacrifice morally undermines the anti-social rationale of that system. Although using some of the *concepts* of socialism, Acland does not use the *word*. This may reflect his still anomalous position as a Liberal MP, but when he does mention his party the term 'faint praise' springs to mind; thus, in assessing the strengths and weaknesses of the party objectives in the interwar years, he notes:

> Their great merit was that each one of them was politically and economically practicable. Their great defect was that although each would have achieved a useful purpose, yet in sum total they would neither have ended unemployment nor inequality, at any rate for years if not for generations.[39]

Party aside, the gravitational pull of *liberalism* may still be acting as a brake on an explicit espousal of socialism – the belief, articulated in *Only One Battle*, that the philosophical resources of liberal radicalism can ground an equitable social policy. Furthermore, and certainly when Acland became the leader of a fledgling political movement, there was an ideological and tactical need to distance himself from competitor movements and parties, especially the Labour Party, that made much of their socialist credentials. This was reinforced by his desire to speak, particularly to the middle classes, in language that would not unduly perturb them.[40]

In terms of war aims what is particularly striking is his broadly warm attitude to the Soviet Union, which is based on a mixture of *realpolitik* and principle; this at a time, as Acland acknowledges, when the Soviet Union, as a consequence of the Nazi–Soviet Pact, was occupying the very country Britain had gone to war over – Poland. The power issue is put baldly: 'We have to face the fact that the Eurasian Continent is now dominated, militarily and politically, by Russia' and that 'it is quite certain that the attitude of Russia will determine the duration of the war';[41] he is also at pains to put the bewildering twists and turns of current Soviet foreign policy in the best possible light, citing the Soviet need to protect its legitimate interests, and Western tardiness; 'I cannot,' he concludes, 'subscribe to the view that Russia has achieved her present position by disgusting and unparalleled duplicity.'[42] In terms of principle, Acland denies that Germany and Russia are equivalent – both 'gangsters';[43] he accepts that 'in both countries religion is persecuted, no one can hold an opposition meeting or an opposition newspaper',[44] but the fundamental difference is that the principles underpinning Soviet society 'are based upon, and arise from, the fundamental conception of the rights of the working man' and not, as in Germany, a narrow nationalism.[45] Furthermore, in a happy marriage of the pragmatic and the moral, a Britain committed to social justice is more likely, in the long run, to gain the crucial support of the USSR.

The social radicalism of *What Now?* is also very evident in Acland's Commons speech in December 1939. Acland uses the occasion to try to position himself anew in parliament, distancing himself from aspects of his past, and establishing the beginnings of a new political agenda. He draws attention to his new voice: '[T]his is a thing,' he says of his radical anti-capitalist sentiments, 'which I have not said before in this House … ',[46] and when a conservative member interjects with 'what the hon. Member is now saying [is] the very opposite of Liberalism'[47] Acland does not deny it but, instead, refers to his political trajectory over the previous years, and to the imperative that MPs always speak the truth regardless of an understandable reluctance to be disloyal to party leaders and to constituency workers. Later on, he again alludes to his new stance in the Commons: 'In my view, which I am explaining in this House for the first time, private capitalism has had its day.'[48] His tone is frequently provocative: he berates those members, from both right and left, who had privately agreed with his critique of government foreign policy but would not go public for fear of losing their seats; and he draws an unattractive parallel between political events in Germany and Britain:

> Differing in this respect from the owners of our own country, the German owners had not succeeded in achieving a mass basis for any party under their own control, and they did the next best thing and financed somebody else's party.[49]

Conventional nostrums will not work in Germany (and, by implication, here too); disloyalty to Hitler will not be promoted by promising the Germans 'a nice little Conservative monarchy, or even a nice little pseudo-Liberal democracy' for ownership and control will still be in the hands of 'the opposite numbers of the Federation of British Industries'.[50] Acland's rhetoric was emphatic: 'the time has come for us to hold everything in common',[51] though as in his pamphlet there was a paucity of detail. Nevertheless, if the reaction of one conservative member is typical – this 'was really a proposal of Socialism in the extreme'[52] – Acland's radical voice had been heard.

In February 1940 Acland brought out *Unser Kampf: Our Struggle*, its title self-consciously counterposing a social response to the elitist individualism of Hitler's *Mein Kampf*. The book appeared in Allen Lane's innovative Penguin Special series with its topical themes, carefully chosen authors, cheap paperback format and incredibly rapid production schedules. Huge sales were achieved. In Acland's case a second impression had to be rushed out later in the month, a third in March, the fourth impression in May, and a revised second edition in August – in all the book sold 152,192 copies.[53] This was to be the book that would dramatically raise Acland's public profile and begin the process that was to lead to the establishment of Common Wealth. Like *What Now?* – indeed, like most of Acland's published output in this period – the book was produced at a very rapid rate, 'written', as he was to say, 'at breakneck speed with negligible time for critical revision',[54] and larded, as he again admitted, with both 'naivete' and 'over-optimism'.[55] The sentiments and, in some instances, the actual wording echoes the December 1939 House of Commons speech. In the Preface there is a degree of distancing from *What Now?* in that *Unser Kampf* is deemed to be an 'elaboration' of the earlier work, where briefly mentioned themes are developed, and there is 'a complete change of emphasis on many points', and some 'errors' are corrected, the new work having benefited from 'the constructive criticism' of *What Now?* by a wide range of readers – though Acland doesn't elaborate on the nature of these changes, and there is no explicit repudiation of any of the key themes of the earlier text.[56] 'Elaboration' does seem to be the appropriate word.

Although this was the period of the so-called 'Phoney War' (September 1939 – May 1940) the nature of the war had altered with the Soviet Union's attack on Finland at the end of November 1939. In *Unser Kampf* Acland differentiates between Russia's move into Poland and her war in Finland. The Polish incursion, he asserts, 'was in my view justified up to the hilt' (on the grounds that (1) Polish resistance to Germany had almost collapsed, (2) 'the people in the territory concerned were actually more Russian than Polish, certainly more Russian than German', and (3) that the Russians were welcomed in by the local population).[57] In Finland, however, given the lack of evidence of any mass Finnish support for the Russian action, 'the aggression, as a thing in itself, must be condemned'.[58] And yet he cannot resist establishing mitigating circumstances to create 'a balanced view'[59] of the Finnish–Soviet war, again, as in *What Now?*, citing the Soviet need to defend itself in a hostile world, and deploying one of his characteristically dotty analogies – in this case the hypothetical position of a capitalist Britain surrounded by socialism, and with Kent as an independent socialist republic, close to the economic and political heart of the UK, that could be a point of entry for socialist forces.[60] Cushioned, however, in Acland's continuing credulity regarding the nature of the USSR lies his strategic belief that a successful outcome of the war for Britain requires the detaching of the Soviet Union from Nazi Germany.

In establishing the *moral* case for social and international justice, *Unser Kampf* reveals a degree of engagement with Christian social teaching not found in

Acland's previous publications. This shift is heralded in the December Commons speech where in his opening sentences he had declared that the doctrine of Common Ownership 'seems to me a quite Christian doctrine', and had wondered how previous generations had managed to reconcile economic individualism with 'Christian tenets'.[61] This case is reiterated in *Unser Kampf* but with textual support from the Bible, and from the *Life of Jesus* by the radical cleric Conrad Noel. As we shall see, Acland's conversion to Christianity *as a faith* still lies in the future, but *Unser Kampf* does suggest a growing engagement with this religious tradition. Thus in the chapter on 'a new morality' he articulates its central imperative in explicit Christian language, 'Love your neighbour as yourself', enabling him to castigate both 'the Church' for failing to live up to this principle and the world for failing to see the essential truth of the injunction in this commandment.[62] He also tops and tails the text with verses from the book of Ezekiel: the frontispiece speaks of God's anger in the face of human wickedness – 'when the land sinneth against me by trespassing grievously, then will I stretch out my hand upon it, and will break the staff of the bread thereof' – but the final page breathes hope: 'Yet behold therein shall be left a remnant that shall be brought forth, both sons and daughters.'

The immediate *political* task outlined in *Unser Kampf* is the ousting of the Chamberlain government. Acland's involvement in the Popular Front campaign had brought him into contact with political figures from across the political spectrum. In late 1939 he became a member of a discussion group initiated by Sir Stafford Cripps; other members included Tory MPs Harold Macmillan and Walter Monckton, various other Liberals and members of Cripps family. Cripps' biographer, Peter Clarke, characterised the group thus:

> What they had in common, it might unkindly be said, was that they were all high-minded toffs, with connections to the aristocracy, landed gentry, or haute bourgeoisie; if not ready to join the Labour Party (which several did later), then already critical of the Chamberlain regime; and most of them practising Christians.[63]

In Cripps' tortuous ideological odyssey of the 1930s he had moved by 1938 from a United Front policy of an alliance of the acceptable left to the Popular Front conception of a broad alliance of democratic forces. He had sent a letter of support to Bartlett in the Bridgwater by-election,[64] and when he issued the famous 'Cripps Memorandum' attempting to get the Labour Party behind the Popular Front (for which he was applauded by Acland)[65] he set in train a set of events that would culminate in his expulsion from the party. The 'Group' was formed in the wake of his ejection, and its formation is interpreted by Clarke as part of the beginnings of a political and ideological realignment in Britain around a 'Progressive' tradition which owed a great deal to the progressive liberalism of the turn of the century.[66] If so, Acland, given his ideological trajectory, was clearly well placed to take advantage of this development.

The discussion of the need for a new government in *Unser Kampf* shows Acland struggling with an old conundrum of radical political thought; as he very much later put it:

> The book attempted some kind of linkage between politics, morality, economics and religion. But what sort of linkage? We never worked it out. Was it the need for profound social change so as to bring forth more moral people; or did we first need to change the people so as to improve the structure of society?[67]

In *Unser Kampf* the removal of the Chamberlain government is deemed to be an 'essential preliminary' step in the project of fundamentally altering the social and economic order; the call is for 'a complete change of government', not a mere 'reshuffle, or an enlargement'; it has to be 'a clean sweep'.[68] Part of Acland's thinking here is that the government, as the creature of large capitalist interests, must necessarily go as part of the extirpation of those interests; it is also a necessary part of a national expiation for the international betrayals since 1931, required to alert global opinion that a fundamental moral shift has occurred in Britain. Thus *prior* to the change of government there had to be a widespread change of 'hearts ... ideas ... and ... aims'.[69] He derives encouragement for his belief that this 'immense task'[70] can be achieved from the experience of the enemy, asking: 'How does our task now compare with that which confronted Herr Hitler in the early 1920s when he set out to rearm Germany and make her master of Europe?'[71] His answer is that Hitler concentrated on creating a 'will' for change, not on the modalities of change, thus 'we cannot attempt to foresee by what stages we shall secure a government inspired by the new ideas. Our problem now is to create the will to demand that it shall be done.'[72]

Acland thus made government change an incredibly difficult task to achieve. It did, however, grant him the luxury of suggesting how the new moral Britain could bring an end to the war. He rejects the 'Stop the War Now' alternative as this would leave Nazi tyranny even stronger. Instead, his hope is that the German people themselves can be persuaded to defy their government and establish peace and justice; but they will only do so on the basis of an approach grounded in the new morality. Acland anticipates this happy new day:

> How would the matter stand under the new direction here suggested?
> 
> I would ask the reader to pause for one moment to consider the passionate thrill of a new hope that would encircle the whole earth in the wake of our new message.
> 
> 'The people of Britain speaking to you.
> 
> 'The World for Humanity! This is our message to you.
> 
> 'People of Germany, – what are we fighting for? How can we possibly gain by killing each other? There is more than enough in this world for

all of us if peoples will only treat each other as brothers. In heaven's name why can't we co-operate for prosperity?'[73]

Germans could be won over, he believes, by cogent arguments, by an appeal to basic moral sentiments – 'You know in your hearts that the treatment you have been persuaded to mete out to these fellow human beings of yours [the Jews] is unworthy of the best traditions of your people'[74] – and by principled action:

> Make test of us now this moment. Send out one man to us now. We will not shoot at him. Let him but put his head over the parapet, at the same moment two of our men will put their heads over ours.[75]

And so on. After this expenditure of utopian energy, Acland ends the book in organisational mode: 'do you *really* mean to help? If so, I would be glad to hear from you at the House of Commons or through Penguin Books, Harmondsworth, Middlesex.'[76] The campaign to construct a movement had begun.

## The return to Christianity

At some point in late 1940 Acland embraced Christianity as a faith.[77] In later reminiscences he used the expression 'recalled to a religious way of life'[78] to make the point that he had grown up with a faith, but possibly also to suggest the presence of a divine hand in his return. His adolescent loss of faith, at Rugby, is attributed to a youthful rationalism: 'I threw over religion with a four-stage argument: "You Christians say that God exists; you ought to be able to prove it; I attend and you prove nothing; so there is no God"';[79] and proceeded to re-write sections of the Prayer Book, 'substituting "Brotherhood of Man" for "God"'.[80] His re-entry into the faith was brought about by reading *Good God* by 'John Hadham', which, he maintained, trumped his earlier intellectual atheism with a better argument. 'Hadham,' he recalled, 'was the first who positively told me that God is unprovable, not because Christians are incompetent, but because people are meant to be free.'[81]

*Good God* followed Acland's *Unser Kampf* in the Penguin Special, appearing some time in February/March 1940, and it was to sell in numbers comparable to its immediate predecessor. 'John Hadham' was the pen name of the theologian and historian James Parkes (1896–1981) who, following his profound effect on Acland, was to play a role in the emergence of Common Wealth, and was to figure in the battles over religion that were to sweep through the leadership of that body. Educated at Oxford after the First World War (in which he had been gassed),[82] he was ordained an Anglican priest in 1926; successfully completing a DPhil on Jewish/Christian relations in 1934, he published his findings as *The Conflict of the Church and the Synagogue* (1934). A member of staff of the Student Christian Movement from 1923, he was an active participant in internationalist movements such as the League of

Nations Union, and a range of Christian and student welfare organisations. From 1928 until 1935 he worked for the International Student Service in Geneva; it was here that he learned from the police that the Swiss Nazi Eisene Front had received orders from the German-based World Anti-Semitic Service (der Antisemitische Weltdienst) to organise his assassination.[83] On returning to England he began his life as a private scholar specialising in analysing anti-Semitism and the relations between Christians and Jews.

*Good God* is a lively and crisply written account of God's dealings with earth ('Of the home life of God I know nothing'[84]). And the claim that so struck Acland is undoubtedly one of its central themes:

> God has decided that all knowledge of himself shall be subjective. It is in that way that he preserves man's free will ... [H]e has made it more and more impossible to prove a matter, the more important it gets, until he has made himself completely unprovable.[85]

But although pivotal to Acland's religious development, the book's immediate effect on him was the *intellectual* clearing of an intellectual blockage. Further development occurred very shortly afterwards:

> A few nights after reading *Good God* there came an impact at first non-verbally; but when it took on words, they could have been: 'And if this Good God is truth, then even *you* might be drawn into some kind of cooperation.'[86]

Over the years Acland struggled to describe this 'indescribable'[87] moment, some form a mystical experience, but freely acknowledged that all he was supplying was metaphors and vague linguistic approximations:

> Shall he say a swelling trumpet chord from all the orchestra of heaven? Shall he say 'a mighty rushing wind' not blowing over and around his body, but raging through all the open spaces between the electrons and the protons and neutrons of which his body is made? The experience ... was utterly real ... It was physical sensation experienced by the body. It was not self-created from inside. It was given.[88]

Whatever this was, Acland was now entering the terrain of belief, and here there was a significant divergence from Parkes. Parkes' God was very much a *personal* God – a being equipped with intellect and emotions with whom terrestrial beings could have a personal relationship. Acland, *at this stage*, did not conceive of God in this way, and the person whose work he turned to, to articulate his own conception of the divine, was Kenneth Ingram.

A good starting point for viewing this phase of Acland's religious thinking is the new book he wrote after *Unser Kampf*, which was entitled *The Forward March* and which appeared in March 1941. The book was also, as we shall see, an ending point in that he used the text – or more precisely, a footnote – to signal a significant new direction in his thinking on the nature of the divine. Religion acquires a new importance in this book: it is deemed 'essential' if the socio-economic changes advocated in the rest of the book are to be achieved.[89] Rounding on current versions of his former self, he asks those who require Christianity to provide 'proof' of its God to read *Good God* which 'proves quite conclusively that God could not exist in a world of free men unless He [note the pious upper-case H] were in fact absolutely unprovable'.[90] The use of scripture, previously noted in *Unser Kampf*, acquires here a new purposiveness and intensity, as he seeks to illustrate that the secular social critique expressed earlier in *The Forward March* can be found in the Gospels. In a properly constituted society there would be a congruence between the religious and the social spirit, and it would become 'possible for the first time in hundreds of years to preach the Christian gospel in terms which make sense in relation to the world which men have to live in from Monday morning to Saturday night.'[91] But when it comes to discussing the nature of God he refers his readers not to Parkes but to Kenneth Ingram: 'My own ideas correspond most closely to those which are presented to us throughout the works of Kenneth Ingram, in particular the *Christian Challenge to Christians.*'[92] And although couched in the sentiments of ecumenism his characterisation of the 'personal' God position could hardly be called respectful:

> I do not have to insist on anyone else agreeing either with me or with Ingram. If someone else finds it more satisfying to 'think' of God as a Being existing in some defined place and related to the Archbishop of Canterbury in much the same way that he is related to the local vicar, there is no need for anyone to quarrel.[93]

However, Acland's identification with Ingram is deceptive. His concern was to stress the radical immensity and otherness of God. Thus he talks of God as 'a Higher Authority, outside man, outside society, outside time, and outside space',[94] something that was anathema to Ingram, and to Macmurray, whose immanent God was in the very substance of time and space, and of which humanity and society partook. He thus seems to have viewed Ingram's stance on a 'personal' God as a theoretical buttressing of an almighty God. And certainly it is possible to find passages in the text of Ingram that Acland recommends, *The Christian Challenge to Christians*, in which Acland could have found encouragement, as in the claim that:

> many of us who loudly proclaim our belief in a personal God do not believe in God at all, and are actually atheists ... The effect of dissociating God from the realities of our own experience is to make Him a finite person confined to an ideal world.[95]

But Ingram's starting point was very different.

Between the first draft of *The Forward March* completed in early December 1940 and the final draft published in March 1941, Acland and Ingram made a considerable stir at the Anglican Malvern Conference held in January 1941. The conference, the original idea of the head of the Industrial Christian Fellowship the Rev. P.T.R. Kirk, had gained the active support of William Temple, the Archbishop of York, and over two hundred participants (overwhelmingly Anglican clergymen) assembled to discuss how the Church should approach post-war social and economic reconstruction.[96] In the first draft of *The Forward March*, although keen to see the Church play a leading role in the project of regenerating Britain, Acland was pessimistic about the outcome of the planned conference: 'It is, of course, too much to hope that the Lambeth Conference will "pass a resolution" in favour of the kind of society which I have described.'[97] Nonetheless he was clearly going to try to do just this. Kirk had been sufficiently impressed by *Unser Kampf* to get its author to give a talk at his church, and Acland had no doubts that this connection was important in getting himself and Ingram invited as key speakers in the section of the conference dealing with 'practical questions': 'assuring me favoured treatment on the Malvern agenda', as he later described it. It also probably did Acland no harm that William Temple was married to his cousin.[98]

It is not clear when Ingram and Acland first met. It is possible that it was one of the fruits of Acland's appeal in *Unser Kampf* for interested people to get in touch with him. Certainly in *The Night is Far Spent* (1941) Ingram, looking back on the early 1940, singled out Acland's call for support in his book as of some significance:

> Of all the movements that were developing at an earlier moment in the war that movement which arose as a result of Sir Richard Acland's book seemed to me to contain the most promising possibilities. I say this mainly because it bore the essential mark of a genuinely revolutionary enterprise, an approach made with a religious understanding – an appeal therefore on religious and moral grounds: and also a programme which involved political action.[99]

We do know that Ingram joined the informal committee Acland established in March 1940 following the popular success of *Unser Kampf*, and immediately became a voluntary worker at the HQ established at Acland's London home[100] – though whether they knew each other before this is not known. Certainly from this time they began a close collaboration that was to endure through the rise and fall of Common Wealth. At Malvern they were in impressive company – other speakers in the conference included T.S. Eliot, Middleton Murry and Dorothy L. Sayers as well as the philosopher D.M. McKinnon and the theologian V.A. Demant; and there were members and supporters of a range of groups and positions such as the Anglo-Catholic, neo-Medievalist Christendom Group and the Moot (heavily influenced by

Karl Mannheim) of which Eliot was a member; but, as one of Temple's biographers put it, 'Sir Richard Acland dominated the proceedings.'[101] This owed a good deal to Acland's canny political skills. Unlike many of the other speakers who brought lengthy speeches which had to be gabbled at an unfeasible rate to meet the limited time, or dense philosophical/theological treatises that completely lost the audience, Acland and Ingram deliberately constructed short, clear presentations that combined accessibility with a measured rate of delivery (as Acland later recalled, 'in the verbatim report of the main speeches my contribution fills 9 pages, Sayers' 21, Demant's 28 and McKinnon's 35').[102] In terms of the content, it says a great deal about Acland – and not all of it flattering – that with his Christianity barely a few months old he felt able to lecture the Archbishop of York, a score of bishops and nearly two hundred other clerics on their duties as Christian pastors. His speech reiterated the familiar themes of his social radicalism, but now inflected with his newly minted Christianity. He begins with a piece of flattery, telling his audience that he intends to describe 'the route by which I have travelled from the back benches of the House of Commons to this much more important position in front of a Conference of the Church of England',[103] a journey he depicts in terms of a move from morality, through the use of Christian ethics, to belief. Still in emollient mood he acknowledges that the Church has done good work preaching the form of individual conduct expected of Christians. *But*, and here the tone changes, in respect of the duty to 'say something about the structural organization of lay society' the Church has underperformed.[104] It is charged with 'unjustifiable caution' in such matters, and its leadership is deemed to be 'less courageous' than the churchmen who spoke out against slavery at the end of the eighteenth century, exemplified by the relative silence on international predation throughout the 1930s, when the injunction to love thy neighbour should have been actively promoted.[105] He accepts that the Church cannot become a political party, with a positive programme, but it should indicate what in the economic and social life of the country is contrary to biblical morality; the Church should say that 'it is the private ownability of the paper shares and documents of title in our great resources which compels us to retain a self-regardant materialistic, and therefore non-Christian way of life', and that the 'ending of this private ownability' will open up 'the possibility of a further advance ... towards the Kingdom of God on earth'.[106]

In Ingram's address the theme of the need for the Church to help generate a new social consciousness is also much in evidence, but it is grounded in a much more self-conscious and explicit radical social theory, which he and Macmurray had been refining throughout the 1930s. This comes out in the vocabulary; the words 'socialism' and 'socialist' appear over a dozen times, while they are entirely absent in Acland's speech; likewise the deployment of 'revolution' and 'revolutionary', again absent in Acland. His formulation of the Church's mission, although at one level echoing Acland, carries resonances absent from the latter's intervention:

socialism is the next stage in the unfolding of God's will in history ... socialism has become the primary religious issue of our time ... This does not mean that the Church should become a political organization. Her mission is rather to proclaim the message and to provide the nucleus of those who will lead the vanguard in the social–political–religious struggle.[107]

The contrast between the two men must have been evident to the listeners at Malvern. Ingram comes over as a militant left-winger, Acland as an earnest social reformer.

At the end of his speech Acland repeated his remark in the first draft of *The Forward March* that 'he did not expect the Lambeth Conference to pass a resolution' embodying his ideas on social reform.[108] Temple provided him with the opportunity to test this hypothesis, for on the final evening of the conference the Archbishop, exploiting the near vacuum (Acland and Ingram excepted) created by the poor level of the interventions, presented an 'astonishing list of "findings" which he just read out to an astounded conference that didn't realise that it had "found" anything of the sort'.[109] Furious that none of these 'findings' mentioned Common Ownership, Acland and Ingram worked into the night duplicating copies of a proposed 'addition' to Temple's statement, which incorporated their critique of private ownership.[110] It is probably worth reproducing, admittedly at some length, the bones of this document, for Acland in later life was to say,

> if there is a single statement which sums up my political faith it is the Addendum which I and Kenneth Ingram moved and seconded to William Temple's findings at the Malvern Conference in 1941 ... Our addendum expressed a belief that I developed during the first half of my political work and have held ever since.

This is the text as presented by Acland:

> There is no structural organisation of society which can bring about the coming of the Kingdom of God on earth, since all systems can be perverted by the selfishness of man. Therefore, the Church as such can never commit itself to any proposed change in the structure of society as being a self-sufficient means of salvation.
>
> But the Church can point to those features of our existing society which, while they can never prevent individual men and women from becoming Christian, are contrary to divine justice and act as stumbling blocks, making it harder for men to live Christian lives. In our present situation we believe that the maintenance of that part of the structure, by which the ultimate ownership of the principal industrial resources of the community can be vested in the hands of private ownership, is such a stumbling block. While these resources can be so owned, men will strive for their ownership for themselves. As a result, a way of life founded on

the supremacy of the economic motive will remain, which is contrary to God's plan for mankind.

The time has come for Christians to proclaim the need for striving towards a form of society in which, while the essential value of the individual human personality is preserved, the continuance of these abuses will no longer be possible.[111]

The proposal of this addition as a resolution next day, one observer noted, 'produced the most animated debate of the conference'.[112] Acland's principal opponent was George Bell, Bishop of Chichester, who detected 'totalitarian' implications in the resolution, and tabled a 'wrecking amendment' which was narrowly carried. The debate brought out a number of visceral feelings in Acland's breast towards the clergy: 'in the discussion I recall seeing a fat little prelate waddling to the microphone and thinking; "If the Church has people who even *look* like that, what hope is there?"'; this turned out to be the Bishop of Bradford, who proceeded to speak *in favour* of Acland's resolution![113] It was subsequently agreed that Acland and Bell should try and produce some form of compromise resolution – which they did, and which was carried unanimously.[114] The ideological meat of the 'compromise' resolution consisted of a small, but fundamentally crucial, change of words in the various drafts – the replacement of 'is' with 'may be'; this occurred in a section dealing with the 'stumbling-blocks' encountered by Christians in their social and economic relations; the result was thus (my italics):

> we believe that the maintenance of that part of the structure of our society, by which the ultimate ownership of the principal industrial resources of the community can be vested in the hands of private owners, *may be* such a stumbling-block.[115]

The 'may be' substituted contexuality for the absolutism of the original 'is'.

Acland's evident unhappiness with these changes (discernible in the pos-conference correspondence between himself and William Temple)[116] did not intrude into a new concluding section added in the final, published, draft of *The Forward March*. Looking back at his fears that the conference would prove largely fruitless, he now happily opined that 'had I foreseen the future I would have written [the concluding paragraphs] not in the tone of warning but in the tone of hope'.[117] And, with less than full candour, he omitted his defeats at the conference, merely reporting that the resolution 'was passed without opposition', and that 'some part of my own ideas was accepted by the drafting committees and the Conference';[118] though he did include the text of the resolution – so the careful reader could (whether or not this was Acland's intention) discern which part of his ideas had not been accepted. But the fact that Acland could spin Malvern as a victory for social reform is a measure of the immediate significance of the conference, and a testimony to Acland's dogged political skills at the conference. It *appeared* to many outside viewers that the Anglican Church had made a significant move to the left. In fact Malvern was a conference of people already inclined, in admittedly different ways, to reform. Bernard Causton, who wrote a brief account of the conference, perceived this climate and applauded Acland's sensitivity to it: 'The author of *Unser Kampf* acutely sensed the sympathetically critical atmosphere of the conference and presented his arguments with considerable skill.'[119] Ingram, in his own presentation, assumed some points of commonality between his approach and that of the conference as a whole, since 'no one, I imagine, would have come to this conference if he did not believe that Christianity must have a social expression'.[120] On the question of why the Acland/Ingram approach made such progress, Ingram, reflecting on the events later, was of the opinion that the other speakers and positions failed to tap into the reformist hopes of the conference; he and Acland had at least something recognisable to offer to this appetite. However, he was less than flattering about the 'average member' of the conference, who 'betrayed no sense of a desperate urgency, precipitated by the world crisis', giving rather 'the impression ... of a degree of complacency'. Worse still, as he also noted, beyond the conference lay the great sea of clergy and lay-people that had felt no urge at all to turn up, and who were not inclined to take on board the conclusions of Malvern. This, combined with the preoccupations of a country fighting a desperate war, Ingram suggested, meant that the Malvern effect was relatively limited.[121] In his own later judgement on these events, Acland maintained that Temple had blunted the impact of the conference by writing an article shortly afterwards in which he completely ignored the Acland/Ingram addition. Nevertheless, he still maintained that 'the Conference, and our addendum, had a significant effect. It allowed people to feel the dynamic elements in the Church were broadly on our side, at least for a time.' That 'time' included Temple's subsequent tenure as Archbishop of Canterbury but came to an end with his death in 1944; Archbishop Fisher, his successor, 'was to guide the Church back to its usual position'.[122] James Parkes, who was also at the Malvern conference, and who met Acland for the first time there, had a much more negative judgement of the proceedings, and was withering in his condemnation: 'the entire inability of the Church of England to face its own need for reform was conspicuous. It was ... [a] miserable ... failure.'[123]

## A personal God

One skips Acland's footnotes at one's peril. He wrote quickly, his ideas altered, the broader context was transformed, he had second thoughts, he changed his mind, and his response, if he could get away with it, was to put the new perspective in a footnote. His publishers no doubt despaired, but for anyone interested in the development of his thought these asides and afterthoughts provide a window on the ongoing critical conversation he was holding with himself. Nowhere is a change of direction more sharply indicated than the footnote to be found on page 104 of *The Forward March*. Acland clearly feels he needs to alert his readers to this development, for he concludes the preface with an injunction: 'The footnotes in this book form an essential part of the argument: they should be read.'[124] The footnote in question is added to the section discussed earlier, where he had recommended Ingram's books on the nature of God, and had distanced himself from the notion of a 'personal' God. Something had clearly happened between December 1940 and March 1941, for the footnote reads (in a curiously insouciant tone):

> By a coincidence it so happens that between writing my typescript and revising the proofs experiences have led me to reject Ingram's views and accept a much more 'personal' idea of God. I still recommend Ingram's books to those who think they do not believe in God at all.[125]

We are not told in the footnote of what Acland's recent momentous 'experiences' consisted. In later autobiographical reflections, Acland reconceptualised his conversion to Christianity in Christian terms. He speaks of three significant events. The first dates to April 1933 when one night he heard his father suffering a violent and prolonged asthma attack. In despair Acland cried out: 'Oh God, stop that noise!' whereupon 'the silence was instantaneous'. He admits that this could have been a coincidence, and also that 'twenty hours later, the impression on me was just about the smallest possible', but nonetheless maintains that 'I was not quite so cocksure about my Humanism. An inner door was ajar to the possibility of truth in religion in general and in Christianity in particular.'[126] The other two events he makes stronger claims about, calling them 'external imperatives' acting upon him, by which he means the intervention of a personal God in his life. The first imperative occurred at Easter 1938 when he was not a Christian, and which animated his moral response to the drift into war. He describes it as a 'sharp experience' that occurred to him one night on Croyde beach in North Devon, and which did not appear to be internally generated:

> It was not Richard Acland having a new idea – a process with which I was familiar. It was an imperative from outside which in words could have been: 'People don't need your pandering promises. Tell them that if they want peace and better times they need to be better people.'[127]

The second external imperative is the event we have already discussed – the non-verbal sense of a possible 'cooperation with God', which followed his reading of *Good God*; this is made clear in his very late *Unpublished Political Autobiography*: 'As on Croyde sands, I knew without possible doubt that this was authenticated from outside myself.'[128] This cannot be the same as the 'experiences' referred to the footnote in *The Forward March* for, quite apart from plural connotation of 'experiences', this would leave no time for Acland to read, absorb, promote and abandon Ingram's view of God. The 'experiences' may certainly have been triggered by the second imperative, but it seems likely that it took Acland some time to work through the implications of this new imperative – time in which his espousal of Ingram occurred. Certainly there is contemporary evidence that Acland's conversion to a personal God was a fairly lengthy and far from smooth transition – and was certainly not fully in place for some time. Thus there is an entry in Acland's private, and unpublished, diary dated 27 October 1943 in which he referred to a dream he had had 'last summer' while thinking of writing a book on God:

> It was sometime last summer that I knew that I had come to the belief in a living God ... At that time I had the only experience which I am pretty sure would be described by one of the New Testament people as meeting God in a dream. In that dream there was, as it were, a slope and at the top was the ground of the people who believe in the living God and at the bottom the other ground, and either people pulling at me were trying to take me upwards, or some other pull was working that way, and I was explaining to people 'I would like to be up at your end, but it's just intellectually dishonest to come your way; I can't make a sham of believing in a living God so as to get these parsons on my side politically.' And saying this I was forging downhill against any pull, when there was something enormous in the way, which was at the same time a wall and the very bottom of the robes of an enormous man, and it said; 'But you DO believe in the living God.' Being aware that this was, indeed, simply a dream, I could not fail to know that it had impressed itself on me more than an ordinary dream, and therefore argued; – 'Now IF this was anything other than a dream there is some reason for its being NOW.' And from there – 'If it had any reason it could only be the reason that you are to push on with the book.'[129]

The account of the dream does seem to suggest that Acland's belief in a living God was not easily won, and that a good deal of psychic turmoil and intellectual doubt accompanied his spiritual journey. Perhaps the use of the plural 'experiences' in *The Forward March* registers a sense of process, the messiness of which has to an extent been tidied up in the neat schematicism of some of the remaining autobiographical material.

Acland considered that he was personally empowered by his belief in God, and further believed that God could intervene in the historical process should it suit his aims. In a letter in early 1943 to a Marxist non-believing member of Common Wealth (Kitty Wintringham – to whom we will return later) Acland wrote that 'for my own part I can only say that a belief in a personal and conscious God is an enormous source of dynamic strength', and, while taking her total scepticism in these matters into consideration, he asked Wintringham seriously to entertain the argument of an interventionist God:

> if you try to line yourself up with the purposes of this God it does *seem* that in most remarkable ways he will set the stage for you, and almost

play the hand for you. I say 'seems' because nothing can be proved. It could be a coincidence.

The examples he gives are remarkable in that they suggest the possibility that God was intervening for the political benefit of Common Wealth. Thus the absence of by-elections in the early days of the movement could be construed as a providential act by the almighty – 'we did NOT have any by-elections in the one period when we could not possibly have coped with them'; and, as a possible example of even greater micro-management by the divine, he cites his decision to hand over his ancestral property to the National Trust, the timing of which, he asserts, deprived opponents of the claim that it was a 'political–personal stunt' by himself. His conclusion is unambiguous in its ambiguity – 'As I say – coincidence or ... '[130]

Acland did not counterpose to a personal God a personal Satan. True, he told Kitty Wintringham that 'the big truth of history ... is the conflict between God and the Devil' but instantly qualified this by insisting on the fundamentally different nature of the two combatants. The Devil is not a being at all but some sort of concentrated expression of human evil, at war with the purposes of God: 'I myself tend to believe that God is a conscious living power, making his plans, winning his triumphs and suffering his disappointments; and that the Devil is a non-conscious summation of all the evil greedy power-seeking elements in human nature.' Conscious, perhaps, of the opacity of this definition of the diabolic he refers Wintringham to what he takes to be Kenneth Ingram's conception of God, which is 'a somewhat similar non-conscious summation of the whole of good'.[131] Out with the conscious Devil goes his abode: Hell. Talk of 'hell flames', he was to write later, is 'crazy or wicked',[132] implying a God, unknown to the Bible, who 'takes pleasure in deliberately punishing even the guilty'. At best he is willing to concede the use of the term 'hell' to signify the psychic conditions humans create for themselves when they cut themselves off from God.[133] Perhaps there is an echo here of Parkes/Hadham in *Good God*, who had also combined a belief in a personal God with a rejection of Hell, opining that the latter doctrine would make God 'a loathsome and incompetent bungler'.[134]

Clearly stung by Acland's footnote in *The Forward March*, Ingram returned to the question of the nature of God in *The Night is Far Spent*. His concern is to counter the impression he believes Acland has created that he (Ingram) rejects any notion of the personality of God. He presents himself as someone engaged in an ongoing struggle to develop a revolutionary theology centred on the conception of God. He concedes deficiencies in his attempt – 'I do not pretend that I have begun as yet to perceive the complete implications of this synthesis'[135] – but nonetheless insists that Acland has misunderstood his views on God – 'I see by a reference in Sir Richard Acland's ... book that I have failed hitherto to explain my own belief satisfactorily.'[136] The ensuing re-articulation of his conception of God seeks to demonstrate that he does have a conception of personality in his account. He distinguishes a 'popular'

Christian conception of God as a person, 'a being with personal moods who occupies a place within (or outside) the universe, and who governs the universe with a much too obviously human, personal bias' from a more sophisticated, adequate conception of divine personality. This draws on the mystical experience that 'man can enter into communion with the universal', becoming 'one with the Spirit of Life', and the biblical metaphor of 'Fatherhood' which is deemed to be 'a symbol which witnesses to the validity of this experience of unity with the whole, as also to the dependency of man upon the reality which surrounds him'.[137] Now this may be a defensible conception of the divine personality, but it serves to demonstrate that Acland's new conception of God is as far away from Ingram as his old.

## *It Must Be Christianity*

In May 1941, following Malvern, Acland produced *It Must Be Christianity*, a pamphlet that was to be of great importance in the struggles over religion in Common Wealth – not because of any intellectual sophistication (which, it has to be said, was far from evident) but because of what it represented and, crucially, what it did not. There is nothing new as regards basic principles; the theoretical interest lies in the attempt to identify and characterise potentially progressive forces in modern society – the human base of fundamental change. The work seeks to be inclusive, but does so in a way that aggravates differences. Acland addresses the pamphlet to two groups that he claims hold the future in their hands – Christians and humanists. It soon becomes apparent, however, that there is actually only *one* progressive force – Christianity – split in two: Christians, and Christians who haven't *yet* realised they are Christians (the humanists). His humanists are progressives who wish to fundamentally alter the nature of society for the good of humanity. However, he asserts, 'surely the overwhelming majority of Humanists, even when they do not accept the existence of any Deity, none the less accept the Christian Ethic.'[138] This claim, insofar as it has any theoretical grounding, possibly represents his take on the Macmurray/Ingram historical hypothesis that progressive movements such as Marxism, though lacking in religious belief, are in some sense religious. Recall Acland's final sentence in the footnote in *The Forward March*: 'I still recommend Ingram's books to those who think that they do not believe in God at all.'[139] And it was this assumption that underpins the decision to give the pamphlet a title around which swirled the debates on religion in Common Wealth – *It Must Be Christianity*. Existing Christianity is still only a potential force for change, his strictures on the failings of the Church remain, but for all his talk of dialogue and mutual appropriation between Christians and humanists – 'these two groups of people should and will substantially merge and pool their respective ideas and philosophies'[140] – the Christian basis of this pooling and merging is not open to question. In time Acland himself acknowledged that the title of the pamphlet was unfortunate in that it was at odds with the political purpose of the work: the piece 'should have been called

*It Must Be the Christian Ethic* because it tried to appeal to Christians and humanists alike without ever inviting the humanists to start believing in God',[141] a concession that nonetheless still failed to understand, or rejected, the objection to the project of Christian hegemony critics perceived in the work.

Acland also takes the opportunity to ventilate what he takes to be theological heterodoxy concerning the doctrine of sin. As at Malvern, he doesn't allow his (freely admitted) recent conversion to stand in the way of speaking his mind – here on the biblical dubiety of what he considers to be the orthodox doctrine of sin: 'Greatly daring I challenge this Doctrine of Sin. I am a mere newcomer to Christianity, but I confess I cannot find in the Gospels any foundation for the heavy emphasis now laid upon this doctrine.'[142] He doesn't provide any evidence for this assertion, but then neither does he actually explain the substance of this 'Doctrine'. Instead he launches two ideas: the sufficiency of divinely grounded human nature for salvation, and the possibility of terrestrial redemption. The 'Doctrine of Sin' would therefore appear to be the proposition that sinfulness precludes the human earning of salvation, which doctrine is to be countered by replacing a hopeless moralism with a constructive teaching:

> Surely Jesus is not *Preaching* to men that which they *ought* to be, but can hardly hope to be because of their sinfulness. He is *telling* them what they *are*, and how they can find their heaven quite literally on earth if only they are alive to their actual nature as God has made it. [Acland's emphasis][143]

The authority trundled out in support of this position is Kenneth Ingram's *The Night is Far Spent* – which is deemed 'vitally important' in dealing with this issue.[144] Certainly one can see an affinity in their accounts. For Ingram,

> Man has within himself the potentialities of salvation ... Because he is so made he desires health, he desires freedom and equality. He desires this because of his real nature. He will strive to obtain what he desires when he has learnt to be real.[145]

However, the subtle but significant difference in emphasis between Acland's Jesus, who *tells* humanity the truth, and Ingram's Jesus, who 'recognized these potentialities',[146] is surely revealing.

## Forward March and the 1941 Committee

We now need to go back in time. Acland's appeal at the end of *Unser Kampf* for people to get in touch with him if they wished actively to promote the book's values and ideas almost immediately began to bear fruit. The book had been published on a Thursday (in February 1940), and on returning to his house after a long weekend he found it very difficult to open the door – the reason being the sheer volume of letters redirected from the House of Commons.[147] Three weeks after publication he had received 850 letters – the vast majority in agreement with his views.[148] In a published analysis of the first five hundred of these, Acland pointed to the broad social spread of the correspondents, and the predominance of people who had either been previously relatively politically apathetic or who had moved away from one of the existing parties.[149] Soon a national conference was called in London (12 March 1940) attended by about 150 of his correspondents, personally invited because of their proximity to the capital and the intelligence of their letters.[150] A committee was established and a name adopted: Acland wanted 'Unser Kampf' – hardly a winning gambit in a country at war with Germany – but the majority preference for 'Our Struggle' prevailed; in time 'Forward March' was substituted, an appellation derived from a speech of Churchill: 'long live the forward march of the common people of all lands towards their true and just inheritance'.[151] A working office was established, and branches began to appear around the country.

Two points are worth making here. Acland conceived of 'Our Struggle'/'Forward March' as a *movement* and not a *political party*. The purpose was not to supplant existing socialist parties but to try to make them more effectively socialist. As the movement consolidated itself, members were encouraged to *join* the Labour Party to push for the policy of Common Ownership, not as a form of Bolshevik entryism, but as part of a desire to play a constructive part in a broader progressive politics.[152] In time, though, with the establishment of Common Wealth, and the increased contestation of by-elections, the question of movement or party became a source of ideological friction. The other point to be made is that the movement had come together through the enthusiasm of, for want of a better word, 'ordinary' people. The bulk were middle class (for although attempts were made to increase working-class participation the results were limited) scattered across Britain in semi-autonomous branches. The movement, although indebted to Acland's rallying call and responding to his initiatives, had a determined and sizeable grass-roots. Acland had not wanted dilettantes – and he had not been disappointed. This was to have consequences for the creation of Common Wealth, which was to emerge out of the merging of two groups – 'Forward March' and the '1941 Committee'. As we shall see later, unlike Forward March the centre of gravity of the 1941 Committee was a fairly select gathering of 'important' people – well-known publishers, writers, academics, journalists and artists; there was no great desire for a mass movement – those local branches that were established never achieved the numbers and internal influence of the branch structure in 'Forward March'. This was to give the latter a distinct advantage in the coming together of the two groups; and when it was achieved very few of the metropolitan stars of the 1941 Committee entered the new organisation – it was to be the Forward March model that was to set the pattern for Common Wealth.

Acland sought to attract stars to Forward March, but he just couldn't achieve it (Stapledon, as we shall see, insofar as he could be called a star, seems to have found Acland, not the other way round). It went spectacularly badly in the case of H.G. Wells. We have Acland's rueful comment on the encounter: 'back in 1940 ... I asked H.G. Wells to join us since he was making noises about the post-war world. I did not realise he hated my guts.'[153] Whether or not Wells did hate Acland's guts before their correspondence in early May 1940, his tone in their exchange of letters was distinctly acerbic. Acland's initial request for co-operation had Wells insisting that his own Declaration of Rights had to be the basis for such co-operation. Acland responded with a notion of functional co-operation among equals – each organisation pursuing those things it did best as part of a common endeavour, for 'you cannot expect them all to take up as their common work the pressing of your particular side of the work'.[154] Wells, in his reply, besides demanding that Acland explain what objections he has to the Declaration, significantly alights on Acland's references to 'leadership'. Acland had at one point said that 'it was quite hopeless' that 'we should all get down and push behind your leadership'.[155] Wells's indignant denial that he sought leadership '*à la* Mosley' is developed to strongly imply that this *was* accurate in the case of Acland, and the letter ends with a rather menacing warning that Wells is now on Acland's case:

> To say you will go ahead without me if I won't come into your present loose, vague proposals for co-operation is, forgive me, silly. You won't leave me behind. You have interested me and I shall follow you like a searchlight.[156]

This letter does not close the door on possible co-operation, so long as Acland falls in with Wells's Declaration. However, Wells seems to have brooded on the matter over the next few days, for he sent a brutal follow-up note (Wells himself called it 'more insulting than ever')[157] where the formerly implicit conclusions on Acland's leadership goals are made explicit:

> I enclose a note on your objections. They bring out the peculiar confused quality of your mind. It slips to and fro between existing conditions and desirable conditions. That is what gives a quality of craziness to your *Unser Kampf* ... I think it is quite impossible to work with or lend countenance to you. You seem to be dreaming of some incoherent combination of progressives, in a movement going nowhere in particular under some foggy 'leadership' of your own ... You will flounder about with this imitation of Hitler for a time and then I suppose we shall hear less and less of you.[158]

Wells annotated the bottom of his draft version of this letter with the deadpan: 'There seems to have been a lull in our correspondence after this.'[159] Acland, nearly forty years later, noted that 'in the long-term his prediction was correct, but for the next five years people heard more of me than of H.G. Wells'.[160] And it was Acland who attempted to get the relationship on to a better footing in February 1941 by sending Wells his latest book, *The Forward March*, with what Wells himself called a 'friendly letter'.[161] In Wells's account of this letter in his 1944 book *'42 to '44: A Contemporary Memoir upon Human Behaviour during the Crisis of the World Revolution* he says that it 'provoked further tart responses on my part'.[162] There are undoubtedly such responses, as in 'why do you write nonsense about "Darwin's theory of evolution" and why do you get your science from an impostor like Gerald Heard?' and 'I guess there's a considerable incompatibility between our intellectual temperaments'; but there is also 'I was glad to have your friendly letter and the book, which I like much better than *Unser Kampf*' and 'I see no reason why we shouldn't co-operate in our common hostility to the reactionaries and unprogressives ... Maybe association will lead to convergence.' More significantly, whereas in his memoir he says that Acland 'displayed a curious disposition to drop the word "Socialism" in favour of "Collective Ownership"',[163] which he attributes to a possible wish on Acland's part to woo the Roman Catholic Church, in his letter to Acland he states, without comment, 'I think "Common Ownership" is a useful phrase.'[164] Hardly 'tart responses'. But Wells in his memoir is attempting to establish a consistency in his response to Acland over time, and in a later missive (28 September 1942), this time not to Acland personally, the savage tone returns. The occasion was the establishment of Common Wealth, when an official (Raymond Gauntlett – CW Political Secretary) wrote to Wells for his support. Wells replied berating Gauntlett, J.B. Priestley and Tom Wintringham (of whom more later) for associating with Acland; the old charges are restated (with variations), and there is an added swipe at Acland's religiosity:

> I am sorry to see that you ... have pinned yourself on to Acland. His intelligence is very limited and unstable, he is as imitative as a monkey (witness *Unser Kampf*), any claptrap that seems to be popular goes into his bag and any 'religious' cant, and his ambition for 'leadership' is uncontrollable. What is 'Common Wealth'? Nothing more nor less than a tail to the flights and plunges of the Acland kite.[165]

By this stage, therefore, 'hated my guts' is certainly appropriate. But both men recognised the will to control in each other – Acland, the relative neophyte, expressed it in more diplomatic terms, while Wells, the grand old man, put it in the punitive tones of a paterfamilias: 'I am not in the leadership business. If I find any dunderheads doing anything of the sort I shall "whip behind".'[166] More worryingly for Acland, this was not the first attempt, and certainly not the last, to draw parallels between himself and Oswald Mosley.

The start of the Acland/Wells correspondence in May 1940 occurred at the moment when the Phoney War was about to come to an end with a vengeance. First, though, Acland was in the House of Commons to witness the end of Neville Chamberlain's premiership in the course of the so-called Norway Debate of 7 and 8 May 1940. 'I sat and listened,' he later recalled 'to the most exciting and portentous debate I had ever attended.'[167] Churchill took over on 10 May, only to face a series of major German victories in Western Europe.

By the end of the month Hitler's forces had reached the Channel, Belgium and the Netherlands had surrendered and the British Expeditionary Force was evacuating from Dunkirk. By the middle of June Paris had fallen and the French were suing for peace. In terms of 'Our Struggle', while Acland continued his barrage of correspondence to build up the organisation, he recognised that in the new context of the war, with an invasion of Britain imminent, people's priorities had shifted: 'With these tremendous events roaring around us, no one was much interested in social changes that might be needed before the war could end. The only questions were about surviving undefeated through the next weeks and months.'[168] This brought new opportunities for work and the merest beginnings of what would prove a fateful relationship. Tom Wintringham entered Acland's field of vision; he was to become one of the founders of Common Wealth, one of its most tireless leaders and, particularly on the issues of morality and religion, *the* most dogged of the critics of Acland.

Wintringham (1898 – 1949),[169] as Acland freely admitted, had an intimidating combination of virtues; he was warrior and politico, scholar and poet combined. After deferring university to join the Royal Flying Corps in the First World War (serving on the Western Front in France as a mechanic and dispatch rider) he graduated from Oxford in 1920 with a degree in history He appears to have joined the Communist Party of Great Britain (CPGB) at the time of its founding in 1920, and remained a member for the next eighteen years. In 1925 Wintringham, along with eleven prominent members of the CPGB, was charged with sedition and sentenced to six months in jail. On his release he became an employee of the party, predominantly as a journalist and editor, and began to gain a reputation as a significant Marxist authority on military affairs. With the coming of the Spanish Civil War he went to Spain in 1936, becoming, in time, Commander of the British Battalion of the International Brigade, where he was wounded at the Battle of Jarama and, much more seriously, at the Battle of Quinto, whereupon he was sent home. In Spain (although married) he had met a young American, Kitty Bowler (who as Kitty Wintringham was to also play an important role in the fortunes of Common Wealth), but on their return to England the party, on the basis of denunciations originating in Communist circles in Spain, denounced Kitty as a 'Trotskyist spy', and when Wintringham refused to leave her he was expelled from the party in 1938. His expulsion was no doubt eased by his growing disillusionment with CPGB policy which he increasingly felt to be sectarian, opportunistic and rigid. His Marxism, however, was not dented by these events.

With the coming of the dark days of May 1940, and the broadcast call of Anthony Eden for the establishment of what was the forerunner of the Home Guard – the Local Defence Volunteers (LDF) – Wintringham believed that his experience with the local militias in the Spanish Civil War could help make the new force an effective military instrument. Since his return to England he had become part of the circle associated with the popular magazine *Picture Post* – notably its proprietor, Edward Hulton, and its editor, Tom Hopkinson – and was employed as a journalist by the publication. Wintringham was convinced, leaving to one side his political considerations, that an armed people was necessary to assist the regular forces, and to carry on the fight in the wake of a military defeat, and he saw the LDF as the nucleus of such a possibility.[170] Acland, who was himself a member of Hulton's select circle (a group, as we shall see that was to be fundamental to the emergence of the 1941 Committee) recalled that Wintringham, along with the military historian and theorist Basil Liddell Hart (1895–1970), approached him with the aim of gaining the assistance of 'Our Struggle' in propagandising their 'Arm the People' campaign. 'Our organization,' he writes 'was already big enough to attract their attention, and we spent about eight weeks pouring their leaflets out to our members for wider distribution.'[171] While the military and the *political* implications of an armed people were clear to Wintringham, given his immersion in Communist theory, it is more likely that Acland was attracted by its military utility and would have seen the political benefits more in terms of a deepening of democracy, rather than a politically potent citizen army. Not all members of the movement agreed with these new activities: 'some wrote in disgust that they had been attracted by the connection between morality and politics and did not want to swamp the population in rifles and hand grenades.'[172] This was very much a minority view. Buoyed up by the popularity of the LDF, Hulton and Wintringham set up, as a piece of private initiative, the legendary training camp at Osterley Park in July 1940 under Wintringham's control, till an impressed but politically concerned War Office took over affairs the following year, dispensing with the 'red' Wintringham, but not his training methods.

Wintringham's boss, Hulton, was a central figure in the emergence of the second organisation that was to feed into Common Wealth, the 1941 Committee. This emerged in the winter of 1940–1 as a gathering of notables who regularly met in Hulton's Mayfair house. It was a loose, fluid group, with people coming and going. There were publishers such as Victor Gollancz and Stanley Unwin, journalists in the form of Kingsley Martin and Ritchie Calder, academics, including C.E.M. Joad and A.D. Lindsay, and the artists Augustus John and David Low – there was even a bishop (Bradford). From the perspective of the later emergence of Common Wealth, other members were the novelist and playwright J.B. Priestley, Wintringham himself (eventually), John Macmurray and Acland.[173] In one sense homogeneous – the members were essentially well heeled and well known – there was, nonetheless, within a broadly common 'progressive' agenda (linking the winning of the war to social reform) a heterogeneity of opinion. To H.G. Wells, who was briefly a member, this diversity spoke of weakness: 'this well-meaning (but otherwise meaningless) miscellany of people,' he waspishly recalled, 'so earnestly and obstinately going in every direction under their vehement professions of unity'.[174] To Acland the Committee provided a new arena for promoting his plans for a radical social movement. Increasingly assisted by Wintringham, he pushed for the adoption by the committee of his Common Ownership proposals, encouraged the move to set up local branches, and sought to steer the organisation away from a ginger-group to something more like Forward March.

In a foretaste of the 'religious' battles that lay ahead in Common Wealth, Acland and Wells crossed swords on the question of religion and education. The Committee itself expressed emollient, if vague, sentiments about the need for 'spirituality' in the modern world, maintaining

> that spiritual values are fundamental for a real civilisation, that man has an individuality which must be preserved, and that the purpose of all the plans we advocate is a nobler quality of life, the fullest development and expression of the human personality.[175]

Following the Malvern conference with, in Wells's words, its 'marvellously pseudo-socialistic pronouncement' in which Acland 'was very active and inspiring', Wells decided that an opportunity has been created 'to define my widening detachment' from the Committee and to 'assist in the disintegration' of the organisation. He therefore tabled a resolution that was sure to ruffle feathers – particularly those of Acland. Mischievously explicit, emollient it was not:

> The 1941 Committee welcomes the belated realization by the Christian Churches of the profound revolutionary quality of the teachings of Jesus of Nazareth but in view of the fact that it has taken the various Christian ecclesiastical organizations nineteen centuries to make that discovery, the 1941 Committee protests strongly against the proposal to hand back education to their sluggish or insincere control. The 1941 Committee calls for a vigorous revision and extension of education throughout the world upon modern lines unencumbered by Christian, Shinto, Jewish or other priestly assumptions.[176]

Having lit the blue touchpaper Wells stood back to view the effect. An immediate consequence was that 'a lively evening' ensued in the Committee. Wells claimed that although 'the consciences of the members were generally with me ... this motion meant death to most of their private schemes' and therefore his proposal was rendered invisible by procedural manoeuvre – 'recorded, but that no action be taken'.[177] To his great regret, he recalled, Acland, 'at whom I was aiming in particular', was absent. In Acland's recollection he certainly gives the impression that he *was* a witness to this rejection of Wells's motion. He referred to the matter in 1942, following the creation of Common Wealth, when a number of Roman Catholic papers had referred to the Wells motion to argue that Common Wealth was anti-Christian. In a letter to the *Catholic Times* Acland, while declaring that neither the 1941Committee nor Forward March were specifically Christian, did stress the strong Christian presence brought to bear on both organisations by himself and (in the case of the 1941 Committee) by John Macmurray, and indicating that Wells was an unrepresentative maverick member of the

Committee. His spin on the meeting is significantly different from that provided by Wells:

> I am sorry that the Wells Resolution on Education has been taken up as a stick with which to beat the 1941 Committee. It is a fact that Wells as an early member of the 1941 Committee presented his resolution to us and asked us to pass it. This proposal aroused heated controversy in which if I remember rightly one or two members present agreed with Wells, but the rest disagreed, some of them with the utmost violence. The resolution was never passed, but it was noted … 'had been received' … As from about one week after this episode Mr Wells took no further part in the work of the 1941 Committee.[178]

Whether or not Wells read this letter is not known, but he certainly did note that the *Catholic Herald* discussed Acland in 'a friendly manner' in 1943, 'recommending him to the politically minded faithful' – a sure sign of a wrong 'un in Wells's eyes.[179] The whole incident was a warning of what could happen when Acland's burgeoning moral/political campaign began to attract strong-minded individuals who construed matters of morality – indeed morality itself – in ways very different to his own.

Throughout 1941 Acland had to carry on his political and literary career from an army hut. He had been conscripted into the army and, waiving his right of exemption as an MP, had been sent to Scotland to become a gunner in an anti-aircraft training regiment where he resolutely refused to seek a commission as an officer. Whereas he loved this time, a move to a regiment near London was less successful. To this push factor was added the pull of political life – particularly his work in Forward March and the 1941 Committee. A strong sense of duty, however, of not wishing to leave the fighting to others, kept him in uniform. The thing that actually persuaded him to leave the services in early 1942 was a political discussion he had with his fellow soldiers one evening over attempts by the government to close down the *Daily Mirror* on the grounds that its criticism of government policy, particularly in scathing cartoons, was undermining morale; this seemed to have so exasperated one soldier that he shouted at Acland: 'And what the bloody hell are you doing piddling around here as a soldier when you're the only one in the whole fucking army that can go and talk for us in the sodding House of Commons?'[180] And so he left the army. Later, clearly musing on the theme of morale, he drew a comparison between his situation and the able-bodied men diverted to travelling concert parties in the war. Their position was justified in terms of raising morale. His political work could, at the very least, be construed in this way: 'even if you only count our effort as "morale boosting" I think we earned our keep'.[181]

Thus, by the summer of 1942 Acland had travelled some distance since he had been elected to the House of Commons in 1935. His liberalism had gradually given way to socialism, but it was a socialism which had retained important elements of his liberal heritage. The resulting synthesis bemused a number of contemporaries who found it difficult to plot Acland on to the ideological map of Britain, and raised the suspicion, articulated by H.G. Wells, that Acland was an opportunistic eclectic interested in personal power. Acland had also become a Christian in the wake of both intellectual reconsideration, prompted by 'Hadham'/Parkes, and mystical experience, and had arrived at the notion of a personal God after a problematic relationship with the ideas of Kenneth Ingram. Compared with Macmurray, Ingram and Stapledon, his was a relatively 'orthodox' religion, but, as with all his beliefs, idiosyncrasies shone through. Finally, he had become an increasingly odd-looking Liberal member of parliament. Appalled by the domestic and international policy of the National Government he became attracted to strategies such as the Popular Front, which spoke of fundamental political realignment in Britain and a focus on movement politics. This was the trajectory that had brought about his creation of Forward March, and his involvement in the 1941 Committee. The next stage in Acland's journey was to involve a new organisation, Common Wealth.

# 5   The moment of Common Wealth

July 1942 saw the emergence of Common Wealth out of Forward March and the 1941 Committee. In terms of the 1941 Committee the vital figure in the merger was the writer and playwright J.B. Priestley (1894–1984). Priestley had become a figure of national importance through his weekly morale-boosting radio broadcasts, and had become chairman of the 1941 Committee. Acland liked and respected Priestley, and the latter clearly thought he could work with Acland. Increasingly the two organisations began to work in concert, though it was clear that both sides sought to produce a merger in which their conceptions and interests predominated. Acland recalled his difficulties in getting the Committee 'to treat us as equals. Their idea was camouflaged absorption',[1] and he himself was busy using his dual membership to steer the Committee down his preferred path. The formal merger took place in London on 26 July 1942, with Priestley becoming president and Acland one of the vice-presidents. Priestley had wanted the new organisation to be called the 'League for Democratic Victory',[2] Acland canvassed for 'Reality' ('it gives you the description of your individual member, – "I am a Realist"'),[3] but it was Tom Wintringham's suggestions – the 'People's Common Wealth Movement' and the 'Common Wealth Freedom Movement' – that, via the adjudication of Priestley, produced 'Common Wealth'.[4]

Acland had no doubts that Forward March had prevailed in the merger. This he attributed to the fundamentally different nature of the two bodies – the centre of gravity of the 1941 Committee was its grandees while Forward March was supported by a national grass-roots organisation; thus Priestley 'had the names ... but ... we had the branches ... We hadn't really amalgamated with The 1941 Committee, we'd eaten it'.[5] Priestley himself quickly felt ill at ease in the new body, and resigned as president within three weeks. As Acland saw it, Priestley, for perfectly good reasons, didn't want to become the full-time leader of a professional political body, having preferred the more relaxed and leisurely ways of the 1941 Committee:

> Priestley's abilities and interests were far wider than mine. I was a politician and nothing else; I had no other abilities and wanted to spend all my time

on it. Priestley had enormous abilities as an author and playwright and wanted to spend less than 24 hours per month on politics.[6]

This good-natured, if spiky, appraisal of Priestley is matched by Priestley's assessment of Acland, contained in an introduction he contributed to Acland's 1943 book *How It Can Be Done*:

> I sometimes hear people say that Acland is 'woolly'. Now that is just what he isn't. He may be intolerant, fanatical, tactless, humourless, too impatient, but he is anything but 'woolly' ... Acland says what he means – though sometimes he is in such a hurry that he does not say it very well – and means what he says. I can write of him with some detachment, for though I agree with most of his conclusions, both his temperament and his approach are different from mine ... He is much more of an Old Testament character, just striding in from the wilderness; whereas I am a more easy-going modern type ... But, in spite of some rumours to the contrary, we arrive in the same place, if only between the covers of this book.[7]

With very few exceptions the big names of the 1941 Committee did not join Common Wealth. Besides Priestley, Vernon Bartlett, MP, the victor of the Bridgewater by-election, joined. Two others should be noted, for their entry was to reverberate in the religious struggles to come – Tom Wintringham and John Macmurray.

## Common Wealth

To his great surprise the person chosen to succeed Priestley as chairman of Commonwealth in October 1942 was that begetter of Acland's conversion the Rev. James Parkes ('John Hadham'). Parkes later speculated that the reason such diverse figures (including Acland and Tom Wintringham) supported him was the fact that he was entirely new to the upper circles (though he had been a member of Forward March), and therefore carried no baggage from the merger manoeuvres and the Priestly split.[8] His wife Dorothy Wickings maintained that the fact that he was a clergyman made him an attractive proposition, as 'a safe cover for the organization'.[9] Acland undoubtedly admired him and owed him a considerable spiritual debt. Religious affinity also figured in the man who had nominated Parkes for membership of the national committee of Common Wealth (whence his elevation to chairman) – Tom Sargant.[10] It is worth saying a little at this point about Sargant because as 1943 dawned ideological opponents within Common Wealth began to lump Acland, Parkes and Sargant together as a troika promoting a transcendentalist and moralistic Christianity.

Tom Sargant (1905–88) grew up in a house with a strong Methodist and Liberal ethos.[11] After Highgate School he was unable to take up a scholarship to Cambridge owing to his father's financial difficulties, instead working in the family business till it folded. Until 1947 he worked in the Royal Mint refinery, rising to a managerial position. He came to Acland's attention through a book he published in 1941 entitled *These Things Shall Be*. It is an idiosyncratic little work, difficult to define. Politically it is broadly leftist in its economic critique – taking to task, for example, Archbishop Temple's statement at Malvern that only excessive interest was unchristian[12] – but is hostile to the existing leftist parties and expresses anti-egalitarian and nationalist, indeed imperialist, sentiments. Theologically, Sargant singles out for praise the contributions at Malvern made by the Rev. V.L. Demant and Dorothy L. Sayers (noting their 'eloquent pleas for the necessity and reasonableness of Christian dogma'[13]), and condemns 'Modernist religion' in the words of 2 Timothy 3:5 as 'having the form of godliness but denying the power thereof';[14] yet he is also attracted to alchemical, occultist, astrological and mystical currents of thought (partly as an alternative to the 'whirlpool of unfathomable arguments and unpicturable concepts' of 'Einstein and his disciples').[15] Acland seems to have been sufficiently impressed to encourage Sargant to join Forward March, and he quickly gravitated to the heights of this movement, and of Common Wealth, serving on a number of leading committees.

Acland was elected president of Common Wealth at the first annual conference of the organisation in April 1943, with Parkes as one of the vice-presidents. The other vice-president was Tom Wintringham.[16] Without diminishing the importance of other figures in the leadership of Common Wealth, particularly the chairman, R.W.G. MacKay, who was a major influence on political strategy and internal organisations,[17] the edgy and often explosive relationship between Acland and Wintringham was at the heart of the ideological drama of the movement. Quite apart from personality differences, Wintringham's atheistic Marxism, which scorned talk of 'morality', and his revolutionary leftism were always going to sit uneasily with the biblical Christianity and parliamentarianism of Acland. Their correspondence reads more like that of a passionate couple than political associates, at times intimate and friendly, at others formal and chilly, sometimes in agreement, often brutally at odds, here compliments, there appalling rudeness. And underlying it all was genuine mutual respect – 'a happy fact', Acland later recalled, 'was that even at the worst moments we retained a good deal of affection and respect for each other'.[18]

Kenneth Ingram and John Macmurray were, in different ways, important figures in Common Wealth. Ingram was one of the nine members of the Policy Committee, the body that supervised the day-to-day running of the organisation.[19] He was also on the governing Executive Committee, where he had a special responsibility for Foreign Affairs and Foreign Policy, and it was his task to introduce debates on these areas at the annual conference.[20] More informally, he was a member of what Acland termed 'our ideational team'. In what was meant as a slapdown to Mackay, the general secretary, Acland indicated to Mackay who were members of this 'team' (and who were not fully!) and its commanding role:

Take our ideational team as it is today [31 August 1943]. Myself, Tom [Wintringham], Ingram, Macmurray, Parkes ... *and* Alan Good [treasurer] and yourself on your ideational sides, because of course no one is quite exclusively of one type or the other. But there it is. That is the ideational team. And unless I'm forced to resign, that team, as an ideational team, sucking up ideas from others and co-ordinating them, discussing them, yes, and taking votes on them in the movement as a whole, but, in brief handling ideas and presenting them to the movement, that team is on top, and the organization as a whole, and you in your capacity as head of the organization as a whole, serve that team.[21]

In Macmurray's case, apart from membership of a little-used appeals committee (which also contained the Rev. Mervyn Stockwood, the future Bishop of Southwark),[22] his role was exclusively 'ideational'. Calder's description of his position in the higher echelons of the movement – 'a 'magisterial grey eminence' – seems about right.[23] Acland in later life spoke of 'all that ... [he] ... had gained by association with Professor John Macmurray, a member of Common Wealth who was unconcerned with our week-to-week problems but was a guide on fundamental issues'.[24] Macmurray's influence had a wide reach with, on occasions, both Acland and Wintringham trading, and disputing the meaning of, Macmurray quotes to substantiate diametrically opposed policies.[25] Macmurray was heavily involved in the creation of a preamble to Common Wealth's constitution with his 'philosophical disquisition' forming the basis of a draft presented to Conference.[26] That both Acland and Wintringham could draw on Macmurray indicates the extent to which Macmurray (and Ingram) occupied a theoretical space that seemed to offer some support to very different positions – Wintringham could point to their admiration for Marxist materialism, and Acland to their religious roots and professed Christianity. These expectations were soon to be put to the test.

Angus Calder's research on Common Wealth enables us to get a sense of the nature of the organisation.[27] He calculated that at its peak Common Wealth had up to fifteen thousand members organised in over three hundred branches; these were spread around the country but with particular concentrations in London and Merseyside, and relative weakness in Wales and Scotland. One fifth of the membership were in the armed forces (which, as the 1945 election revealed, was an important location for radical hopes). The membership was predominantly middle class and relatively young (with a preponderance of 30- to 45-year-olds). Thanks to the generosity of its treasurer Alan P. Good (who contributed over £30,000 to the movement) and of Acland himself Common Wealth was able to afford a well-staffed London office, and a polished propaganda effort, though finances were in time to become dangerously stretched.

A fundamental part of Common Wealth strategy was to get involved in by-elections. There was a wartime electoral truce between the Conservative, Labour and Liberal parties where vacant seats were not contested. Common

Wealth decided that when a Conservative seat was vacated they would either support a likely independent socialist candidate or put forward a candidate of their own. 'I was assailed in the Smoking Room [of the Commons],' Acland recalled, 'with a virulence quite abnormal as between one MP and others. I was breaking the Party Truce! I was revealing, or even creating, disunity in the face of the enemy.'[28] Even before the creation of Common Wealth, when the 1941 Committee and Forward March had been working together, an opportunity arose. One evening in May 1942 the journalist Tom Driberg heard on the radio that the Conservative MP for Maldon had died. Driberg lived in the constituency, and recalled a conversation he had had with Tom Hopkinson, editor of *Picture Post*, and member of the 1941 Committee, about the need to contest Conservatives in by-elections. 'There was something else, too,' Driberg later wrote.

> On the carpet in front of my gas fire was stretched out, naked, the slender, rangy form of my Canadian soldier friend, S. I must have betrayed some interest at the brief news item ... I must even have said something to the effect that I might stand for Parliament myself. I remember that he hooted with laughter and said such words as 'You'd never do it – and, if you did, you'd never make it.' Perhaps this challenge fortified my recollection of Tom Hopkinson's approach.[29]

Once Driberg had put his name forward (as an independent candidate under the slogan 'A Candid Friend for Churchill')[30] things moved with great rapidity. To Acland the atmosphere must have reminded him of the Bridgwater contest. As there, support came from all sorts of people and across the political spectrum. Driberg was immensely impressed by Acland's electoral savvy:

> Despite his almost George Washington reputation for Christian integrity ... Acland is no starry-eyed dreamer: I know of no one better versed in the tactics and technique of modern electioneering – and he could lecture key workers and helpers on how to do a job while at the same time infecting them with enthusiasm for it.[31]

Acland laid out a route-map for Driberg: 'It's now 13 days to polling day; we must spend nine days organising and four days winning.'[32] And win they did. Possibly assisted by news of the military disaster in North Africa that was the fall of Tobruk, Driberg romped home – a second independent candidate polled 1,476 votes, the Tory candidate got 6,226 votes, but Driberg received a commanding 12,219 votes; this in a constituency that in 1935 had given the Conservative 17,072 votes against the Labour candidate's 9,264 – the Conservative vote had thus dropped by 22 per cent.[33]

The first actual Common Wealth MP was Acland himself. With the creation of Common Wealth Acland's status as a Liberal MP, long anomalous, was no longer sustainable. It would appear that he officially ceased to be a Liberal

MP on 30 September 1942.[34] It was probably at this time that by means of an audacious bluff he managed to prevent the Liberal Party from replacing him as MP for North Devon. As he noted, with some understatement, 'London Liberal headquarters was naturally concerned at having one of the few Liberal seats represented by a Socialist', and, he believed, wanted to replace him with a person he describes as 'one of the most un-Liberal men who ever walked' (Harcourt Johnson). A crucial meeting was held in North Devon where Acland offered the party a choice: he could either resign immediately and then fight a by-election against the new official Liberal candidate or the party could let him stay put and he would promise not to fight the seat in the first post-war election. He then left the meeting to its deliberations: 'I sat on the sea's edge for some two hours while they debated their decision; I didn't at that time see much chance of winning if they chose the first alternative. But they chose the second.'[35] And so Acland remained the MP for North Devon until 1945 when he honoured his agreement and fought for Common Wealth in another constituency.

By the time of the 1945 General Election Acland had been joined by three Common Wealth MPs, all the products of by-election victories: Eddisbury (April 1943), Skipton (January 1944) and Chelmsford (April 1945). Of the remaining nine constituencies in which Common Wealth had put up a Common Wealth candidate (as opposed to supporting an Independent) only Tom Wintringham came close to victory in North Midlothian in February 1943 with 48 per cent of the vote, and just under nine hundred votes behind.[36] Even where it failed it received significant vote swings, as in the five by-elections it contested in early 1944, where it registered swings of between 6 and 11 per cent in its favour. Acland maintained that since two groups that tended to vote left were disenfranchised (21- to 25-year-olds, because the electoral register had not been updated since 1939, and those on military service) he calculated that the swings would have been in the order of 16–21 per cent;[37] in this vein he suggested that it was no coincidence that Common Wealth's arithmetically most successful result – Chelmsford, where Millington 'turned the 12,000 Conservative majority of 1935 into a 6,000 majority for Common Wealth ... [A] swing of 28.3 per cent in our favour' – occurred in the wake of the revision of the 1939 electoral register.[38] In total Common Wealth received almost 100,000 votes over the twelve by-elections.[39] Its wins showed that Common Wealth was able to contest very varied types of constituency, including places in which other left-wing parties had feared to tread. Thus Eddisbury was an almost totally rural constituency in Cheshire, so alien to the Labour Party that they had never once attempted to field a candidate.[40] Skilful candidate selection, and enthusiastic and industrious canvassing by Common Wealth members and local volunteers were also paramount. Thus three young servicemen, Warrant Officer John Loverseed, Wing-Commander Ernest Millington and Lieutenant Hugh Lawson, were the victors at Eddisbury, Chelmsford and Skipton, and each was assisted by hundreds of diligent canvassers. Again, as in Acland's campaigns in Bridgwater and Maldon, the candidates were able to gain, for a variety of reasons, support from members, and supporters, of other parties and from those with no previous political affiliation. Among those by-elections in which Common Wealth supported other socialist candidates, as in their backing of Jennie Lee (Independent Labour Party) for Bristol Central in February 1943, the contest Acland looked back on with most enjoyment was that of West Derbyshire in February 1944.[41] This constituency had been in the grip of the Tory Devonshire family since its creation in 1885, apart from a brief period from 1918 to 1923 when a Liberal cobbler, Charles Frederick White, won the seat. In the by-election the Conservative candidate was the Duke of Devonshire's son, Lord Hartington. With a certain degree of symmetry the cobbler's son, Charlie White, announced his candidacy as an Independent Labour. Acland immediately sprang into action and parachuted in an electoral team; 'our organisation ran his whole campaign,' he later wrote. This was just the sort of contest that appealed to Common Wealth activists and supporters – 'No one mentioned Common Ownership,' Acland recalled. 'It was democratic right against feudal privilege. Hartington never had a chance.' Churchill and the coalition government sent support and speakers to Hartington, while leftists from the Communist Party to the Labour Party threw in their lot with White. Hartington got 11,775 votes, but White emerged victorious with 16,336, which Acland reckoned was a 17 per cent swing 'in our favour'.[42]

In terms of its ideology Common Wealth's official statements can be found in the central policy documents published by the organisation, notably the *Common Wealth Manifesto* authorised by conference. At the heart of these declarations are two perennial Common Wealth concepts – Common Ownership and Vital Democracy.

*Common Ownership*  This is the theme most deeply rooted in Acland's own theoretical odyssey. All 'great productive resources'[43] are to be 'wholly transferred'[44] to Common Ownership. The *Manifesto* provides a sizeable list of these resources: all land, all credit and investment institutions, all fuel and power, all water-supply, all transport, all 'important materials' (such as iron, chemicals, etc.), all industries manufacturing capital equipment, all large enterprises manufacturing everyday goods, and 'all large-scale trading and distributive enterprises'.[45] In line with a long-standing conviction of Acland's, compensation would be paid to existing owners but on a sliding scale, with the 'smallest owners' receiving 100 per cent of the value of their assets, while the largest would receive only a very small percentage of asset value.[46] Ownership was strictly distinguished from 'control' where there is merely government regulation of private ownership, which, it is argued in *Questions and Answers About Common Wealth's Policy*, rapidly degenerates into 'the private ownership of public control' – the road to 'Fascism', where capital totally captures the state.[47] Private property will still exist, as in housing, but nothing that 'will enable you to live as a parasite on the labour of others'.[48] Common Ownership is to be expressed through democratic planning mechanisms with a 'major plan' to be constructed by 'the elected representatives of the community';[49] implementation at the plant level is to be in the hands of salaried managers, technicians and workers. In arguing this Common Wealth sought to rebut claims that Common Ownership would involve bureaucratic control by 'a whole lot of civil servants'.[50]

*Vital Democracy* This was a term that emerged out of the 1941 Committee rather than Forward March. The aim is to create 'a democracy which is a living freedom, not dead, formal or buried in red tape'.[51] A whole range of political/constitutional changes are demanded, with the focus very much on the parliamentary – how one is to refresh its membership, make it more efficient, more representative, more effective, how it can be supplemented by other institutions. Some proposals are immediately political: the end of the electoral truce and updating of the electoral register – both necessary to 'renew parliament' by unfreezing the party pattern determined by the election of 1935.[52] Some measures are concerned with electoral reform. Thus the first-past-the-post single-member-constituency contest is rejected, as is any form of plural voting. Instead, proportional representation with the single transferable vote is to be introduced with constituencies electing between three and five members. Attendance at the polling station is to be made compulsory – though with the right to register a non-vote or a negative-vote, and the franchise has to be extended to include all men and women over the age of 18.[53] At the constitutional level the House of Lords is to be abolished,[54] and Scotland and Wales are to have their own devolved assemblies. Local government is to be encouraged, with local councils given greater competencies and powers and restrictions on the local franchise removed.[55] Since Vital Democracy was deemed to be about ensuring maximum participation by individuals, the term was also used to designate participation in the social and economic sphere as in various schemes of industrial democracy designed to facilitate worker input into the production process, spreading the democratic from the purely political sphere.[56] From this aspect Vital Democracy could be viewed as encapsulating the democratic principles underpinning Common Ownership.

*Other themes* Common Wealth had a series of international and geopolitical aspirations. Acland had long called for a dismantling of the old model of European colonial empires, and this was included in the *Common Wealth Manifesto* under the slogan 'Freedom for the Colonies'. The goal was 'that at the earliest possible moment, steps be taken to give the colonial people full economic and political self-government'. India, in particular, was singled out as ripe for independence, and specific measures to transfer power to the Indians were outlined.[57] There were also long-term aspirations towards 'world unity'. A democratic European Federation was called for to begin to transcend the dangers inherent in claims to national sovereignty. At an even grander level a World Council was envisaged to supervise the activities of a World Economic Council and to implement the decisions of a World Court.[58]

Many years later, Acland argued that developments in the war undermined the possibility that Common Wealth's most ambitious plans would be achieved, and that from the middle of 1942 he 'half understood' this to be the case.[59] His argument was that in the early days of the war, when Britain was the last power fighting the Nazis and very close to defeat, he could make the plausible case that the only way military defeat could be staved off was by radical social reorganisation – social justice and winning the war were thus inextricably linked. The entry into the war of the USSR and, above all, the USA transformed matters. It was now possible to argue that military victory could be achieved without a thoroughgoing social transformation. 'In retrospect,' he argued, 'America's entry was associated with the defeat of our political ideas.' This dawning realisation, he argued, became more widespread, and marked the political and ideological strategy of Common Wealth:

> Our conversations shifted ... We talked less about changes needed to win the war and more about changes we hoped would be made in a victorious post-war Britain. Slowly we stopped believing in a thoroughly socialist country after the war and settled instead for the nationalisation of a few major industries as a satisfactory step in the first five post-war years.[60]

How much of this is hindsight it is difficult to determine. It can, however, be said that in the by-election campaigns Common Wealth candidates were very keen to stress the tangible social and economic benefits that their election to parliament would help to promote. Much of this coalesced around the call for the full implementation of the Beveridge Report (1942) with its plans for a welfare state, which the government had shelved. Whatever the ultimate aspirations of the Common Wealth activists their willingness to throw their weight behind Beveridge positioned them *in reality* in the tide of leftist welfarism. In this sense Acland's half-understanding of the trajectory of Common Wealth was not inaccurate.

## The debates about religion

The historian Paul Addison has called Common Wealth 'an idealistic movement'.[61] Now 'idealistic' is a notoriously slippery concept, and would have been – and was – rejected by significant members of Common Wealth, who associated the word with unacceptable political and philosophical positions which they defined as 'idealism'. But 'idealistic' does convey an important flavour of the organisation. In the main Common Wealth had grown out of bodies that had brought together people deeply dissatisfied with the opportunistic and hypocritical politics of the 1930s, and who yearned for a new social order – people who had frequently become estranged from former party loyalties, or who previously had no such loyalties. Once established Common Wealth was able to further attract people of a similar disposition. In the 'summary' to the *Common Wealth Manifesto* the 'purpose and programme' of the movement is summed up thus: 'It is no use tinkering with the past. It is no use compromising between past and future. We must reject the past, and begin to build a new social order'[62] – a critical and anticipatory sentiment that was common to all the sections of the movement.

Before looking at the deep divisions underlying such unity, however, we should note an act of Acland's that contained a strong measure of personal idealism – the transfer of his West Country family estates to the National Trust in 1943–4, which, at 17,000 acres was, and remains, the largest ever single acquisition by the Trust. As Mary Hilson and Joseph Melling show in their study of this transfer, it was not a simple gift on Acland's part; he in effect sold his estates to the Trust, but at nothing like their market value.[63] His motivations included a fear that death duties would lead to the break-up of the estates, a desire to pump money into a debt-ridden Common Wealth, the need to purchase a London property appropriate for a political leader, and a frankly political eye for how the act would play out in Common Wealth and in the country.[64] He could even, as we saw earlier, view it as evidence of a divine providence looking after the fortunes of Common Wealth (CW), as he wrote to a sceptical Kitty Wintringham at the time:

> The handing of my property to the National Trust is the result of thought and negotiation stretching back to December; the event comes just so late that CW has already proved, by its by-election results, that it owes nothing to a 'political–personal stunt' by 'its leader'; and yet just soon enough so that in the negotiations that must be going on between us and Labour, and within Labour, our enemies are deprived of their slickest and easiest argument, namely that CW is another Mosley show under a new Mosley.[65]

None of which should detract from the fact that Acland was also acting on a principled opposition to the private ownership of large estates, a principle he had been articulating in his publications and speeches for some time, and which he now, in the face of some fierce family opposition,[66] was putting into practice in his own affairs.

This element of idealism was, as previously stated, very evident in Common Wealth. However, when the issue of the foundations of belief and action was raised it became crystal clear that the sources of idealism in the membership were radically heterogeneous. Common Wealth's rise had brought into its fold individuals with hugely divergent world views, divisions evident in the highest reaches of the movement. Furthermore, Acland, the person most associated with Common Wealth, was the author of *It Must Be Christianity* and made no bones about the importance he attached to his Christian faith, and the movement's chairman, after Priestley, was a Church of England clergyman – the Rev. James Parkes. Inevitably, therefore, the debate about philosophical and political foundations would become a struggle over the role of religion and morality – a struggle, moreover, that would continue unresolved through the life of the movement till the 1945 General Election imposed its own

152  *The moment of Common Wealth*

closure. Before turning to the multi-faceted battle that commenced in 1943, let us begin with a couple of individual skirmishes – the Rev. George Jager's critique of Macmurray and Ingram and his anxiety about Acland's association with the pair, and Olaf Stapledon's assault on *It Must Be Christianity*.

### 'Orthodoxy' vs 'religion' – the Rev. George Jager

This occurred in the period of the birth of Common Wealth. Throughout 1941 and into 1942, flushed with the relative success of their interventions at Malvern, Acland and Ingram addressed gatherings of clergy around the country promoting the link between Christianity and Common Ownership. In early 1942 nine-tenths of a conference of 200 clergy in Liverpool called for a further conference where practical measures to bring about Common Ownership could be discussed.[67] Two months later this conference met in Leicester under the auspices of the Left Book Club. It is clear that various shades of left-wing clergy were present: James Parkes, who was a participant, told Angus Calder that he remembered 'one Rector of an Anglican Church hissing through clenched teeth at another that he was a "Trotskyite"'.[68] The conference established the Council of Clergy and Ministers for Common Ownership – a body that was to be rapidly captured by Communist sympathisers.[69] Ingram was elected secretary of the Council and the Bishop of Bradford its president. It was the apparent closeness between Acland and Ingram that disturbed one participant, the Rev. George Jager, Vicar of Billesley. Shortly after the conference Jager wrote to Acland – a letter that Acland intriguingly annotated with the words 'Very Important'.[70] As we have already seen, by this date (June 1942) Acland had publicly broken, via the *Forward March* footnote, with Ingram's conception of God, but either Jager was unaware of this fact, or he was aware of it but thought Acland had not sufficiently distanced himself from his Malvern colleague (Jager too had been at Malvern).[71] Jager in his letter to Acland upbraided him for his practice of 'pairing ... [himself] with Kenneth Ingram when appealing to Christians and their ministers';[72] and he was forthright in his condemnation of Ingram, and of Macmurray:

> you should know that to me, and, judging from an S.C.M. [Student Christian Movement] theological conference that I attended, to the most alive of the ministers of my generation, the names of Ingram and Macmurray stand for a school of theological thought that we have considered and rejected.

Although finding one or two things in Ingram acceptable Jager condemns Ingram for 'his shallow empirical ("does it work for me?") approach', his 'very arbitrary use of words', 'seeing only in them the meaning that he wishes to see' (a trait 'he ... shares with Macmurray'), and his 'assumption that Jesus was a Marxist'. Ingram and Macmurray are deemed to be old hat, frozen in the 'Modernism' of their twenties. Instead, Jager recommends such 'live parsons' as the Bishop of Bradford and William Temple who are left-wing in politics but '"right wing" in theology', and among thinkers of the past the Victorian Christian Socialist F.D. Maurice, 'who found the basis of his political unorthodoxy in deepening, instead of contradicting, the orthodox religious thought of his time, and all time'. Jager ends his letter with a warning that Acland's association with Ingram is in serious danger of alienating the more orthodox Christian supporters of Forward March:

> I am sure that [Ingram] ... is a valuable member of the Forward March committee, but I do strongly suggest that when you are appealing to Church people, you should not, without very serious further consideration, gratuitously associate yourself with one who is chiefly known among us as the unrepentant exponent of a discarded heresy.
>
> This is a long and rather blunt letter, and it has taken me a long time to write. I write it because I am very anxious that your very live political thought should so separate itself from what is really alive *and true* in theology.

There is certainly evidence that Jagers' claim about a generational shift in British theology was shared in theological circles at the time. An article in a theological journal from the early months of the war asserted that 'the older men are to a greater or lesser degree liberals, while the younger are demanding a return to dogma'.[73] Calder argues that the decline of 'Modernism' from its heyday in the 1920s had been notably assisted by the growing popularity of the theology of Karl Barth with its strong sense of the mighty gap between God and humanity.[74] And it is the case that John Macmurray viewed Barth as a negative though potent force whose transcendentalism generated depoliticisation. As he wrote to a correspondent in 1936:

> I don't think you can combine Barth and me ... Barth's *effect* is to push God farther into the sky, whatever he may *say*. He releases Christians, by his emotional effect, from their own immanent responsibility. They cannot understand history – so why try?[75]

Thus, while Macmurray would have repudiated Jager's claims as to heresy, he would have recognised the background to which Jager was referring.

Since we don't possess Acland's response to Jager we have to infer its content from Jager's next letter.[76] Evidently Acland was at pains to reassure Jager that he had indeed broken theologically with Ingram, for Jager says that 'he was very glad to get' the reply and heartened, it would appear, by Acland's account of his theological relationship with Ingram, adopts a confessional tone: 'you may well be right in claiming that "Ingramism" is an essential stage on many folks' pilgrimage towards full Christian belief; and I passed through something like it myself'. But he is not done castigating Acland – 'I still think that it was misplaced modesty for you to have linked your name with Ingram's for the Leicester conference. I think it was partly responsible for what seemed to me to be the disappointing small attendance at Leicester.' In one final sortie, written a couple of months later, Jager, now vice-chairman of the Regional Common Wealth Committee on the basis of his attendance at the Church Union Summer School of Sociology in Oxford, returns to his attack on Ingram and Macmurray.[77] In the case of Macmurray he reiterates his point about him having no influence on significant Christian theology, though as a politically inclined cleric he does concede merit in Macmurray's desire to unite theory and practice. Turning to Ingram, Jager provides evidence that the root of the hostility of many clergymen to Ingram is his work on sexuality: 'I had confirmation of my point that your connection with Ingram is not helpful with these churchpeople, though it is his books on sex which really damn him in their eyes.' Taken in connection with the controversy between Ingram and William Temple over Ingram's *Sex-Morality Tomorrow*, which revealed that Anglican lay people, the Bishop of London and Temple himself found Ingram's views on sexuality deeply provocative, Jager's remark indicates that to a number of laity and clergy (including at least one member of Common Wealth) Ingram's sexual unorthodoxy marks him out as more than simply a maverick theologian – a person, indeed, to quote Temple, with 'extremely unsound and dangerous views' on sexuality.[78]

It is difficult to know whether this interchange had any significant effect on Acland, though the annotated 'Very Important' is significant. It must surely have concentrated his mind on how he differed from Ingram, and there is no evidence of any further public theological double-acts involving himself and Ingram. It would also have alerted him to the possible political costs of offending more mainstream theological positions. Furthermore, the fact that, as Calder notes, 'Anglican clergy ... were often prominent in the formation of branches' of Common Wealth would not have been lost on Acland.[79] Certainly in the later battle with the radicals he did everything he could to avoid statements that might appear provocative to the more 'orthodox' appearing in official Common Wealth documents.

### 'Must It Be Christianity?' Olaf Stapledon

Unlike Acland, Ingram and Macmurray, Stapledon was primarily a regional member of Common Wealth.[80] His home was on the Wirral peninsula, and it was here that his political work was based. This was where he wrote material in support of the organisation, and from where he occasionally travelled down to London on Common Wealth business. It was in Cheshire, Lancashire and North Wales that he gave his talks, raised funds, helped in by-elections and generally took part in local branch activities. He was therefore not a part of the central London leadership – being chairman of the Merseyside branch of Common Wealth was more than enough to a man who was not naturally drawn to the daily disciplines of political life.[81] Stapledon began his association in the early Our Struggle/Forward March days. In early May 1940 he is to be seen selling tickets for a meeting to be addressed by Acland in Liverpool. His observations on Acland are mixed: 'He is not an orator or a great leader,' he wrote to his daughter, but 'he has the right approach, and gets hold of the middle class people';[82] similarly to Naomi Mitchison: 'not a great leader, but I think he struck the right note for the moment'.[83] It would appear that Stapledon began to gain greater visibility as a Forward March member and activist because he was to be part of the Forward March team that negotiated the birth of Common Wealth with the 1941 Committee in the middle of 1942.[84] In 1943, given the closeness of the Eddisbury constituency to his own home it was not surprising that he was an energetic canvasser for Common Wealth's first by-election victor, John Loverseed (and with his wife hosted a celebratory lunch for the new MP).[85] In his papers are preserved lecture notes for talks he gave explaining and promoting Common Wealth principles in a range of North West venues, from Preston to Wrexham, and from St Helens to Ellesmere Port. He published articles in the *Common Wealth Review*, and a short pamphlet, *Seven Pillars of Peace*, in Common Wealth's 'Popular Library' series (a series that also contained Ingram's *Religion and the New Society* and, flagged but not published, *Personal and Social Values* by John Macmurray). Acland must have been sufficiently impressed by his performance to ask Stapledon to agree to stand as a Common Wealth candidate for the Wirral as soon as the first post-war General Election was called. Stapledon declined, on the grounds that he would make 'a very mediocre politician'.[86] In *Youth and Tomorrow* (1946) he gave some sense of why he had thrown in his lot with Common Wealth:

> Everywhere I found a new outlook emerging. The rise of the new political movement called Common Wealth was one of the many symptoms of this change. People seemed to be in the midst of a painful process of sloughing an old cramping skin from their minds, and exposing a fresh, more supple, more sensitive and at first more vulnerable one, but one that would be in the long run better suited for life in a new kind of world.[87]

Following the drubbing at the 1945 General Election, when almost all of the leading figures of the movement left (including Acland and Ingram[88]) Stapledon retained his membership, and continued to work for the reduced but surviving Common Wealth, until his death in 1950.[89]

Stapledon was at ease with the basic political and social values of Common Wealth, and extolled Common Ownership and Vital Democracy in his talks and speeches. He recognised Acland's virtues as a politician and was willing to quote his exhortations to service, fellowship and community. But *It Must Be Christianity* really stuck in his craw. He disagreed with many of the claims of that work, and clearly found the title of the work to be both tendentious and provocative. As far as we know there was no epistolatory exchange on these matters between Stapledon and Acland, and we don't know to what extent, if any, Acland was aware of Stapledon's criticisms. What we do know is that Stapledon took his objections on the road to public and branch meetings. His critique of Acland, although grounded in his own distinctive – some might say idiosyncratic – philosophical viewpoint, has a broader significance in that it represents an undoubted current in Common Wealth who were not wedded to Christian *beliefs* but, unlike, say, some of the Marxists, were not hostile to 'morality' as such, and who wanted a stress on the 'spiritual' purposes of Common Wealth.

In late August 1942, barely a month after the founding of Common Wealth, Stapledon addressed a meeting organised by Common Wealth in Ellesmere Port; the import of the title of his talk, and the intended target, would surely not have been lost on many in the audience: '*Must* It Be Christianity?' As Acland did in *It Must Be Christianity* Stapledon begins with the fact of the diversity of views in the movement as regards basic values, and runs with Acland's dualistic characterisation of progressive forces as divided between Christians and humanists. His lecture notes begin with four bullet points: 'Importance of this question for Common Wealth ... many supporters are Christians ... many supporters are non-Christians, Humanists ... *disputes* are constantly arising'.[90] This is the political terrain in which he has to work. Furthermore, Acland, the person publicly most associated with Common Wealth, has asserted the centrality of Christianity in his pamphlet. Stapledon's difficult political task is therefore to reconcile Christian and humanist interests while simultaneously not seeming to repudiate totally Acland's endorsement of the Christian tradition. Acland, we recall, sought to convince his readership that humanists were really Christians who hadn't fully appreciated that fact, as in his later characterisation of Tom Wintringham, 'although we differed about morality he really does qualify for "They who do the work of God shall be called the children of God"'.[91] Stapledon has a few dialectical tricks of his own. He appears, at first, to be meeting Acland halfway in that he calls for the 'reassertion of Christian morality (but not Christian doctrine)';[92] and indeed this is a concession, since it suggests that there must be some Christian dimension in the way forward. The rejection of Christian doctrine, as we saw in Chapter 3, rests on Stapledon's conviction that humans are incapable of generating systematic and accurate metaphysical knowledge of the universe, and that therefore Christian *beliefs* insofar as they claim to be knowledge are fundamentally without substance. The concession to Acland on Christian morality is, however, less than it seems. Much of what constitutes Christian morality is, for Stapledon, merely the derivative of false beliefs – 'loss of belief wrecks morality ... our whole culture is "living on its capital" (so far as morality is concerned) i.e. on the tradition of Christianity which arose out of former belief'.[93] Furthermore, Christianity's historical reliance on actual 'capital' pollutes the source of its moral teaching. When Stapledon comes to identify the positive core of 'Christian morality' it is devoid of specifically Christian doctrine, and is, in effect, an assertion of the 'spiritualism' discussed in Chapter 3, of the need to be an instrument of the spirit. The need for Christian morality boils down to nothing more than the assertion, which Stapledon makes in another talk, that 'every religion contains a pinch of true religion',[94] and Christianity is no exception. Not that humanism has all the answers either, and Stapledon points to its currents of shallow materialism, utilitarianism, instrumentalism and hostility to religion; but its positive historical achievements such as its concern with human equality and enlightenment need also to be noted. Stapledon thus believes that it is possible to deal creatively with the fact of Christian and humanist diversity, 'since we can agree on essentials and "agree to differ" about the rest';[95] this entails a dialectical synthesis of 'Christianity' and humanism, and a tolerant pluralism for remaining areas of disagreement. The answer to the question 'Must It Be Christianity?' is thus ambiguous – in a sense it is 'yes', but to a 'Christianity' without Christianity, a conception light years away from Acland's.

## Crisis

Among the central leadership of Common Wealth the 'religious' issue began to grow critical from early 1943, with things coming to a head in November of that year when memos and letters flew back and forth, crisis meetings were held, resignations were threatened and personal relations hit a new low. The main energy was generated by a conflict between the Marxists and Acland (and those associated with him by the Marxists, namely Parkes and Sargant). But the conflict drew in figures outside these two nodes, most notably Macmurray and Ingram. The Marxist struggle was conducted by Tom Wintringham and by a figure of whom we need to have some background, Kitty Wintringham.

Katharine (Kitty) Bowler (1908–66) was born in New England, and attended Bryn Mawr where she studied economics and politics.[96] Left-wing, though not Communist, she worked for the League Against War and Fascism, and International Labour Defence, eventually arriving in Spain in the midst of the Civil War, where she met Tom Wintringham in September 1936, and they quickly became lovers. From the perspective of the Communist leadership in Spain, Kitty's non-party status and vigorously expressed independent views, her unconventional relationship with Tom Wintringham (who was married, and to one of the founder members of the Communist Party of Great Britain), her new career as a journalist and her efforts to get actively involved in the Republican cause were all reasons for concern, and she was taken into custody, charged with being a Trotskyite spy and intensively interrogated (using sleep deprivation) over three days and nights, with execution a real possibility. On her release she was to play an important role in nursing Tom when he was severely wounded in battle. Back in England the CPGB mounted a campaign against Kitty, eventually expelling Tom when he refused to separate from her. After Wintringham obtained a divorce they were married in January 1941. It is important to stress that, as a member of Common Wealth, Kitty Wintringham was very much her own person – smart, theoretically savvy, and feisty – and that as well as the shared battles she and Tom fought in the movement she had the added struggle of getting her own voice heard, of not being rendered peripheral or invisible as woman and wife. In the heated debates over religion in November 1943, this issue surfaced in all its rawness.

On the issue of philosophical foundations it must have appeared to the Wintringhams, as it did to Stapledon, that the opposition was in possession of the high ground. Common Wealth, like Forward March before it, appeared to be joined at the hip with *It Must Be Christianity*. Acland did nothing to dispel this impression; indeed, in 1943 he let the text be reprinted in the collection to which Stapledon had reluctantly submitted his own confession of lack of faith – Ernest W. Martin's *In Search of Faith* (see Chapter 3). As a consequence, much of the Wintringhams' campaign is *reactive*, trying to dismantle the more egregious elements of Acland's past ideological influence, and resisting the new products of his energetic and fecund mind. This said, Acland was to acknowledge that Tom Wintringham's resolute advocacy of Marxism did cause him genuinely to develop an appreciation of the virtues of Marxism, and one can see in the development of his ideas in the Common Wealth period an attempt to incorporate ideas from this source. However, it was the claim that Marxism was *the* meta-narrative that he stubbornly resisted, for this was a challenge to the true meta-narrative, Christianity.

In March 1943 Acland, in the midst of a fairly edgy exchange of letters with Kitty Wintringham about the relative claims of Christianity and Marxism, sought her opinion on the synopsis of a book he was planning to write, provisionally entitled *Revolutionaries Should Be Christians*. Acland's letter of 6 March had raised the temperature in a slighting and *ad hominem* reference to the inadequacies of humanism:

> You humanists are perpetually casting back for some sure form of guidance in all emergencies. Wells wants his 'Rights of man', you want your line or theory. There ain't no such creature as will do the job for you – only God. Sorry but I mean it.[97]

Kitty replied on 7 March accusing Acland of intellectual confusion: 'you have assumed that theory is to the humanist, what God is to the religious man. This is to show a profound misconception of not merely Marxism but the scientific method.'[98] On 9 March Acland countered with the claim that the right use of reason and scientific method brings knowledge of

> the big truth of history, to which all minor events are referable ... the conflict between God and the Devil ... [I]t is only when you see history in terms of this struggle that you become fully conscious (or as fully conscious as is now possible) not only of what you are doing, but of what you should do and why you should do it.[99]

He maintains that he is not rejecting Marxism; indeed, he refers to his 'immense indebtedness' to Tom Wintringham for showing him that 'Marxism is an essential part of the mental equipment of any contemporary politician', *but*, since Marxism is primarily about the effects of the economy upon individuals it is only 'a part of the whole truth', and 'great mental distortion has been caused by Marxism strutting around as if it were the whole'.[100] And, with a neat piece of footwork, he deftly moves from saying that he is going to thank Tom in the preface to his new book to asking Kitty to comment on the synopsis.

The synopsis of *Revolutionaries Should Be Christians* because it is so unformed shines a light on Acland's visceral Christocentric conception of the world at this time. The most notable section is that dealing with 'the world before Christ', which seems more akin to the war of all against all in Hobbes's state of nature than to any even vaguely historical account, though unlike Hobbes Acland claims to be writing history:

> Stage one, possibly human beings living, either like sheep or like wolves, with no ascertainable system of social cohesion. As soon as any system of social cohesion – power structures … For countless centuries the history of mankind all over the world was the story of the rise and fall of one power structure after another. There was absolutely no 'rhyme or reason' in it; nothing to make one assume that it would at any future time be anything different.[101]

The prose is at times almost risibly childlike as Acland dredges up imagined scenes of physical and sexual violence:

> Meanwhile the quality of life for ordinary men was absolutely hopeless. Slavery was assumed. Men could be flogged to death for a dirty look, or for fun. Daughters could be sold to buy food, and it was thought normal that they be manhandled by every slave trader's agent through whose hands they passed, unless they were pretty enough to earn big money by being sold as virgins.[102]

The Old Testament world, so central to the Christianity of Macmurray and, latterly, Ingram, is fleetingly introduced to reinforce the contrast with the world of the New Testament:

> Christ said nothing new. Almost every word he spoke had been spoken before by other prophets who had had followings which had not generated sufficient dynamic to impinge on the situation at all. It cannot be proved that he was God, nor can it be proved that he rose from the dead, but SOMETHING happened in or around 34 AD which started something happening which had never happened before.[103]

With Christ, history forms a pattern for the first time, as novel 'power structures' emerge out of the collapse of their predecessors in a benign incline of progress. Here one senses an echo of Macmurray, whom Acland had been reading over the past two years, but with a personal God clearly rejected by Macmurray. In Acland's reworking, subsequent history 'is the record of the brilliant generalship by which God out-manoeuvres his opponent',[104] and another tableau is provided:

> The battle of the Marne was fought and won by God in the Circus Maximus at the time of Nero. Here hundreds of the men and women who had found this new faith were eaten in front of tens of thousands of people. But instead of running away and screaming they were eaten on their knees singing praises and crying forgiveness to those who had condemned them.[105]

Again, there is a naive, yet vivid, earnestness to that little detail – 'instead of running away and screaming'.

Not surprisingly, neither Kitty nor Tom Wintringham was impressed with the synopsis. In a document produced at the height of the crisis in November 1943 they assailed Acland's outline. It was woeful history in its characterisation of the period before Christ as patternless and featureless, oblivious of features of the ancient world which were to be crucial in the development of the modern:

> it writes off the development of monotheism, of Confucianism, of Greek philosophy, natural science and democracy, of Roman law, etc. – not to mention the Stoic proclamation of universal brotherhood at Pergamon and the wave of slave revolts that culminated with Spartacus.[106]

When they sent Acland a copy of this document he was clearly hurt and angry, for he wrote in the margin next to the section quoted above: 'Cheat. If I can't put to you a half-developed idea at top speed without you quoting it as authority ... hell!'[107] The Wintringhams deemed the piece to be riddled with what they termed theocratic dualism – dualist because of its transcendental God, and theocratic in investing God with all effective agency: 'It implies that human society before Christ has no value, and since Christ no value except that due to direct divine intervention.'[108] Schooled in the rigours of Marxist dialectics, and convinced, therefore, of the crucial importance of sound theory Acland seemed to the Wintringhams devoid not merely of any understanding of Marxism, but of any understanding of theory as such. Their caste pride in arduous intellectual labour was affronted by what they viewed as a form of mental incontinence. As Kitty Wintringham exasperatedly wrote to Kenneth Ingram in March 1943:

> The real difficulty, I think, is that he has a superficial nodding acquaintance with all sorts of ideas but no real knowledge or comprehension of what the present body of human knowledge – science, history, philosophy, psychology, dialectics, etc. – mean to other people ... And the jumble

within his mind is at times appalling. The result is that quite unconsciously he gets bright ideas, hurls them out quite without realising that he is insulting the intelligence of others, who have spent years of patient study and research comprehending the present body of man's knowledge.[109]

Relations between Acland and the Wintringhams worsened over the summer of 1943. In the space of twelve days Acland completed a new book, eventually published as *How It Can Be Done*, and sent it to Tom Wintringham for comments.[110] In his diary for 5 August 1943 Acland records that, in the course of a phone call with Wintringham, Tom had informed him that 'he had sent me four pages of sad comment on my book' and that Tom 'didn't quite know what's left at the end of [his] criticism'.[111] It is an indication of the growing strain between the two men that Acland felt he could predict what Tom would say, namely that his draft was not grounded in Marxist principles:

> I think I will find that his criticism arises from the fact that my proposals 'aren't in the book'. But there isn't a book on overthrowing capitalism, except the Marxist–Socialist book, and that book is closed. It is closed because its theories have been proved in practice to be unreal to the task of overthrowing capitalism.[112]

He also reveals that the stakes are high in this matter: 'it will take more than Tom to prevent me from publishing this book. I'd walk out of Common Wealth and try again from nothing rather than not publish it.'[113]

Kitty Wintringham's letter to Kenneth Ingram in March, previously referred to, was an attempt to get Ingram on board on the clarification of basic issues about belief. The Wintringhams felt that Ingram was ideologically much closer to them than to Acland, and indeed both of them cited Ingram's work on a number of occasions, particularly *The Night Is Far Spent* (1941); in one document they say that Ingram's recent books 'are easy for a Marxist to recognise as parallel, or nearly so, to Marxist beliefs'.[114] They also believed that Acland would be more prepared to listen to Ingram on these matters than to themselves: 'therefore the appeal to you, we have a common basis of ideas, but I feel you would know how to use words that would be more comprehensible to Dick'.[115] She maintained, not particularly plausibly, that she had 'definitely dodged the religious issue' in the past, because 'Tom had said he wanted to tackle this major issue, together with you'.[116] Whether through Kitty Wintringham's prompting or for some other reason, Ingram clearly got into discussion with Acland, for on 26 October Tom Wintringham was asked by Acland to discuss some 'questions' with himself and Ingram. Wintringham agreed, but rejected the venues suggested by Acland, instead suggesting that a 'week-end' discussion be arranged where, among others, John Macmurray and James Parkes might participate.[117] Acland agreed, but was later bitterly to regret admitting Macmurray to the proceedings.

Not that Acland himself didn't attempt to influence the composition of the meeting, notably in the case of Kitty Wintringham, whom he pointedly did not ask to take part. In the ensuing exchange of correspondence about this Acland argued that her exclusion was based on her personal failings, while Kitty maintained that it was because of her gender. Common Wealth had by this time developed policy on the role of women, and had a Women's Policy Sub-Committee. In August 1942 Acland had circulated for comments a draft leaflet on 'Men and Women' which had argued that men and women are different but complementary, deploying an unfortunate image to convey this: 'it is the difference between a nut and a bolt, two things which fit together to make a stronger and more useful whole'.[118] 'Common Wealth,' the leaflet continued,

> is dead against all those men who regard women as a charming but frivolous appendage in what ought to be a purely man's world. But equally we cannot believe that success will be achieved under the leadership of those masculine women who want to run the whole show as a fight between women and men.[119]

The specific proposals that emerged from the Women's Policy Sub-Committee spoke of equality before the law, equality of opportunity, equal remuneration for equal work, pay for the 'housewife', family allowances, adequate health-care provision and labour-saving devices in the home.[120] Common Wealth was also to publish in 1944 a short pamphlet, *Women and Politics*, more combative about the exclusion of women from decision-making processes, by Elaine Burton (1904–91), of whom Acland was later to say, in a telling phrase, that she 'seemed to talk less about Common Wealth than what would become known as Women's Liberation'.[121] Acland therefore approached his exchange with Kitty Wintringham on the assumption that he was sympathetic, indeed actively sympathetic, to the rights of women, but his understanding of the position of women differed markedly from that of Kitty herself.

In response to Acland's suggestion that they should merely have a private chat about his views rather than Kitty attend the proposed weekend meeting, she cut to the chase about the systematic marginalisation of women in Common Wealth:

> I am driven to the reluctant conclusion that it is just another instance of sex-discrimination in CW. It is a tragic fact that particularly at the top of CW it is considered sufficient to murmur a few kindly words on appropriate occasions or pass a resolution or two, but *in practice* to relegate women to 'their proper places'. This is a field where a change of outlook on the part of both men and women in the movement is urgently needed.[122]

To say that Acland's reply was tactless would be a gross understatement. Having opined 'that all men have a distinct bias in ignoring women' he proposed that Common Wealth's press officer Mary Seaton be invited to the meeting, and asked Kitty to 'convey to Tom my suggestion that she be asked to attend'. Even he realised that this was an outrageous suggestion, and in a postscript admitted 'that my request that you act as post office ... is ... put in for the one and only purpose of being absolutely bloody' but, ending in the truly negative, he adds: 'I am absolutely dead tired and simply cannot retype the whole page so as to leave it out. I must apologise and hope you will forgive me an almost deliberate unkindness' – a piece of breathtaking insensitivity! Elsewhere in the letter he asserted that his not wanting her at the conference 'has relatively little to do with your sex' – the reason was that although she had 'a scintillating and rapier-like mind', she also had 'a more chaotically disorderly brain than anyone I've ever met who has the same store of knowledge'.[123]

In her reply Kitty argued that the invitation to Mary Seaton, a person she maintained had little knowledge of Marxism and no interest in questions of morality, indicated Acland's opportunism and tokenism:

> in order to prove me wrong you think it is only necessary to produce a woman – the first one handy. Women do not ask for special privileges as women but to be judged and treated as people, as equals, on the basis of their qualifications and not of their sex.[124]

Returning to her experience as a member of Common Wealth she speaks of the exclusions, ready blame, inadequate praise, and of being subsumed as a wife:

> From the moment I came into CW it has been drummed into my ears 'You can't do that because you are a woman and/or a wife' ... By bitter experience I have found that ... I get full credit for everything I do wrong, very little credit for any good work (which is either credited to Tom or taken as a matter of course).[125]

She also charges Acland with attempting to rig the conference by only allowing one Marxist (Tom) against three 'religious anti-materialists' (Acland, Parkes and Sargent) and three 'religious materialists' (including Kenneth Ingram; Macmurray, as we shall see, did not in the end take part in this meeting). And she asserts her own right and qualifications to be at the conference:

> I believe it would be true to say that with the exception of Tom there is no more qualified Marxist in the movement, nor one who has taken the trouble to search for a good working basis of agreement with the religious element in CW, than myself.[126]

Acland, however, was not for budging, and Kitty Wintringham did not take part.

The meeting was scheduled for 20 and 21 November. In the weeks before the event a positive blizzard of paper descended on the leadership of Common Wealth as people sought to define their positions. Three papers are of particular note and were produced by Acland, the Wintringhams and Ingram. Acland's was a 'Memorandum On Common Wealth Theory'. The document shows that he had travelled a distance from *It Must Be Christianity*, much of this due to the pressure of the Wintringhams; as Kitty Wintringham reminded Acland in their November exchange of letters, 'Under this treatment you first consented to at least read some Marx, Engels and Macmurray and listen seriously to Ingram.'[127] Unlike *It Must Be Christianity* with its notion that humanists were Christians in the making, the 'Memorandum' begins with Macmurray's analysis of the Jewish mind in *The Clue to History* to argue that both Christians and Marxists (or more accurately sophisticated Christians and Marxists) can both legitimately claim to be embodying the unity of the ideal and the material. He acknowledges the fundamentally different grounding of the two traditions, and that 'at some stage this difference of faith may be divisive', but as far as enlightened Common Wealth members *should* be concerned 'this is not divisive for any practical purpose now'.[128] Insofar as there is divisiveness, this is due to the presence of unreconstructed Christians and Marxists in the movement, and to misunderstandings derived from the use of very different vocabulary. He can't, however, resist, by way of a postscript, asserting that the Marxists have been more successful in getting their conception of the unity of the ideal and the material over than the Christians. This little barb aside, the 'Memorandum' is above all a political document; Acland *had* genuinely come to appreciate elements of the Marxist case but the paper was conceived as a weapon in his war of manoeuvre in Common Wealth. As regards his own deep beliefs, in October he had produced in seventy hours a draft of a book whose title was suggestive of strong unreconstructed dimensions in Acland – 'Are You Sure You Don't Believe in God?' He had also agreed to collaborate with Parkes on a religious play.[129] The degree of travel from *It Must Be Christianity* needs to be seen in this light.

The Wintringhams offered 'Fellowship or Morality?', an aggressive piece of Marxist scholasticism, twenty-five pages long, with nine main sections, and fifty-nine sub-sections. Opponents' writings were examined with a forensic intensity for evidence of theoretical and political malpractice, and this fed into an arraignment based on distinct categories of error. The Wintringhams accept as a definition of their 'philosophical' beliefs (they use inverted commas to distance themselves from the idealist connotations of philosophy) the section on dialectical and historical materialism contained in that Moscow-approved theoretical bible of the CPGB, *The History of the Communist Party of the Soviet Union*. They also recommend a number of texts by Marx and Engels (*The German Ideology, Ludwig Feuerbach and the End of Classical German Philosophy, Theses on Feuerbach* and *Anti-Dühring*) and in the course of their indictments use both Macmurray and Ingram as friendly authorities. The villains are Sargant, Parkes and Acland. They are 'the principal exponents of the tendencies leading to sectarianism' in Common Wealth, and, indeed, are 'in danger of leading at some future point of time, towards a Fascism based upon religious illusion'.[130] Sargant is found guilty of 'Idealist Platonism' because of his assertion that an 'absolute right', a moral law, exists, that should govern human society.[131] Parkes's crime is 'Theocratic Idealism', a belief that governments get their legitimacy from their 'wisdom', which is the intrusion of an illegitimate religious conception – wisdom 'is the priestly word'.[132] Acland gets the lion's share of attention and is dealt with under two counts: 'Irrationality' and 'Dualism'. Acland's 'Irrationality' is deemed to take a number of forms: an opposition to theory, or a belief that it is relatively unimportant; the substitution of mythical religious material or low-grade political pragmatism in the place of theory; the rating of the subjective over the objective; and a general muddled inability to think clearly. He also, they argue, falls foul of Macmurray's strictures on 'Dualism'.[133] Acland's conception of God, his privileging of the 'Idea', as in his 'ideational team', the 'utopian perfectionism'[134] (citing Ingram's use of the category) of his rejection of the doctrine of sin are all viewed as manifestations of his dualist disposition. All three men, therefore, arrive at 'moralism', whereby an essentially external moral code is meant to act as a guide for human activity. Given that the preferred moral code is a product of an earlier level of development – revealed in the link between 'morality and 'mores', and 'principles' and 'prince' – it acts as an historical drag on the present. For this reason the Wintringhams do not wish to use the word 'morality'. Again, following Macmurray, they do accept that there is a 'true morality' – the 'morality of friendship', which is generated in the course of collective social practice, but argue that it should be called, not morality, but 'democratic procedure on its formal side and on its spiritual side, love'.[135] Furthermore, the crucial distinction, which they claim Acland misses, is not between Christianity and Marxism, but between idealism and Christianity. A revolutionary non-idealist Christianity (no doubt thinking of Macmurray and Ingram) can work in politics with Marxism, an idealist Christianity cannot.[136]

The claim that Common Wealth might become Fascist did not originate with the Wintringhams. The career of another idiosyncratic leftist baronet who had led his supporters into Fascism – Sir Oswald Mosley – was fresh in the memory, and the temptation to read Acland from this perspective was one that a number of opponents could not resist. In May of 1943, in *What is Common Wealth?* R. Page Arnot for the CPGB, after pointing to a French example, Marcel Deat, who had moved from a member of the Socialist Party to a Vichy supporter, alighted on the Mosley case: 'the first stage to Mosley's British Union of Fascists was the formation of *The New Party* whose middle-class following carried on vaguely socialist propaganda while separating themselves from the Labour movement.'[137] This reference to Mosley's New Party is the key to why the Wintringhams were so worried by the possibility of an unwelcome change in direction for Common Wealth. When Common Wealth was formed, like its predecessor Forward March it was a *movement*, not a *party*; it did not see itself as a competitor to the various parties of the left, but as a facilitator of left unity – hence the absence of the word 'party' in all three of the alternative titles for the movement. However, once Common Wealth began to field candidates under its own name, and expand and refine its national organisation, some members did begin to see themselves as members of a party, locked in a battle with alternative parties. By the time of the October/November debates Acland was also clearly of this opinion. At the very end of November in a draft leaflet, speaking of Common Wealth he wrote: 'We have become, and almost all of us think rightly become – amongst other things a political party.'[138] The Wintringhams were well aware that this was Acland's view, and in 'Fellowship or Morality?' they refer to the 'sectarianism that seeks ... to change CW from a movement into a party against all other parties'.[139] This went against their passionate understanding of the purpose of Common Wealth as an instrument to create a popular front of the left nationally and internationally, and they adapted a statement of Marx in *The Manifesto of the Communist Party*: 'CW does not form a separate party opposed to other Left parties ... It has no interests separate and apart from those of the people as a whole.'[140] From their perspective Acland was seeking to create a party, with himself as leader, espousing an ideology grounded on a narrow and conservative moralistic Christianity. Drawing on examples as varied as Ulster unionism, the Ku Klux Klan, Father Coughlin and Mosley's Blackshirts, they asserted 'that in Britain a constituent part of any effective Fascist development will take a religious form ... will be a pseudo-religion',[141] with the implication that Acland with his party and his ideology could provide the basis of such a development.

The third document is Ingram's 'Draft Policy Document'. Produced five days before the weekend meeting, it emphatically illustrates the sharp division on basics involved in the Acland/Wintringhams struggle. This is not because Ingram takes sides in the document but rather because he allows the dispute to be visibly highlighted, as a dispute, as two different paths that can be taken. Thus the first three paragraphs set the scene by justifying Common Wealth's existence in terms of the distinct principles it advocates and defends. Paragraph 4 begins to indicate what these values and objectives are, with section (a) talking about the need for a new social order, and (b) on the need to unite the middle and working classes in the struggle for that order. Then, in section (c), after a few words about Vital Democracy and 'brotherhood', one finds two passages arranged side by side on the page. On one side, this:

> Society is composed of individuals, and if CW is to promote a new social conception its propaganda must include a moral appeal addressed to individual men and women. CW must present its case not on the ground of economic expediency, not on the plea that its programme, when fulfilled, will materially benefit the individual; but on the claim that its principles should be supported because they are right.[142]

On the other, this:

> While the note of CW propaganda should be an insistence that its programme is demanded in the interests of social justice, CW must be careful to avoid the dangers inherent in any moral and idealist appeal. The new

society will be built up not by calling on men and women to embrace a new moral outlook, but primarily out of the experience which they gain from their common action in the political struggle.[143]

Although slightly softened by Ingram's prose and with its deep foundational roots out of sight, here, literally in graphic form, was the impasse that was somehow to be sorted out in the days to come.

## Two meetings

In fact, the outcome of the weekend meeting was to be significantly shaped by a meeting held a couple of days earlier, when Acland and Tom Wintringham went to see John Macmurray.[144] It is not clear at what point the original arrangement, that Macmurray be a participant at the weekend meeting, was changed, nor whose idea it was. Acland was always to regret what happened at the meeting with Macmurray, but there is no evidence that he went reluctantly: indeed, to the contrary, the depth of his unhappiness at the outcome speaks of the disappointment of high expectations. Macmurray was his former tutor and a man he admired, one whose books he had been reading of late – he was also a fellow Christian. Wintringham, also, must have expected a good deal of sympathy, given his understanding of the relative closeness of Macmurray's revolutionary Christianity to his own Marxism. If this was his expectation it was to be fulfilled. In Acland's dejected notes on the meeting – a real transcript of pain – we can see how badly things went for him. Macmurray's opening remarks were a hammer blow for Acland: 'Macmurray starts by saying that as between R.A. and T.W. he comes down almost wholly on the side of T.W. because he thinks it is absolutely essential to start from Marxism.'[145] Macmurray brought out his long-standing arguments about the primacy of action, and the dangers of descending into utopianism – in Acland's paraphrase: 'it is no use for individuals to start talking about what they would like the state of society to be, what it ought to be' and 'you must stop imagining some utopian better state of society'. A clearly exasperated Acland, who had come to the meeting in the first place for Macmurray's advice, was confronted with an intellectual who seemed unwilling to use either his intellect or his imagination to talk about what should be done. Macmurray appeared to be all thought and no thought:

> In the whole of the discussion it was impossible to get from Macmurray one sentence which implied that CW was an organisation which, so to speak, ought to exist. He deliberately said, – 'All our unfreedoms come from wrong thinking' and, in another context, 'I always run like a hare from those who ask me what they ought to do.'

Macmurray then launched into an attack on the Church: the charge, 'the same as Marx's; that it is Idealist'. Acland's transcendental personal God is rejected out of hand: 'You Christians, I tell them, do not have a religious core and centre to your lives. You really create for yourselves a God who would cease to exist if you stopped believing in him.' Macmurray conceded that there were dangers in the contemporary development of Marxist theory, notably that there might be a reductionist preoccupation with biology, whereas in the case of Christianity the 'danger is that they will think that God enables them to dispense with blue books'. These dangers are not of equal strength, however:

> Macmurray says that he fears the Christian danger much more than he fears the Marxist danger, and that he therefore thinks the absolutely essential job now is to start work on Marxism, so as to reinterpret it in line with the present developing situation. You must do this, he says, because it is from Material facts that your main challenge is now coming.

In retrospect Acland kicked himself for allowing himself to be put in a situation which brought out his doubts about his own intellectual ability, and which prevented him from mounting a sufficiently robust defence against Macmurray and Wintringham:

> I was at a double disadvantage: it was a two-to-one struggle; in the last resort I had more respect for my opponents' brains than for my own. Tom had won a first class history degree at Oxford [in fact he hadn't[146]] and he nearly died of wounds in Spain. I was a public speaker, an almost fortuitous MP, and author of a slap-happy little book that made me the leader of our movement.[147]

At the time, as he wrote up his notes on the meeting, Acland was torn between genuine respect for Macmurray's learning and a resentment that the professor, who took virtually no part in the day-to-day activities of Common Wealth, was preaching the centrality of 'action' to Acland, who was permanently active in the service of that organisation, not to mention the quotidian political grind of ordinary members:

> We should be supremely grateful to him for by no means secret association with our movement. We should respect and draw upon his wisdom. But we should also remember that if we took the whole of his advice, we would all become Macmurrays. Now one or two Macmurrays is splendid ... but 10,000 Macmurrays cannot form a part of the cutting. But if his wisdom and judgment are correct, the very situation now requires that somewhere a sharp cutting edge shall be put on it. CW is part of the total blade. It is at the moment the only part of the blade. We can perhaps say that this part of the blade is at the moment making a more valiant and painstaking effort to sharpen itself up than any other part. This is being done, at the moment, by five or ten thousand members and friends of CW. It could not be done by five or ten thousand Macmurrays.[148]

This feeling was aggravated by the fact that Macmurray was leading a life of scholarly calm and independence which a side of Acland clearly desired. The strain of navigating a political organisation, with its ocean-going egos, and the inevitable compromises it entailed, pulsates through a heartfelt little passage:

> Oh God please arrange matters so as to release me from any part in this God-awful work of wrestling inside a political organisation, which means in fact enduring in one's body and mind one's tiny share of the actual pains of social childbirth; and let me become a free writer and preacher of thoughts which may some other day lead to a religious and political revolution and reintegration organised by other men.

He clearly found the experience with Macmurray and Wintringham distressing, and still did thirty or forty years later when he composed his fragments of autobiography. In a very human fashion he used these compositions to state what he did not state at the time – the cutting rejoinder that had not been made; in essence that whatever Macmurray and Wintringham thought of his theoretical errors, he had created Common Wealth and made it successful, and had done it on the basis of those beliefs so belittled by the duo, and would continue to do so if left alone by obstructive Marxism:

> Had I known as much as I know now, I could have stood up to the pair of them. Even with what little I knew, I could have done better than I did. I could have said: 'The test of any theory is that it works in practice. In Britain we can't win without at least two thirds of the salaried middle classes on our side. Up to now, with these people, socialist propaganda has almost totally failed. I come with an amalgam – maybe a careless amalgam – of politics–morality–economics–religion; and in Common Wealth you see a positive response. Leave us free to explore a winning line.'[149]

But he hadn't said this at the time, or at least, he believed, not sufficiently clearly and forcefully, and he felt that the meeting had left him politically weakened.

The weekend meeting duly took place. It was chaired by François Lafitte (1913–2002), social scientist and *Times* journalist, one-time CPGB activist (and briefly, in Vienna, a Soviet agent) who had come into Common Wealth through both the 1941 Committee and Forward March.[150] It would seem that the other participants were Acland, Parkes, Sargant, Ingram, Wintringham, the Rev. George McLeod (later Moderator of the Church of Scotland) and the general secretary of Common Wealth, John Mure.[151] The goal was to somehow produce a leaflet that would embody the Common Wealth stance on its basic foundations. From the start of the meeting, commencing with a report on Macmurray's position, Acland was on the back foot.[152] He decided that his best option was to get an acknowledgement in the document of the equal status of Christianity and Marxism in Common Wealth. Wintringham, fortified by the Macmurray judgement, and seeing therefore an opportunity to press for the hegemony of Marxism, refused. Acland, ever the street fighter, offered a compromise: the document would state that in the world in general Marxism and Christianity both have equal dangers, 'but then say the Christian dangers apply particularly to CW because of its origins'. We do not know what the other participants contributed to the discussion, but one assumes that given the diversity of opinion Wintringham concluded that Acland's offer was the best he could get, for the compromise was accepted.

## The struggle continues

Acland, of course, hadn't the slightest intention of letting matters rest there. On the day the meeting finished he confided to his diary that the struggle was continuing: 'if we can hold to the present basis for a time, then let there be no doubt that we are going to win out on top'.[153] This optimism was partly based on his belief that whereas Christianity deeply pervaded British society, Marxism was an abstruse science, the preserve of a minority: 'For every man who responds favourably to the name of Marx in this country, there are ten thousand who respond to the name of Christ.' He contrasts 'the tomes and tomes' of Marxist theory required by its advocates with Christianity's four books of the Gospel, where 'most of the relevant passages are already known by heart to at least half the people'. 'Oh yes,' he concluded, 'I am quite satisfied we will win out. In as little as two hundred years Marx will be as small a figure as Calvin or Voltaire.' In the meantime he was going to use every trick in the book to get things back on track in Common Wealth.

So began seven months of intrigue and counter intrigue, acrimonious meetings and correspondence, seemingly endless drafts of documents, with much hot air and bad temper. Acland used the winter months to try to claw back ground. He had the advantage of being in charge of redrafting the leaflet on Common Wealth policy, assisted by Kenneth Ingram who, although sympathetic to aspects of the Wintringhams' perspective, was a good organisation person, with feelings of loyalty to Acland, and whose disposition was towards compromise and a tolerant eclecticism. More specifically, Ingram had none of the intense dislike of 'morality' talk found in the Wintringhams. Quite the reverse. In *Religion and the New Society* he had no doubts that 'Common Wealth has drawn support and kindled enthusiasm chiefly because from the first it sounded a moral-religious note'.[154] As we saw in Chapter 2, Ingram's discussion of homosexuality was very much concerned with its moral status, and in the significantly entitled *Sex-Morality Tomorrow* (1940), the book that got him into such trouble with the Church of England, his progression beyond the orthodox Christian moral condemnation of homosexuality had been achieved by his adoption of a morality of love. The Wintringhams too had spoken of love but this was in terms of an alternative to moral language, not the fusion envisaged by Ingram. From Ingram's perspective contestation on the level of the moral was to strike at the very citadel of Christianity's historical understanding of sexual behaviour. This gave an existential edge to Ingram's moral discourse. Acland's God was not his, but a concern with establishing the boundaries between permissible and impermissible behaviour must have seemed a more worthwhile enterprise than the Wintringhams' abandonment of the vocabulary of the ethical.

On the specific issue of homosexuality there is no evidence of any policy discussions of this issue within Common Wealth. As to attitudes, apart from Ingram's there is almost total silence. We have the much later memories of Ernest Millington, the RAF officer who won Chelmsford for Common Wealth in April 1945; in his dealings with Tom Driberg his attitude might be characterised as a circumscribed tolerance:

> I took the liberal view that his sexuality was his own business ... He had in his flat, as I remember, a slender Italian youth as housekeeper ... I dismissed the young man as a live-in-lover. That was his business and that of the boy.[155]

When, however, he finally got to hear of the extent of Driberg's active sex life he cut off all further contacts: 'I had nothing to gain and much to lose in self-respect by allowing myself contact with groups that entertained themselves with homosexual orgies ... It was a dreadful shame that the needs of his lower self prevailed and left him basically unfulfilled.'[156] Driberg himself in his autobiography confessed his failure to integrate his sexual, religious and political impulses, invoking the concept of schizophrenia to map his three 'conflicting compulsions ... all, it seemed, mutually irreconcilable ... "deviant" sex, "exotic" religion [i.e. Roman Catholicism] – and Left-wing politics'.[157] Matt Cook cites Driberg's remark to illustrate what he takes to be a feature of the years following the Second World War, but which surely also applies to the war years, the failure of left-wing parties to see anything political (in a positive sense) about the issue of homosexuality, which 'had come to be seen as a social problem and personal tragedy and not as integral to any discourse of rights or a broader left-wing political agenda'.[158] Furthermore, as the Jagar/Acland and Temple/Ingram correspondence reveals, sexual unorthodoxy would not be without potential political costs.

As to Acland's views on homosexuality, we have relatively little to go on. His only considered piece on sexual morality, an essay entitled 'Chastity or What?' dates from two decades after the events of Common Wealth, and in the meantime the highly influential Wolfenden Committee, itself a product of changing attitudes to homosexuality, had recommended the partial decriminalisation of homosexual acts. Acland is also distinctly ambiguous in his essay when discussing homosexuality. Since his principal purpose is to defend chastity *before marriage* and monogamy *within marriage* as part of a critique of the call for a 'relaxation' of sexual morality, his room for manoeuvre in assessing homosexuality is not great. He does, however, wish to distance himself from what he terms the 'authoritarian views' of some contemporary clergy.[159] Thus he considers a pamphlet published by the Society of Friends in 1963, *Towards a Quaker View of Sex*, whose liberal views had provoked a deal of criticism at the time. The chapter on homosexuality had commended the Wolfenden Report and called for a rethink of traditional Christian attitudes to homosexual behaviour. Maddeningly, Acland noted that he agreed 'with most of the Quaker group's conclusions about homosexuality' but failed to indicate his points of disagreement.[160] It is difficult to believe that he could have endorsed the view of the Quaker authors – a view which in effect echoes Ingram's position of twenty-five years earlier – that there is

> no reason why the physical nature of a sexual act should be the criterion by which the question whether or not it is moral should be decided. An act which ... expresses true affection between two individuals and gives pleasure to them both, does not seem to us to be sinful by reason *alone* of the fact that it is homosexual.[161]

This would seem to follow from Acland's response to another recent publication, *No New Morality* by Canon Douglas Rhymes of Southwark Cathedral. Acland wished to defend Rhymes from the charge that he 'approves of homosexuals',[162] arguing that

> of course Canon Rhymes does not do anything of the sort. He only wants us to change the law in accordance with the Wolfenden recommendations, and to extend a little charity rather than condemnation to those who have to face life with strong homosexual tendencies,[163]

which does suggest that Acland considered homosexual activity immoral but not deserving of pariah status or criminalisation, and that he wished to encourage those homosexuals who chose the difficult path of chastity – a position significantly different from the Ingram/'Quaker' approach.[164] Acland also thought that the authors of the Quaker booklet and Rhymes had brought down trouble on their own heads. His political instincts were affronted by what he saw as their gross naivety; in the case of the Quakers, 'They wrote in such terms that their report was predictably heralded under such headlines as "Quaker Group Rejects Church View of Sex"',[165] and in that of Rhymes,

> I have no sympathy whatever ... Because in these days it is not good enough to be as harmless as a dove; one must at least try to be as wise as a serpent as well. Canon Rhymes ought to have known about being misunderstood.[166]

Reinforcement of the view that back in the days of Common Wealth Acland would not have encouraged any such ventures into this dangerous terrain.

We should also note the internal constraints operating within Ingram: his unwillingness to publicly identify as a homosexual, his positive remarks presented as the judicious judgement of a disinterested authorial voice – internal pressures understandable given the external legal and social climate. To expect a symmetry with the positions of Macmurray, Stapledon and Acland is naive – the silence is the story, the dog did not bark. We have to adjust our calibration if we want to find any hints of inputs from Ingram into the production of ideas in Common Wealth that draws on his sexual theorising. The use of the moral as a weapon against religious, social and legal conservatism has already been mentioned. We might also speculate that his stress on the need for Common Wealth to somehow prefigure in its social relationships the society to come forms a link with his views on friendship and bonding. Thus in the draft policy document he wrote before the fateful meetings in late 1943 he spoke of the need 'to build up in CW, in the relations between members, and between branches, regions and H.Q., the spirit of the new society' and for 'the encouragement, so far as is possible, of opportunities for closer relationships within the branches and groups'.[167] This was a theme he was to return to in an article for the *Common Wealth Review*, 'Symbolism and Emotion': a sign of real success for the movement would be when outsiders 'are able to say of us: "there's a real unity of friendliness among these Common Wealth people. They are showing us in their relationships with each other the possibilities of the new society."'[168]

Be that as it may, Ingram's approach, in the context of the battle over religion in the leadership, was to move the debate away from assuming an unbridgeable chasm between Christianity and humanism towards conceiving of the conflict in terms of two dispositions, idealism (understood not in Macmurray's early-Marx sense, but in the colloquial affirmative sense) or an attraction to principles, and Realism, the desire to get things done. This distinction, which is meant to cut across the Christian/humanism divide, enables him to argue that the conflict in Common Wealth is not zero-sum but rather two sides that can and should be united:

> both elements are essential. CW could not hope to arouse enthusiasm if it failed to insist on high principles and to inspire a wider vision. ... Similarly, if CW were not to constitute itself an effective political organization and to pursue an immediate policy, its principles would remain unrealized ideals.[169]

Again, this could bridge more easily to Acland's notion of Common Wealth as morality in action than it could to Wintringhams' 'unification' of thought and action under Marxist hegemony. And indeed, when Ingram tried out his distinction on Wintringham his response was to deploy the Macmurrian sense of 'Idealism', Ingram's idealists were not one aspect of a potential fruitful synthesis but unrealistic, conservative drags on the historical process: 'it is not action they are against but facts'.[170]

Together, Ingram and Acland got down to work. As early as December Acland was crowing to his diary: 'I think I won out over the Wintringhams in eight words. "It is easier to criticise than to draft."'[171] He had, however, to get his draft through a five-person committee, two of whom were Ingram and himself, with Kitty Wintringham as a third, and in Calder's words the meeting 'seems to have been disputacious'.[172] In particular Acland could not prevent the ensuing internal leaflet *Common Wealth and the New Year* that was printed in February 1944 from containing a passage that was both highly critical of organised Christianity and markedly warm towards Marxism:

> In particular, Christians should not forget that in recent decades organised institutional Christianity *as a whole* has either divorced itself from the daily struggle in society and in men's individual lives or served as a support for reaction. A few individual Christians have been exceptions to the general rule, and some sections of institutional Christianity have supported certain social reforms. They are signs of a changing attitude to-day; but in general, from 1839 to 1939, Humanists (and particularly Marxists) showed a higher level of effort and self-sacrifice in the actual work of changing the structure of society than organised Christianity. The most spectacular recent example was the self-sacrifice and courage shown by members of the International Brigade in Spain.[173]

The hand of the Wintringhams was particularly visible here. When, however, the leaflet was debated at the annual conference, the above passage clearly caused offence. Common Wealth conferences, as Calder has argued, had far more people in favour of the type of views associated with Acland, Parkes and Sargant than it did those supportive of the Wintringhams' position.[174] Certainly there is evidence that there was some disquiet in the movement that the attempt to avoid moral appeals was linked to an increasing Marxist influence in the higher echelons of Common Wealth. There is, for example, a letter from a branch secretary (John Ferguson) to Kitty Wintringham in November 1943 after she had rejected an article he had submitted to the house journal. He was stung by her criticism that his essay had not understood the 'essential interdependence of economics and politics',[175] and was moved to a piece of pointed reminiscence:

> When I joined the 'Forward March' in 1941 I joined it because it stood for politics based not on economic theories nor on class interests but on moral principles ... Because in those days we would not have spoken of 'the essential interdependence of economics and politics', we should have regarded both as based on moral issues.

His conclusion left little doubt as to his sense of the source of this revision, and of what he might be driven to do:

> I do not see why there should not be any number of Marxists inside CW. But if CW has become an avowedly Marxist movement then it has

changed sadly in the past two years, and I for one shall have to reconsider my position with regard to the movement.

Ironically, Acland himself helped fuel the opposition at this conference by attempting to take on board some of the Macmurray/Wintringhams criticism of 'moralism', and stressing the need for 'scientific analyses'; his speech, Calder argues, 'clearly displeased some of his most fervent admirers'.[176] In attempting to defend *Common Wealth and the New Year* Acland referred back to the power of moral language in the early days of the movement but argued that now, although such appeals were still a dynamic force, they also posed potential dangers: first, they threatened to cut off the movement from what he termed 'those organisations, which had been engaged for many decades in the struggle for a new society'[177] – an echo here of elements of the Wintringhams' perspective on the centrality of the Marxist movement – and second, a point that surely must have gone down badly with significant sections of the conference, moral language risked 'attracting people who had little political experience' and a number of people who had been so attracted 'responded most sluggishly to our request that they should go canvassing'. The response of most of those who spoke had much more in common with John Ferguson's letter to Kitty Wintringham than it did with Acland's presentation. Even before Acland had spoken, a Mr Porter had complained of how over the past year the movement had been 'reoriented', with the downplaying of the moral. One speaker detected a drift to 'materialism' within Common Wealth, while another complained of the failure to get *Common Wealth and the New Year* approved by the membership. Significant figures in the organisation weighed in: Harry Roff, vice-chairman of Common Wealth, argued that organised religions and Marxist parties were entirely different phenomena and could not be simplistically compared, while Tom Sargant deplored the fact that *Common Wealth and the New Year* maligned Christianity to the benefit of Marxism. Tom Wintringham alone argued against this tide of opinion, initially trying to win time with a bit of procedural chicanery – that the document be referred back to the membership, but that 'for the present ... [it] ... should be used as a guide for action' – and then, seeking to gloss the critique of moralism in terms of an embedding of the moral in action, he denied 'that a separate moral can be made, if it is shut off from the actions of the world'. In a subsequent letter to Tom Wintringham, Acland particularly cited the intervention of Sargant, which he argued received 'pretty strong support' from the Conference 'or rather by certain sections of it'.[178] The upshot was that when Common Wealth came to publish *Common Wealth and the New Year* it included, on page 8, an added note that publicly revealed the dissension in the ranks on these matters: 'This leaflet was produced for the Common Wealth Conference, 1944. Certain parts of it, particularly on pages 6 and 7, were criticised. It was agreed at the Conference that the leaflet be referred to the movement for consideration and amendment.'[179]

Despite his own contribution – which doesn't seem to have been a Machiavellian ploy – Acland was undoubtedly encouraged by the turn of events at the conference, and used the occasion of the republishing of the leaflet under the new title, the year having long ceased to be 'new', of *Common Wealth in 1944* to excise the offending passage, leaving the field to the preceding pre-existing paragraph which breathed pure Acland/Ingram:

> Both Christians and non-Christians, Marxists and non-Marxists are found within CW. Some find this surprising. But both the Marxist and Christian philosophies are based on high ideals; both are based on the conception of the brotherhood of man, which both are passionately determined to achieve. We believe that through our work together the area of consonance in our social ideas will increase, not only in Common Wealth, but in a wider People's Movement.[180]

An angry Wintringham accused Acland of, in effect, abusing his position, and of reviving the quarrel of the previous November;[181] the latter, clearly relishing Wintringham's discomfiture, replied, with a brutal candour, that power relations had shifted – in *his* favour:

> I am sorry if the cutting of the phrases in condemnation of the Churches was 'sharp practice'. It may have been. I have noticed, in these matters, that there is always a tendency for those who are relatively less anxious for a document to be published to get their way in detail. Last December, when I wanted the document and others didn't I found myself forced to tolerate these phrases ... It is possible that I have taken a fraudulent advantage of the relatively reversed positions.[182]

He also could not resist giving a kicking to Wintringham's supporter at the dreadful meeting in November, John Macmurray. In response to Wintringham's citation of Macmurray's warning about the danger of Christian Socialism unintentionally exposing people to reactionary Christian ideas, Acland sought to put Macmurray in his place: 'you must not use Macmurray's fears as if they constituted a veto in CW.'[183] Since Macmurray had been more or less elevated to this status the previous year, with Acland at the sharp end, this must have been sweet to write!

And there things remained. Neither side could deliver a killer punch. The Wintringhams failed to get the hegemony of Marxism established, and Acland had to put up with an attenuated version of his Godly vision. As Acland was later ruefully to admit: 'The quarrel was never resolved either by compromise or by victory for either Tom or myself. Maybe we wore one another out.'[184] As Common Wealth entered the final year of its effective existence, overt disagreement continued, but in a new political context where Common Wealth was fighting for its life. In an important sense external forces were to bring Common Wealth down. However, the internal religious conflicts, in themselves and as aspects of broader political and philosophical differences, would have on their own seriously weakened, and possibly – at least in its current form – destroyed Common Wealth. As we saw, the Wintringhams' objection to moral language was of a piece with their opposition to seeing Common Wealth as a party rather than as a movement, both flowing from a thoroughgoing Marxist project. It is difficult to see how the broad-church Common Wealth, the product of the space created by the wartime truce, could have held together with the return of 'normal' politics. As it was, Common Wealth had been battered by the religious disputes, and the new political climate was to put it under further stress, exacerbating tensions and promoting disintegration.

## Endgame

It was the Labour Party that ultimately determined Common Wealth's fate. Labour's participation in the wartime electoral truce, and in the coalition government, had created the political space in which Common Wealth had flourished. From the end of 1943 it seemed only a matter of time before victory in the war was achieved. What would Labour now do? And what should Common Wealth do? Internally both the Labour Party and Common Wealth were sufficiently heterogeneous politically for there to be very different answers available to those two questions. With the benefit of hindsight the writing was on the wall for Common Wealth when the Labour Party proscribed them in 1943, making membership of Common Wealth 'incompatible' with membership of the Labour Party, on the grounds that it was a rival electoral organisation that had sought to encourage Labour members to break the electoral truce in by-elections.[185] It may be true, as G.D.H. Cole argued, that the ban was not 'rigidly enforced',[186] and that, as Calder documents, Common Wealth did have friends in the Labour Party, but it spoke volumes about the Labour Party leadership's view of Common Wealth. The implications of this stance for Common Wealth rather depended on what Labour would do vis-à-vis the electoral truce and the coalition government. In his later autobiographical reflections Acland spoke of 'one miracle that could have saved us',[187] namely that if Labour had remained in a coalition government after the war (and this Churchill was to propose) and fought a General Election as a coalition then Common Wealth could have prospered as the credible alternative on the left. When, however, it became clear that Labour, after much internal heart-searching, was going to leave the coalition and fight a General Election independently, Common Wealth, with options diminishing, had to do some hard thinking. Very shortly before Labour's official decision to fight, Common Wealth started to explore the possibility of becoming affiliated to the Labour Party.[188] Despite a good deal of objection in the regions, and Acland's initial opposition, the leadership came to the conclusion that this move represented their best option, and approaches were made to Labour and a meeting arranged (chaired for Labour by Harold Laski). Common Wealth asked for either affiliation or some sort of electoral arrangement whereby Labour would give Common Wealth a free run in certain constituencies. Labour wanted Common Wealth simply to dissolve and its members to join Labour as individuals. After several months without an answer, Common Wealth had a raspberry blown to them in a speech made by James Walker of the Labour National Executive Committee, at Labour's Annual Conference in December 1944. Common Wealth, Walker sneered, had been set up

> by a rich man who decided he would found a Party in order to become a leader – that is the easiest and cheapest way to become a leader. The Communists claim that their programme is based on the economics of Marx and Engels, but when I look at the Common Wealth Party I begin to think that their policy is based on the economics of Marks and Spencer. They are out looking for cheap seats, and they have nothing at all to offer the Labour Party.[189]

At a more elevated level it became clear that Labour feared that the admission of Common Wealth would start a stampede of proposals for affiliation from a whole range of leftist groups, above all from the CPGB.[190] Acland's later opinion was that 'from Labour's point of view, win or lose the impending General Election, it was far better to be on their own than to admit a factious idealistic group on their left'.[191]

Common Wealth now had their answer. One response to this rejection was that some Common Wealth members simply jumped ship and joined Labour. Even before December this had been happening, most notably the galling loss to Labour of one of the three Common Wealth MPs, John Loverseed, the victor of Eddisbury,[192] and he was quickly joined by Mackay, the former chairman, who was one of those who had always seen Common Wealth as merely a surrogate for Labour. Common Wealth as a whole weathered these incidents, though its finances looked increasingly shaky, and Mackay's defection, and the loss of some other officials weakened its administrative structure.[193] Now, however, they were faced with the prospect of fighting a General Election in which the Labour Party would be a declared opponent. Acland could not conceal his sense that things were not going well; in a leaflet he conceded that Common Wealth 'would not be able to dominate the electoral situation in Britain in 1945. We shall have to make our contribution as best we may by putting up our own candidates in a certain number of constituencies.'[194] There were things to cheer about, above all the stunning Common Wealth by-election victory at Chelmsford in April 1945 which turned the 1935 Conservative majority of 16,624 into a Common Wealth majority of 6,431.[195] But, crucially, Labour had not contested the seat, and in the two-hander between Common Wealth and the Conservatives, the former had the anti-Tory vote to itself. Chelmsford may also have reinforced the Common Wealth view that there were a significant number of constituencies where it could win but Labour could not, and therefore sustained the belief that Common Wealth could credibly go it alone in the forthcoming General Election. But they would have to fight the election with the handicap of simultaneously urging voters to support Labour in the generality of constituencies, while opposing Labour candidates in the chosen battlegrounds.

In the run-up to the General Election forty-six seats were considered possible targets, but in the end this shrank to twenty-three. Among the candidates were Acland, Tom and Kitty Wintringham and Sargant. Ingram had been the candidate for one of the discarded possibles, and in the North West Stapledon canvassed for the Common Wealth candidate for Fylde, Karl Heath. In just seven of the contests Common Wealth had no Labour opponent. Used to targeted by-elections, the organisational and financial resources of Common Wealth, weakened by personnel defection and financial shortfall, were inadequate to the task of simultaneously fighting twenty-three seats. 'In general', Calder found that the 'branches and regions seemed to have rushed into the election without much preparation or constructive forethought'.[196] Indicative of this picture of confusion and unpreparedness is Acland's decision to stand for Putney, in the wake of him honouring his commitment to the Liberal Party not to stand again in North Devon. According to his diary the maestro of the by-election made a foolish judgement based on faulty information:

> If anyone ever wants to know by what careful calculations I went to Putney the answer is, – no calculations at all, – just a stupid muddle. Carol Bunker [the National Agent] plus some members of the Putney Branch had some queer idea that the Putney Labour Party had ceased to exist and would not fight; I was away on holiday in Westmorland when Churchill forced on the election; I asked for Putney on the strength of their reports which turned out to have no shadow of foundation whatever.[197]

Elsewhere he described the ensuing campaign as 'perhaps the most politically wretched three weeks of my life';[198] his Diary instanced the bad reception he received from the working-class population of Putney: 'It is spiritually wearing to be booed by children in working class streets and to get hostile glares from men building prefabricated houses on bomb-damaged sites.'[199] In Fylde, as elsewhere, the prospect of a struggle with Labour caused trouble in Common Wealth ranks. Stapledon, in his speeches backing Karl Heath, had to justify why Common Wealth was risking splitting the socialist vote, and he recounted the recent history of relations with Labour; '*CW asked for affiliation* & electoral cooperation. But Labour refused, with contempt. Confirming our worst fears! *Yet CW supports Labour nearly everywhere ... But CW must have MPs* as mouthpiece. Therefore ... select seats where Labour has no chance. Therefore Fylde.'[200] Unfortunately for Heath, support for Labour was rife among Common Wealth branches in the region. Subsequent post-mortems showed that out of fourteen branches examined, three did no work for Heath, and over half actively supported the Labour candidate; one report concluded that

180   *The moment of Common Wealth*

the region did 'far more work for the Labour Party than for its own CW candidate'.[201]

The election was a prolonged affair lasting from 5 to 19 July (to accommodate local holidays), and the results, given the size of the poll and the need to count the overseas service vote, were not available until the 26th. Acland clearly sensed that things had not gone well for Common Wealth, predicting on the close of the polls that 'fully half of our candidates will have lost their deposits'.[202] Ingram, following a tour of a number of the constituencies in which Common Wealth had stood, wrote to Acland on 13 July. The letter must have confirmed Acland's forebodings; Ingram was down-beat about the possible results, and the tone is one of consolation and defiance. He also highlighted the baleful effect of the seemingly schizophrenic strategy of opposing Labour candidates while calling for a Labour administration:

> I want only to record my impressions after having toured round a fair number of CW constituencies. I daresay we may do badly, so far as electoral results are concerned: and the first reaction to that may incline us to defeatist and despairing conclusions, leading even to resignations by our weaker brethren. But I am quite convinced that that will be a false and merely temporary judgment. For the moral which ultimately arises is that Common Wealth has been immensely strengthened by the ordeal of this Contest ... This hasn't been our election. We were inevitably placed with one hand tied behind our backs because we were working for the return of a Labour Government – as the best alternative in the existing situation – and yet combating Labour.[203]

The results in fact were considerably worse than Acland had anticipated. There was one piece of good news – Millington held on to Chelmsford, with a reduced majority, but with a higher vote (24,548 to 27,309).[204] As in the April by-election Labour had not stood, and it was the presence or absence of Labour that determined the magnitude of Common Wealth's poll in specific constituencies. In the sixteen constituencies where there was Labour opposition all the Common Wealth candidates lost their deposits. This included Acland, who had not expected to lose *his*; he came third with 2,686 votes, behind the Conservatives (16,356) and Labour (12,469); it also included Hugh Lawson, previously Common Wealth MP for Skipton, who kept his promise to Labour not to contest that seat again, and was duly massacred in Harrow West (Lawson 2,462, Conservatives 28,617, Labour 18,961, Liberals 7,462). Stapledon was quite right that Labour would not win Fylde, which went to the Tories (37,930), but Labour polled 22,102 votes to Karl Heath's 1,784. In North Midlothian Kitty Wintringham's 3,299 votes probably provided the one example in the election where Common Wealth intervention did have a decisive effect on the outcome – unfortunately it was to the detriment of Labour, which was just pipped at the post by a Conservative majority of 1,177. Eight Common Wealth candidates in constituencies contested by Labour received less than 1,000 votes each. Of the total Common Wealth vote of 110,634 the sixteen Labour-contested constituencies delivered only 23,632 votes (21.3 per cent); the remaining 87,002 votes (78.6 per cent) came from the seven non-Labour-contested constituencies. The best of the losing candidates in these latter constituencies were Tom Wintringham with 14,435 votes (42.6 per cent of the poll) at Aldershot, Moeran at Thirsk and Malton (13,572 votes; 39.9 per cent) – both in straight fights with the Tories – and Checkland at Ecclesall (Sheffield) (12,045 votes; 35.9 per cent). The remaining three, including Sargant at Petersfield (Hampshire) with 6,600 votes and 18.5 per cent of the poll, all saved their deposits.

It was a dreadful result. Acland, long prone to bouts of depression, was 'in the bottom' for twenty-four hours.[205] In his later reminiscences he credits a visit from Tom Wintringham with snapping him out of this state by articulating a way forward. Past battles not withstanding, Acland's genuine respect for Tom is evident (though he is silent here about Kitty!):

> I've spoken disparagingly of this very great man. Although we differed about morality he really does qualify for 'They who do the work of God shall be called the children of God.' He said, at once, 'Richard, I think we should set course to wind up Common Wealth and join the Labour party as individuals.' I took about three minutes to think of it, and realised that the whole depression had gone.[206]

In subsequent years he did grapple with the question of whether this was in fact the correct thing to do. He recalled that his reasoning at the time was that Labour was now the only show in time, having captured that widespread urge for social change that Common Wealth so benefited from during the war years. To have retained a separate and oppositional existence would have seemed curmudgeonly and out of kilter with the times, not to mention being totally ineffective: '"Join us in not trusting Labour to do a proper job!" Perhaps it could have been a viable slogan in the late 1950s; but not in the last half of 1945.'[207] And yet he couldn't help reflecting on the fact that Common Wealth, like Forward March before it, had attracted in significant numbers people who had not been engaged in or with politics in the past, and his hunch was that with the ending of the effective life of Common Wealth these people in the main retreated from politics, thereby helping to create the conditions which led to Conservative electoral dominance in the 1950s and early 60s. He was therefore forced to conclude that, 'it remains an open question whether we should have tried to soldier on'.[208]

One final defeat awaited him, for he failed to get his proposal to disband accepted.[209] The central leadership was initially split between those who called for the winding up of Common Wealth and those, such as Ingram and Sargant, who wanted Common Wealth to continue as a propaganda organisation within the Labour Party. Eventually this second view was rejected as unrealistic, and the leadership pulled behind the dissolution option. This met intense opposition within many branches in the regions (though a majority of members and branches were in favour of dissolution) and from many service members overseas. They wished Common Wealth to carry on, harrying the Labour Party and positioning itself so as to be at the centre of a left-wing realignment when Labour began to fail. C.A. Smith, the leader of this opposition, flung Common Wealth's previous concern with morality in the face of its leadership:

> CW has existed to proclaim certain truths and ethical principles which have to be placed in the forefront of the propaganda of a Socialist party. I ask now how has the fact that 12 million people voted for a Labour Government changed the importance of that fact?[210]

A special conference was called for 16 September to resolve the issue. In Acland's subsequent telling, Smith expected to lose, and was taken aback when Acland suggested that the opposition would carry the day:

> As he left, I said: 'You realise you're bound to win?' 'Win!?!?' 'But of course; we shall have a gathering of branch officers and the only item on the agenda will be "That we all stop being branch officers".' I've never seen a fellow so taken aback. But of course I was right. And C.A. Smith got all the Common Wealth assets and all the debts.[211]

A significant factor was also the speech of Common Wealth's sole remaining MP, Millington, who pledged to stay in that capacity if the organisation continued to exist. This the conference agreed to do, by a vote of 119 to 89. The same day all the key members of the leadership resigned from Common Wealth: Acland, Ingram, Tom Wintringham, Kitty Wintringham, Sargant and others (Parkes had drifted away from membership some time before, and given Macmurray's somewhat ethereal relationship to the movement his absence from these proceedings, quite apart from his recent move to Edinburgh, is comprehensible). Up in West Kirby, Olaf Stapledon remained a member. The organisation he continued to support, and which retained the name Common Wealth, did not rapidly disappear, in fact it was not finally dissolved until 1993, but it was to be a mere shadow of its former self (graphically symbolised by Millington himself taking the Labour Whip in 1946).[212] The Moment of Common Wealth was well and truly over.

# Conclusion

So what roads did Macmurray, Ingram, Stapledon and Acland take following the split within Common Wealth? Three of the four were in their fifties or sixties in September 1945: Macmurray was 54, Stapledon 59 and Ingram 63; Acland was much younger, at 38. Let us therefore briefly look at their subsequent lives, before ending with a few words on the broader significance of the four and their movement.

## Stapledon

Stapledon was to live five more years after the Common Wealth split. He was conscious that his literary reputation was fading, with his back catalogue gradually going out of print and relatively little interest in his new fiction. Intellectually as hungry as ever, he began to spend time on an issue that had always interested him – the 'paranormal' (particularly telekinesis and telepathy). The universe, whether in his fictional depictions or in philosophical treatments, had always had a marked element of the uncanny, not least the numinous presiding 'spirit'; it now appeared to him more mysterious than ever, with, as he put it in *Enquiry*, a journal of 'psychical research', 'the whole universe of ordinary experience ... a superficies behind which lie unimaginable depths of existence',[1] and he greeted some of the latest findings of psychic investigators with a 'cautious acceptance'.[2] Politically he kept up his membership of Common Wealth; as one of their few remaining 'names' the party HQ plied him with invitations to speak and write for the organisation, and to sit on committees and join delegations, though as Acland had found there were limits to Stapledon's toleration of day-to-day politics. When he was asked to stump up some of the £350 required to acquire a canvassing car for a candidate he must have sent a fairly dusty reply, for an anxious letter arrived from Hubert Wilson, the hon. treasurer of Common Wealth, evidently trying to smooth ruffled feathers – 'I quite appreciate your own position as I know, of course, that political action does not in any case make a strong appeal to you';[3] when questioned by US Immigration in 1949 as to his political affiliations he prefaced the 'Fabian Society' and the 'British Soviet Society' with 'I am a member of "Common Wealth" a very small political party in England but

I am not active in it.'[4] He also became increasingly associated with movements that sought, in the context of growing hostility between the USSR and the Western powers, to promote world peace. Thus he worked with the National Peace Council (as did Ingram and Macmurray), agreeing to sit on a commission it set up to examine 'the problems of "East–West" relations'. This led to a final essay of political theory, 'The Conflict of Values: The Bridge Between' – in an edited volume published by the NPC – a 'bridge' constructed between a defence of 'Marxist Values' by Professor Hyman Levy of London University, and a vindication of 'Christian Values' by moral philosopher and former Malvern Conference speaker, Donald Mackinnon.[5] Stapledon also attended international peace conferences, most spectacularly in 1949 when he was, for reasons that remain opaque, the sole member of an eighteen-person British delegation to an international peace conference in New York to be granted a visa; indeed, he was to be the only representative from Western Europe.[6] A photograph exists of him standing next to the composer Dmitri Shostakovich, the unwilling figurehead of the Soviet delegation;[7] it was a taxing visit with hostile demonstrations and an unfriendly press. His final novel, *A Man Divided*, was published in 1950. Later that year, on 6 September, he suffered a fatal heart attack at the age of 64.

## Ingram

Preserved in the Stapledon Papers at Liverpool University is Kenneth Ingram's contribution to a fitful correspondence he conducted with Stapledon in the late 1940s. Neither a profound nor a particularly intimate exchange, it does give a little snapshot of Ingram's life as he entered his late sixties. Still the vigorous political animal, he can be glimpsed meeting MPs in the House of Commons, attending a reception at the Soviet Embassy, and discussing plans to become part of some delegation to Yugoslavia. Gregarious and intellectually energetic, he asks Stapledon to propose him for membership of the Authors' Club, invites him to address a small discussion club he regularly attends (the Grecian Club), and talks of his own membership of the Interplanetary Society when he hears that Stapledon is to give a lecture there.[8] The correspondence would appear to have been initiated by Ingram's pique at the lack of critical response to his latest book, *Communist Challenge: Good or Evil?* (1948). He wrote to Stapledon, including a copy of the book, lamenting the fact that he had 'never had a book which has been so ignored by reviewers'[9] and asking Stapledon to give him his opinion of the work. It would appear that Stapledon made appreciative noises (that it contained two favourable citations of Stapledon's *Philosophy and Living* might have helped) for Ingram wrote back, 'Thank you very much for your letter. It is just what I want.'[10] The National Peace Council (NPC) also gave them a common point of reference. Ingram was, and continued to his death to be, a very active member of the body: he was on its Executive Committee (and, like Stapledon, on the East–West Commission), and became in time vice-chairman of the organisation. He contributed a small piece, 'Can the Two Worlds Co-operate?' to the NPC volume containing Stapledon's essay on values, and produced a Council pamphlet, *Negotiation – Not Appeasement*, and a short history of the institution in 1958.[11] Related to these concerns, and also building on his experience as foreign affairs spokesperson for Common Wealth, Ingram was to produce two histories of international relations, *Years of Crisis: An International History 1919–1945* (1946) and *History of the Cold War* (1955). One wonders what Stapledon made of Ingram's chapter, 'Will Christianity Survive?' in *Communist Challenge: Good or Evil?* The validation of the philosophical and political resources of Christianity contained in it could hardly have been to his taste. In fact, there are signs in that work of a move towards a more conservative theology on Ingram's part. This turn is very evident in Ingram's final book, *Is Christianity Credible?* (1963), published when he was in his eighties, just a couple of years before his death. Still committed to a politically engaged religion, he self-consciously distances himself from elements of his 1930s religious radicalism:

> [T]here was a time when what seemed to me the ineffectiveness of the Churches moved me to despair. I formed the conclusion that a spiritual revival must emanate from some source entirely independent of ecclesiasticism. But I am now convinced that this was temperamental, an impulsive and wrong conclusion. I believe that such a revival will be conceived within the womb of orthodoxy, and not from a source which is independent of the main current of Christian tradition.[12]

Part of this is a desire to ground matters firmly in the theological traditions of Christianity, and partly a reworked conception of God that places more emphasis on the transcendent element within immanence, and conveys a more personal deity, one who has 'purposes' and can 'communicate' with humanity. Absent, palpably absent, from his post-war writings is any detailed treatment of sexuality, which, as we saw in Chapter 2, may have been attendant on Archbishop Temple's intervention following the publication of *Sex-Morality Tomorrow*. However, in *Is Christianity Credible?* the old fire burns for the briefest of moments when he commends an Anglican committee's report on homosexuality for 'rejecting the injustice and moral absurdity of the existing law'.[13] And that was that. Ingram died on 28 June 1965; he was 83 years old.

## Macmurray

In a letter to Stapledon in November 1949, Ingram reported that John Macmurray had stayed with him for a night before departing to the Gold Coast to write a report on its university.[14] Macmurray's trip was one aspect of his life following the war, that of a respected educationalist particularly concerned with educational development in the then 'colonies'. He was also invited to give public lectures both at home and abroad, most prominently the highly prestigious Gifford Lectures in 1953 and 54.[15] However, recognition in these respects could not conceal from him the fact that as a philosopher he was increasingly seen as old-fashioned and irrelevant; 'seen', in fact, is probably the wrong word for what was in effect a gradually fading visibility. The most brutal registration of this turn of events is provided in the autobiographical reflections of Macmurray's 1946 successor in the Grote Chair at London University, A.J. Ayer. In one version (for there are two) he deploys the imagery of dereliction to suggest, by the bombed-out premises of University College, London, with its philosophy department consisting 'of two tiny rooms in one of the outlying and more dilapidated parts of the college', the poor state of philosophical study under Macmurray's tenure, part of a double dereliction of duty by the latter, who it is implied had given no leadership in the subject and had then 'abandoned' the department for Edinburgh.[16] Ayer plays the whole situation for laughs, complete with an English member of staff who dressed and acted like a 'stage Frenchman', and Macmurray's former secretary, 'a Greek lady', who had become a junior lecturer in ethics. Philosophically the two men had little in common. In his second shot at the story, Ayer portrays Macmurray as a last gasp of Balliol idealism, one who 'liked to preach his doctrines outside academic circles' but who 'unfortunately ... did not display the same enthusiasm for invigorating his department';[17] he dismissively records that he 'knew next to nothing' of Macmurray's published work, and using the gap between Macmurray relinquishing the chair and his acceptance of it (which was two years, but he believed to be seven) he felt 'absolved from the usual courtesy of bestowing even a perfunctory encomium on my predecessor' in his inaugural lecture, instead dedicating it to his former tutor, Gilbert Ryle.[18] Macmurray's assessment of Ayer for the appointment committee, while much more respectful, nonetheless viewed the younger man as representing a trend that was in important respects impoverishing philosophy: 'Narrowly logical – though a leading light of the new logical school. I should think most unsuitable for you.'[19] Unfortunately for Macmurray it was Ayer and Ryle who were to be at the heart of philosophical development in Britain in the immediate years to come.

Ayer was not alone in using the imagery of preaching to characterise Macmurray. In the 1944 volume which deemed Macmurray to be one of 'ten modern prophets', it was noted that although Macmurray was a professor of philosophy, 'by temperament he is less a metaphysician than a preacher'.[20] It also, though without the offensive tones of Ayer, spoke of the lack of a definitive statement of his overarching philosophical views: 'He has not given us as yet any comprehensive philosophical treatise, but his various essays on religious, philosophical and sociological themes, his "tracts for the times" are full of profound thought and imaginative insight.'[21] An invitation to give the Gifford Lectures at Glasgow University in 1953 and 1954 provided an opportunity for Macmurray to present such a 'definitive statement', and the subsequent two-volume reworking of these lectures in *The Self as Agent* (1957) and *Persons in Relation* (1961) are the nearest he ever got to a formal statement of his basic philosophical beliefs. Although these works were to be at the centre of the revival of interest in Macmurray's work in the 1990s (initially, at least, stimulated by Tony Blair's endorsement) their abstract quality makes them curiously bloodless when compared to the richly embedded works of the 1930s. Nor, despite Macmurray's kind words towards aspects of the linguistic turn in British philosophy in the books, did they warm the contemporary big beasts of philosophy to his work. Dorothy Emmet, herself a former student of Macmurray, recalled that Gilbert Ryle used the title of one of the volumes as an occasion for mirth; as editor of *Mind* Ryle had been sent *The Self as Agent* for review: 'When I give my Gifford Lectures,' Ryle said, 'I shall take that title but separate the syllables in the last word [hence "The Self as a Gent"].'[22] Macmurray's biographer John Costello deploys a striking metaphor to bring out the response of analytical philosophers to Macmurray's work:

> To analytic ears, Macmurray's work was tonal music written in a fiercely atonal era and played on cumbersome early, even foreign, instruments. They simply walked out of the hall scornfully or – and this applies to most of them – on the basis of negative reviews by their friends, never even went inside to hear the music for themselves.[23]

Between the publication dates of the two volumes Macmurray and his wife Betty became members of the Society of Friends in 1959. We saw in the first chapter Macmurray's heartfelt declaration in 1934 that he was above all a Christian standing outside the Churches. His decision to become a Quaker seems to have hinged on an appreciation of the doctrinal inclusiveness of this denomination – the 'absence of definitive doctrinal beliefs – indeed ... an objection to them', in which he found an echo of his critique of the theoretical bias in Christianity, and which offered the prospect of a practical, communal life.[24] The previous year he had finally retired from his chair in Edinburgh. In the sixteen years of his retirement he continued to write articles and pamphlets, but after *Persons in Relation* came out in 1961 no further major books. Aged 85, he was to die on 21 June 1976.

## Acland

It is easy to forget just how much younger Acland was than Stapledon, Ingram and Macmurray. In November 1945 he celebrated his thirty-ninth birthday, and was to live another forty-four years. After leaving Common Wealth in 1945 he had joined the Labour Party, and was thought of sufficiently highly by Herbert Morrison that he was offered the chance to contest a by-election at Gravesend in 1947 as the Labour Party candidate. Gravesend had gone to Labour in 1945 after being in Tory hands since 1924 but the sitting MP, Garry Allighan, had been expelled from the Commons for making false allegations and corruption. This and the fact that Labour had done badly in the recent municipal elections (including in Gravesend) meant that there was a real chance that the seat might revert to the Conservatives. But if anyone could win a by-election it was Acland. Campaigning under what one might consider a rather risky slogan for a member of the governing party – 'Tough Times: So What?' – he duly won the seat, though with a majority reduced from 7,056 to 1,675.[25] As ever, he was not to everyone's taste, including some fellow party members; Hugh Gaitskell, who had spoken for him in the campaign, though pleased with the result was scathing about the victor:

> The Gravesend by-election result has cheered everybody up immensely. Those who know, of course, are not enthusiastic about Acland coming back to the House. What a bore he is! ... He hardly condescended to shake hands and uttered no word of thanks afterwards.[26]

Still, he managed to improve his electoral performance in the years to come, for at the General Election in 1950 he increased his majority to 5,571 and in 1951 to 5,755.[27] He was, however, to part company with the Labour Party over the issue of nuclear weapons, an issue which was to lead him in 1958 to be one of the founder members of the Campaign for Nuclear Disarmament (CND).[28] In the wake of Atlee's decision to back Churchill's proposal to manufacture British hydrogen bombs in 1955, Acland resigned from his seat to force a by-election. Unfortunately Churchill chose that moment to stand down, whereupon Eden called a General Election. As Acland recalled, this transformed his chances because 'no one noticed an isolated anti-nuclear candidate in a single constituency'.[29] He came third behind the Conservative victor (22,058), and the new Labour candidate (19,149), just saving his deposit with a not unrespectable 6,514 votes.[30] So ended his parliamentary career, in which over twenty years he had represented three parties – Liberal, Common Wealth and Labour. Now, aged 49, his life took a new direction for he applied for a job as an assistant teacher at Wandsworth School in London (his grandfather had, after all, been Gladstone's minister of education), initially as an RE teacher (at which he was so bad that he 'had to ask the headmaster to relieve [him] of these ... duties'[31]) and then, for four years, as a teacher of maths and physics.[32] In January 1960 his experience at the school was deemed 'just' sufficient to get him a lecturing post at St Luke's College of Education in Exeter (whose premises had been partly funded by earlier Aclands), thus allowing him to return permanently to his beloved Devon,[33] and he remained at the college until his retirement in 1974.

Politically he maintained strained relations with the Labour Party, writing in *The Next Step* (1974): 'I have at different times joined the Labour Party, spectacularly resigned from the Labour Party, rejoined the Labour Party, and now failed to renew my subscription to the Labour Party.'[34] Hilson and Melling reveal that when the Social Democratic Party emerged at the beginning of the 1980s, Acland 'aligned himself' with this breakaway from

Labour.³⁵ Common Wealth was always to hold a treasured place in his memory; as he wrote in 'A Personal Postscript' to one of the chapters of *The Next Step*:

> it would be good to reconstitute something like Common Wealth; but refined, of course, by the knowledge and the social experience that have come to us since 1945 ... It was all very exciting. Naturally I want to believe that the same sort of thing is needed all over again.³⁶

Francis Wheen, in his biography of Tom Driberg, unearths a moment when it seemed to Acland that this was a possibility. Unfortunately it was a madcap scheme by Driberg in 1969 to start a new political movement centred on his new friends Mick Jagger and Marianne Faithfull. He wrote to Acland, who as we saw played a crucial part in his entering parliament, seeking his support, and got an enthusiastic response which returned to the experience of Common Wealth. Driberg in return ran with this theme: 'Perhaps Common Wealth was a not-quite-right rehearsal?' The plans soon petered out, with Jagger and Faithfull proving difficult to pin down. The final act was a meeting in London between Driberg, Acland and the Trotskyist journalist Paul Foot, who had reluctantly been drawn into Driberg's plans; following Foot's rejection of a rejuvenated Common Wealth, Foot and Acland were prevailed upon by Driberg, in Foot's jaundiced words, to go to 'some ghastly gay bar in one of those shady streets in Soho, where he [Driberg] flirted in a quite appalling manner with the waiters'.³⁷

Acland continued to bring out books over the years: *Public Speaking* (1946) provided, on the basis of his political career, a how-to guide for tyro political speakers; *Nothing Left to Believe* (1949) returned to the political/religious concerns that had animated his books in the early 1940s ('I want to write about the unchanging Christian truth in the context of our changing world'³⁸); *Waging Peace* (1958) outlined his case against nuclear weapons; *Why So Angry?* (1958) set itself the modest task of 'working out ... an acceptable relationship between one person and the whole maelstrom of contemporary world history';³⁹ *We Teach Them Wrong* (1963) dwelt on the problems of teaching religion to children, and in his words 'was quite well reviewed, went into three editions and produced no effect whatever',⁴⁰ while *The Next Step* (1974) contained his latest thoughts on the political way forward for Britain, and a typically eccentric Acland preface containing the surreal 'I hope to add a footnote in Chapter 13 at about 9.0 a.m. on March 1st' and the grandiloquent 'This book is not a piece of journalism. Its time span is from before 3,000,000,000 BC to at least the middle of the twenty-second century.'⁴¹ His final book, *Hungry Sheep*, appeared in 1988 the year that he turned 82. The energy and enthusiasm are as strong as ever, as is the passionate following of contemporary social and political developments, and of recent theoretical work upon these trends. The deep moral sense is there also, a capacity to empathise with human suffering, and a desire to castigate oppression; also the use of telling examples, in one case from his family's past:

> As lately as in 1853, John Creech, in search of work, walked twenty-five miles from my great great grandfather's estate near Porlock to my great great uncle's estate near Tiverton. Finding none, he walked twenty-four of the miles back before dying in the snow on Dunkery Beacon. Next day his widow came begging and the vicar gave her a shilling.[42]

The book shows his socialist principles to be still in place, and the commitment to Common Ownership of the major resources of society still intense. The broader argument is about the need to see all of this from a religious perspective, though one at variance from much of institutional Christianity. At one point he calls himself 'a not very devout Christian',[43] which is not a piece of pious self-deprecation but is an expression of his inner struggles over faith and belief. In one of his unpublished autobiographical fragments from 1978 he talks of his religious life in the years after his mystical experience in distinctly melancholic tones:

> I have talked about a trumpet blast from heaven or a gale wind through the interstices of my body. It would be nice to say the experience transformed my life. At first, I was enthusiastically confident of the new faith as any convert. For fifteen years I tried hard to take it seriously. But this did not last, and by now I cannot be sure that my daily life would be seriously different if I were not a nominal Christian.[44]

Even in the midst of these dark reflections, however, he asserts a continuing belief in the presence of the divine in the progress of humanity, using a quote from *The Significance of Jesus* by W.R. Maltby (1929) which he had returned to time and again since reading it shortly after his conversion in 1940:

> There is, however, one aspect of religious truth from which I have not wavered, and this record should include the sentence which I have several times described as the lodestar of my personal endeavour. It comes from *The Significance of Jesus* [pp. 39–40] 'there is, I believe, already within our reach, a nobler more reasonable, more comprehensive message than ever our fathers knew – and this not because we are wiser or even more sincere than they, but because it is not for nothing that the Spirit of God has been at work upon the minds of men during these years of amazing research and fearless interrogation'.[45]

It would seem that in later life he became what Hilson and Melling refer to as a 'Quanglican', namely an Anglican with distinct Quaker sympathies, and they cite a source that claims that Acland was latterly a member of both the Anglican Church and the Society of Friends.[46] In *Hungry Sheep* there is a move away from the Anglicanism of his time in Common Wealth towards a position much closer to the views held then by Kenneth Ingram, who is not mentioned, and John Macmurray, who is. He talks of 'all that I gained by association with Professor John Macmurray', particularly about 'the on-going conflict between Christianity understood as the eternal purposes of Jesus, and "Christianity" as offered at any particular time by the institution that works in his name'. Macmurray, he asserts, 'showed us how to look at religion in a twentieth-century way', but he adds, and here one catches an echo perhaps of their fateful interview at the height of the religious conflict in Common Wealth, 'but he hardly wrote a line which would help us to understand the twentieth century', adding, 'In what follows I shall try to avoid making this mistake'.[47] One thing he could not avoid were more of those wonky, slightly batty metaphors that had always peppered his works, the prize probably going to: 'If we want a more likely mental image of Jesus as he was seen by his contemporaries, we might picture the kind of man whom eight international forwards would like to have behind them at scrum half.'[48] Anyway, this was his final book. He died on 24 November 1990, two days short of his eighty-fourth birthday.

## Secularism and its tensions

'To-day religion is once more "in the air",' wrote Olaf Stapledon in the late 1940s:

> We have passed through a long period when 'advanced thinkers' rejected it as sheer superstition ... But to-day not only 'advanced thinkers' but hosts of ordinary people have learnt the lesson. They recognize that ... religion (in some sense of that ambiguous word) must come back into its own.[49]

Today religion is once more back on the agenda. Not that it ever went away, but at the moment many of our own 'advanced thinkers' – one thinks for example of Žižek, Badiou and Habermas – have placed religion at the heart of their current speculations, and this is different. The talk now is of the emergence of a postsecular era. Clearly one can point to the rise of militant religious/political projects (graphically manifested in 9/11) as a causal factor in this new focus, but the 'turn to religion'[50] in philosophy and social theory was underway before these tumultuous events. Perhaps it makes sense to talk of postsecularism as the most recent manifestation of a recurring phenomenon within the rise of modern secularism, with Stapledon and his fellow thinkers representing an earlier recurrence.

In *God's Funeral*, A.N. Wilson refers to Thomas Carlyle's discussion in 1832 of Boswell's *Life of Johnson*. Carlyle contrasts the religious and spiritual Dr Johnson with the great sceptical philosopher David Hume, characterising them as 'the two half-men of their time' and asserting, 'who so should combine the intrepid Candour and decisive scientific Clearness of Hume, with the

Reverence, the love and devout Humility of Johnson, were the whole man of a new time'.[51] Articulated here is an emphatic sense of the Janus face of modern secularism, from one aspect an invigorating humanism, but from the other an enervating sense of the diminishment or even loss of the dimension of the sacred; there is also the conviction that this need not be so. Currently such ideas are very much in evident in recent postsecular thinking. In its left/liberal form as understood by, say, John Caputo, postsecularism involves 'a certain *iteration* of the Enlightenment by another means, the production of a New Enlightenment, one that is enlightened about the limits of the old one':[52] in other words, a defence of the political and social achievements of liberal modernity but one that does not entail the marginalisation or denial of the religious. Perhaps, therefore, we can speak of a recurring point of resistance to these perceived negative features of secularism. Postsecularism is then to be understood, in Hent de Vries's words, 'not as an attempt at historical periodization ... but merely as a topical indicator for – well, a problem',[53] and not a new one, though in a new context. As Charles Taylor has argued in his monumental *A Secular Age*, North Atlantic secularism was nurtured in, and emerged out of, Western Christendom; he rejects what he terms 'subtraction stories' of the emergence of modern exclusive humanism, 'that humans ... lost, or sloughed off, or liberated themselves from certain earlier, confining horizons, or illusions, or limitations of knowledge'; in short, 'an acceptable form of exclusive humanism had to be imagined. And this couldn't be done overnight. Nor could it arise in one leap, but it came to be in a series of phases, emerging out of earlier Christian forms.'[54] Terry Eagleton in his spirited critique of the 'new atheism' of Richard Dawkins and Christopher Hitchens (out of which he mischievously constructs a composite 'Ditchkins') uses Nietzsche's parity of disrespect for both Liberalism and Christianity to likewise highlight the degree of continuity between the two: 'Friedrich Nietzsche did not oppose liberalism to Christianity in the manner of Ditchkins. He saw them as pretty much of a piece and condemned them both ... Secular liberalism is in no sense the "natural" antidote to religious faith.'[55] The fractured legacy was always there to be rediscovered. Thus, Taylor argues that the culture of modern Western society has experienced what he terms 'cross-pressures'; on the one hand there is the appeal of 'narratives of closed immanence', world views which do not need, and do not seek, the dimension of transcendence to give shape or meaning to life and the world, but on the other hand there is a recurring sense of the inadequacy of this closure; the result has been the creation of 'a number of middle positions, which have drawn from both sides'.[56] He situates Carlyle as a product of these cross-pressures, and provides an account of the recurrence of these pressures on figures such as Matthew Arnold, and in literary creations such as Mrs Humphry Ward's *Robert Elsmere*. Here the various narratives of 'loss of faith' are not simplistically seen as exemplars of 'subtraction' theories of the decline of religion, but as personal struggles of individuals caught in the grip of conflicting impulses, between the unacceptability of Christianity for those who have deeply internalized the immanent order (or come to see themselves totally within it), on the one hand, and a strong dissatisfaction with the flatness, emptiness of the world, and/or the inner division, atomism, ugliness or self-enclosed nature of human life in modernity.[57]

Rather than a 'loss of faith', it is more an attempt to salvage what is deemed to be affirming in Christianity, but in a form that excises what is deemed to be objectionable in traditional dogmatic forms of this faith.

The interwar thinkers discussed in this book to an extent anticipate some of the analytical and normative moves to be found in contemporary postsecular theorising. Whatever else it might be, Macmurray's *The Clue to History* is an attempt to unravel the tensions and contradictions to be found within emergent modern secularism, and he is as adamant as Taylor that the story is not simply about loss and disenchantment. Likewise, Habermas's call that the 'major religions must reappropriate the normative foundations of the liberal state *on their own premises*'[58] echoes Ingram's long struggle to do this in relation to homosexuality, something which Habermas still considers a mighty ask (for it is 'necessary to revise attitudes and prescriptions that (as with the dogmatic prejudice against homosexuality ... ) claim support from ... long-standing traditions of interpretations of the holy scriptures').[59] Then there is the impulse, found in all four writers, to expand the definition of the religious. Stapledon, for example, using the fact that 'God' is absent in the word 'religion', deploys an ancient etymology of the term (*religare* – to re-bind) to argue for the religious status of science, which 'in giving man a sense of his indissoluble unity with the rest of the cosmos ... has been almost literally *religious*, binding, harmonizing'.[60] In similar vein – leaving aside the reference to 'Christian', which Stapledon would not have relished – the contemporary Italian philosopher Gianni Vattimo, casting his gaze over the period of the Enlightenment, opines that

> Voltaire was more religious than the Jesuits ... because the Jesuits were becoming guardians of the traditional order of society, while Voltaire was leading the case for the society of man. In many senses ... what seemed to be 'less Christian' was actually 'more Christian'.[61]

Acland's recommendation of Ingram's books 'to those who think they do not believe in God at all' is also in this territory.[62]

Common Wealth provided a political home for this group of idealists, and for a plethora of other such idealisms. The whole enterprise crackled with utopian energy. It was unlike existing parties. That there was intense internal debate as to whether Common Wealth was a party or a movement suggests the unusual nature of this organisation. Much of its membership was attracted by the idea that it had a different, indeed higher, calling than its political competitors, hence its capacity to draw in people disillusioned with existing parties, and those who had previously not been politically active. Kenneth Ingram, reflecting on his decision to join Forward March, saw Acland's creation as providing 'some corporate expression' for a 'quickening of perception' in society.[63] For Ingram the goals of Common Wealth had an austere, selfless quality to them – they were about moral rectitude, not material advantage: it is not 'a cause which will bring gain to its adherents'; rather, 'it expresses at this stage of social development what both true Christianity and true Humanism demand'.[64] The heterogeneity of the idealism attracted to the new body was to Ingram a source of strength and an indication of authenticity, and, as we saw, Common Wealth could encompass both the orthodox Christian clergyman the Rev. George Jager and the Marxist Wintringhams. Ingram sought to give a dialectical glow to this plurality – 'a specifically Christian body would not have contained the necessary antithesis: and a thesis cannot by itself produce a synthesis'[65] – but, as shown in Chapter 5, the conflict over fundamental visions introduced dangerous levels of instability. The overarching context provided a temporary space in which this extraordinary venture could briefly thrive. The electoral truce threatened seriously to inhibit the proper political treatment of the problems and opportunities produced by wartime conditions, and Common Wealth skilfully responded to the widespread discontent at this state of affairs. The sheer depth of the challenges threatening Britain powerfully stimulated the appetite for political and social innovation, and made the unthinkable thinkable. 'This war,' wrote Olaf Stapledon in 1942, 'is teaching us, slowly, painfully, surely.'[66] The lessons learnt were to sweep Labour to power, but that victory surely owes something to Acland's dogged determination to prevent politics becoming another casualty of war.

# Notes

**Introduction**

1 Contemporary photograph of blackboard showing the result in A. Calder, *The People's War: Britain 1939–45*, London: Jonathan Cape, 1969, Illustration no. 63 (between pages 512 and 513).
2 R. Rorty, 'Religion as Conversation-Stopper', in R. Rorty, *Philosophy and Social Hope*, London: Penguin, 1999, p. 169. He was subsequently to modify his argument, distinguishing between the pernicious role of 'ecclesiastical organizations' that promulgate 'orthodoxy' and acquire 'economic and political clout' and parish-level 'congregations'; the former 'are the target of secularists like myself'; R. Rorty, 'Religion in the Public Square: A Reconsideration', *Journal of Religious Ethics*, 31:1, 2003, p. 141. My thanks to Michael Bacon for pointing out this article to me.
3 J. Habermas, *Between Naturalism and Religion*, Cambridge: Polity, 2008; C. Taylor, 'A Catholic Modernity?' in J.L. Heft (ed.) *A Catholic Modernity?* New York and Oxford: Oxford University Press, 1999.
4 Tom Wintringham to Kenneth Ingram, 16 July 1944. Wintringham Papers, Liddell Hart Centre for Military Archives, King's College London, 3/6/2.
5 J.B. Coates, *Ten Modern Prophets*, London: Frederick Muller, 1944. The others were Gerald Heard, Aldous Huxley, Julian Huxley, C.E.M. Joad, D.H. Lawrence, John Middleton Murry, H.G. Wells and Karl Marx.
6 Coates, *Ten Modern Prophets*, p. 7.
7 J. Macmurray, *The Clue To History*, London: Student Christian Movement Press, 1938, p. 28.
8 J.E., 'Review of *Sex-Morality Tomorrow*', *International Journal of Psychoanalysis*, 22, 1941, p. 176.
9 O. Stapledon, 'Outgrowing a Great Religion', Stapledon Papers, Liverpool University, F.13.21.
10 In the Acland Papers at Exeter University.
11 A.L.R. Calder, 'The Common Wealth Party 1942–1945', unpublished DPhil thesis, University of Sussex, 1968.
12 J.E. Costello, *John Macmurray: A Biography*, Edinburgh: Floris Books, 2002, pp. 81–2.
13 K. Ingram, *Modern Thought on Trial*, London: Philip Allan, 1933, pp. 17–19.
14 R. Crossley, *Olaf Stapledon: Speaking for the Future*, Liverpool: Liverpool University Press, 1994, p. 144.
15 He claimed (in 1974) that his 'first political memory (and I'm really rather proud of it)' was when he was sent to Coventry at school 'for saying in comment on atrocity stories by German soldiers, that probably much the same sort of thing

was done by British, French and Russian troops'; R. Acland, *Personal Political Memoirs*, p. 1. Acland Papers, University of Exeter, EUL MS 104/4 (1).
16 Costello, *John Macmurray*, p. 74.
17 Ibid., Chapter 13, pp. 256–62, 267–70, 275–8; also D. Ormrod, 'The Christian Left and the Beginnings of Christian–Marxist Dialogue, 1935–45', in J. Obelkevich, L. Roper and R. Samuel (eds), *Disciplines of Faith: Studies in Religion, Politics and Patriarchy*, London: Routledge & Kegan Paul, 1987, pp. 435–50.
18 K. Ingram, *The Night Is Far Spent*, London: George Allen & Unwin, 1941, p. 78.
19 In an interview with Angus Calder in the 1960s he said that he joined the Labour Party after leaving the army (he had previously been a Tory), and was 'on and off a member since'; Angus Calder, interview with Kenneth Ingram, 20 January 1965, tape recording 15/7, Common Wealth Papers, University of Sussex. Also, in a memoir of his mother he noted that in the 1930s 'her own religious and social and political outlook had expanded in much the same directions as my own ... At the General Election of 1935 she spent afternoons and evenings addressing envelopes for our Labour candidate'; K. Ingram, 'Portrait of a Mother', in K.A. Ingram, *Towards Old Age*, London: Quality Press, 1945, pp. 29–30; K. Ingram, *Modern Thought on Trial*, London: Philip Allan, 1933, p. 238.
20 O. Stapledon, *New Hope For Britain*, London: Methuen, 1939, p. 133.
21 Crossley, *Olaf Stapledon*, p. 94.
22 O. Stapledon, 'Why I am a Socialist', Stapledon Papers, F.13.18.
23 Crossley, *Olaf Stapledon*, pp. 231–2, pp. 259–61.
24 Acland, *Personal Political Memoirs*, p. 10.
25 Ibid., p. 1.
26 O. Stapledon, 'Do We Need a New Religion?' (January 1943), Stapledon Papers, F.32.5.
27 Ibid.
28 Acland, *Personal Political Memoirs*, 1974, p. 15.
29 Stapledon, *New Hope for Britain*, p. 158.
30 K. Ingram, *Christianity – Right or Left?* London: George Allen & Unwin, p. 82.
31 E. Bloch, *Heritage of Our Times*, Cambridge: Polity Press, 1991, p. 140.
32 R. Acland, *The Forward March*, London: George Allen & Unwin, 1941, p. 30.
33 *Report of a Religious Delegation to Spain – April 1937*, London: Victor Gollancz, 1937, p. 12.
34 Ibid., p. 13.
35 Ibid., p. 9.
36 *Hansard*, House of Commons Debates, vol. 321, 25 March 1937, c. 3129.
37 Crossley, *Olaf Stapledon*, pp. 238–9.
38 R. Acland, *Unser Kampf: Our Struggle*, Harmondsworth: Penguin, 1940, pp. 82–3.
39 J. Macmurray, 'Religion in Soviet Russia' (typescript and manuscript, 1943), p. 1; Macmurray Papers, Edinburgh University, Gen. 2162.2.39.
40 Ibid., p. 6.
41 O. Stapledon, 'Religion To-Day', *Faith and Freedom*, 3:2 (8), Spring 1950, p. 52; also O. Stapledon 'The Conflict of Values: The Bridge Between', in a collection of essays (without a named editor), *Two Worlds in Focus: Studies of the Cold War*, London: National Peace Council, 1950, p. 51.
42 Quoted in C. Collette, 'Questions of Gender: Labour and Women' in B. Brivati and R. Heffernan (eds), *The Labour Party: A Centenary History*, Houndmills: Macmillan, 2000, p. 409.

**1 John Macmurray**

1 Quoted in F.G. Kirkpatrick, *John Macmurray: Community Beyond Political Philosophy*, Lanham: Rowman and Littlefield, 2005, p. 157.

2 J. Warren, 'Blair's Guru', *The Philosophers' Magazine*, fourth quarter 2006, pp. 41–4; also M. Bevir and D. O'Brien, 'From Idealism to Communitarianism: The Inheritance and Legacy of John Macmurray', *History of Political Thought*, 24:2, 2003, pp. 305–29, and J. Rentoul, *Tony Blair: Prime Minister*, London: Warner Books, 2001, pp. 41–3.
3 See the vague generalities in T. Blair, 'Foreword', in P. Conford (ed.), *The Personal World: John Macmurray on Self and Society*, Edinburgh: Floris Books, 1996, pp. 9–10. Gareth Dale in his recent study of Karl Polanyi, who was to encourage Macmurray in his reading of the early Marx, is clearly exasperated by Blair's claim of affinity: 'one must wonder either at the former prime minister's command of philosophy or at his capacity to speak the truth'; *Karl Polanyi: The Limits of the Market*, Cambridge: Polity, 2010, p. 40.
4 For biographical information on Macmurray see J. Costello, *John Macmurray: A Biography*, Edinburgh: Floris, 2002; and 'Macmurray, John (1891–1976)', *Oxford Dictionary of National Biography*, Oxford: Oxford University Press, 2004.
5 The document is undated but talks about how Macmurray 'entered' Glasgow University as a student 'a quarter of a century ago', which yields 1934 as the date of writing. Internal evidence, particularly the range of themes, suggests it cannot be much later than this. The catalogue of the John Macmurray Collection at Regis College Library, University of Toronto, suggests 'c.1934' (Macmurray's biographer John E. Costello kindly sent me a copy of this catalogue).
6 John Macmurray, 'Here I Stand', p. 1. Macmurray Papers, Edinburgh University, Gen.2162.2.53.
7 Ibid., p. 2.
8 Ibid.
9 Ibid., p. 4.
10 John Macmurray, *Search for Reality in Religion*, London: Friends Home Service Committee, 1965, p. 21.
11 Ibid., p. 25. Macmurray does not specify the date of the conference, but his biographer confidently asserts the 1932 date (Costello, *John Macmurray*, p. 197). Andrew Collier's guess of 1919 for the conference seems implausible (A. Collier, 'Macmurray and Marx: The Philosophy of Practice and the Overcoming of Dualism', in D. Fergusson and N. Dower (eds), *John Macmurray: Critical Perspectives* New York: Peter Lang, 2002, p. 69.)
12 David Leopold says that the 1956 translation by Martin Milligan was preceded by a translation by Ria Stone but this was only circulated in mimeographed form, and he has never seen a copy; *The Young Karl Marx: German Philosophy, Modern Politics, and Human Flourishing*, Cambridge: Cambridge University Press, 2007, p. 4, note 13. Frank G. Kirkpatrick maintains that Macmurray 'was the first English scholar to make use of the 1932 collection of Marx's early writings'; *John Macmurray*, p. 27; presumably 'English' here means 'native English-speaking' scholar. In Chapters 3 and 4 of his book Kirkpatrick provides a valuable discussion of the relationship between Macmurray and Marx.
13 J. Macmurray, 'The Early Development of Marx's Thought', in J. Lewis, K. Polanyi and D.K. Kitchin (eds), *Christianity and the Social Revolution*, London: Victor Gollancz, 1935. Macmurray's citation shows that he had access to the two-volume 1932 Leipzig edition of the early works: S. Landshut and J.P. Mayer (eds), *Der Historische Materialismus: Die Frühschriften*, Leipzig: Alfred Kröner Verlag, 1932. On Macmurray's relationship with Polanyi see Costello, *John Macmurray*, pp. 200–2, pp. 222–35. Polanyi's acquaintance with the *Manuscripts* is evident in his own essay in *Christianity and the Social Revolution*, 'The Essence of Fascism', especially pp. 374–6. When Polanyi came to live in England in the 1930s his relationship with Macmurray flourished, and he became deeply involved with the Christian Left. His sophisticated understanding of the

Manuscripts can be seen in 'Notes of a Week's Study on The Early Writings of Karl Marx and Summary of Discussions on British Working Class Consciousness', *Christian Left Group Bulletin* 2, 1 January 1938 (although anonymous, Fred Block provides convincing evidence for Polanyi's authorship in 'Karl Polanyi and the Writing of *The Great Transformation*', *Theory and Society*, 32, 2003, p. 303, footnote 12). In this work Polanyi calls Marxism 'prophetic teaching ... the most important since Jesus' (p. 2), adding that Marx 'came very near to defining the personal' but did not 'quite achieve this definition; it is still complex and tentative compared with Macmurray's present formulation' (p. 10). For a study of Polanyi see Dale, *Karl Polanyi: The Limits of the Market*.
14 I deal with this more fully in V. Geoghegan, 'Religion and Communism: Feuerbach, Marx and Bloch', *The European Legacy*, 9:5, 2004, pp. 585–95.
15 L. Feuerbach, *The Essence of Christianity*, New York: Harpers & Row, 1957, p. xxxvi.
16 Ibid., p. 12.
17 K. Marx, *Contribution to the Critique of Hegel's Philosophy of Law. Introduction*, in K. Marx and F. Engels, *Collected Works*, vol. 3, London: Lawrence and Wishart, 1975, p. 175.
18 K. Marx, *Economic and Philosophic Manuscripts of 1844*, Marx and Engels, vol. 3, p. 272.
19 Marx, *Contribution to the Critique of Hegel's Philosophy of Law. Introduction*, Marx and Engels, vol. 3, p. 176.
20 K. Marx, *On the Jewish Question*, Marx and Engels, vol. 3, p. 159. See also W. Breckman's discussion of this issue in *Marx, the Young Hegelians, and the Origins of Radical Social Theory: Dethroning the Self*, Cambridge: Cambridge University Press, 1999, pp. 292–7.
21 Marx, *Contribution to the Critique of Hegel's Philosophy of Law. Introduction*, Marx and Engels, vol. 3, p. 176.
22 I. Berlin, *Flourishing: Letters 1928–1946*, ed. Henry Hardy, London: Pimlico, 2005, p. 115; see also: M. Ignatieff, *Isaiah Berlin: A Life*, London: Chatto and Windus, 1998, p. 71. A fact worth noting is Berlin's relative weakness in German: 'I sat there reading ... the Marx–Engels *Ausgabe*, in German, badly – my German is not good – with dictionaries, but if I could read anything in translation, I did it, the same way as I used cribs at school'; Berlin, *Flourishing*, p. 115.
23 I. Berlin, *Karl Marx: His Life and Environment*, London: Thornton Butterworth, 1939, p. 33, p. 79.
24 Ibid., p. 77.
25 Ibid., p. 97. One might note in contrast Jonathan Wolf's recent comment that *On The Jewish Question* 'is possibly one of the most important and influential works of political philosophy of the last two hundred years'. *Why Read Marx Today?* Oxford: Oxford University Press, 2002, pp. 3–4.
26 I. Berlin, *Karl Marx: His Life and Environment*, fourth edition, Oxford: Oxford University Press, 1978, p. x, p, xii.
27 K. Marx and F. Engels, *Selected Works*, London: Lawrence and Wishart, 1970, pp. 584–5.
28 F. Mehring, *Karl Marx: The Story of His Life*, Ann Arbor: University of Michigan Press, 1962, Chapters 2 and 3.
29 G.V. Plekhanov, *Fundamental Problems of Marxism*, London: Lawrence and Wishart, n.d., pp. 13–33.
30 E.H. Carr, *Karl Marx: A Study in Fanaticism*, London: Dent, 1934, pp. 68–9, p. 305.
31 Ignatieff, *Isaiah Berlin*, p. 71.
32 Berlin, *Karl Marx*, fourth edition, p. x.
33 Berlin, *Flourishing*, p. 200.

34 Carr's judgement comes from an unpublished 'Autobiographical Sketch' (1980) quoted in J. Haslam, *The Vices of Integrity: E.H. Carr, 1892–1982*, London: Verso, 1999, p. 53.
35 E.P. Lam, 'Does Macmurray Understand Marx?', *Journal of Religion*, 20:1, 1940, p. 53.
36 Ibid., p. 65.
37 Costello's biography is a great source for following the emergence of the early ideas of Macmurray; there is also a very useful discussion of this issue in Chapter 2, 'An Intellectual Biography of John Macmurray: From Evangelicalism to Marxism', of Frank G. Kirkpatrick's *John Macmurray*.
38 D. Emmet, *Philosophers and Friends: Reminiscences of Seventy Years in Philosophy*, Basingstoke: Macmillan, 1996, p. 4; Bevir and O'Brien, 'From Idealism to Communitarianism', p. 307. As we shall see, both Stapledon and Acland were undergraduates at Balliol – Stapledon a few years before Macmurray, Acland much later (Ingram did not go to university).
39 Emmet, *Philosophers and Friends*, p. 4.
40 John Macmurray, 'The Conception of Society', in E. McIntosh (ed.), *Selected Philosophical Writings*, Exeter: Imprint Academic, 2004, p. 96.
41 Ibid., p. 101.
42 J. Macmurray, *Freedom in the Modern World*, London: Faber & Faber, 1932, p. 127.
43 J. Macmurray, *Interpreting the Universe*, London: Faber & Faber, 1933, p. 22.
44 Ibid., p. 158.
45 J. Macmurray, *The Philosophy of Communism*, London: Faber & Faber, 1933, p. 36.
46 Macmurray, 'The Early Development of Marx's Thought', p. 219.
47 Ibid.
48 D. McLellan (ed.), *Karl Marx: Selected Writings*, second edition, Oxford: Oxford University Press, 2000, p. 53.
49 Macmurray, 'The Early Development of Marx's Thought', pp. 230–1.
50 McLellan (ed.), *Karl Marx: Selected Writings*, p. 34.
51 Macmurray, 'The Early Development of Marx's Thought', p. 229.
52 E. Bloch, *The Principle of Hope*, Oxford: Basil Blackwell, 1986, p. 1286.
53 E. Bloch, *Atheism in Christianity: The Religion of the Exodus and the Kingdom*, New York: Herder and Herder, 1972, p. 210.
54 Bloch, *The Principle of Hope*, p. 274.
55 Bloch, *Atheism in Christianity*, p. 209.
56 E. Bloch, *The Utopian Function of Art and Literature: Selected Essays*, Cambridge, MA: MIT Press, 1988, p. 50.
57 Bloch, *The Principle of Hope*, p. 1199.
58 Bloch, *Atheism in Christianity*, p. 9.
59 Bloch, *The Principle of Hope*, p. 1201.
60 Macmurray, 'Here I Stand', p. 1.
61 J. Macmurray, 'Reflections on H.G.W's [H.G. Wood] Reflections on Communism and Christianity', pp. 11–12, Macmurray Papers, Gen. 2162.2.30. The manuscript is undated, but probably dates from 1933/4 when H.G. Wood was actively publishing on this theme; see H.G. Wood, *The Truth and Error of Communism*, London: Student Christian Movement Press, 1933; also Wood's 'The Truth and Falsity of Communism', published in a pamphlet which also contained Macmurray's 'The Challenge of Communism'. These were originally speeches given by Wood and Macmurray at a meeting of the Industrial Christian Fellowship, 30 January 1934, in (no ed.) *Christianity and Communism*, London: The Industrial Christian Fellowship, 1934.
62 Macmurray, 'Reflections', p. 3.
63 See V. Geoghegan, *Utopianism and Marxism*, London: Methuen, 1987; reprinted with new introduction, London: Peter Lang, 2008.

64 Macmurray, *The Philosophy of Communism*, p. 43.
65 J. Macmurray, *The Clue to History*, London: Student Christian Movement Press, 1938, p. 8.
66 Ibid., p. 9.
67 Ibid., p. 13.
68 Ibid., p. 15.
69 J. Macmurray, *Reason and Emotion*, London: Faber & Faber, 1935, p. 248.
70 Macmurray, *The Philosophy of Communism*, p. 80.
71 Macmurray, *Freedom in the Modern World*, p. 205.
72 Macmurray, *The Philosophy of Communism*, p. 66.
73 Ibid.
74 Ibid., p. 67.
75 Ibid., p. 73.
76 John Macmurray, 'Christianity and Communism: Towards a Synthesis', in Lewis *et al.* (eds), *Christianity and the Social Revolution*, p. 519.
77 Ibid., p. 511.
78 J. Macmurray, *Creative Society: A Study of the Relation of Christianity to Communism*, London: Student Christian Movement Press, 1935, p. 27.
79 Ibid., p. 91.
80 Ibid., p. 79.
81 Ibid., pp. 84–5.
82 Ibid., p. 87.
83 Macmurray, *Freedom in the Modern World*, pp. 70–1.
84 Macmurray, *The Clue to History*, p. 28.
85 Ibid., p. 34.
86 Ibid., p. 32.
87 C. Taylor, 'A Catholic Modernity?', in J.L. Heft (ed.), *A Catholic Modernity?* New York and Oxford: Oxford University Press, 1999, p. 13.
88 R. Rorty, *Philosophy and Social Hope*, London: Penguin, 1999, p. 171.
89 Ibid.
90 Kirkpatrick speaks of 'a great deal of ambiguity in Macmurray's treatment of the concept of God'; *John Macmurray*, p. 86, note 4.
91 K. Ingram, *The Christian Challenge to Christians*, London: George Allen & Unwin, 1938, p. 80.
92 Quoted in Costello, *John Macmurray*, p. 270. Macmurray's emphasis.
93 Macmurray, *Reason and Emotion*, p. 210.
94 Macmurray, *The Clue to History*, p. 122.
95 Ibid., p. 127.
96 Ibid., p. 146.
97 Ibid., p. 148.
98 Ibid., p. 146.
99 Ibid.
100 Ibid. p. 164
101 Ibid., p. 166.
102 C. Taylor, 'Modes of Secularism', in Rajeev Bhargava (ed.), *Secularism and Its Critics*, Delhi: Oxford University Press, 1998, p. 38.
103 Taylor, 'A Catholic Modernity?', p. 18.
104 Ibid., p. 19.
105 Macmurray, *The Clue to History*, p. 169.
106 Ibid., p. 192.
107 Ibid., p. 196.
108 Ibid., p. 203.
109 Ibid., p. 205.
110 Macmurray, *Creative Society*, p. 85.

111 Ibid., p. 76.
112 J. Macmurray, 'The Challenge of Communism', pp. 24–5.
113 Geoghegan, *Utopianism and Marxism*, pp. 79–84.
114 Macmurray, 'The Challenge of Communism', p. 32.
115 Ibid., p. 25.
116 Ibid., pp. 27–8.
117 Ibid., p. 32.
118 Macmurray, *The Clue to History*, pp. 153–4.
119 Ibid., p. 208.
120 Ibid.
121 Ibid.
122 Ibid., p. 209.
123 Ibid.
124 Macmurray, *The Philosophy of Communism*, p. 86.
125 Ibid.
126 Ibid. p. 93.
127 Ibid., p. 92.
128 Ibid., p. 88.
129 Macmurray, *Creative Society*, p. 180.
130 Ibid., p. 182.
131 Ibid., p. 183.
132 Ibid., p. 184.
133 Macmurray, *The Clue to History*, p. 213.
134 Ibid.
135 Ibid., pp. 218–19.
136 Ibid., pp. 222–3.
137 Ibid., p. 223.
138 Ibid., p. 224.
139 Ibid., pp. 226–7.
140 See J. Macmurray, 'Fascism and Christianity', in *The Christian Answer to Fascism*, London: The Christian Left, 1938, p. 16.
141 Macmurray, *The Clue to History*, p. 232.
142 Ibid., pp. 230–1.
143 Ibid., p. 221.
144 Ibid., p. 237.
145 Ibid.
146 J. Macmurray, *The Foundation of Economic Reconstruction*, London: National Peace Council, 1942, pp. 3–4.
147 J. Macmurray, *Constructive Democracy*, London: Faber & Faber, 1943, p. 7.
148 Ibid.
149 J. Macmurray, 'War to Peace', *Industrial and Personnel Management*, September/October 1943, p. 147.
150 J. Macmurray, *Challenge to the Churches*, London: Kegan Paul, Trench, Trubner, 1941, p. 13.
151 J. Macmurray, *Conditions of Freedom*, London: Faber & Faber, 1950, pp. 90–1.
152 J. Macmurray, *Through Chaos to Community?* London: National Peace Council, 1944, p. 15.
153 Ibid., pp. 15–16.
154 Costello, *John Macmurray*, pp. 148–50.
155 J. Macmurray, *A Crisis of Culture: The USSR and the West*, London: National Peace Council, 1947, p. 3.
156 Ibid., p. 2.
157 Ibid., p. 12.
158 Ibid.

159 J. Macmurray, *The Self as Agent*, New York: Harper and Brothers, 1957, p. 16, p. 17.
160 J. Macmurray, *Persons in Relation*, London: Faber & Faber, 1961, pp. 155–6.
161 Macmurray, *Persons in Relation*, p. 153.
162 Ibid., p. 154.
163 Macmurray, *Conditions of Freedom*, p. 68.
164 Macmurray, 'War to Peace', p. 150.
165 Macmurray, *Search for Reality in Religion*, p. 25.

## 2 Kenneth Ingram

1 I mainly use the terms 'homosexual' and 'homosexuality' in this chapter. It is a way of bridging the gap between Ingram's time and today, since the terms were widely used in the period under discussion and are still very much in use in the contemporary world. That these words carry a shifting freight of ideological baggage I don't deny. It is a messy compromise.
2 See, for example, Roger Lloyd in *Revolutionary Religion: Christianity Fascism and Communism*, London: Student Christian Movement Press, 1938, who talks of 'the impressive testimony of many of the best Christians, notably Kenneth Ingram and John Macmurray' (p. 167).
3 For biographical information see: T. d'Arch Smith, 'Introduction', *The Quorum. A Magazine of Friendship*, North Pomfret, VT: Elysium Press, Asphodel Editions, 2001, pp. 3–4; K. Ingram, 'Portrait of a Mother' in K. Ingram, *Towards Old Age*, London: Quality Press, 1945, pp. 7–37; K. Ingram, *Taken at the Flood*, London: George Allen & Unwin, 1943, pp. 125–39; J.E. Costello, *John Macmurray: A Biography*, Edinburgh: Floris, 2002, pp. 259–78.
4 For date of birth see entry for Ingram in 'New General Catalog of Old Books and Authors'. Online. Available HTTP: www.authorandbookinfo.com/ngcoba/in.htm (accessed 26 September 2010).
5 See John Maiden, 'The Anglican Prayer Book Controversy of 1927–28 and National Religion', PhD thesis, University of Stirling, 2007, p. 204. Online. Available HTTP: https://dspace.stir.ac.uk/dspace/handle/1893/247 (accessed 26 September 2010).
6 E. Waugh, *Brideshead Revisited*, Harmondsworth: Penguin, 1962, p. 28.
7 Ingram, *Taken at the Flood*, p. 126; see also Ingram, 'Portrait of a Mother', pp. 16–17.
8 Anglo-Catholicism, it should be noted, was far from monolithic, as Kenneth Leech argues in 'Beyond Gin and Lace: Homosexuality and the Anglo-Catholic Subculture', originally published in Ashley Beck and Ros Hunt (eds), *Speaking Love's Name; Homosexuality: Some Catholic and Socialist Perspectives*, London: The Jubilee Group, 1988. Online. Available HTTP: www.anglocatholicsocialism.org/lovesname.html (accessed 26 September 2010).
9 L. Dowling, *Hellenism and Homosexuality in Victorian Oxford*, Ithica: Cornell University Press, 1994. On Victorian 'Uranian' Hellenism also see: M.M. Kaylor, *Secreted Desires: The Major Uranians: Hopkins, Pater and Wilde*, Brno, Czech Republic: Masaryk University Press, 2006.
10 L.A. Hall, '"Disinterested Enthusiasm for Sexual Misconduct": The British Society for the Study of Sex Psychology, 1913–47', *Journal of Contemporary History*, 30:4, October 1995, p. 666; also D.C. Weigle, 'Psychology and Homosexuality: The British Sexological Society', *Journal of the History of the Behavioral Sciences*, 31:2, April 1995, pp. 137–48.
11 T. d'Arch Smith, 'Introduction', *The Quorum*, pp. 1–15.
12 K. Ingram, *England at the Flood-Tide*, London: The Damian Press, 1924, pp. 14–15.
13 Ibid., p. 14.

14 On Carpenter see Sheila Rowbotham's fine biography, *Edward Carpenter: A Life of Liberty and Love*, London: Verso, 2008, particularly pp. 280–5.
15 On this see H. Oosterhuis and H. Kennedy, *Homosexuality and Male Bonding in Pre-Nazi Germany*, New York and London: Harrington Park Press, 1991. The authors push the claim of *Der Eigene* to be the first gay journal in the world.
16 M. Arnold, *Culture and Anarchy and Other Writings*, ed. Stefan Collini, Cambridge: Cambridge University Press, 1993, p. 128.
17 Ingram, *England at the Flood-Tide*, p. 18.
18 Ibid., p. 17.
19 Ibid., p. 18.
20 Ibid., pp. 18–19.
21 Ibid., p. 24.
22 See S. Heschel, *The Aryan Jesus: Christian Theologians and the Bible in Nazi Germany*, Princeton: Princeton University Press, 2008.
23 On Carpenter's anti-Semitism see V. Geoghegan, 'Edward Carpenter's England Revisited', *History of Political Thought*, 24:3, 2003, pp. 521–2. Tom Harrisson in a 1941 study of all the British books dealing with the war published since 1939 found that among the novels 'nearly half worked in a Jew somehow or other, and only in one case was the reference not unfavourable'. Harrisson argued that there was a generational factor here as wartime exigencies had largely removed the young from publishing, leaving the field to those 'who had their minds made up before the last war'; Tom Harrisson, 'War Books', *Horizon*, 4:24, 1941, pp. 420–1, p. 420.
24 Ingram, *England at the Flood-Tide*, p. 68.
25 Ibid., p. 121.
26 Ibid., p. 115.
27 Ibid., p. 149.
28 Ibid., p. 181.
29 K. Ingram, *An Outline of Sexual Morality*, London: Jonathan Cape, 1922, p. 71.
30 Ibid., p. 73.
31 Ibid., p. 72.
32 D. Hilliard, 'UnEnglish and Unmanly: Anglo-Catholicism and Homosexuality', *Victorian Studies*, 25:2, 1982, p. 184.
33 T. d'Arch Smith, *Love in Earnest: Some Notes on the Lives and Writings of English 'Uranian' Poets from 1889 to 1930*, London: Routledge & Kegan Paul, 1970; see also D.H. Mader, 'The Greek Mirror: The Uranians and Their Use of Greece', *Journal of Homosexuality*, 49:3–4, 2005, pp. 377–420. Following d'Arch Smith, Mader includes Ingram with two other writers whom he describes as 'close to or in the Uranian movement'; p. 383.
34 A.K. Ingram, *Boys: What They Are and How to Manage Them*, London: A.R. Mowbray, 1911, p. 3.
35 Ingram was himself actively involved in the Scouting movement and was the author of *A Manual for Church of England Scouts*, London: A.R. Mowbray, 1913. The tone was very much 'healthy body, healthy mind' – among the tips for avoiding 'impure' thoughts and acts was jumping out of bed the moment one woke up.
36 A.K. Ingram, *The Greater Triumph: A Story of Osborne and Dartmouth*, London: A.R. Mowbray, 1911; *Basil Verely: A Study of Charterhouse Life* London: A.R. Mowbray, 1912.
37 Ingram, *An Outline of Sexual Morality*, p. 83.
38 Ibid.
39 Ibid.
40 A modern anthology of his poetry exists: Rev. E.E. Bradford, *To Boys Unknown*, London: The Gay Men's Press, 1988.
41 T. d'Arch Smith, *Love in Earnest*, pp. 117–23, p. 137.

42 Weigle, 'Psychology and Homosexuality', p. 148, n. 38. The lecture was eventually published: G. Ives, *The Graeco-Roman View of Youth*, n.p.: The Cayme Press, 1926. Neil McKenna argues that Oscar Wilde and Lord Alfred Douglas were early members of the Order of Chaeronea (N. McKenna, *The Secret Life of Oscar Wilde*, London: Arrow Books, 2004, p. 270), while Thomas Wright, citing Ives's loan of books to Wilde and Douglas, suggests that 'Ives's book collection may even have been a "purple" [i.e. homosexual] equivalent of Mudie's circulating library. As a "subscriber", Wilde had access to all the important homosexual literature of the day'; T. Wright, *Oscar's Books*, London: Vintage, 2009, p. 206.
43 W. Paine, *Shop Slavery and Emancipation: A Revolutionary Appeal to the Educated Young Men of the Middle Class*, London: P.S. King and Son, 1912, p. 107; also W. Paine, *A New Aristocracy of Comradeship*, London: Leonard Parsons, 1920. The publisher, bibliophile and writer Callum James has discovered that Paine was the same person as William Anderson, author of *The Counter Exposed* and *The Servitude of the Shop*: 'Sat, Jan 10, 2009 – William Paine-Anderson: Erotic Socialism II'. Online: Available HTTP: http://callumjames.blogspot (accessed 15 March 2009). T. d'Arch Smith, *Love in Earnest*, p. 141.
44 See Hubert Kennedy's 'Afterword' to Sagitta/Mackay's 1926 novel about a 15-year-old male prostitute, *The Hustler*, n.p.: L Xlibris, 2002, pp. 296–311; also H. Kennedy, *Anarchist of Love: The Secret Life of John Henry Mackay*, San Francisco: Peremptory Publications, 2002.
45 Benedict Friedländer, in Oosterhuis and Kennedy, *Homosexuality and Male Bonding in Pre-Nazi Germany*, p. 78.
46 'George Cecil Ives: An Inventory of His Papers at the Harry Ransom Humanities Research Center'. Online. Available HTTP: www.lib.utexas.edu/taro/uthrc/00060/hrc-00060.html (accessed 26 September 2010); Weigle, 'Psychology and Homosexuality', p. 141.
47 Oosterhuis and Kennedy, *Homosexuality and Male Bonding in Pre-Nazi Germany*, p. 30.
48 E. Carpenter, *Ioläus: An Anthology of Friendship*, London: Swan Sonnenschein, 1906, pp. 210–12; E. Carpenter, *The Intermediate Sex: A Study of Some Transitional Types of Men and Women*, London: George Allen & Unwin, 1916, p. 49.
49 Carpenter, *The Intermediate Sex*, Chapter 3.
50 Ingram, *An Outline of Sexual Morality*, p. 82.
51 Ibid., p. 75.
52 K. Ingram, *The Symbolic Island*, London: The Damian Press, 1924, p. 22.
53 Ibid., p. 161.
54 Ibid.
55 Ibid., pp. 147–8.
56 Ibid., pp. 214–15.
57 I rely heavily here on Oosterhuis and Kennedy, *Homosexuality and Male Bonding in Pre-Nazi Germany*, particularly pp. 183–239.
58 K. Ingram, *Modern Thought on Trial*, London: Philip Allan, 1933, p. 238.
59 Ingram, *Taken at the Flood*, pp. 126–8; Ingram, 'Portrait of a Mother', pp. 29–30; K. Ingram, *Towards Christianity: The Religious Progress of the World*, London: Student Christian Movement Press, 1939, pp. 25–8.
60 Ingram, 'Class Hatred', in *The Quorum*, pp. 32–3.
61 K. Ingram, *The Modern Attitude to the Sex Problem*, London: George Allen & Unwin, 1930, p. 10.
62 Ibid., p. 75.
63 Ibid., p. 72.
64 Ibid., p. 84.
65 Ibid.
66 Ibid., p. 78.

67 Ibid., pp. 78–9.
68 Ibid., p. 79.
69 Ibid., p. 77.
70 Ibid., p. 154.
71 Ibid.
72 Ibid., p. 146.
73 Ibid., p. 84. This is not to say that he thought all male homosexuals were effeminate.
74 Ibid., p. 150.
75 Ibid., p. 102.
76 Ibid., p. 153.
77 K. Ingram, *Midsummer Sanity*, London: Philip Allan, 1933, pp. 12–13.
78 Ibid., p. 45.
79 Ibid., p. 44.
80 Ibid., p. 46.
81 Ibid., p. 48.
82 Ibid.
83 T. d'Arch Smith, *Love in Earnest*, p. 163.
84 Ingram, *Midsummer Sanity*, pp. 48–9.
85 Ibid., p. 51.
86 Ibid., p. 154.
87 Ibid., p. 48.
88 Ibid., pp. 117.
89 See M. Houlbrook, *Queer London: Perils and Pleasures in the Sexual Metropolis, 1918–1957*, Chicago and London: University of Chicago Press, 2005, pp. 78–9.
90 Ingram, *Midsummer Sanity*, p. 294.
91 Ibid., pp. 295–6.
92 Paul Webb, 'Introduction' to Bradford, *To Boys Unknown*, p. 14.
93 'Review of *An Outline of Sexual Morality*', *Times Literary Supplement*, 8 June 1922, p. 383.
94 'Review of *The Modern Attitude to the Sex Problem*', *Times Literary Supplement*, 29 May 1930, p. 463.
95 'Review of *Sex-Morality Tomorrow*', *Times Literary Supplement*, 12 October 1940, p. 523.
96 Houlbrook, *Queer London*, p. 232.
97 K. Ingram, *Christianity – Right or Left*, London: George Allen and Unwin, 1937, p. 151.
98 Ibid., p. 152.
99 *Report of a Religious Delegation to Spain, April 1937*; see also Ormrod, 'The Christian Left and the Beginnings of Christian–Marxist Dialogue, 1935–45', in J. Obelkevich *et al.* (eds), *Disciplines of Faith: Studies in Religion, Politics and Patriarchy*, London: Routledge & Kegan Paul, 1987, pp. 435–50; also Costello, *John Macmurray*, Chapter 13.
100 Ingram, *Taken at the Flood*, p. 128.
101 See Costello, *John Macmurray*, p. 258.
102 Macmurray, *Reason and Emotion*, p. 134. The quote is from Galatians 3:28.
103 Macmurray, *Reason and Emotion*, pp. 100–1.
104 Ibid., p. 133. Matthew 5:8.
105 Macmurray, *Reason and Emotion*, pp. 129–30.
106 Ibid., p. 138.
107 J. Macmurray, *The Clue to History*, London: Student Christian Movement Press, 1938, p. 42.
108 K. Ingram, *And He Shall Come Again*, London: Heinemann, 1938, p. 10.
109 Ingram, *Christianity – Right or Left*, pp. 83–4.

110 K. Ingram, *'It is Expedient ... '*, London: Geoffrey Bles, 1935, p. 49.
111 Ibid., p. 56.
112 Ibid., pp. 56–7.
113 K. Ingram, *The Christian Challenge to Christians*, London: George Allen & Unwin, 1938, especially Chapter 2.
114 K. Ingram, *Sex-Morality Tomorrow*, London: George Allen & Unwin, 1940, pp. 34–5.
115 Ibid., p. 47.
116 Ingram, *Modern Thought on Trial*, p. 113.
117 Ingram, *Sex-Morality Tomorrow*, p. 62.
118 Ibid., p. 173.
119 Ibid., p. 42.
120 Ibid., p. 121.
121 Ibid., p. 116.
122 Ibid.
123 K. Porter and J. Weeks (eds), *Between the Acts: Lives of Homosexual Men 1885–1967*, London: Routledge, 1991, p. 99.
124 Ingram, *Sex-Morality Tomorrow*, p. 165.
125 Ibid., p. 161.
126 Houlbrook, *Queer London*, p. 163.
127 Ibid., p. 164.
128 Ingram, *Sex-Morality Tomorrow*, p. 68.
129 Ibid., p. 119.
130 Ibid., p. 59.
131 Ibid., p. 60.
132 Ibid., p. 150.
133 Ibid., p. 152.
134 Ibid., p. 127.
135 Ibid., p. 152.
136 There is some circumstantial evidence that he thought the age of consent should be around 16; Ingram, *Sex-Morality Tomorrow*, p. 125:

> It is evident that any State, however liberal, would be compelled to prevent any sexual intercourse where one of the parties was below the age of consent. But in a large number of cases it may legitimately be claimed that youths over sixteen or seventeen are liable to be persuaded unduly ... In the heterosexual sphere the age of consent has to be fixed arbitrarily, although it is realized that it does not correspond in every individual case to the stage when a mature will-power has been evolved.

137 Ingram, *Sex-Morality Tomorrow*, p. 154.
138 Ibid., pp. 159–60.
139 Ibid., p. 162.
140 Ibid., p. 164.
141 K. Ingram, *Christianity and Sexual Morality – A Modernist View*, London: The Union of Modern Free Churchmen, 1944.
142 Letter from Miss L.A. MacMunn to William Temple, 3 July 1942. W. Temple 30f. 83, Lambeth Palace Library.
143 Letter from W. Temple to Kenneth Ingram, 4 July 1942. Temple 30f. 84.
144 Letter from W. Temple to Miss L.A. MacMunn, 4 July 1942. Temple 30f. 85.
145 Letter from Kenneth Ingram to William Temple, 7 July 1942. Temple 30f. 86.
146 Ingram, *Taken at the Flood*, p. 134.
147 Letter from Lord Quickswood to William Temple, 11 July 1942. Temple 30f. 87.
148 Letter from William Temple to Lord Quickswood, 20 July 1942. Temple 30f. 91.

149 Letter from Kenneth Ingram to William Temple, 24 July 1942. Temple 30f. 92.
150 Kenneth Ingram, Insert document, Temple 30f, 93.
151 Ingram to Temple, 24 July 1942. Temple 30f. 92.
152 There was, of course, his 1944 pamphlet *Christianity and Sexual Morality: A Modernist View*. This was, however, only twenty-two pages long, and was written for a relatively marginal liberal Congregationalist organisation, the Union of Modern Free Churchmen; it did not go beyond the ideas expressed in *Sex-Morality Tomorrow*, and was restrained in tone, with youthful homosexual activity discussed in terms of it not preventing the emergence of heterosexual relations later in life:

> Many a schoolboy is still told that if he indulges in homosexual practices he may render himself physically incapable of marrying, and that in some way or other he will wreck his career if he persists ... The facts, so far as I have been able to investigate them, point almost invariably in the opposite direction. Most of these early practices seem to leave no mark whatever, physical or psychological, on the subsequent experiences of the persons concerned.
> (p. 20)

153 Letter from the Rev. George Jager to Richard Acland, 24 August 1942, Common Wealth Papers I, University of Sussex, 8/107.
154 Houlbrook, *Queer London*, Chapter 10.
155 K. Ingram, *Is Christianity Credible?* London: The Faith Press, 1963, p. 153.
156 Houlbrook, *Queer London*, p. 232–6.
157 P. Wildeblood, *Against the Law*, Harmondsworth: Penguin, 1957, pp. 12–13. On the 1950s and 1960s more generally, see Houlbrook, *Queer London*, Chapter 10, and M. Cook, 'Queer Conflicts: Love, Sex and War', in Matt Cook (ed.), *A Gay History of Britain: Love and Sex between Men since the Middle Ages*, Oxford: Greenwood World Publishing, 2007, pp. 167–77.
158 There is an attenuated echo of the 'pedagogic eros' in Ingram's final novel, *Storm in a Sanctuary* (1954) where, unrelated to the plot, a cathedral organist and choirmaster, Dr Spede, talks of his preference for the company of his choristers:

> I prefer the company of my boys to adults ... I prefer my boys to any group of contemporaries. It's just because they are undeveloped and immature and incomplete that they are so attractive. There are endless possibilities in them. It's fascinating to imagine what they may become.
> (*Storm in a Sanctuary*, London: Ernest Benn, 1954, pp. 50–1)

**3 Olaf Stapledon**

1 Robert Crossley's biography *Olaf Stapledon: Speaking for the Future*, Liverpool: Liverpool University Press, 1994, is invaluable for anyone interested in Stapledon. For studies of Stapledon's works see L.A. Fiedler, *Olaf Stapledon: A Man Divided*, New York: Oxford University Press, 1983; J. Kinnaird, *Olaf Stapledon*, Mercer Island, WA: Starmont House, 1986; and P. McCarthy, *Olaf Stapledon*, Boston: Twayne, 1982; see also the collection of essays in P. McCarthy, C. Elkins and H. Greenberg (eds), *The Legacy of Olaf Stapledon*, New York: Greenwood, 1989.
2 Crossley, *Olaf Stapledon*, p. 13, p. 197.
3 Ibid., p. 145.
4 Olaf Stapledon to Ernest W. Martin, 31 January 1941 (in the possession of the author).
5 Ibid.

6 Olaf Stapledon to Ernest W. Martin, 14 December 1944 (in the possession of the author).
7 Ibid.
8 Ibid.
9 Ibid.
10 Olaf Stapledon to Ernest W. Martin, 3 January 1945 (in the possession of the author).
11 Olaf Stapledon to Ernest W. Martin, 16 January 1945 (in the possession of the author).
12 Stapledon to Ernest W. Martin, 3 January 1945.
13 Ibid.
14 Ibid.
15 Stapledon to Ernest W. Martin, 16 January 1945.
16 O. Stapledon, 'The Great Certainty', in Ernest W. Martin (ed.), *In Search of Faith: A Symposium*, London: Lindsay Drummond, 1943, p. 37.
17 Ibid.
18 Ibid., p. 39.
19 Ibid., p. 38.
20 Ibid., p. 37.
21 O. Stapledon, *Waking World*, London: Methuen, 1934, p. 14.
22 Stapledon to Ernest W. Martin, 3 January 1945.
23 O. Stapledon, 'Personality and Liberty', *Philosophy*, 24:89, April 1949, p. 147.
24 Stapledon to Ernest W. Martin, 3 January 1945.
25 Stapledon, 'The Great Certainty', p. 56.
26 Ibid., p. 57.
27 O. Stapledon, *Latter-Day Psalms*, Liverpool: Henry Young and Sons, 1914, p. 11.
28 Ibid., pp. 41–2.
29 Ibid., p. 12.
30 Ibid. p. 93.
31 S. Nadler, *Spinoza: A Life*, Cambridge: Cambridge University Press, 1999, pp. 186–8.
32 R. Scruton, *Spinoza: A Very Short Introduction*, Oxford: Oxford University Press, 2002, p. 72, p. 124.
33 Nadler, *Spinoza*, p. 220. Frederic Jameson discerns a Spinozan element in Stapledon in *Archaeologies of the Future: The Desire Called Utopia and Other Science Fictions*, London: Verso, 2005, p. 131.
34 O. Stapledon, *Philosophy and Living*, Harmondsworth: Penguin, 1939, vol. 2, p. 346.
35 Ibid., p. 425.
36 O. Stapledon, *A Modern Theory of Ethics*, London: Methuen, 1929, p. 184.
37 O. Stapledon, *Odd John*, London: Methuen, 1935.
38 O. Stapledon, *The Flames*, London: Secker and Warburg, 1947.
39 Stapledon, *Waking World*, p. 188.
40 O. Stapledon, *Saints and Revolutionaries*, London: Heinemann, 1939, p. 142.
41 T. Moylan, *Demand the Impossible: Science Fiction and the Utopian Imagination*, New York: Methuen, 1986.
42 O. Stapledon, *Last and First Men* and *Last Men in London*, Harmondsworth: Penguin, 1972, pp. 326–7.
43 O. Stapledon, *Star Maker*, London: Orion, 2003, p. 270.
44 Ibid., p. 164.
45 Ibid., p. 200.
46 Ibid., p. 248.
47 D. Hume, *Dialogues Concerning Natural Religion*, London: Penguin, 1990, p. 79.
48 Ibid.

49 The case for a strong influence can be found in Fiedler, *Olaf Stapledon*, pp. 43–7, and for a weaker influence in Robert Crossley, 'Famous Mythical Beasts: Olaf Stapledon and H.G. Wells', *Georgia Review*, 36, Fall 1982, pp. 619–39.
50 O. Stapledon, 'Mr Wells Calls in the Martians', *The London Mercury*, 36, 1937, p. 295.
51 R. Crossley (ed.), 'The Correspondence of Olaf Stapledon and H.G. Wells 1931–42', in G. Wolfe (ed.), *Science Fiction Dialogues*, Chicago: Academy Chicago, 1982, p. 35. Robert Crossley reveals that in 1911 while reading Wells's *New Worlds for Old* Stapledon 'boldly declared "I am a socialist"'; Crossley, *Olaf Stapledon*, p. 94.
52 Crossley, 'The Correspondence of Olaf Stapledon and H.G. Wells', p. 35.
53 Crossley, *Olaf Stapledon*, p. 198.
54 Ibid.
55 Stapledon, *Waking World*, p. 12.
56 Stapledon, 'Mr Wells Calls in the Martians', p. 296.
57 Stapledon, *Waking World*, pp. 12–13.
58 Stapledon, 'Mr Wells Calls in the Martians', p. 296.
59 Crossley, 'The Correspondence of Olaf Stapledon and H.G. Wells', p. 46.
60 Ibid., p. 45.
61 Ibid.
62 Ibid., p. 46.
63 Ibid., p. 45.
64 O. Stapledon, 'Some Thoughts on H.G. Wells's *You Can't Be Too Careful*', in Robert Crossley (ed.), *An Olaf Stapledon Reader*, Syracuse: Syracuse University Press, 1997, p. 204.
65 See Stapledon, *Philosophy and Living*, vol. 2, p. 307, and Stapledon, *Waking World*, p. 2.
66 Stapledon, *Philosophy and Living*, vol. 2, p. 377.
67 Ibid., pp. 371–2.
68 Ibid., p. 319.
69 Ibid., p. 320.
70 Ibid., pp. 321–2.
71 Ibid., p. 321.
72 Ibid., p. 458.
73 O. Stapledon, 'Israel's Part', *The London Mercury*, 39:233, March 1939, p. 554.
74 O. Stapledon, 'Christianity and Marxism', *The New Leader*, 16 March 1946, p. 6.
75 Stapledon, 'Israel's Part', p. 554.
76 O. Stapledon, 'Religion To-Day', *Faith and Freedom*, 3:2 (8), Spring 1950, p. 52; also O. Stapledon 'The Conflict of Values: The Bridge Between', in a collection of essays (without a named editor), *Two Worlds in Focus: Studies of the Cold War*, London: National Peace Council, 1950, p. 51.
77 See V. Geoghegan, 'Ideology and Utopia', *Journal of Political Ideologies*, 9:2, 2004, p. 130.
78 Stapledon, *Waking World*, pp. 271–2.
79 O. Stapledon, *New Hope for Britain*, London: Methuen, 1939, p. 158.
80 O. Stapledon, *Youth and Tomorrow*, London: St Botolph, 1946, p. 58.
81 Ibid., p. 85.
82 Stapledon, *Saints and Revolutionaries*, p. 99.
83 Stapledon, *New Hope for Britain*, p. 139.
84 Ibid., p. 145.
85 Ibid., p. 147.
86 Ibid., p. 160.
87 O. Stapledon, *Beyond the Isms*, London: Secker and Warburg, 1942, p. 159.
88 Stapledon, *Star Maker*, p. 31.
89 Ibid., p. 38.

90 Ibid., p. 41.
91 Stapledon, *Waking World*, pp. 160–3, pp. 205–16.
92 Stapledon, *Star Maker*, p. 42.
93 Ibid.
94 Stapledon, *A Modern Theory of Ethics*, p. 258.
95 Stapledon, *Waking World*, p. 182.
96 Stapledon, *Beyond the Isms*, p. 24.
97 Ibid., p. 24.
98 Olaf Stapledon, *Sirius*, Harmondsworth: Penguin, 1964, p. 125.
99 Stapledon, *Philosophy and Living*, vol. 2, p. 427.
100 Stapledon, *Beyond the Isms*, p. 53.
101 He was also critical of the Communists on other grounds – particularly on their perceived authoritarian tendencies.
102 Stapledon, *Beyond the Isms*, p. 127.
103 Stapledon, *Philosophy and Living*, vol. 2, p. 427.
104 Stapledon, *A Modern Theory of Ethics*, p. 267.
105 Ibid., p. 267, p. 266.
106 E.V. Rieu, 'Preface', in Olaf Stapledon, *The Opening of the Eyes*, London: Methuen, 1954, p. vi.
107 Ibid., p. vii.
108 S. Moskowitz, 'Olaf Stapledon: Cosmic Philosopher', in O. Stapledon, *Darkness and the Light*, Westport, CT: Hyperion Press, 1974, no page numbers in essay.
109 Communication to Sam Moskowitz quoted in the 'authorized biography' in S. Moskowitz (ed.), *Far Future Calling: Uncollected Science Fiction and Fantasies of Olaf Stapledon*, Philadelphia: Oswald Train, 1979, p. 64.
110 Moskowitz, 'Olaf Stapledon: Cosmic Philosopher', no page number.
111 Quoted in Moscowitz, *Far Future Calling*, pp. 64–5.
112 Agnes Stapledon to Ernest Martin, 30 September – 2 October 1981 (in possession of author).
113 'I am come as Time, the waster of the peoples' (*Bhagavad Gita*, trans. Swami Prabhavananda and Christopher Isherwood, New York: Signet, 2002, p. 94). This would appear to be the passage remembered by the scientist Robert Oppenheimer on witnessing the first detonation of the atom bomb: 'I remembered the line from … the *Bhagavad Gita*: "Now I have become Death, the destroyer of worlds"' (J. Bernstein, *Robert Oppenheimer: Portrait of an Enigma*, Chicago: Ivan R. Dee, 2004, p. 199).
114 Crossley, *Olaf Stapledon*, pp. 323–5, pp. 365–7; she was a cousin of the Queen Mother.
115 Stapledon, *The Opening of the Eyes*, p. 70.
116 Crossley, *Olaf Stapledon*, p. 250; Fiedler, *Olaf Stapledon*, pp. 130–3.
117 Stapledon, *The Opening of the Eyes*, p. 8.
118 Ibid., p. 17
119 Ibid., pp. 92–3.

**4 Sir Richard Acland**

1 E.R. Punshon, *Night's Cloak*, London: Victor Gollancz, 1944, p. 25. I owe the reference to Punshon's book to A.L.R. Calder's thesis on Common Wealth, 'The Common Wealth Party 1942–1945', unpublished DPhil thesis, University of Sussex, 1968, vol. 2, p. 165.
2 For biographical material see 'Sir Richard Thomas Dyke Acland (1906–90)', *Oxford Dictionary of National Biography*, Oxford: Oxford University Press, 2004; Calder, 'Common Wealth', vol. 1, pp. 16–18. There are no fewer than three unpublished attempts at autobiography in the Acland Papers at Exeter University:

'Personal Political Memoirs', 1974, EUL MS 104/4 (1) (dating from 1974); the other two are both contained in one volume entitled 'An Un-Named Book. An Argumentative Autobiography', EUL MS 104/4 (1). To distinguish them for referencing purposes one will be referred to as 'An Un-Named Book. An Argumentative Autobiography [70s]' (as it dates from the late 1970s), and the other as 'An Un-Named Book. An Argumentative Autobiography [80s]' (dating from the late 1980s).
3 Acland, 'Personal Political Memoirs', p. 1.
4 J.E. Costello, *John Macmurray: A Biography*, Edinburgh: Floris, 2002, p. 120.
5 Virtually all the standard reference books say that he was MP for Barnstaple, but in any biographical information provided by Acland himself on book covers and the like he always called himself MP for North Devon.
6 Acland, 'An Un-Named Book. An Argumentative Autobiography [70s]', p. H45.
7 Calder, 'Common Wealth', vol. 1, p. 17.
8 R. Acland, *Why So Angry?* London: Victor Gollancz, 1958, pp. 67–8.
9 *Hansard*, House of Commons Debates, vol. 317, 6 November 1936, c. 420.
10 Ibid., 423.
11 D. Dutton, *A History of the Liberal Party*, Houndmills, Basingstoke: Palgrave, 2004, pp. 68–136.
12 M. Baines, 'Liberal Nadir, 1935–56', *Liberal Democrat History Group*. Online. Available HTTP: www.liberalhistory.org.uk (accessed 23 November 2008).
13 See M. Pugh, 'The Liberal Party and the Popular Front', *English Historical Review*, 121:494, December 2006, pp. 1327–50.
14 Calder, 'Common Wealth', vol. 1, p. 17.
15 Pugh, 'The Liberal Party', p. 1332.
16 Ibid., pp. 1330, 1332.
17 R. Acland, *Only One Battle*, London: Victor Gollancz, 1937, p. 14.
18 Ibid., p. 206.
19 Ibid., p. 110.
20 Ibid., p. 53.
21 Ibid., p. 55.
22 Ibid., pp. 61–2.
23 Ibid., p. 149.
24 Ibid., p. 142.
25 Ibid., p. 155.
26 Acland, 'An Un-Named Book. An Argumentative Autobiography [70s]', p. H77.
27 See Pugh, 'The Liberal Party', pp. 1342–3; see also I. McLean, 'Oxford and Bridgwater', in C. Cook and J. Ramsden (eds), *By-Elections in British Politics*, London: Macmillan, 1973, pp. 140–64.
28 Acland, 'An Un-Named Book. An Argumentative Autobiography [70s]', p. H77.
29 Calder, 'Common Wealth', vol. 1, p. 17.
30 Pugh, 'The Liberal Party', pp. 1342–3.
31 R. Acland, *This Way to Death: A Critical Examination of Government Foreign Policy*, London: n.p., 1938.
32 *Hansard*, House of Commons Debates, vol. 339, 5 October 1938, c. 383.
33 Ibid., c. 392.
34 Acland, 'Personal Political Memoirs', 1974, p. 6.
35 *Hansard*, House of Commons Debates, vol. 339, c. 389.
36 *Hansard*, House of Commons Debates, vol. 345, 15 March 1939, c. 512.
37 Acland, 'An Un-Named Book. An Argumentative Autobiography [70s]', p. H90.
38 R. Acland, *What Now? Memorandum on the World Situation September 1939 by Sir Richard Acland, MP*, n.p.o.p.: n.p., n.d. [1939], no page numbers – the quote is on the first page of the main text.
39 Ibid., third page.

40 Calder, 'Common Wealth', vol. 1, pp. 26–7.
41 *What Now?* thirteenth page.
42 Ibid., fourteenth page.
43 Ibid., sixteenth page.
44 Ibid., fifteenth page
45 Ibid., sixteenth page.
46 *Hansard*, House of Commons Debates, vol. 355, 5 December 1939, c. 587.
47 Ibid., c. 589.
48 Ibid., c. 591.
49 Ibid., c. 590.
50 Ibid., c. 591.
51 Ibid., c. 587.
52 Ibid., c. 591.
53 Calder, 'Common Wealth', vol. 1, p. 19; see also J. Lewis, *Penguin Special: The Life and Times of Allen Lane*, London: Penguin, 2006, p. 199.
54 Acland, 'An Un-Named Book. An Argumentative Autobiography [70s]', p. H92.
55 Ibid., p. H94.
56 R. Acland, *Unser Kampf: Our Struggle*, Harmondsworth: Penguin, 1940, p. viii.
57 Ibid., p. 81.
58 Ibid., p. 83.
59 Ibid., p. 84.
60 Ibid., pp. 84–5.
61 House of Commons Debates, vol. 355, c. 587.
62 Acland, *Unser Kampf*, pp. 31–52.
63 P. Clarke, *The Cripps Version: The Life of Sir Stafford Cripps 1889–1952*, London: Penguin, 2002, p. 107.
64 Ibid., p. 79.
65 B. Pimlott, *Labour and the Left in the 1930s*, Cambridge: Cambridge University Press, 1977, p. 176.
66 Clarke, *The Cripps Version*, pp. 107–9.
67 R. Acland, *Hungry Sheep*, Basingstoke: Marshall Pickering, 1988, p. 3.
68 Acland, *Unser Kampf*, p. 139.
69 Ibid., p. 141.
70 Ibid.
71 Ibid., p. 142.
72 Ibid., p. 143.
73 Ibid., pp. 153–4.
74 Ibid., p. 155.
75 Ibid., p. 157.
76 Ibid., p. 160.
77 Acland in his address to the Malvern Conference in early January 1941 refers to his conversion as happening 'within the last few months or even weeks'; *Malvern 1941: The Life of the Church and the Order of Society*, London: Longmans, Green, 1941, p. 153.
78 Acland, *Hungry Sheep*, p. 3.
79 Ibid., p. 1.
80 Acland, 'An Un-Named Book. An Argumentative Autobiography [70s]', p. H8.
81 Acland, *Hungry Sheep*, p. 4.
82 For biographical material see his autobiography: J. Parkes, *Voyage of Discoveries*, London: Victor Gollancz, 1969; also 'Parkes, James William (1896–1981)', *Oxford Dictionary of National Biography*, Oxford: Oxford University Press, 2004, and H. Chertok, *He Also Spoke as a Jew: The Life of the Reverend James Parkes*, London and Portland, OR: Vallentine Mitchell, 2006.
83 Parkes, *Voyage of Discoveries*, p. 130.

84　J. Hadham, *Good God: A Study of His Character and Activities*, Harmondsworth: Penguin, 1940, p. 9. The frontispiece has 'Sketches of' instead of 'A Study of'.
85　Ibid., p. 44.
86　Acland, 'An Un-Named Book. An Argumentative Autobiography [80s]', p. 2.9.
87　R. Acland, 'Sleep-Walking in the Desert', in B. Dixon (ed.), *Journeys in Belief*, London: George Allen and Unwin, 1968, p. 18.
88　R. Acland, *We Teach Them Wrong: Religion and the Young*, London: Victor Gollancz, 1963, p. 174. In his last book, *Hungry Sheep*, Basingstoke: Marshall Pickering, 1988, Acland shared the fact that his mother had experienced a similar epiphany as a child. He quoted her third-person account of lying on a sunny bank surrounded by the familiar trees and flowers of the countryside:

> All at once, quite without prelude, an astonishing radiance welled up on all these familiar things and in the child herself. They were no longer just themselves, separate objects with edges of their own; they were that radiance, and the radiance was unbounded, glorious love.
> (p. 122)

89　R. Acland, *The Forward March*, London: George Allen & Unwin, 1941, p. 94.
90　Ibid., p. 95.
91　Ibid., p. 101.
92　Ibid., p.103.
93　Ibid.
94　Ibid., p. 104.
95　K. Ingram, *The Christian Challenge to Christians*, London: George Allen & Unwin, 1938, p. 82.
96　For Malvern see *Malvern 1941: The Life of the Church and the Order of Society*, London: Longmans, Green, 1941; also J. Kent, *William Temple: Church, State and Society in Britain, 1880–1950*, Cambridge: Cambridge University Press, 1992, pp. 148–67, and F.A. Iremonger, *William Temple Archbishop of Canterbury: His Life and Letters*, Oxford: Oxford University Press, 1948, pp. 429–34.
97　Acland, *The Forward March*, p. 107.
98　Acland, 'An Un-Named Book. An Argumentative Autobiography [70s]', pp. H110, H113.
99　Ingram, *The Night is Far Spent*, p. 107.
100　Calder, 'Common Wealth', vol. 1, pp. 21–2.
101　Iremonger, *William Temple*, p. 430.
102　Acland, 'An Un-Named Book. An Argumentative Autobiography [80s]', p. 2.10; on Ingram's comments on the 'academic' dullness of many of the papers see: K. Ingram, 'The Church and Social Thinking', in S.G. Evans (ed.), *Return to Reality: Some Essays on Contemporary Christianity*, London: Zeno, 1954, pp. 197–8.
103　R. Acland, 'Practical Questions I', *Malvern 1941*, p. 153.
104　Ibid., p. 154.
105　Ibid., p. 154, pp. 156–7.
106　Ibid., pp. 161–2.
107　K. Ingram, 'Practical Questions II', *Malvern 1941*, p. 177.
108　Acland, *Malvern 1941*, p. 162.
109　Acland, 'Personal Political Memoirs', p. 6. The 'findings' are contained in *The Life of the Church and the Order of Society*, London: The Industrial Christian Fellowship, 1941.
110　Acland, 'An Un-Named Book. An Argumentative Autobiography [80s]', p. 2.10.
111　Acland, 'An Un-Named Book. An Argumentative Autobiography [70s]', pp. H3–4.
112　B. Causton, 'The Scene of the Conference', in *Malvern 1941*, p. 3.
113　Acland, 'Personal Political Memoirs', p. 7.

214  *Notes*

114 Kent, *William Temple*, pp. 157–9; Causton, *Malvern 1941*, p. 3.
115 Iremonger, *William Temple*, p. 431.
116 Kent, *William Temple*, pp. 158–9; Iremonger, *William Temple*, pp. 431–2.
117 Acland, *The Forward March*, p. 108.
118 Ibid., p. 108, p. 110.
119 Causton, *Malvern 1941*, p. 3.
120 Ingram, *Malvern 1941*, pp. 175–6.
121 Ingram, 'The Church and Social Thinking', p. 197; also Angus Calder, Interview with Kenneth Ingram 20 January 1965, tape recording 15/7, Common Wealth Papers 1, University of Sussex.
122 Acland, 'An Un-Named Book. An Argumentative Autobiography [70s]', p. H113.
123 Parkes, *Voyage of Discoveries*, p. 163.
124 Acland, *The Forward March*, p. 11.
125 Ibid., p. 104.
126 Acland, 'An Un-Named Book. An Argumentative Autobiography [70s]', p. H27.
127 Acland, *Hungry Sheep*, pp. 3–4.
128 Acland, 'An Un-Named Book. An Argumentative Autobiography [80s]', p. 2.9.
129 Diary of Richard Acland, 27 October 1943, Common Wealth Papers 1, 8/269.
130 Richard Acland to Kitty Wintringham, 9 March 1943, Common Wealth Papers 1, 8/118–19; the specific remarks are included in an accompanying document, 'First Draft of Book under some such title as; – REVOLUTIONARIES SHOULD BE CHRISTIANS', 8/120–2.
131 Richard Acland to Kitty Wintringham, 9 March 1943. Common Wealth Papers 1, 8/118–19.
132 R. Acland, *Nothing Left to Believe?* London: Longmans Green, 1949, p. 46.
133 Ibid., p. 48.
134 Hadham, *Good God*, p. 76.
135 Ingram, *The Night is Far Spent*, pp. 116–17.
136 Ibid., p. 117.
137 Ibid.
138 R. Acland, *It Must Be Christianity*, n.p.o.p.: n.p. [1941], p. 9.
139 Acland, *The Forward March*, p. 104.
140 Acland, *It Must Be Christianity*, p. 7.
141 Acland, 'An Un-Named Book. An Argumentative Autobiography [70s]', p. H118.
142 Acland, *It Must Be Christianity*, p. 12.
143 Ibid., pp. 12–13.
144 Ibid., p. 13.
145 K. Ingram, *The Night is Far Spent*, London: George Allen & Unwin, p. 124.
146 Ibid.
147 Acland, 'Personal Political Memoirs', p. 7.
148 Calder, 'Common Wealth', vol. 1, p. 20.
149 Ibid., pp. 20–1.
150 Acland, 'An Un-Named Book. An Argumentative Autobiography [80s]', p. 2.4.
151 Acland, 'An Un-Named Book. An Argumentative Autobiography [70s]', p. H96.
152 Calder, 'Common Wealth', vol. 1, pp. 107–9.
153 Acland, 'An Un-Named Book. An Argumentative Autobiography [70s]', p. H106.
154 H.G. Wells, *'42 to '44: A Contemporary Memoir upon Human Behaviour during the Crisis of the World Revolution*, London: Secker & Warburg, 1944, p. 161.
155 Ibid., p. 160.
156 Ibid., p. 162.
157 Ibid.
158 Ibid., pp. 162–3.
159 D.C. Smith (ed.), *The Correspondence of H.G. Wells*, vol. 4, London: Pickering & Chatto, 1996, p. 263,

Notes 215

160 Acland, 'An Un-Named Book. An Argumentative Autobiography [70s]', p. H106.
161 Smith, *The Correspondence of H.G. Wells*, vol. 4, p. 291.
162 Wells, *'42 to '44*, p. 162.
163 Ibid.
164 Smith, *The Correspondence of H.G. Wells*, vol. 4, p. 291.
165 Wells, *'42 to '44*, p. 165.
166 Ibid., p. 162.
167 Acland, 'An Un-Named Book. An Argumentative Autobiography [70s]', p. H97.
168 Ibid., p. H99.
169 For biographical information see H. Purcell, *The Last English Revolutionary: Tom Wintringham 1898–1949*, Thrupp: Sutton Publishing, 2004; also 'Wintringham, Thomas Henry (Tom) (1898–1949)', *Oxford Dictionary of National Biography*, Oxford: Oxford University Press, 2004.
170 See Purcell, *The Last English Revolutionary*, Chapters 11 and 12; also D. Fernbach, 'Tom Wintringham and Socialist Defense Strategy', *History Workshop Journal*, 14:1, 1982, pp. 63–91; and S. Cullen, *Home Guard Socialism: A Vision of a People's Army*, Warwick: Allotment Hut Booklets, 2006.
171 Acland, 'An Un-Named Book. An Argumentative Autobiography [70s]', pp. H99–100.
172 Ibid., p. H100.
173 Calder, 'Common Wealth', vol. 1, p. 51.
174 Wells, *'42 to '44*, p. 164.
175 Calder, 'Common Wealth', vol. 1, p. 55.
176 Wells, *'42 to '44*, p. 164.
177 Ibid.
178 Untitled typescript (marked in red at top of front page: X unity – Merger Period) [1942], Wintringham Papers, Liddell Hart Centre for Military Archives, King's College London, 3/6/2, p. 3.
179 Wells, *'42 to '44*, p. 165.
180 Acland, 'Personal Political Memoirs', p. 9.
181 Ibid.

## 5 The moment of Common Wealth

1 A.L.R. Calder, 'The Common Wealth Party 1942–1945', unpublished DPhil thesis, University of Sussex, 1968, vol. 1, p. 104.
2 Acland, 'Personal Political Memoirs', 1974, Acland Papers, Exeter University, EUL MS 104/4 (1), p. 12.
3 H. Purcell, *The Last English Revolutionary*, Thrupp: Sutton Publishing, 2004, p. 216; letter from Richard Acland to Tom Wintringham, 12–6.42, Wintringham Papers, Liddell Hart Centre for Military Archives, King's College London, 3/6/2.
4 Purcell, *The Last English Revolutionary*, p. 216.
5 R. Acland, 'Personal Political Memoirs', p. 13.
6 R. Acland, 'An Un-Named Book. An Argumentative Autobiography [70s]', Acland Papers, EUL MS 104/4 (1), pp. H147–8.
7 J.B. Priestley, 'Introduction', in Richard Acland, *How It Can Be Done*, London: Macdonald, 1943, pp. 11–12.
8 J. Parkes, *Voyage of Discoveries*, London: Gollancz, 1969, p. 182–3.
9 See H. Chertok, *He Also Spoke as a Jew: The Life of the Reverend James Parkes*, London and Portland, OR: Vallentine Mitchell, 2006, p. 342.
10 Parkes, *Voyage of Discoveries*, p. 182.
11 For biographical information see 'Sargant, Thomas (1905 – 1988)', *Oxford Dictionary of National Biography*, Oxford: Oxford University Press, 2004.

12 T. Sargant, *These Things Shall Be*, second edition, London: William Heinemann, 1942, p. 28.
13 Ibid., p. 94.
14 Ibid., p. 95.
15 Ibid., p. 89, p. 88.
16 Calder, 'Common Wealth', vol. 1, p. 157.
17 Mackay only joined Common Wealth in 1943 and left in 1944. In this period Calder does consider him one of the leading three (with Acland and Wintringham) in Common Wealth; Calder, 'Common Wealth', vol. 2, pp. 102–3. On MacKay see K. Gildart, 'An Australian Socialist in England: Kim Mackay, the British Left, and European Federalism, 1934 – 1960'. Online. Available HTTP: www.historycooperative.org/proceedings/asslh/gildart.html (accessed 26 September 2010).
18 Acland, 'An Un-Named Book. An Argumentative Autobiography [70s]', pp. H175–6.
19 Calder, 'Common Wealth', vol. 1, p. 197.
20 A. Calder, taped interview with Kenneth Ingram, 20 January 1965; Common Wealth Papers 1, University of Sussex, Tape Recordings.
21 This is a section of a letter from Acland to Tom Wintringham indicating what he intended to say to Mackay in a forthcoming meeting; Richard Acland to Tom Wintringham, 31 August 1943; Wintringham Papers, 3/6/2.
22 Calder, 'Common Wealth', vol. 2, p. 97.
23 Calder, 'Common Wealth', vol. 1, p. 117.
24 R. Acland, *Hungry Sheep*, Basingstoke: Marshall Pickering, 1988, p. 9.
25 Tom Wintringham to Richard Acland [1944]; Wintringham Papers, 3/6/3.
26 Calder, 'Common Wealth', vol. 1, p. 152.
27 Calder, 'Common Wealth'; I rely heavily here on the useful summary of his findings in A. Calder, *The People's War: Britain 1939–45*, London: Jonathan Cape, 1969, pp. 546–50.
28 R. Acland, 'An Un-Named Book. An Argumentative Autobiography [80s]', Acland Papers, EUL MS 104/4 (1), p. 3.2.
29 T. Driberg, *Ruling Passions: The Autobiography of Tom Driberg*, London: Quartet Books, 1978, p. 180.
30 F. Wheen, *The Soul of Indiscretion: Tom Driberg: Poet, Philanderer, Legislator and Outlaw*, London: Fourth Estate, 2001, p. 171.
31 Ibid., p. 181.
32 Wheen, *The Soul of Indiscretion*, p. 174.
33 P. Addison, *The Road to 1945: British Politics and the Second World War*, London: Pimlico, 1994, p. 159.
34 Online. Available HTTP: www.hansard.millbanksystems.com/people/mr-richard-acland (accessed 30 March 2009).
35 Acland, 'Personal Political Memoirs', p. 10.
36 Calder, 'Common Wealth', vol. 2, p. 180.
37 Acland, 'An Un-Named Book. An Argumentative Autobiography [80s]', p. 3.3.
38 Ibid., p. 3.10.
39 Calculated from figures in F.W.S. Craig (ed.), *British Parliamentary Election Results 1918–1949*, Glasgow: Political Reference Publications, 1969.
40 P. Addison, 'By-Elections of the Second World War', in C. Cook and J. Ramsden (eds), *By-Elections in British Politics*, London: Macmillan, 1973, p. 185.
41 For an account of this by-election see Calder, 'Common Wealth', vol. 1, pp. 242–7; also G.H. Bennett, 'The Wartime Political Truce and Hopes for Post War Coalition: The West Derbyshire By-Election, 1844', *Midland History*, 17, 1992, pp. 118–35.
42 Acland, 'An Un-Named Book. An Argumentative Autobiography [80s]', pp. 3.8–3.9.
43 *Common Wealth Manifesto: A New Social Order*, fourth edition, London: CW Publishing, 1944, p. 2.

44 Ibid., p. 8.
45 Ibid.
46 Ibid.
47 *Questions and Answers about Common Wealth's Policy*, London: CW Publishing, n.d. [1944], p. 8.
48 Ibid., p. 6.
49 Ibid., p. 1.
50 *Common Wealth Manifesto*, p. 1.
51 Ibid., p. 2.
52 Ibid., p. 4.
53 Ibid., p. 5.
54 Ibid.
55 Ibid., pp. 5–6.
56 *Questions and Answers*, p. 1.
57 *Common Wealth Manifesto*, p. 12.
58 Ibid, pp. 13–15.
59 Acland, 'An Un-Named Book. An Argumentative Autobiography [70s]', p. H135.
60 Ibid.
61 Addison, *The Road to 1945*, p. 160.
62 *Common Wealth Manifesto*, inside cover.
63 M. Hilson and J. Melling, 'Public Gifts and Political Identities: Sir Richard Acland, Common Wealth, and the Moral Politics of Land Ownership in the 1940s', *Twentieth Century British History*, 11:2, 2000, pp. 176–7.
64 Hilson and Melling, pp. 156–82.
65 Richard Acland to Kitty Wintringham, 9 March 1943; Common Wealth Papers 1, 8/120–2.
66 His wife Anne was initially very opposed to the plan, and it took months before she reluctantly came on board; Hilson and Melling, pp. 173–4.
67 Calder, 'Common Wealth', vol. 1, p. 40.
68 Ibid., p. 41.
69 Ibid.
70 Letter from the Rev. George Jager to Richard Acland, 2 June 1942, Common Wealth Papers I, 8/95–6.
71 *Malvern 1941*, p. 231.
72 Jager to Acland, 2 June 1942.
73 The Rev. E.L. Mascall (in *Theology*, December 1939). Quoted in F.A. Iremonger, *William Temple Archbishop of Canterbury: His Life and Letters*, Oxford: Oxford University Press, 1948, p. 608.
74 Calder, *The People's War*, p. 478.
75 Quoted in J.E. Costello, *John Macmurray: A Biography*, Edinburgh: Floris, 2002, p. 270; Macmurray's emphasis. Costello also notes that Macmurray did acknowledge Barth's personal opposition to the Nazis (p. 414, note 19).
76 Jager to Acland, 6 June 1942, 8/97.
77 Jager to Acland, 24 August 1942, 8/107–8.
78 W. Temple to Miss L.A. MacMunn, 4 July 1942, Temple 30f.85, Lambeth Palace Library.
79 Calder, 'Common Wealth', vol. 2, pp. 135–6.
80 For biographical material on Stapledon I am heavily reliant on R. Crossley, *Olaf Stapledon: Speaking for the Future*, Liverpool: Liverpool University Press, 1994.
81 Crossley, *Olaf Stapledon*, pp. 306–7.
82 Ibid., p. 278.
83 'Letter to Naomi Mitchison', in R. Crossley (ed.), *An Olaf Stapledon Reader*, Syracuse: Syracuse University Press, 1997, p. 281.
84 Crossley, *Olaf Stapledon*, p. 288.

85 Ibid., p. 305.
86 Ibid., p. 307.
87 O. Stapledon, *Youth and Tomorrow*, London: St Botolph, 1946, p. 64.
88 Macmurray's semi-detached 'grey eminence' status makes it difficult to track his membership of Common Wealth.
89 Among Stapledon's papers at Liverpool University is a receipt for Common Wealth membership dues for himself and his wife dated 21 March 1949. He died the following year. Stapledon Papers, Liverpool University, H6.C.1.9.
90 O. Stapledon, 'Must It Be Christianity?' p. 1, Stapledon Papers, F.48.5.
91 Acland, 'Personal Political Memoirs', p. 15.
92 Stapledon, 'Must It Be Christianity?' p. 1.
93 Ibid., p. 2.
94 O. Stapledon, 'Do We Need a New Religion?' Stapledon Papers, F.32.5.
95 Stapledon, 'Must It Be Christianity?' p. 1.
96 For biographical material on Kitty Wintringham see Purcell, *The Last English Revolutionary*; also 'Wintringham, Thomas Henry (Tom) (1898–1949)', *Oxford Dictionary of National Biography*, Oxford: Oxford University Press, 2004.
97 Richard Acland to Kitty Wintringham, 6 March, 1943; Wintringham Papers, 3/6/2. This letter, as is Kitty Wintringham's reply, is included in extract form in a letter Kitty sent to Kenneth Ingram in March 1943.
98 Kitty Wintringham to Richard Acland, 7 March, 1943, Wintringham Papers, 3/6/2.
99 Richard Acland to Kitty Wintringham, 9 March, 1943, Common Wealth Papers I, 8/118–19.
100 Ibid.
101 R. Acland, 'First Draft Synopsis of Book under some such title as; – REVOLUTIONARIES SHOULD BE CHRISTIANS', Common Wealth Papers I, University of Sussex, 8/120–2.
102 Ibid.
103 Ibid.
104 Ibid.
105 Ibid.
106 Tom and Kitty Wintringham, 'Fellowship or Morality?' Common Wealth Papers I, 8/334–60, p. 16.
107 Ibid.
108 Ibid.,
109 Kitty Wintringham to Kenneth Ingram, [March] 1943; Wintringham Papers, 3/6/2.
110 Richard Acland, Diary, 28 July 1943, Acland Papers, EUS 104/1. Photocopy of originals held in the Common Wealth Papers 1; also Calder, 'Common Wealth', vol. 1, p. 211.
111 Acland, Diary, 5 August.
112 Ibid.
113 Ibid. He did indeed publish it and took on board a number of Wintringham's criticisms; Calder, 'Common Wealth', vol. 1, p. 212.
114 Wintringhams, 'Fellowship or Morality?' p. 4.
115 Kitty Wintringham to Kenneth Ingram, [March] 1943.
116 Ibid.
117 Tom Wintringham to Richard Acland, 26 October 1943, Wintringham Papers, 3/6/2.
118 Richard Acland, 'Men and Women', Wintringham Papers, 3/3/5.
119 Ibid.
120 'Final Draft of Women's Policy Sub-Committee', Wintringham Papers, 3/3/5.
121 Acland, 'An Un-Named Book. An Argumentative Autobiography [70s]', p. H174. On Elaine Burton see 'Burton, (Frances) Elaine, Baroness Burton of Coventry (1904–91)', *Oxford Dictionary of National Biography*, Oxford: Oxford University Press, 2004.

122 Kitty Wintringham to Richard Acland, 10 November 1943, Wintringham Papers, 3/6/2.
123 Richard Acland to Kitty Wintringham, 11 November 1943, Wintringham Papers, 3/6/2.
124 Kitty Wintringham to Richard Acland, November 1943, Common Wealth Papers I, 8/293–7.
125 Ibid.
126 Ibid.
127 Ibid.
128 Richard Acland, 'Memorandum on Common Wealth Theory', Common Wealth Papers 1, 8/301–3.
129 'Common Wealth', vol. 1, p. 213.
130 Wintringhams, 'Fellowship or Morality?' p. 2.
131 Ibid., p. 3.
132 Ibid., p. 9.
133 Ibid., p. 15.
134 Ibid., p. 18. K. Ingram, *The Night Is Far Spent*, London: George Allen & Unwin, pp. 123–4.
135 Wintringhams, 'Fellowship or Morality?' p. 21.
136 Ibid., p. 19.
137 R. Page Arnot, *What is Common Wealth?* London: Communist Party of Great Britain, 1943, p. 5.
138 Richard Acland, 'Draft Leaflet Arising from Weekend Discussion 20/21.11.43', p. 1, Common Wealth Papers I, 8/322–32.
139 Wintringhams, 'Fellowship or Morality?' p. 22.
140 Ibid., p. 23.
141 Ibid., p. 21.
142 Kenneth Ingram, 'Draft Policy Document', 15 November 1943, pp. 2–3, Common Wealth Papers I, 8/315–18.
143 Ibid.
144 Calder, 'Common Wealth', vol. 1, pp. 215–16.
145 Richard Acland, 'Report on MacMurray to Me & Tom as Prepared for Conference', Common Wealth Papers I, 8/308–11. I have corrected Acland's spelling of Macmurray.
146 According to Hugh Purcell, 'he obtained his BA in Modern History though he did not distinguish himself. (The [post-war] shortened course was not graded so it is impossible to say how badly he did)'; *The Last English Revolutionary*, p. 21.
147 Acland, 'An Un-Named Book. An Argumentative Autobiography [80s]', p. 3.5.
148 Acland, *Report on MacMurray*.
149 Acland, 'An Un-Named Book. An Argumentative Autobiography [80s]', p. 3.7.
150 N. Deakin, *Besieging Jericho: Episodes from the Early Career of François Lafitte (1931–1945)*, Cercles Occasional Papers Series, 2004. Online. Available HTTP: www.cercles/n11/deakin.pdf (accessed 27 April 2009).
151 Calder, 'Common Wealth', vol. 1, pp. 214–15.
152 Richard Acland, Diary, 21 November 1943, Common Wealth Papers I, 8/274.
153 Ibid.
154 Kenneth Ingram, *Religion and the New Society*, London: Common Wealth Publications, [1943?], p. 8.
155 E. Millington, *Was That Really Me?* n.p.o.p: Fultus Books, 2006, pp. 131–2.
156 Ibid., pp. 132–3.
157 Driberg, *Ruling Passions*, p. 16.
158 M. Cook, 'From Gay Reform to Gaydar', in M. Cook (ed.), *A Gay History of Britain: Love and Sex between Men since the Middle Ages*, Oxford: Greenwood World Publishing, 2007, p. 186.

159  R Acland, 'Chastity or What?' in Richard Sadler (ed.), *Sexual Morality: Three Views*, London: Arlington Books, 1965, p. 23.
160  Ibid., p. 18.
161  *Towards a Quaker View of Sex*, London: Friends Home Service Committee, 1963, p. 36. Emphasis in text.
162  Acland, 'Chastity or What?', p. 22
163  Ibid.
164  Not that the pamphlet was official Quaker policy. Its publication drew fire from other Quakers, and a second edition was issued the following year with a number of more orthodox changes, including a number of deletions and subtle word changes in the chapter on homosexuality; *Towards a Quaker View of Sex*, revised edition, London: Friends Home Service Committee, 1964.
165  Acland, 'Chastity or What?', p. 18.
166  Ibid., pp. 22–3.
167  Kenneth Ingram, 'Draft Policy Document', 15 November 1943, p. 3, Common Wealth Papers I, 8/315–18.
168  Quoted in Calder, 'Common Wealth', vol. 2, p. 61.
169  Kenneth Ingram, 'Memorandum', 27 November 1943, Common Wealth Papers I, 8/369–71.
170  Tom Wintringham to Kenneth Ingram, 16 July 1944, Wintringham Papers, 3/6/2.
171  Acland, Diary, 11 December 1943.
172  Calder, 'Common Wealth', vol. 1, pp. 216–17.
173  *Common Wealth and the New Year*, London: St Clement's Press, 1944. Wintringham Papers, 3/4/2.
174  Calder, 'Common Wealth', vol. 1, p. 208.
175  John Ferguson to Kitty Wintringham, 3 November 1943, Wintringham Papers, 3/3/2.
176  Calder, 'Common Wealth', vol. 1, p. 219.
177  For an account of this section of the conference see *Report of the Second Conference held at the Royal Hotel, Woburn Place, London, WC1. Easter 1944*, London: Common Wealth Publishing, 1944, pp. 26–8.
178  Richard Acland to Tom Wintringham, 7 June 1944, Common Wealth Papers I, 8/415–17.
179  *Common Wealth and the New Year*, p. 8. Wintringham Papers, 3/4/2.
180  *Common Wealth in 1944*, London: Common Wealth Publishing, 1944, p. 6.
181  Tom Wintringham to Richard Acland [n.d., but clearly early June 1944], Common Wealth Papers I, 8/414.
182  Richard Acland to Tom Wintringham, 7 June 1944.
183  Ibid.
184  Acland, 'An Un-Named Book. An Argumentative Autobiography [70s]', p. H178.
185  Calder, 'Common Wealth', vol. 1, p. 147.
186  G.D.H. Cole, *A History of the Labour Party from 1914*, London: Routledge & Kegan Paul, 1948, p. 410.
187  Acland, 'An Un-Named Book. An Argumentative Autobiography [70s]', p. H188.
188  On this see Calder, 'Common Wealth', vol. 1, pp. 286–96.
189  Ibid., p. 293.
190  Ibid., p. 294.
191  Acland, 'An Un-Named Book. An Argumentative Autobiography [80s]', p. 3.11.
192  Calder, 'Common Wealth', vol. 1, p. 238.
193  Ibid., p. 295, p. 313.
194  Quoted in Calder, 'Common Wealth', vol. 1, p. 301.
195  Craig, *British Parliamentary Election Results 1918–1949*, p. 349.
196  Calder, 'Common Wealth', vol. 1, p. 314.
197  Quoted in Calder, 'Common Wealth', vol. 1, p. 317.

198 Acland, 'An Un-Named Book. An Argumentative Autobiography [70s]', p. H192.
199 Quoted in Calder, 'Common Wealth', vol. 1, p. 325.
200 Olaf Stapledon, 'COMMON WEALTH: Vote for Karl Heath', Stapledon Papers, F.10.7.
201 Calder, 'Common Wealth', vol. 1, p. 324. Robert Crossley says that in the 1945 election Olaf Stapledon 'campaigned for both Common Wealth and Labour Candidates' (*Olaf Stapledon*, p. 323); presumably, though, not in the same constituency.
202 Ibid., p. 235.
203 Kenneth Ingram to Richard Acland, 13 July 1945, Common Wealth Papers I, 8/441–2.
204 All results taken from Craig, *British Parliamentary Election Results 1918–1949*.
205 Acland, 'Personal Political Memoirs', p. 15.
206 Ibid.
207 Acland, 'An Un-Named Book. An Argumentative Autobiography [80s]', p. 3.12.
208 Ibid.
209 On this see Calder, 'Common Wealth', vol. 1, pp. 327–33.
210 Calder, 'Common Wealth', vol. 1, p. 329.
211 Acland, 'Personal Political Memoirs', p. 15. Interviewed by Calder in the 1960s Smith was not kind to Acland, calling him 'a chronic poseur ... always thinking of his own image'. Cited in Gildart, ' An Australian Socialist in England: Kim Mackay'.
212 On the post-war life of Common Wealth see: D.L. Prynn, 'Common Wealth – A British "Third Party" of the 1940s', *Journal of Contemporary History*, 7:1–2, 1972, pp. 177–9; also J. Callaghan, 'Common Wealth and the Communist Party and the 1945 General Election', *Contemporary British History*. 9:1, 1995, pp. 75–6.

**Conclusion**

1 O. Stapledon, 'Data for a World View; 2. Paranormal Experiences', *Enquiry*, 1:2, 1948, p. 18.
2 From his letter to Aage Marcus (6 February 1948) in R. Crossley (ed.), *An Olaf Stapledon Reader*, Syracuse: Syracuse University Press, 1997, p. 290.
3 Hubert Wilson to Olaf Stapledon, 7 May 1947, Stapledon Papers, Liverpool University, H6.C.1.3/H6/C.1.3.
4 R. Crossley, *Olaf Stapledon: Speaking for the Future*, Liverpool: Liverpool University Press, 1994, p. 30.
5 O. Stapledon, 'The Conflict of Values: The Bridge Between', in a collection of essays (without a named editor), *Two Worlds in Focus: Studies of the Cold War*, London: National Peace Council, 1950, pp. 44–60.
6 For the visit see Crossley, *Olaf Stapledon*, pp. 10–17, pp. 371–81.
7 Ibid., p. 375.
8 Kenneth Ingram to Olaf Stapledon, 2 May 1950, Stapledon Papers, H1.I.7/H1/I/1–7.
9 Kenneth Ingram to Olaf Stapledon, 8 June 1948, Stapledon Papers, H1.I.1/H1/I/1.
10 K. Ingram, *Communist Challenge: Good or Evil?* London: Quality Press, 1948, p. 23, p. 75; Kenneth Ingram to Olaf Stapledon, 30 June 1948, Stapledon Papers, H1.I.2/H1/I/2.
11 K. Ingram, 'Can the Two Worlds Co-operate?', *Two Worlds in Focus: Studies of the Cold War*, London: National Peace Council, 1950, pp. 61–7; *Negotiation – Not Appeasement*, London: National Peace Council, 1951; *Fifty Years of the National Peace Council 1908–1958*, London: National Peace Council, 1958.
12 K. Ingram, *Is Christianity Credible?* London: The Faith Press, 1963, p. 151.
13 Ibid., p. 153.
14 Kenneth Ingram to Olaf Stapledon, 28 November 1949, Stapledon Papers, H1.I.6/H1/I.6.

15 For Macmurray's post-war years see J.E. Costello, *John Macmurray: A Biography*, Edinburgh: Floris, 2002, pp. 304–400.
16 A.J. Ayer, *Part of My Life*, London: Collins, 1977, p. 307, p. 310. Ayer's biographer follows his subject's steer: 'the philosophy department that Ayer found when he arrived in 1946 was in a sad state'; B. Rogers, *A.J. Ayer: A Life*, London: Chatto & Windus, 1999, p. 206.
17 A.J. Ayer, *More of My Life*, Oxford: Oxford University Press, 1985, p. 16.
18 Ibid., p. 23.
19 Costello, *John Macmurray*, p. 308.
20 J.B. Coates, *Ten Modern Prophets*, London: Frederick Muller, 1944, p. 100.
21 Ibid.
22 D. Emmet, *Philosophers and Friends: Reminiscences of Seventy Years in Philosophy*, London: Palgrave Macmillan, 1996, p. 53. Costello relates a much more disparaging version of Ryle's reflection on *The Self as Agent* where Ryle is purported to have said: 'Macmurray's first volume should have been entitled: *The Self as a Gent!*'; *John Macmurray*, p. 332.
23 Costello, *John Macmurray*, p. 332.
24 J. Macmurray, *Search for Reality in Religion*, London: Friends Home Service Committee, 1969, p. 69, pp. 70–5.
25 R. Acland, *Hungry Sheep*, Basingstoke: Marshall Pickering, 1988, p. 4; 1947 by-election results. Online. Available HTTP: www.geocities.com/by_elections/47.html#gravesend (accessed 26 September 2010); G.D.H. Cole, *A History of the Labour Party from 1914*, London: Routledge & Kegan Paul, 1948, p. 476.
26 P.M. Williams (ed.), *The Diary of Hugh Gaitskell 1945–1956*, London: Jonathan Cape, 1983, p. 49.
27 UK General Election results, February 1950, October 1951. Online. Available HTTP: www.psr.keele.ac.uk/area/uk/ge50/i.10.htm; www.psr.keele.ac.uk/area/uk/ge51/i.10.htm (both accessed 26 September 2010).
28 A.F. Havighurst, *Britain in Transition*, Chicago: Chicago University Press, 1985, p. 466. A photo showing him at a silver jubilee celebration of CND can be found at: www.topfoto.co.uk/gallery/CND/ppages/ppage97.html (accessed 26 September 2010). Acland's closing lines in *Waging Peace* (1958) include the name and address of CND, and the 'hope that steadily increasing numbers will join in its work'; *Waging Peace*, London: Frederick Muller, 1958, p. 161.
29 Acland, *Hungry Sheep*, p. 7.
30 UK General Election results, May 1955. Online. Available HTTP: www.psr.keele.ac.uk/area/uk/ge55/i.10.htm (accessed 26 September 2010).
31 R. Acland, *We Teach Them Wrong: Religion and the Young*, London: Victor Gollancz, 1963, p. 9.
32 Acland, *Hungry Sheep*, p. 7.
33 Ibid; 'History of St Luke's'. Online. Available HTTP: http://education.exeter.ac.uk/pages.php?id=133 (accessed 26 September 2010).
34 R. Acland, *The Next Step*, Exeter: self-published by Richard Acland, 1974, p. 162.
35 M. Hilson and J. Melling, 'Public Gifts and Political Identities: Sir Richard Acland, Common Wealth, and the Moral Politics of Land Ownership in the 1940s', *Twentieth Century British History*, 11:2, 2000, p. 164.
36 Ibid., p. 179.
37 All of this is taken from F. Wheen, *The Soul of Indiscretion: Tom Driberg: Poet, Philanderer, Legislator and Outlaw*, London: Fourth Estate, pp. 368–72.
38 R. Acland, *Nothing Left to Believe?* London: Longmans, Green, 1949, p. x.
39 R. Acland, *Why So Angry?* London: Victor Gollancz, 1958, p. 12.
40 Acland, *Hungry Sheep*, p. 8.
41 Acland, *The Next Step*, p. 7.
42 Acland, *Hungry Sheep*, p. 111.

43　Ibid., p. 134.
44　Richard Acland, 'An Un-Named Book. An Argumentative Autobiography [70s]', Acland Papers, Exeter University, EUL MS 104/4 (1), H102–3.
45　Ibid., pp. H103–4.
46　Hilson and Melling, 'Public Gifts and Political Identities', *Twentieth Century British History*, p. 162, p. 164–5. The source is T. Copley, *Teaching Religion*, pp. 71–5.
47　Acland, *Hungry Sheep*, p. 9.
48　Ibid., p. 137.
49　O. Stapledon, 'The Meaning of "Spirit"', in P. Albery and S. Read (eds), *Here and Now No. 5*, London: The Falcon Press, 1949, p. 72.
50　The phrase is taken from H. de Vries, *Philosophy and the Turn to Religion*, Baltimore: Johns Hopkins University Press, 1999.
51　A.N. Wilson, *God's Funeral*, London: John Murray, 1999, p. 60.
52　J.D. Caputo, *Religion*, London: Routledge, 2001, p. 60.
53　H. de Vries, 'Introduction: Before, Around, and Beyond the Theologico-Political', in H. de Vries and L.E. Sullivan (eds), *Political Theologies: Public Religions in a Post-Secular World*, New York: Fordham University Press, 2006, p. 2.
54　C. Taylor, *A Secular Age*, Cambridge, MA: The Belknap Press of Harvard University Press, 2007, p. 22, pp. 27–8.
55　T. Eagleton, *Reason, Faith, and Revolution: Reflections on the God Debate*, New Haven and London: Yale University Press, 2009, p. 18.
56　Taylor, *A Secular Age*, p. 595.
57　Ibid, p. 391.
58　J. Habermas, *Between Naturalism and Religion*, Cambridge: Polity, 2008, p. 261. Habermas's emphasis.
59　J. Habermas, 'Religious Tolerance – The Pacemaker for Cultural Rights', *Philosophy*, 79, 2004, p. 13.
60　O. Stapledon, *Waking World*, London: Methuen, 1934, p. 130. See also Crossley, *Olaf Stapledon*, p. 214. Cicero suggests a different, though equally God-free, etymology – *relegere* – to re-read. See V. Geoghegan, 'Utopia and the Memory of Religion', in M.J. Griffin and T. Moylan (eds), *Exploring the Utopian Impulse: Essays on Utopian Thought and Practice*, Oxford: Peter Lang, 2007, pp. 101–3.
61　G. Vattimo, 'A Prayer for Silence', in J.W. Robbins, *After the Death of God*, New York: Columbia University Press, 2007, p. 97.
62　R. Acland, *The Forward March*, London: George Allen & Unwin, 1941, p. 104.
63　K. Ingram, *Taken at the Flood*, London: George Allen & Unwin, 1943, p. 129.
64　Ibid., p. 134.
65　Ibid.
66　O. Stapledon, *Beyond the Isms*, London: Secker and Warburg, 1942, p. 9.

# Bibliography

**Manuscript sources**

Acland Papers, Exeter University
Common Wealth Papers, Sussex University
Macmurray Papers, Edinburgh University
Stapledon Papers, Liverpool University
Temple Papers, Lambeth Palace Library
Wintringham Papers, Liddell Hart Centre for Military Archives, King's College London
Letters from Olaf Stapledon to Ernest.W. Martin (1941–45), and Agnes Stapledon to Ernest W. Martin (1981), in author's possession.

**Printed sources**

*Acland*

*Only One Battle*, London: Victor Gollancz, 1937.
*This Way To Death: A Critical Examination of Government Foreign Policy*, London: n.p., 1938.
*What Now? Memorandum on the World Situation September 1939 by Sir Richard Acland, M.P.*, n.p.o.p, n.p., n.d. [1939].
*Unser Kampf: Our Struggle*, Harmondsworth: Penguin, 1940.
*It Must Be Christianity*, n.p.o.p., n.p., n.d. [1941].
'Practical Questions. I' in *Malvern 1941: The Life of the Church and the Order of Society*, London: Longmans, Green, 1941, 153–62.
*The Forward March*, London: George Allen & Unwin, 1941.
*What It Will Be Like*, London: Victor Gollancz, 1942.
*How It Can Be Done*, London: Macdonald, 1943.
*Nothing Left to Believe?* London: Longmans, Green, 1949.
*Waging Peace*, London: Frederick Muller, 1958.
*Why So Angry?* London: Victor Gollancz, 1958.
*We Teach Them Wrong: Religion and the Young*, London: Victor Gollancz, 1963.
'Chastity or What?' in R. Sadler (ed.), *Sexual Morality: Three Views*, London: Arlington Books, 1965, 1–32.
'Sleep-Walking in the Desert', in B. Dixon (ed.), *Journeys in Belief*, London: George Allen and Unwin, 1968, 15–24.
*The Next Step*, Exeter: self-published by Richard Acland, 1974.
*Hungry Sheep*, Basingstoke: Marshall Pickering, 1988.

## Ingram

*Boys: What They Are and How to Manage Them*, London: A.R. Mowbray, 1911.
*The Greater Triumph: A Story of Osborne and Dartmouth*, London: A.R. Mowbray, 1911.
*Basil Verely: A Study of Charterhouse Life*, London: A.R. Mowbray, 1912.
*A Manual for Church of England Scouts*, London: A.R. Mowbray, 1913.
*An Outline of Sexual Morality*, London: Jonathan Cape, 1922.
*England at the Flood-Tide*, London: The Damian Press, 1924.
*The Symbolic Island*, London: The Damian Press, 1924.
*The Modern Attitude to the Sex Problem*, London: George Allen & Unwin, 1930.
*Midsummer Sanity*, London: Philip Allan, 1933.
*Modern Thought on Trial*, London: Philip Allan, 1933.
*'It is Expedient ... '*, London: Geoffrey Bles, 1935.
*Christianity – Right or Left?* London: George Allen & Unwin, 1937.
*And He Shall Come Again*, London: Heinemann, 1938.
*The Christian Challenge to Christians*, London: George Allen & Unwin, 1938.
*Towards Christianity: The Religious Progress of the World*, London: Student Christian Movement Press, 1939.
*Sex-Morality Tomorrow*, London: George Allen & Unwin, 1940.
'Practical Questions II' in *Malvern 1941: The Life of the Church and the Order of Society*, London: Longmans, Green, 1941, 165–79.
*The Night is Far Spent*, London: George Allen & Unwin, 1941.
*Religion and the New Society*, London: Common Wealth Publications, n.d., [1943?].
*Taken at the Flood*, London: George Allen & Unwin, 1943.
*Christianity and Sexual Morality – A Modernist View*, London: The Union of Modern Free Churchmen, 1944.
'Portrait of a Mother', in K.A. Ingram, *Towards Old Age*, London: Quality Press, 1945, 7–37.
*Years of Crisis*, London: George Allen & Unwin, 1946.
*Communist Challenge: Good or Evil?* London: Quality Press, 1948.
'Can the Two Worlds Co-operate?', in (no editor) *Two Worlds in Focus: Studies of the Cold War*, London: National Peace Council, 1950, 61–7.
*Negotiation – Not Appeasement*, London: National Peace Council, 1951.
*Storm in a Sanctuary*, London: Ernest Benn, 1954.
'The Church and Social Thinking', in S. G. Evans (ed.), *Return to Reality: Some Essays on Contemporary Christianity*, London: Zeno, 1954, 192–210.
*History of the Cold War*, London: Darwen Finlayson, 1955.
*Fifty Years of the National Peace Council 1908–1958*, London: National Peace Council, 1958.
*Is Christianity Credible?* London: The Faith Press, 1963.
'Class Hatred', in *The Quorum: A Magazine of Friendship*, North Pomfret, VT: Elysium Press/Asphodel Editions, 2001, 28–33.

## Macmurray

*Freedom in the Modern World*, London: Faber & Faber, 1932.
*Interpreting the Universe*, London: Faber & Faber, 1933.
*The Philosophy of Communism*, London: Faber & Faber, 1933.

'The Challenge of Communism', in (no editor) *Christianity and Communism*, London: The Industrial Christian Fellowship, 1934, 14–32.
*Creative Society: A Study of the Relation of Christianity to Communism*, London: Student Christian Movement Press, 1935.
*Reason and Emotion*, London: Faber & Faber, 1935.
'Christianity and Communism: Towards a Synthesis', in J. Lewis, K. Polanyi and D.K. Kitchin (eds), *Christianity and the Social Revolution*, London: Victor Gollancz, 1935, 505–26.
'The Early Development of Marx's Thought', in J. Lewis, K. Polanyi and D.K. Kitchin (eds), *Christianity and the Social Revolution*, London: Victor Gollancz, 1935, 209–36.
'Fascism and Christianity', in (no editor), *The Christian Answer to Fascism*, London: The Christian Left, 1938, 13–17.
*The Clue to History*, London: Student Christian Movement Press, 1938.
*Challenge to the Churches*, London: Kegan Paul, Trench, Trubner, 1941.
*The Foundation of Economic Reconstruction*, London: National Peace Council, 1942.
*Constructive Democracy*, London: Faber & Faber, 1943.
'War to Peace', *Industrial and Personnel Management*, September/October 1943, 146–50.
*Through Chaos to Community?* London: National Peace Council, 1944.
*A Crisis of Culture: The USSR and the West*, London: National Peace Council, 1947.
*Conditions of Freedom*, London: Faber & Faber, 1950.
*The Self as Agent*, New York: Harper and Brothers, 1957.
*Persons in Relation*, London: Faber & Faber, 1961.
*Search for Reality in Religion*, London: Friends Home Service Committee, 1969.
'The Conception of Society', in E. McIntosh (ed.), *Selected Philosophical Writings*, Exeter: Imprint Academic, 2004, 95–107.

## Stapledon

*Latter-Day Psalms*, Liverpool: Henry Young and Sons, 1914.
*A Modern Theory of Ethics*, London: Methuen, 1929.
*Waking World*, London: Methuen, 1934.
*Odd John*, London: Methuen, 1935.
'Mr Wells Calls in the Martians', *The London Mercury*, 36, 1937, 295–6.
'Israel's Part', *The London Mercury*, 39:233, March 1939, 553–4.
*New Hope For Britain*, London: Methuen, 1939.
*Philosophy and Living*, Harmondsworth: Penguin, 1939.
*Saints and Revolutionaries*, London: Heinemann, 1939.
*Beyond the Isms*, London: Secker and Warburg, 1942.
'The Great Certainty', in E.W. Martin (ed.), *In Search of Faith: A Symposium*, London: Lindsay Drummond, 1943, 37–59.
'Christianity and Marxism', *The New Leader*, 16 March 1946, 6.
*Youth and Tomorrow*, London: St Botolph, 1946.
*The Flames*, London: Secker and Warburg, 1947.
'Data for a World View; 2', Paranormal Experiences', *Enquiry* 1:2, 1948, 13–18.
'Personality and Liberty', *Philosophy*, 24:89, April 1949, 144–56.
'The Meaning of "Spirit"', in P. Albery and S. Read (eds), *Here and Now No. 5*, London: The Falcon Press, 1949, 72–82.
*A Man Divided*, London: Methuen, 1950.
'Religion To-Day', *Faith and Freedom*, 3:2 (8), Spring 1950, 49–53.

'The Conflict of Values: The Bridge Between', in a collection of essays (no editor) *Two Worlds in Focus: Studies of the Cold War*, London: National Peace Council, 1950, 44–60.
*The Opening of the Eyes*, London: Methuen, 1954.
*Sirius*, Harmondsworth: Penguin, 1964.
*Last and First Men* and *Last Men in London*, Harmondsworth: Penguin, 1972.
*Darkness and the Light*, Westport, CT: Hyperion Press, 1974.
'The Correspondence of Olaf Stapledon and H.G. Wells 1931–42', ed. R. Crossley, in Gary Wolfe (ed.), *Science Fiction Dialogues*, Chicago: Academy Chicago, 1982, 27–57.
'Letter to Aage Marcus', in R. Crossley (ed.), *An Olaf Stapledon Reader*, Syracuse: Syracuse University Press, 1997, 289–90.
'Letter to Naomi Mitchison', in R. Crossley (ed.), *An Olaf Stapledon Reader*, Syracuse: Syracuse University Press, 1997, 281–2.
'Some Thoughts on H.G. Wells's *You Can't Be Too Careful*', in R. Crossley (ed.), *An Olaf Stapledon Reader*, Syracuse: Syracuse University Press, 1997, 203–6.
*Star Maker*, London: Orion, 2003.

**Secondary sources**

Addison, P., 'By-Elections of the Second World War', in C. Cook and J. Ramsden (eds), *By-Elections in British Politics*, London: Macmillan, 1973, 165–90.
*The Road to 1945: British Politics and the Second World War*, London: Pimlico, 1994.
Arnold, M., *Culture and Anarchy and Other Writings*, ed. S. Collini, Cambridge: Cambridge University Press, 1993.
Arnot, R. Page., *What is Common Wealth?* London: Communist Party of Great Britain, 1943.
Ayer, A.J., *Part of My Life*, London: Collins, 1977.
——*More of My Life*, Oxford: Oxford University Press, 1985.
Baines, M., 'Liberal Nadir, 1935–56', *Liberal Democrat History Group*. Online. Available HTTP: www.liberalhistory.org.uk (accessed 23 November 2008).
Bennett, G.H., 'The Wartime Political Truce and Hopes for Post War Coalition: The West Derbyshire By-Election, 1944', *Midland History*, 17, 1992, 118–35.
Berlin, I., *Karl Marx: His Life and Environment*, London: Thornton Butterworth, 1939.
——*Karl Marx: His Life and Environment*, fourth edition, Oxford: Oxford University Press, 1978.
——*Flourishing: Letters 1928–1946*, ed. Henry Hardy, London: Pimlico, 2005.
Bernstein, J., *Robert Oppenheimer: Portrait of an Enigma*, Chicago: Ivan R. Dee, 2004.
Bevir, M. and D. O'Brien, 'From Idealism to Communitarianism: The Inheritance and Legacy of John Macmurray', *History of Political Thought*, 24:2, 2003, 305–29.
*Bhagavad Gita*, trans. Swami Prabhavananda and Christopher Isherwood, New York: Signet, 2002.
Blair, T., 'Foreword', in Philip Conford (ed.), *The Personal World: John Macmurray on Self and Society*, Edinburgh: Floris Books, 1996, 9–10.
Bloch, E., *Atheism in Christianity: The Religion of the Exodus and the Kingdom*, New York: Herder and Herder, 1972.
——*The Principle of Hope*, Oxford: Basil Blackwell, 1986.
——*The Utopian Function of Art and Literature: Selected Essays*, Cambridge, MA: MIT Press, 1988.
——*Heritage of Our Times*, Cambridge: Polity Press, 1991.

Block, F., 'Karl Polanyi and the Writing of *The Great Transformation*', *Theory and Society*, 32, 2003, 275–306.
Bradford, E.E., *To Boys Unknown*, London: The Gay Men's Press, 1988.
Breckman, W., *Marx, the Young Hegelians, and the Origins of Radical Social Theory: Dethroning the Self*, Cambridge, Cambridge University Press, 1999.
'Burton, (Frances) Elaine, Baroness Burton of Coventry (1904–91)', *Oxford Dictionary of National Biography*, Oxford: Oxford University Press, 2004.
Calder, A.L.R., 'The Common Wealth Party 1942–1945', unpublished DPhil thesis, University of Sussex, 1968.
—— *The People's War: Britain 1939–45*, London: Jonathan Cape, 1969.
Callaghan, J., 'Common Wealth and the Communist Party and the 1945 General Election', *Contemporary British History*, 9:1, 1995, 62–79.
Caputo, J.D., *Religion*, London: Routledge, 2001.
——'Spectral Hermeneutics: On the Weakness of God and the Theology of the Event', in Jeffrey W. Robbins (ed.), *After the Death of God*, New York: Columbia University Press, 2007, 47–85.
Carpenter, E., *Ioläus: An Anthology of Friendship*, London: Swan Sonnenschein, 1906.
—— *The Intermediate Sex: A Study of Some Transitional Types of Men and Women*, London: George Allen & Unwin, 1916.
Carr, E.H., *Karl Marx: A Study in Fanaticism*, London: Dent, 1934.
Causton, B., 'The Scene of the Conference', in *Malvern 1941: The Life of the Church and the Order of Society*, London: Longmans, Green, 1941, 1–8.
Chertok, H., *He Also Spoke as a Jew: The Life of the Reverend James Parkes*, London and Portland, OR: Vallentine Mitchell, 2006.
Clarke, P., *The Cripps Version: The Life of Sir Stafford Cripps 1889–1952*, London: Penguin, 2002.
Coates, J.B., *Ten Modern Prophets*, London, Frederick Muller, 1944.
Cole, G.D.H., *A History of the Labour Party from 1914*, London: Routledge & Kegan Paul, 1948.
Collette, C., 'Questions of Gender: Labour and Women', in B. Brivati and R. Heffernan (eds), *The Labour Party: A Centenary History*, Houndmills: Macmillan, 2000, 402–21.
Collier, A., 'Macmurray and Marx: The Philosophy of Practice and the Overcoming of Dualism', in D. Fergusson and N. Dower (eds), *John Macmurray: Critical Perspectives*, New York: Peter Lang, 2002, 69–76.
*Common Wealth Manifesto: A New Social Order*, fourth edition, London: CW Publishing, 1944.
Cook, M., *London and the Culture of Homosexuality, 1885–1914*, Cambridge: Cambridge University Press, 2003.
——'Queer Conflicts: Love, Sex and War', in M. Cook (ed.), *A Gay History of Britain: Love and Sex between Men since the Middle Ages*, Oxford: Greenwood World Publishing, 2007, 145–77.
——'From Gay Reform to Gaydar', in M. Cook (ed.), *A Gay History of Britain: Love and Sex between Men since the Middle Ages*, Oxford: Greenwood World Publishing, 2007, 179–214.
Costello, J. E., *John Macmurray: A Biography*, Edinburgh: Floris, 2002.
CND, online. Available HTTP: www.topfoto.co.uk/gallery/CND/ppages/ppage97.html (accessed 26 September 2010).
Craig, F.W.S. (ed.), *British Parliamentary Election Results 1918–1949*, Glasgow: Political Reference Publications, 1969.

Crossley, R., 'Famous Mythical Beasts: Olaf Stapledon and H.G. Wells', *Georgia Review*, 36, Fall 1982, 619–39.
——*Olaf Stapledon: Speaking for the Future*, Liverpool: Liverpool University Press, 1994.
——(ed.), *An Olaf Stapledon Reader*, Syracuse, New York: Syracuse University Press, 1997.
Cullen, S., *Home Guard Socialism: A Vision of a People's Army*, Warwick: Allotment Hut Booklets, 2006.
Dale, G., *Karl Polanyi: The Limits of the Market*, Cambridge: Polity, 2010.
d'Arch Smith, T., *Love in Earnest: Some Notes on the Lives and Writings of English 'Uranian' Poets from 1889 to 1930*, London: Routledge & Kegan Paul, 1970.
——'Introduction', *The Quorum. A Magazine of Friendship*, North Pomfret, VT: Elysium Press, Asphodel Editions, 2001, 1–15.
de Vries, H., 'Introduction: Before, Around, and Beyond the Theologico-Political', in Hent de Vries and Lawrence E. Sullivan (eds), *Political Theologies: Public Religions in a Post-Secular World*, New York: Fordham University Press, 2006, 1–88.
Deakin, N., *Besieging Jericho: Episodes from the Early Career of François Lafitte (1931–1945)*, Cercles Occasional Papers Series, 2004. Online. Available HTTP: www.cercles/n11/deakin.pdf (accessed 27 April 2009).
Dowling, L., *Hellenism and Homosexuality in Victorian Oxford*, Ithica: Cornell University Press, 1994.
Driberg, T., *Ruling Passions: The Autobiography of Tom Driberg*, London: Quartet Books, 1978.
Dutton, D., *A History of the Liberal Party*, Houndmills, Basingstoke: Palgrave, 2004.
Eagleton, T., *Reason, Faith, and Revolution: Reflections on the God Debate*, New Haven and London: Yale University Press, 2009.
Emmet, D., *Philosophers and Friends: Reminiscences of Seventy Years in Philosophy*, London: Palgrave Macmillan, 1996.
Engels, F., *Ludwig Feuerbach and the End of Classical German Philosophy*, in K. Marx and F. Engels, *Selected Works*, London: Lawrence and Wishart, 1970.
Fernbach, D., 'Tom Wintringham and Socialist Defense Strategy', *History Workshop Journal*, 14:1, 1982, 63–91.
Feuerbach, L., *The Essence of Christianity*, New York: Harpers & Row, 1957.
Fiedler, L. A., *Olaf Stapledon: A Man Divided*, New York: Oxford University Press, 1983.
Geoghegan, V., *Utopianism and Marxism*, London: Methuen, 1987; reprinted with new introduction, London: Peter Lang, 2008.
——'Edward Carpenter's England Revisited', *History of Political Thought*, 24:3, 2003, 509–27.
——'Ideology and Utopia', *Journal of Political Ideologies*, 9.2, 2004, 123–38.
——'Religion and Communism: Feuerbach, Marx and Bloch', *The European Legacy*, 9:5, 2004, 585–95.
——'Olaf Stapledon: Utopia and Worship', *Utopian Studies*, 13:3, 2005, 347–64.
——'Utopia and the Memory of Religion', in M. J. Griffin and T. Moylan (eds), *Exploring the Utopian Impulse: Essays on Utopian Thought and Practice*, Oxford: Peter Lang, 2007, 101–15.
'George Cecil Ives: An Inventory of His Papers at the Harry Ransom Humanities Research Center'. Online. Available HTTP: www.lib.utexas.edu/taro/uthrc/00060/hrc-00060.html (accessed 26 September 2010).
Gildart, K., 'An Australian Socialist in England: Kim Mackay, the British Left, and European Federalism, 1934 – 1960'. Online. Available HTTP: www.historycooperative.org/proceedings/asslh/gildart.html (accessed 26 September 2010).

## Bibliography

Gravesend By Election Results. Online. Available HTTP: www.geocities.com/by_elections/47.html#gravesend (accessed 26 September 2010).
Habermas, J., 'Religious Tolerance – the Pacemaker for Cultural Rights', *Philosophy*, 79:1, 2004, 5–18.
—— *Between Naturalism and Religion*, Cambridge: Polity, 2008.
Hadham, J. (James Parkes), *Good God: A Study of His Character and Activities*, Harmondsworth: Penguin, 1940.
Hall, L. A., '"Disinterested Enthusiasm for Sexual Misconduct": The British Society for the Study of Sex Psychology, 1913–47', *Journal of Contemporary History*, 30:4, October 1995, 665–86.
*Hansard*, House of Commons Debates. Online. Available HTTP: www.hansard.millbanksystems.com
Harrisson, T., 'War Books', *Horizon*, 4:24, 1941, 416–37.
Haslam, J., *The Vices of Integrity: E.H. Carr, 1892–1982*, London: Verso, 1999.
Havighurst, A.F., *Britain in Transition*, Chicago: Chicago University Press, 1985.
Heschel, S., *The Aryan Jesus: Christian Theologians and the Bible in Nazi Germany*, Princeton: Princeton University Press, 2008.
Hilliard, D., 'UnEnglish and Unmanly: Anglo-Catholicism and Homosexuality', *Victorian Studies*, 25:2, 1982, 181–210.
Hilson, M. and J. Melling, 'Public Gifts and Political Identities: Sir Richard Acland, Common Wealth, and the Moral Politics of Land Ownership in the 1940s', *Twentieth Century British History*, 11:2, 2000, 156–82.
'History of St Luke's'. Online. Available HTTP: http://education.exeter.ac.uk/pages.php?id=133 (accessed 26 September 2010).
Houlbrook, M., *Queer London: Perils and Pleasures in the Sexual Metropolis, 1918–1957*, Chicago and London: The University of Chicago Press, 2005.
Hume, D., *Dialogues Concerning Natural Religion*, London: Penguin, 1990.
Ignatieff, M., *Isaiah Berlin: A Life*, London: Chatto and Windus, 1998.
Iremonger, F.A., *William Temple Archbishop of Canterbury: His Life and Letters*, Oxford: Oxford University Press, 1948.
Ives, G., *The Graeco-Roman View of Youth*, n.p.o.p.: The Cayme Press, 1926.
J.E. 'Review of *Sex-Morality Tomorrow*', *International Journal of Psychoanalysis*, 22, 1941, 174–6.
James, C., 'Sat., Jan. 10, 2009 – William Paine-Anderson: Erotic Socialism II'. Online. Available HTTP: http://callumjames.blogspot (accessed 15 March 2009).
Jameson, F., *Archaeologies of the Future: The Desire Called Utopia and Other Science Fictions*, London: Verso, 2005.
Kaylor, M. M., *Secreted Desires: The Major Uranians: Hopkins, Pater and Wilde*, Brno, Czech Republic: Masaryk University Press, 2006.
Kennedy, H., 'Afterword', to John Henry Mackay, *The Hustler*, n.p.: L Xlibris, 2002.
—— *Anarchist of Love: The Secret Life of John Henry Mackay*, San Francisco: Peremptory Publications, 2002.
Kent, J., *William Temple: Church, State and Society in Britain, 1880–1950*, Cambridge: Cambridge University Press, 1992.
Kinnaird, J., *Olaf Stapledon*, Mercer Island, WA: Starmont House, 1986.
Kirkpatrick, Frank G., *John Macmurray: Community Beyond Political Philosophy*, Lanham: Rowman and Littlefield, 2005.
Lam, E.P., 'Does Macmurray Understand Marx?', *Journal of Religion*, 20: 1, 1940, 47–65.

Landshut, S. and J.P. Mayer (eds), *Der Historische Materialismus: Die Frühschriften*, Leipzig: Alfred Kröner Verlag, 1932.
Leech, K., 'Beyond Gin and Lace: Homosexuality and the Anglo-Catholic Subculture', originally published in A. Beck and R. Hunt (eds), *Speaking Love's Name; Homosexuality: Some Catholic and Socialist Perspectives*, London: The Jubilee Group, 1988. Online. Available HTTP: www.anglocatholicsocialism.org/lovesname.html (accessed 26 September 2010).
Leopold, D., *The Young Karl Marx: German Philosophy, Modern Politics, and Human Flourishing*, Cambridge: Cambridge University Press, 2007.
Lewis, J., *Penguin Special: The Life and Times of Allen Lane*, London: Penguin, 2006.
McCarthy, P., C. Elkins and H. Greenberg (eds), *The Legacy of Olaf Stapledon*, New York: Greenwood, 1989.
McKenna, N., *The Secret Life of Oscar Wilde*, London: Arrow, 2004.
McLean, I., 'Oxford and Bridgwater', in C. Cook and J. Ramsden (eds), *By-Elections in British Politics*, London: Macmillan, 1973, 112–29.
McLellan, David (ed.), *Karl Marx: Selected Writings*, Oxford: Oxford University Press, 2000.
'Macmurray, John (1891–1976)', *Oxford Dictionary of National Biography*, Oxford: Oxford University Press, 2004.
Mader, D.H., 'The Greek Mirror: The Uranians and Their Use of Greece', *Journal of Homosexuality*, 49:3–4, 2005, 377–420.
Maiden, J., 'The Anglican Prayer Book Controversy of 1927–28 and National Religion', PhD thesis, University of Stirling, 2007, p. 204. Online. Available HTTP: https://dspace.stir.ac.uk/dspace/handle/1893/247 (accessed 26 September 2010).
Marx, K., *Contribution to the Critique of Hegel's Philosophy of Law*, in K. Marx and F. Engels, *Collected Works*, Vol. 3, London: Lawrence & Wishart, 1975, 3–129.
—— *Contribution to the Critique of Hegel's Philosophy of Law. Introduction*, in K. Marx and F. Engels, *Collected Works*, Vol. 3, London: Lawrence & Wishart, 1975, 175–87.
—— *On the Jewish Question*, in K. Marx and F. Engels, *Collected Works*, Vol. 3, London: Lawrence & Wishart, 1975, 146–74.
Mehring, F., *Karl Marx: The Story of His Life*, Ann Arbor: University of Michigan Press, 1962.
Millington, E., *Was That Really Me?* n.p.o.p: Fultus Books, 2006.
Moskowitz, S (ed.), *Far Future Calling: Uncollected Science Fiction and Fantasies of Olaf Stapledon*, Philadelphia: Oswald Train, 1979.
——'Olaf Stapledon: Cosmic Philosopher', in Olaf Stapledon, *Darkness and the Light*, Westport, CT: Hyperion Press, 1974, (no page numbers).
Moylan, T., *Demand the Impossible: Science Fiction and the Utopian Imagination*, New York: Methuen, 1986.
Nadler, S., *Spinoza: A Life*, Cambridge: Cambridge University Press, 1999.
'New General Catalog of Old Books and Authors'. Online. Available HTTP: www.authorandbookinfo.com/ngcoba/in.htm (accessed 26 September 2010).
Oosterhuis, H. and H. Kennedy, *Homosexuality and Male Bonding in Pre-Nazi Germany*, New York and London: Harrington Park Press, 1991.
Ormrod, D., 'The Christian Left and the Beginnings of Christian–Marxist dialogue, 1935–45', in J. Obelkevich, L. Roper and R. Samuel (eds), *Disciplines of Faith: Studies in Religion, Politics and Patriarchy*, London: Routledge & Kegan Paul, 1987, 435–50.

Paine, W., *Shop Slavery and Emancipation: A Revolutionary Appeal to the Educated Young Men of the Middle Class*, London: P.S. King and Son, 1912.
—— *A New Aristocracy of Comradeship*, London: Leonard Parsons, 1920.
Parkes, J., *Voyage of Discoveries*, London: Victor Gollancz, 1969.
'Parkes, James William (1896–1981)', *Oxford Dictionary of National Biography*, Oxford: Oxford University Press, 2004.
Pimlott, B., *Labour and the Left in the 1930s*, Cambridge: Cambridge University Press, 1977.
Plekhanov., G.V., *Fundamental Problems of Marxism*, London: Lawrence and Wishart, n.d.
[Polanyi, K.], 'Notes of a Week's Study on the Early Writings of Karl Marx and Summary of Discussions on British Working Class Consciousness', *Christian Left Group Bulletin* 2, 1 January 1938.
—— 'The Essence of Fascism', in J. Lewis, K. Polanyi and D.K. Kitchin (eds), *Christianity and the Social Revolution*, London: Victor Gollancz, 1935, 359–94.
Porter, K. and J. Weeks (eds), *Between the Acts: Lives of Homosexual Men 1885–1967*, London: Routledge, 1991.
Priestley, J.B., 'Introduction', in R. Acland, *How It Can Be Done*, London: Macdonald, 1943, 5–13.
Prynn, D.L., 'Common Wealth – A British "Third Party" of the 1940s', *Journal of Contemporary History*, 7:1–2, 1972, 169–79.
Pugh, M., 'The Liberal Party and the Popular Front', *English Historical Review*, 121: 494, December 2006, 1327–50.
Punshon, E.R., *Night's Cloak*, London: Victor Gollancz, 1944.
Purcell, H., *The Last English Revolutionary: Tom Wintringham 1898–1949*, Thrupp: Sutton Publishing, 2004.
*Questions and Answers about Common Wealth's Policy*, London: CW Publishing, n.d., [1944?].
Rentoul, J., *Tony Blair: Prime Minister*, London: Warner Books, 2001.
*Report of a Religious Delegation to Spain – April 1937*, London: Victor Gollancz, 1937.
*Report of the Second Conference held at the Royal Hotel, Woburn Place, London, WC1. Easter 1944*, London: Common Wealth Publishing, 1944.
'Review of Kenneth Ingram, *An Outline of Sexual Morality*', *Times Literary Supplement*, 8 June 1922, 383.
'Review of Kenneth Ingram, *The Modern Attitude to the Sex Problem*', *Times Literary Supplement*, 29 May 1930, 463.
'Review of Kenneth Ingram, *Sex-Morality Tomorrow*', *Times Literary Supplement*, 12 October 1940, 523.
Rhymes, D., *No New Morality: Christian Personal Values and Sexual Morality*, London: Constable, 1964.
Rieu, E.V., 'Preface', in Olaf Stapledon, *The Opening of the Eyes*, London: Methuen, 1954, vii–ix.
Rogers, B., *A.J. Ayer: A Life*, London: Chatto & Windus, 1999.
Rorty, R., 'Religion as Conversation-Stopper', in *Philosophy and Social Hope*, London: Penguin, 1999, 168–74.
—— 'Religion in the Public Square: A Reconsideration', *Journal of Religious Ethics*, 31:1, 2003, 141–9.
Rowbotham, S, *Edward Carpenter: A Life of Liberty and Love*, London: Verso, 2008.
Sargant, T, *These Things Shall Be*, second edition, London: William Heinemann, 1942.

'Sargant, Thomas (1905–1988)', *Oxford Dictionary of National Biography*, Oxford: Oxford University Press, 2004.
Satty, H.J., and C.C. Smith, *Olaf Stapledon: A Bibliography*, Westport, CT, and London: Greenwood, 1984.
Scruton, R., *Spinoza: A Very Short Introduction*, Oxford: Oxford University Press, 2002.
'Sir Richard Thomas Dyke Acland (1906–90)', *Oxford Dictionary of National Biography*, Oxford: Oxford University Press, 2004.
Smith, D.C. (ed.), *The Correspondence of H.G. Wells, Vol. 4 (1935–46)*, London: Pickering & Chatto, 1996.
Taylor, C., 'Modes of Secularism', in R. Bhargava (ed.), *Secularism and Its Critics*, Delhi: Oxford University Press, 1998, 31–53.
——'A Catholic Modernity?' in J.L. Heft (ed.), *A Catholic Modernity?* New York and Oxford: Oxford University Press, 1999, 13–37.
——*A Secular Age*, Cambridge, MA: The Belknap Press of Harvard University Press, 2007.
*The Life of the Church and the Order of Society*, London: The Industrial Christian Fellowship, 1941.
*Towards a Quaker View of Sex*, London: Friends Home Service Committee, 1963.
*Towards a Quaker View of Sex*, revised edition, London: Friends Home Service Committee, 1964.
UK General Election Results, February 1950, October 1951, May 1955. Online. Available HTTP: www.psr.keele.ac.uk/area/uk/ge50/i.10.htm; www.psr.keele.ac.uk/area/uk/ge51/i.10.htm; www.psr.keele.ac.uk/area/uk/ge55/i.10.htm (all accessed 26 September 2010).
Vattimo, G., 'A Prayer for Silence', in John D. Caputo and G. Vattimo, *After the Death of God*, ed. J.W. Robbins, New York: Columbia University Press, 2007, 89–113.
——'Towards a Nonreligious Christianity', in John D. Caputo and G. Vattimo, *After the Death of God*, ed. J.W. Robbins, New York: Columbia University Press, 2007, 27–46.
Warren, J., 'Blair's Guru', *The Philosophers' Magazine*, fourth quarter 2006, 41–4.
Waugh, E., *Brideshead Revisited*, Harmondsworth: Penguin, 1962.
Weigle, D.C., 'Psychology and Homosexuality: The British Sexological Society', *Journal of the History of the Behavioral Sciences*, 31:2, April 1995, 137–48.
Wells, H.G., *'42 to '44: A Contemporary Memoir upon Human Behaviour during the Crisis of the World Revolution*, London: Secker & Warburg, 1944.
Wheen, F., *The Soul of Indiscretion: Tom Driberg: Poet, Philanderer, Legislator and Outlaw*, London: Fourth Estate, 2001.
Wildeblood, P., *Against the Law*, Harmondsworth: Penguin, 1957.
Williams, Phillip M. (ed.), *The Diary of Hugh Gaitskell 1945–1956*, London: Jonathan Cape, 1983.
Wilson, A.N., *God's Funeral*, London: John Murray, 1999.
'Wintringham, Thomas Henry (Tom) (1898–1949)', *Oxford Dictionary of National Biography*, Oxford: Oxford University Press, 2004.
Wolf, J., *Why Read Marx Today?* Oxford: Oxford University Press, 2002.
Wood, H.G., *The Truth and Error of Communism*, London: Student Christian Movement Press, 1933.7
Wright, T., *Oscar's Books*, London: Vintage, 2009.

# Index

1941 Committee 1, 138–40; Acland, Sir Richard 134, 138–40, 141; emergence 138; Forward March/1941 Committee merging 7, 134, 142, 155; Hulton, Edward 137, 138; Macmurray, John 7, 138, 139; members 138, 142; Priestley, J.B. 7, 136, 138, 142–43; religious debate 139–40; Vital Democracy 149; Wells, H.G. 138, 139–40; Wintringham, Tom 138

Acland, Sir Richard 2, 3, 6, 8, 109–41, 187–91, 194; 1941 Committee 134, 138–40, 141; biographical notes 1, 3, 6, 8, 110, 116, 129–30, 140, 187–88, 191, 199, 212, 213; Communism 111; Conservative Party 112, 114, 115; Fascism/Nazism 12, 112, 115, 117, 118, 120–21, 134; Forward March 7, 83, 133–38, 141, 142; homosexuality 171–72; idealism 113, 151; Labour Party 114, 116, 134, 187–88; Liberal MP 2, 6, 10, 110–21, 140, 141, 146–47, 188, 211; Malvern Conference 10, 80, 124–28, 133, 139, 212; Marxism 113, 158–59, 164, 170; morality 2, 6, 7, 10, 11, 14, 118–19, 120, 129, 140, 156, 189; Popular Front 6, 111–12, 113, 119, 141; Soviet Union 116–17, 118; Spanish Civil War 12, 13; utopianism 121; war 8–9, 115–16, 140, 194, 195–96; *see also* Acland, Sir Richard and Common Wealth; Acland, Sir Richard and religion; Acland, Sir Richard, works

Acland, Sir Richard and Common Wealth 1, 2, 4, 7, 109, 110, 118, 132–33, 134, 141, 142–82; Common Ownership 119, 126, 134, 136, 138, 151, 190, 217; Ingram, Kenneth 3, 7, 10, 80, 122, 123–24, 129, 131–32, 133, 141, 152, 191, 194; Macmurray, John 3, 7, 10, 167–69, 191; Parkes, Rev. John/'Hadham' 6, 7, 121–22, 128, 131, 141; social radicalism 6, 10, 110, 112–14, 116, 117, 120, 125, 134, 138, 140–41, 190; Stapledon, Olaf 3, 7, 154–57; Wells, H.G. 135–36, 138, 139–40, 141, 158; Wintringham, Tom 11, 136, 137–38, 144, 158, 161; *see also* Common Wealth

Acland, Sir Richard and religion 2, 3, 6, 11, 14, 122–23, 141, 190; atheism 110; Christianity 10–11, 110, 118–19, 121–28, 133, 141, 145, 151, 156, 158–59, 190, 212, 213; Church of England 3, 10, 124–28; God 11, 122, 123, 128–32, 141, 152, 159–60, 165, 167, 193; the Marxist/Christianity struggle 144, 145, 151–52, 157–70, 173, 174–77, 194; 'Quanglican' 190; religious/secular relationship 2, 6, 8

Acland, Sir Richard, works: *Forward March* 14, 122–24, 126, 127, 128–29, 130, 131, 132, 135, 152; *How It Can Be Done* 161, 218; *Hungry Sheep* 189–91, 213; *It Must Be Christianity* 132–33, 151, 154–57, 158, 164; *The Next Step* 188, 189; *Nothing Left to Believe* 189; *Only One Battle* 112, 116; *Public Speaking* 189; *Revolutionaries Should Be Christians* 158, 159–60; *Unpublished Political Autobiography* 129; *Unser Kampf (Our Struggle)* 6–7, 14, 118–24, 128, 133–34, 135, 136; *Waging Peace* 189; *This Way to Death* 115; *We Teach Them Wrong* 189; *What It Will Be Like and How It Can be Done* 14, 143; *What Now?*

*Index* 235

*Memorandum on the World Situation September 1939 by Sir Richard Acland, MP* 116, 117, 118; *Why So Angry?* 189
agnosticism 3, 6, 89, 102, 106, 107; *see also* Stapledon, Olaf and religion
Anglo-Catholicism/Church of England 56, 58, 191; Acland, Sir Richard 3, 10, 124–28; homosexuality 5, 53, 55, 56, 57, 60, 63, 70; Ingram, Kenneth 3, 5, 9, 53–54, 55–64, 75, 80–81, 202; Reformation 37, 58; Temple, William, Archbishop of Canterbury 5, 10, 80–83, 153; *see also* Christianity; God; religion
anti-Semitism 122, 203; Ingram, Kenneth 5, 57–58, 63; Nazism 31, 46–47, 115
aristocracy 56, 61, 100–101, 119
Arnold, Matthew 57, 192
atheism 11, 14, 51, 102, 107, 110; Bloch, Ernst 24; Communism 29; Feuerbach, Ludwig 18; socialism 71

Bauer, Bruno 19–20, 47
Berlin, Isaiah 19, 198; *Karl Marx: His Life and Environment* 19–20
Blair, Tony 15, 187, 197
Bloch, Ernst 12, 24–25, 99–100, 101, 103
Bowes-Lyon, Lilian 107, 108, 210
Bradford, Bishop 127, 138, 152, 153
Buddhism 11, 49
by-elections: Common Wealth 1, 110, 114, 119, 131, 143, 145–46, 147–48, 150, 154, 155, 178, 179, 180; Conservative Party 1, 145–46; Labour Party 177, 180, 187–88; *see also* election

Calder, Angus 152, 153, 154, 177, 196; 'The Common Wealth Party 1942–45' 7, 145
capitalism 71, 75, 161; Acland, Sir Richard 116, 117, 120; Fascism 12; Macmurray, John 27, 29, 36, 44; Marx, Karl 17, 23
Carpenter, Edward 56, 57, 58, 60, 61–62, 64, 70, 77, 80; *The Intermediate Sex* 56, 57, 62, 70
Chamberlain, Neville 115, 119, 120, 136
Chelmsford 2, 147, 171, 178, 180
Christian Left 3, 9, 197; Ingram, Kenneth 3, 9, 54, 55, 71, 202; Macmurray, John 3, 9, 54

Christianity 10; Acland, Sir Richard 10–11, 110, 118–19, 121–28, 133, 141, 145, 151, 156, 158–59, 190, 212, 213; Bible/Gospels 11, 30, 38, 40, 72, 73, 75, 98, 119, 123, 133, 159, 170, 193; Common Wealth: the Marxist/ Christianity struggle 7–8, 137, 144, 145, 151–52, 157–70, 173, 174–77, 194; Communism 53; criticism 10–11; doctrine of sin 133, 165; Enlightenment 11; European history 4, 31, 35–38, 50; Fascism 43; hegemony 49, 133; history 36–38; homosexuality 11, 53, 55, 69; Ingram, Kenneth 10–11, 53, 57, 58, 71, 86, 170–71, 185 (immanentist materialist Christianity 3, 75, 81, 185); institutional Christianity 8, 10, 14, 16, 37–38, 67, 81, 103, 174, 185, 190, 195; liberal democracy 18–19, 23, 192; Macmurray, John 10–11, 14, 15, 23, 24, 30–32, 35–38, 41, 46, 49–50, 52, 81, 159, 167–68, 187; Marx, Karl 18–19, 23; monasticism 37–38, 56; morality 53; secularism 38; sexuality 5, 53; Stapledon, Olaf 6, 10, 14, 85–88; universalism 36–37, 49–50, 89; war 8; *see also* Anglo-Catholicism; God; morality; religion; secularism
Churchill, Sir Winston 111, 115, 134, 136, 146, 148, 177, 179, 188
Common Ownership 2, 148; Acland, Sir Richard 119, 126, 134, 136, 138, 151, 190, 217; Common Wealth 2, 148–49, 151, 152, 155; *see also* Common Wealth
Common Wealth 1, 7, 14, 142–82, 189, 193–94; 1945 General Election 147, 151, 155, 177–81; by-elections 1, 110, 131, 145–46, 147–48, 150, 154, 178, 179; Common Ownership 2, 148–49, 151, 152, 155; *Common Wealth and the New Year* 174, 175–76; *Common Wealth Manifesto* 148, 149, 150–51; crisis 157–67, 170–77; dissolution 8, 155, 176–82; emergence 1, 2, 13, 14, 110, 118, 134, 142, 165, 194; Fascism 148, 164, 165, 166; Forward March/ 1941 Committee merging 7, 134, 142, 155; foundational values 4, 7, 14, 169; homosexuality 154, 170–72; idealism 150, 151, 165, 167, 173, 193; *It Must Be Christianity* 132–33, 151, 154–57, 158; Labour Party 177–82; morality 151, 156, 163, 164, 165, 166, 170,

173–75, 177, 182; movement/political party 165, 177, 193; religious debates 1, 3, 7–8, 11, 132, 137, 139, 144, 145, 150–77, 191, 194; religious/secular relationship 14; socialism 1, 9, 14; swing in its favour 2, 147, 148, 178; themes 148–50; two meetings 162–63, 167–70; Vital Democracy 2, 149, 155; wartime electoral truce 1, 110, 145–46, 149, 177, 194; *see also* Acland, Sir Richard; Common Wealth, branches/ regions; Common Wealth, committees; Common Wealth, membership; Ingram, Kenneth; Macmurray, John; Stapledon, Olaf

Common Wealth, branches/regions 1, 7, 145, 147, 154, 179–80, 181–82; Chelmsford 147, 171, 178, 180; London 7, 154, 145; Merseyside 7, 13, 145, 154; Scotland 145; Wales 145, 154; Wirral 7, 154, 155

Common Wealth, committees: Appeals Committee 7; Executive Committee 7, 144; 'ideational team' 7, 144–45; Policy Committee 7, 144; Women's Policy Sub-Committee 162

Common Wealth, membership 1, 2, 14, 142–43, 145, 147–48, 151, 181, 182, 193; Acland, Sir Richard 110, 118, 132–33, 134, 142–82 (founder 1, 2, 4, 7, 109, 141; 'Memorandum On Common Wealth Theory' 164); Ferguson, John 174–75; Ingram, Kenneth 4, 7, 54, 55, 83, 144, 152–82, 183–85, 187, 191, 193, 194 ('Draft Policy Document' 166–67, 173); Jager, Rev. George 152–54, 194; MacKay, R.W.G. 144, 178, 216; Macmurray, John 4, 7, 143, 144, 145, 153, 154, 161, 167–69, 174, 176, 182, 218; the military 2, 145, 147; Millington, Ernest 147, 171, 180, 182; Parkes, Rev. James/ 'Hadham' 143, 151, 152, 157, 161, 163–65, 169, 174, 182; Priestley, J.B. 7, 136, 138, 142–43, 151; Sargant, Tom 7, 143–44, 157, 164, 169, 174, 175, 179, 181, 182; Smith, C.A. 182, 221; Stapledon, Olaf 4, 7, 154–57, 158, 179, 182, 183–84, 218; Wintringham, Kitty 137, 157–58, 160–66, 174, 179, 180, 182; Wintringham, Tom 136, 137, 142, 143, 144, 147, 157, 160, 161, 164–66, 174–76, 179, 181, 182 ('Fellowship or Morality?' 164–66)

Communism: Acland, Sir Richard 111; atheism 29; Great Britain 9, 30, 137, 157, 164, 165, 178; Ingram, Kenneth 9; Macmurray, John 17, 23, 24, 25, 27, 28–29, 30–32, 40–44, 47, 51; materialism 104; religion 23, 24, 29, 42, 104; Soviet Communism 4, 11, 13–14, 15, 17, 36, 40–42; Stapledon, Olaf 88, 99, 100, 101, 104, 106, 210; Wintringham, Tom 7, 14, 137, 157; *see also* Marx, Karl; Marxism; Soviet Union

Conservative Party (Tory) 2, 101, 148, 181; Acland, Sir Richard 112, 114, 115; by-elections 1, 145–46; Fascism 112; National Government 6, 39, 111, 112, 115, 141

Costello, John E. 50, 187, 199, 217, 222
Cripps, Sir Stafford 119
Crossley, Robert 95, 107, 209, 221

democracy: Common Ownership 148, 149; education 100; liberal democracy 17, 18, 23, 44, 47, 192; Macmurray, John 23, 32, 39, 44, 48, 49, 50; Stapledon, Olaf 100–101; Vital Democracy 2, 149, 155; Western democracies 11, 13, 17
Driberg, Tom 146, 171, 189

Eagleton, Terry 192
economics 101; 1930s economic crisis 100; economic determinism 98–99; Fascism 43, 44; Macmurray, John 30, 38, 39, 48, 49, 52, 98; Marxism 30, 39, 52, 98–99, 102; *see also* capitalism; Common Ownership; Marx, Karl
Eden, Anthony 111, 115, 137, 188
election: 1938 General Election 6, 115, 196; 1945 General Election 8, 147, 151, 155, 177–81; 1950 General Election 188; Cairo, mock election 2; electoral register 2, 147, 149; wartime electoral truce 1, 110, 145–46, 149, 177, 194; *see also* by-elections
Eliot, T.S. 124–25
Engels, Friedrich 64, 164, 178; *Ludwig Feuerbach and the End of Classical German Philosophy* 20; *The Origin of the Family, Private Property and the State* 34
Enlightenment 45, 193; Christianity 11; New Enlightenment 192; religion 2–3, 11, 34, 39; secularism 192
Europe: history 4, 31, 35–38, 50

Index 237

Fascism 4, 11–12, 24, 45, 148; Christianity 43; Common Wealth 148, 164, 165, 166; economics 43, 44; Great Britain 12, 13; Ingram, Kenneth 11–12, 63–64, 71; Macmurray, John 31, 40, 43–48, 49, 217; Mosley, Sir Oswald 9, 63, 165; socialism 12; Stapledon, Olaf 11–12, 100, 101; *see also* Nazism

Feuerbach, Ludwig 17–18, 19, 20–21, 22–23, 30, 33, 104; *The Essence of Christianity* 17–18

Forward March 1, 3; Acland, Sir Richard 7, 83, 133–38, 141, 142; emergence 133–34; Forward March/1941 Committee merging 7, 134, 142, 155; Ingram, Kenneth 7, 83, 194; members 134, 142, 143, 144, 153, 181; movement/political party 134, 165; socialism 134; Stapledon, Olaf 7, 134, 154–55; *see also* Acland, Sir Richard

freedom: Macmurray, John 27, 36, 37, 38, 39, 42, 45, 49–50, 51–52

Freud, Sigmund 45, 95, 102–3

Germany 8, 24, 44, 45, 48, 100, 115; *Der Eigene* 57, 61, 62, 63, 203; Hitler, Adolf 31, 44, 45, 46, 63, 115, 117, 118, 120, 135, 137; homosexuality 57, 61–62, 63; *see also* Nazism

Great Britain 44; British Society for the Study of Sex Psychology (BSSSP) 53, 56, 61; Communism 9, 30, 137, 157, 164, 165, 178; Fascism 12, 13; idealism 21; political parties 101; Soviet Union 49; Victorian Britain 55, 58, 64, 66, 68, 153; Victorian Hellenism 56, 57, 59–60

God: Acland, Sir Richard 11, 122, 123, 128–32, 141, 152, 159–60, 165, 167, 193; Ingram, Kenneth 75, 122, 123, 129, 131–32, 185, 193; Macmurray, John 11, 29, 32, 35, 71, 99, 153; Stapledon, Olaf 3, 6, 91–92, 94, 97, 99, 103, 105–8, 156, 193; *see also* Christianity; religion

Habermas, Jürgen 3, 191, 193
Hegel, Georg 23, 24, 30, 34, 35, 36
historical materialism 7, 28, 164; *see also* Marx, Karl
Hobbes, Thomas 51, 159
homosexuality 5, 7, 9, 55–71, 75–80, 83–84, 170–72, 193, 202, 207; Acland,
Sir Richard 171–72; age of consent 61, 70, 79, 83–84, 206; Anglo-Catholicism 5, 53, 55, 56, 57, 60, 63, 70; Bradford, Rev. E.E. 61, 69; British Society for the Study of Sex Psychology (BSSSP) 53, 56, 61; chastity 73, 82, 171, 172; Christianity 11, 53, 55, 69; Common Wealth 154, 170–72; d'Arch Smith, Timothy 56, 61, 67, 203; definition 77; *Der Eigene* 57, 61–62, 63, 203; Germany 57, 61–62, 63; Hirschfeld, Magnus 57, 61; Ives, George 56, 61, 204; law reform 70, 83; lesbianism 66, 77; love 75–76, 78, 170; medicalisation of 57, 59; 'Order of Chaeronea' 56, 204; Paine, William 61, 204; pederasty 5, 55, 60–63, 65–66, 67–68, 69, 70–71, 79, 83–84, 207; *The Quorum* 56, 61, 64, 68, 69; *Towards a Quaker View of Sex* 172, 220; Uranian movement 67, 74, 203; Victorian Hellenism 56, 57, 59–60; Wilde, Oscar 60, 204; *see also* Carpenter, Edward; Ingram, Kenneth

humanism 24; Acland, Sir Richard 113, 129, 132, 133, 156, 158, 164; Christian/humanism divide 173, 174, 194; secularism 192; Stapledon, Olaf 92–93, 95, 156–57; *see also* Marxism

Hume, David 94, 191; *Dialogues Concerning Natural Religion* 94

idealism: Acland, Sir Richard 113, 151; British idealism 21; Common Wealth 150, 151, 165, 167, 173, 193; Macmurray, John 21, 23, 33, 35, 186

India 41, 49–50, 149; *Bhagavad Gita* 107, 210

Ingram, Kenneth 2, 4–5, 8, 53–84, 184–85, 193; anti-Semitism 5, 57–58, 63; biographical notes 1, 3, 4–5, 8, 53, 54, 185, 199; bisexuality 5, 62, 65, 66, 76, 78, 79–80; Christian Left 3, 9, 54, 55, 71, 202; Communism 9; 'deviant' sexuality 5, 53, 59, 77; Fascism 11–12, 63–64, 71; Forward March 7, 83, 194; homosexuality 5, 7, 9, 55–71, 75–80, 83–84, 170, 202, 207; Labour Party 9, 196; Malvern Conference 10, 80, 124, 125–26, 128; Marxism 5, 9, 58, 71–75; morality 53, 59, 66, 73, 75–76, 78, 170; Nazism 73; pederasty 5, 55, 60–63, 65–66, 67–68, 69, 70–71, 79, 83–84, 207; secularism 8, 53; sexual activity and marriage 5, 55, 60, 75, 82; sexuality 53, 59, 66, 70, 75, 76, 78, 80, 154; socialism 5, 9, 64, 68, 71–75, 125–26; Soviet Union 71; utopianism 59, 64, 84; women 58–59, 63, 65, 66, 70; *see also* homosexuality; Ingram, Kenneth and Common Wealth; Ingram, Kenneth and religion; Ingram, Kenneth, works

Ingram, Kenneth and Common Wealth 4, 7, 54, 55, 83, 144, 152–82, 183–85, 173, 187, 191, 193, 194; Acland, Sir Richard 3, 7, 10, 80, 122, 123–24, 129, 131–32, 133, 141, 152, 191, 194; Ingram's role 7, 83, 173; Macmurray, John 3, 4, 5, 54, 64, 71–75, 125; religious debates 7–8; *see also* Ingram, Kenneth

Ingram, Kenneth and religion: Anglo-Catholicism 3, 5, 9, 53–54, 55–64, 75, 80–81, 202; Christianity 10–11, 53, 57, 58, 71, 86, 170–71, 185; God 75, 122, 123, 129, 131–32, 185, 193; immanentist materialist Christianity 3, 75, 81, 185; religious/ secular relationship 2, 8, 53; Temple, William 5, 80–83, 154, 185

Ingram, Kenneth, works 54, 55, 60, 69–70, 154; *The Changing Order* 55; *Christian Challenge to Christians* 123; *Christianity and Sexual Morality – A Modernist View* 54, 80, 207; *Communist Challenge: Good or Evil?* 184, 185; *England at the Flood-Tide* 56, 59; *The Faded Vision* 55; *History of the Cold War* 185; *Is Christianity Credible?* 185; *'It is Expedient ... '* 73–74; *A Manual for Church of England Scouts* 103; *Midsummer Sanity* 67–69, 71, 74; *The Modern Attitude to the Sex Problem* 53, 54, 64–67, 70, 76, 77, 79; *The Night is Far Spent* 124, 131–32, 133, 161; *An Outline of Sexual Morality* 53, 54, 56, 59, 60–61, 62, 65, 66, 67, 70, 77; *Religion and the New Society* 54, 155, 170; *Sex-Morality Tomorrow* 5, 53, 54, 70, 75–82, 83, 154, 170, 185, 207; *The Symbolic Island* 62–63; *Years of Crisis: An International History 1919–1945* 185

Islam 49

Italy 12, 43, 45, 48, 100; Mussolini 45, 46, 112; *see also* Fascism

Japan 49

Judaism 19, 58; Macmurray, John 31, 32, 33, 34, 46–47, 73, 74, 99; *see also* anti-Semitism

Kant, Immanuel 51
Keynes, John Maynard 10, 110, 111

Labour Party 2, 8, 14, 101, 111, 187–88, 194; Acland, Sir Richard 114, 116, 134, 187–88; Blair, Tony 15, 187, 197; Common Wealth 177–82; economics 101; Ingram, Kenneth 9, 196; Macdonald, Ramsay 39
League of Nations 10, 44–45, 48, 121
Left Book Club 112, 114, 152
Lenin, Vladimir 88, 98
Lewis, C.S. 107
Liberal Party 2, 101; 1935 Election 111; Acland, Sir Richard 2, 6, 10, 110–21, 140, 141, 146–47, 188, 211; Popular Front 111; Sinclair, Sir Archibald 111
Liberalism 110, 116, 117, 119, 140, 192; liberal democracy 17, 18, 23, 44, 47
Local Defence Volunteers (LDF) 137, 138
Luther, Martin 15, 37

MacKay, R.W.G. 144, 178, 216
Macmurray, John 2, 5, 15–52, 73, 185–87; 1941 Committee 7, 138, 139; Ayer, A.J. 186, 222; biographical notes 1, 3, 4, 8, 15–16, 34, 187, 197, 199; Bloch, Ernst 24–25; Christian Left 3, 9, 54, 202; Communism 17, 23, 24, 25, 27, 28–29, 30–32, 40–44, 47, 51; Costello, John E. 50, 187, 199, 217, 222; democracy 23, 32, 39, 44, 48, 49, 50; dualism 19, 22, 32–33, 35, 36, 39, 43, 52, 165; economics 30, 38, 39, 48, 49, 52, 98; Fascism/Nazism 31, 40, 43–48, 49, 217; Feuerbach, Ludwig 17–18, 19, 20–21, 22–23, 30, 33; freedom 27, 36, 37, 38, 39, 42, 45, 49–50, 51–52; friendship 28, 29, 32, 51, 52, 72–73, 165; Hegel, Georg 23, 24, 30, 34, 35, 36; history 32–41, 52, 99; idealism 21, 23, 33, 35, 186; Judaism 31, 32, 33, 34, 46–47, 73, 74, 99; Marxism 4, 5, 9, 14, 16, 17–32, 40, 51–52, 71–75, 97, 167–68, 197; science 14, 22, 31, 39, 99; secularism 8, 38, 193; socialism 9, 15, 39–40, 48, 125; Soviet Union 4, 14, 15, 17, 40–43, 44, 45, 48–49, 51–52, 99; state

22, 23, 37, 40, 43, 45, 48, 49, 51; *Ten Modern Prophets* 4, 186; utopianism 25, 27–28, 29, 41; war 8, 21, 48–51; *see also* Macmurray, John and Common Wealth; Macmurray, John and religion; Macmurray, John, works; Marx, Karl
Macmurray, John and Common Wealth 4, 7, 143, 144, 145, 153, 154, 161, 167–69, 176, 182, 218; Acland, Sir Richard 3, 7, 10, 167–69, 191; Ingram, Kenneth 3, 4, 5, 54, 64, 71–75, 125; Macmurray's role 7, 168; religious debates 7–8; Stapledon, Olaf 3, 97–99; *see also* Common Wealth
Macmurray, John and religion 3, 4, 10–11, 22, 23, 24–25, 29, 32, 34, 51, 52, 99; Christ and Marx 4, 10, 17, 25–27, 30–32, 197; Christian outside the Churches 8, 10, 14, 16, 25, 86, 187; Christianity 10–11, 14, 15, 23, 24, 30–32, 35–38, 41, 46, 49–50, 52, 81, 159, 167–68, 187; God 11, 29, 32, 35, 71, 99, 153; Jesus 4, 10, 23, 25, 26, 27, 30–32, 35, 37, 39, 45, 46, 72, 73, 75, 159; Kingdom of Heaven 4, 14, 23, 26–27, 29, 30, 31, 34, 49, 52, 71, 99; religious/secular relationship 2, 4, 8, 22–26, 33, 34, 50–51
Macmurray, John, works 99; *Challenges to the Churches* 49; *The Clue To History* 4, 8, 26, 30, 31, 33, 34–36, 42, 45, 47–48, 99, 164, 193; 'The Conception of Society' 21–22; *Conditions of Freedom* 49; *Creative Society* 30, 44, 99; 'The Early Development of Marx's Thought' 17, 197; 'Here I Stand' 15–17, 25; *Interpreting the Universe* 22; *Persons in Relation* 51, 186–87; *The Philosophy of Communism* 25–26; 'Reflections on H.G.Wood's Reflections on Communism and Christianity' 25, 199; *The Self as Agent* 51, 186–87, 222; *Through Chaos to Community?* 49
Malvern Conference 184; Acland, Sir Richard 10, 80, 124–28, 133, 139, 212; Ingram, Kenneth 10, 80, 124, 125–26, 128; Temple, William 124, 126, 127, 128, 144
Martin, Ernest W. 86–87, 88, 89, 106, 158; *In Search of Christianity* 86, 87, 158

Marx, Karl 9, 64, 97, 195; alienation 18, 19–20, 21; Berlin, Isaiah: *Karl Marx: His Life and Environment* 19–20, 21; Carr, E.H.: *Karl Marx: A Study in Fanaticism* 20, 21; *Communist Manifesto* 26, 97, 166; *Contribution to the Critique of Hegel's Philosophy of Law. Introduction* 17, 19, 22; *Critique of Hegel's 'Philosophy of Right'* 23; critique of religion 17, 18–19, 20, 22, 51, 104; *Economic and Philosophical Manuscripts of 1844* 17, 19, 30, 197–98; Feuerbach, Ludwig 17–18, 19, 20–21, 22–23; *German Ideology* 22; historical materialism 7, 28, 164; ideology 18; liberal democracy 17, 18, 23, 44, 47; Mehring, F.: *Karl Marx: The Story of His Life* 20; *On the Jewish Question* 17, 18, 19–20, 22, 23, 47, 198; Plekhanov, G.V.: *Fundamental Problems of Marxism* 20; *Ten Modern Prophets* 4; state 18–19; *see also* Marxism
Marxism: Acland, Sir Richard 113, 158–59, 164, 170; Common Wealth: the Marxist/Christianity struggle 7–8, 137, 144, 145, 151–52, 157–70, 173, 174–77, 194; economic determinism 98–99; economics 30, 39, 52, 98–99, 102; historical materialism 7, 28, 164; Ingram, Kenneth 5, 9, 58, 71–75; Macmurray, John 4, 5, 9, 14, 16, 17–32, 40, 51–52, 71–75, 97, 167–68, 197; morality 2; Plekhanov, G.V.: *Fundamental Problems of Marxism* 20; Polanyi, Karl 198; religion 2, 98, 102–3, 132; Stapledon, Olaf 6, 87–88, 97–99, 102–3; Wintringham, Tom 7, 137, 145, 164; *see also* Marx, Karl
the military: Common Wealth 2, 145, 147; disenfranchised 2, 147; Wintringham, Tom 137, 138
Millington, Ernest 147, 171, 180, 182
morality: Acland, Sir Richard 2, 6, 7, 10, 11, 14, 118–19, 120, 129, 140, 156, 189 (politics moral basis 2, 6, 118–19, 129); Common Wealth 151, 156, 163, 164, 165, 166, 170, 173–75, 177, 182; Ingram, Kenneth 53, 59, 66, 73, 75–76, 78, 170; Stapledon, Olaf 93, 100, 105
Mosley, Sir Oswald 135, 151; Fascism 9, 63, 165
Murry, John Middleton 124, 195

National Government 6, 39, 111, 112, 115, 141
National Peace Council 55, 184–85
National Trust 131, 151
Nazism 11, 12, 63, 100, 101, 136–37; Acland, Sir Richard 12, 112, 115, 117, 118, 120–21, 134; anti-Semitism 31, 46–47, 115; economics 44; Hitler, Adolf 31, 44, 45, 46, 63, 115, 117, 118, 120, 135, 137 (*Mein Kampf* 118); homosexuality 63; Ingram, Kenneth 73; Macmurray, John 31, 40, 43–48, 49, 217; Stapledon, Olaf 100, 101; *see also* Fascism
Nietzsche, Friedrich 24, 94, 192

Parkes, Rev. John/'Hadham' 7, 121–22, 128, 131, 141; Common Wealth 143, 151, 152, 157, 161, 163–65, 169, 174, 182; *Good God* 6, 7, 121, 122, 123, 129, 131
Polanyi, Karl 17, 197–98
Popular Front 6, 111–12, 113, 119, 141
Priestley, J.B. 7, 136, 138, 142–43, 151
the Quakers 113, 187; Acland, Sir Richard: 'Quanglican' 190; homosexuality 172; Macmurray, John 187; *Towards a Quaker View of Sex* 172, 220

racism 47, 73; *see also* anti-Semitism
religion 3, 193; Buddhism 11, 49; Common Wealth, religious debates 1, 3, 7–8, 11, 132, 137, 139, 145, 150–77, 191 (the Marxist/Christianity struggle 144, 145, 151–52, 157–70, 173, 174–77, 194; 'orthodoxy' vs 'religion' 152–54); Communism 23, 24, 29, 42; critique 10–11, 17, 18–19, 20, 22, 51, 104; Enlightenment 2–3, 11, 34, 39; institutional religion 23; Islam 49; Marxism 2, 98, 102–3, 132; nature of 3, 11, 68; the 'religious turn' 2, 10–11, 191; Soviet Union 42–43, 99; Wells, H.G. 96–97; *see also* Acland, Sir Richard and religion; Anglo-Catholicism; Christianity; God; Ingram, Kenneth and religion; Judaism; Macmurray, John and religion; religious/secular relationship; Stapledon, Olaf and religion
religious/secular relationship 2, 3, 10, 38; Acland, Sir Richard 2, 6, 8; Common Wealth 14; Ingram, Kenneth 2, 8, 53; Macmurray, John 2, 4, 8, 22–26, 33, 34, 50–51; Stapledon, Olaf 2, 8, 102–5; *see also* religion; secularism
Rorty, Richard 2, 34, 195
Rousseau, Jean-Jacques 22, 40, 51

Sargant, Tom 7; Common Wealth 7, 143–44, 157, 164, 169, 174, 175, 179, 181, 182; *These Things Shall Be* 144
satan/devil 91, 107, 131, 158
science: Macmurray, John 14, 22, 31, 39, 99; Stapledon, Olaf 102
secularism 67, 68, 96, 191–94; Caputo, John 192; Ingram, Kenneth 8, 53; Macmurray, John 8, 38, 193; modern secularism 3, 8, 191, 192, 193; post-secularism 2, 38, 191, 192–93; Stapledon, Olaf 8, 96, 102–5, 191; *see also* religion; religious/secular relationship; Rorty, Richard
sexuality 53, 59, 66, 70, 75, 76, 78, 80, 154, 171; 'deviant' sexuality 5, 53, 59, 77, 171; Macmurray, John 5; pederasty 5, 55, 60–63, 65–66, 67–68, 69, 70–71, 79, 83–84, 207; sexual activity and marriage 5, 55, 60, 75, 82; *see also* Ingram, Kenneth; homosexuality
Smith, C.A. 182, 221
Social Democratic Party 188
socialism 9–10; Acland, Sir Richard: social radicalism 6, 10, 110, 112–14, 116, 117, 120, 125, 134, 138, 140–41, 190; atheism 71; Common Wealth 1, 9, 14; Fascism 12; feudal socialism 5, 9, 64; Forward March 134; Ingram, Kenneth 5, 9, 64, 68, 71–75, 125–26; Macmurray, John 9, 15, 39–40, 48, 125; materialism 71, 97; religion 9; Stapledon, Olaf 6, 9–10, 106, 209; *see also* Communism; Marx, Karl; Marxism
Soviet Union 12, 49, 71, 150; Acland, Sir Richard 116–17, 118; Macmurray, John 4, 14, 15, 17, 40–43, 44, 45, 48–49, 51–52, 99; militant atheism 14; Plekhanov, G.V. 20; religion 42–43, 99; Soviet Communism 4, 11, 13–14, 15, 17, 36, 40–42; Stapledon, Olaf 14, 87
Spanish Civil War 4, 7, 12–13, 47, 137; Acland, Sir Richard 12, 13; Ingram, Kenneth 71; Macmurray, John 47, 71;

Stapledon, Olaf 12, 13; Wintringham, Tom 7, 137, 157, 168
Spinoza, Baruch 35, 92, 105
Stapledon, Olaf 2, 5–6, 85–108, 183–84; biographical notes 1, 3, 4, 5–6, 8, 85, 106–7, 155, 184, 199, 218; Communism 88, 99, 100, 101, 104, 106, 210; Crossley, Robert 95, 107, 209, 221; ethics 93, 100, 105; Fascism/Nazism 11–12, 100, 101; Forward March 7, 134, 154–55; humanism 92–93, 95, 156–57; ideology 99–102; Martin, Ernest W. 86–87, 88, 89, 106, 158; Marxism 6, 87–88, 97–99, 102–3; secularism 8, 96, 102–5, 191; socialism 6, 9–10, 106, 209; Soviet Union 14, 87; Spanish Civil War 12, 13; Spinoza, Baruch 92, 105; war 8, 85, 107, 194; Wells, H.G. 94–97, 209; *see also* Stapledon, Olaf and Common Wealth; Stapledon, Olaf and religion; Stapledon, Olaf, works
Stapledon, Olaf and Common Wealth 4, 7, 154–57, 158, 179, 182, 183–84, 218; Acland, Sir Richard 3, 7, 154–57; Forward March/1941 Committee merging 7, 155; Macmurray, John 3, 97–99; Merseyside 7, 13, 154; the Wirral 7, 85, 154, 155; *see also* Common Wealth
Stapledon, Olaf and religion 3, 5–6, 11, 12, 85, 102–4, 155–57, 191, 193; agnosticism 3, 6, 89, 102, 106, 107; Christianity 6, 10, 14, 85–88, 156; faith 88–90; God/unknowable 'spirit'3, 6, 91–92, 94, 97, 99, 103, 105–8, 156, 193; 'personality in community' 6, 89; religious but not Christian 5–6, 85–108, 156; religious/secular relationship 2, 8, 102–5; tension between his principles 6, 90, 92, 97, 105, 107; utopia and worship 6, 90–94, 101, 104, 105, 107, 108
Stapledon, Olaf, works 85, 90–95, 209; 'The Conflict of Values: The Bridge Between' 184; *The Flames* 92; *Last and First Men* 5, 85, 90, 93, 95; *Last Men in London* 85; *Latter-Day Psalms* 91–92; *A Man Divided* 184; *A Modern Theory of Ethics* 105; *New Hope for Britain* 101; *Odd John* 92; *The Opening of the Eyes* 105–6, 107–8; *Saints and Revolutionaries* 96; *Sirius* 92, 103–4;

*Star Maker 5,* 85, 90, 92, 93–94, 101–2, 107; *Waking World* 102; *Youth and Tomorrow* 155
state: Macmurray, John 22, 23, 37, 40, 43, 45, 48, 49, 51; Marx, Karl 18–19

Taylor, Charles 3, 8, 34, 38, 192–93; religion and secularism 3, 34, 38; *A Secular Age* 8, 192–93
Temple, William 10, 153; Ingram, Kenneth 5, 80–83, 154, 185; Malvern Conference 124, 126, 127, 128, 144

United States 18, 50, 150
utopianism 93, 193; Acland, Sir Richard 121; Bloch, Ernst 12, 24–25; Ingram, Kenneth 59, 64, 84; Macmurray, John 25, 27–28, 29, 41; More, Thomas 41; Stapledon, Olaf: utopia and worship 6, 90–94, 101, 104, 105, 107, 108

Vattimo, Gianni 193
Vital Democracy 2, 149, 155; *see also* Common Wealth
Voltaire, François-Marie 170, 193

war: Acland, Sir Richard 8–9, 115–16, 140, 194, 195–96; Cold War 4; inter-war years 4, 9, 15, 48; Macmurray, John 8, 21, 48–51; 'No More War' movement 9; Stapledon, Olaf 8, 85, 107, 194; World War I 41, 64, 112; World War II 1, 75, 107, 150 (Phoney War 118, 136); *see also* Spanish Civil War
Wells, H.G. 61, 195: *'42 to '44* 136; Acland, Sir Richard 135–36, 138, 139–40, 141, 158; *First and Last Things* 96; *God the Invisible King* 96; *New Worlds for Old* 9; religion 96–97; Stapledon, Olaf 94–97, 209; *The Star* 95; *The War of the Worlds* 95; *You Can't Be Too Careful* 97
Wintringham, Kitty 7, 130, 131, 151; Common Wealth 137, 157–58, 160–66, 174, 179, 180, 182; *see also* Common Wealth
Wintringham, Tom 3, 7, 137–38, 168, 219; Acland, Sir Richard 11, 136, 137–38, 144, 158, 161; Common Wealth 136, 137, 142, 143, 144, 147, 157, 160, 161, 164–66, 174–76, 179, 181, 182; Common Wealth: the

Marxist/Christianity struggle 7–8, 137, 144, 145, 151–52, 157–70, 173, 174–77, 194; Communist Party 7, 14, 137, 157; Home Guard 7, 137; Marxism 7, 137, 145, 164; the military 137, 138; *Picture Post* 137; Spanish Civil War 7, 137, 157, 168; *see also* Common Wealth

women: Common Wealth 162–63; Ingram, Kenneth 58–59, 63, 65, 66, 70; Women's Policy Sub-Committee 162; *see also* Wintringham, Kitty

For Product Safety Concerns and Information please contact our EU
representative  GPSR@taylorandfrancis.com
Taylor & Francis Verlag GmbH, Kaufingerstraße 24, 80331 München, Germany

www.ingramcontent.com/pod-product-compliance
Lightning Source LLC
Chambersburg PA
CBHW070559300426
44113CB00010B/1327